ISRAEL
From Conquest to Exile

ISRAEL

From Conquest to Exile

A Commentary on Joshua–2 Kings

John J. Davis
John C. Whitcomb

BMH

BOOKS

BMH BOOKS
P.O. Box 544
Winona Lake, Indiana 46590
1-800-348-2756

Combined cloth edition as *History of Israel*—4 printings

Combined paper edition: First printing, June 1989
Second printing, May 1994

ISBN: 0-88469-238-8

Printed in the United States of America

PREFACE

This volume is a study of Israel's history from the time of the conquest through the fall of the kingdoms of Israel and Judah. The focus is upon the biblical text rather than the various theories of Israel's history as reconstructed by contemporary critics.

The present book is a composite of three earlier volumes published separately under the titles, *Conquest and Crisis, The Birth of a Kingdom*, and *Solomon to the Exile*. The first two were authored by John J. Davis and the latter by John C. Whitcomb. The chapters that follow are not a mere reprint of that material. Corrections, revisions, and stylistic changes, in addition to improvement in the graphics, have been incorporated into this new publication.

The purpose of the authors has been to come to grips with the essential teachings of the biblical text from Joshua through II Kings. Comparisons are consistently made with parallel portions of Scripture as well as with specific and general allusions in the New Testament. In an effort to broaden and enhance the interpretation of given passages, appropriate references are made to the Hebrew text and archaeological discoveries.

The style adopted for this study is clearly informal and reflects a reverent attitude toward the authority and sanctity of Scripture. It is the authors' intention that these biblical books be understood not merely as the reflections of Israel's search for her God, but especially as the Lord's unique revelation of Himself to His people. Even the most casual comparison of the biblical material to contemporary historiography will make it clear that the Bible is unique in its approach to Israel's history. The embarrassing failures of her great leaders are not hidden by the historians, but, under the inspiration of the Holy Spirit, are made lessons to all who would follow the Lord in a sinful world.

The authors have approached the Old Testament text with full confidence that the original words (which have been marvelously and providentially preserved through the centuries) were inspired of God and therefore absolutely inerrant. This concept was taught by the Lord Jesus Christ (Matt. 5:18; John 10:35) and His apostles (II Tim. 3:15-17; II Peter 1:19-21), and is everywhere assumed in the Old Testament. Since extended quotations from the biblical text have been omitted for lack of space, it is urged that the student approach this study with both an open Bible and a ready heart.

CONTENTS

ILLUSTRATIONS

TIME AND GENEALOGY CHARTS

MAPS

TRANSLITERATION

HEBREW

Consonants			Vowels	
א -'	ט -ṭ	פ -p,p̱	ָ -ā,ŏ	ֱ -ĕ
ב -b,ḇ	י -y	צ -ṣ	ַ -a	ִ -i
ג -g,g̱	כ -k,ḵ	ק -q	ֲ -ă	ִי -î
ד -d,ḏ	ל -l	ר -r	הָ -â	וֹ -o
ה -h	מ -m	שׂ -ś	ֶ -e	ֳ -ŏ
ו -w	נ -n	שׁ -š	ֵ -ē	ֹ -ō
ז -z	ס -s	ת -t,ṯ	ֵי -ê	וּ -û
ח -ḥ	ע -'		ְ -e	ֻ -u

GREEK

α,ᾳ -a	ζ -z	λ -l	π -p	φ -ph
β -b	η -ē	μ -m	ρ -r	χ -ch
γ -g	θ -th	ν -n	σ,ς -s	ψ -ps
δ -d	ι -i	ξ -x	τ -t	ω -ō
ε -e	κ -k	ο -o	υ -u	' -h

Part One

CONQUEST AND CRISIS

Studies in Joshua, Judges and Ruth

John J. Davis

JOSHUA

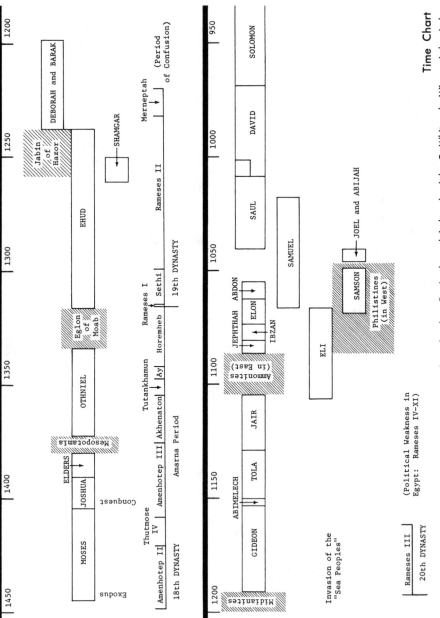

Time Chart

Based on the chart Patriarchs and Judges by John C. Whitcomb, Winona Lake, Ind.

1

INTRODUCTION

I. THE SURVIVAL OF A NATION

The record of Israel's exodus from the land of Egypt and preservation in the barren wilderness of Sinai constitutes one of the most captivating stories in the Bible. Equally thrilling are the accounts of Israel's conquest of the land of Canaan under the leadership of the man Joshua. The years spent in conquest and settlement were crucial ones in the history of Israel. A comprehensive record of these events is found in the first eight books of the Bible. The first five books, known as the Pentateuch, give us the history of the Hebrews *up to* their entrance into the land of Canaan, while the books of Joshua, Judges and Ruth continue that history by describing the conquest and settlement *in* the land of Canaan.

In this chapter we will examine the historical, cultural and religious setting for the conquest and settlement era as illuminated by recent archaeological and historical studies.

A. Historical Setting

1. The Biblical Data

When did the conquest of Canaan take place? This question must be considered before one attempts to describe the cultural setting for these events. At present there is an absence of agreement upon this question. Many scholars, refusing to accept the historical accuracy of the numbers of the Bible, date these events in the thirteenth century B.C.[1] Others, following the chronological data given in several key texts, date the conquest in the fourteenth century B.C. The latter view appears to be the preferable view in the light of Biblical evidence and Egyptian history. According to I Kings 6:1 the exodus from Egypt took place 480 years before the fourth year of Solomon. The date for the fourth year of Solomon is generally regarded as 966 B.C. This would mean that the exodus took

---

[1]Yohanan Aharoni, *The Land of the Bible*, trans. A. F. Rainey (Philadelphia: The Westminster Press, 1962), p. 178, note 10.

place about 1446/5 B.C. In order to arrive at the date for the
beginning of the conquest under Joshua, one need only deduct
the 40 years spent in the wilderness (Exod. 16:35; Num. 14:33-
34). The campaigns of Joshua, therefore, began about 1405
B.C.[2] The judge Jephthah places 300 years between Israel's
sojourn at Heshbon and about the second year of his judgeship
(Judg. 11:26). If we add 38 years to cover the period from the
exodus to Heshbon and 144 years from Jephthah to the fourth
year of Solomon, we find that the total number of years between
the exodus and Solomon's fourth year is about 482.[3] This ac-
cords well with the information given in I Kings 6:1. The
chronological setting for the events recorded in the Book of
Joshua should be considered as the fourteenth century B.C.
According to Caleb's statement in Joshua 14:10 the major battles
recorded in Joshua 1:1–14:1 lasted for a period of about
seven years.[4]

2. Egypt and Palestine

The information obtained by archaeological research and a
careful study of the Biblical records indicate that the exodus
should be placed in the middle of the fifteenth century B.C.
(i.e., 1445 B.C.). This would mean that Joseph rose to power
during the Twelfth Dynasty in Egypt, i.e., in the nineteenth century B.C. Exodus 1:8 informs us that a "new king" rose up
against Egypt.[5] This undoubtedly refers to one of the Hyksos

---

[2]John Rea, "The Time of the Oppression and Exodus," *Grace Journal*
(Winona Lake: Grace Theological Seminary, 1961), Vol. 2, No. 1.
. . . . , "New Light on the Wilderness Journey and the Conquest,"
Grace Journal, Vol. 2, No. 2.

[3]The extra two years can probably be adjusted on the basis of overlapping
judgeships during this period.

[4]According to Caleb's statement, 45 years had passed since the giving of
the promise to him (Josh. 14:10). That promise was given to him 38 years
before the crossing of the Jordan (cf. Num. 14:24). The major battles,
therefore, took about seven years. Josephus (*Ant.* V.1.19) gives the duration of the conquest as five years.

[5]The Hebrew expression translated "rose up over Egypt" is *wayāqām
melek ḥādāš 'al miṣrāyim* and is better rendered "rose up *against* Egypt."
Note the use of this expression elsewhere (Deut. 19:11; 28:7; Judg. 9:18;
20:5; II Sam. 18:31; II Kings 16:7).

kings who ruled in the Delta area. The Hyksos dominated lower
Egypt for about 150 years and in the middle of the sixteenth
century were driven out of Egypt. This brought about a revival
of native Egyptian rule and the establishment of the Eighteenth
Dynasty in the land. It is interesting to note that the Israelites
were not driven out with the Hyksos even though they both lived
in the Delta area. The Eighteenth Dynasty pharaohs continued
to enslave the Israelites until the Lord raised up Moses to lead
them out of the land in 1445 B.C. This great exodus probably
took place during the reign of Amenhotep II (1450-1423 B.C.).[6]
It is significant, indeed, that the Lord should deliver His people
from Egypt when Egypt was enjoying unparalleled economic
growth and political control over countries to the north. What
better way could the Lord demonstrate His sovereign power
over the nations of the world and prove conclusively that Israel
was indeed His "son" and "firstborn" (cf. Exod. 4:22)?

When Israel was about to enter Canaan, another amazing
turn of events took place. Egypt, which had unqualified control over Palestine, began to weaken under the leadership of
Pharaoh Amenhotep III (1410-1372 B.C.). Throughout the latter years of his reign and during the reign of his son Akhenaton
(1380-1363 B.C.) there was a decided decline in interest in
Palestinian holdings and the result was that many of the petty
kings of Palestine revolted from Egyptian rule. Other cities in
Palestine were quite frustrated over the lack of defense provided
by these pharaohs and in desperation wrote many letters to
Amarna, the capital city of Akhenaton, pleading for help. These
letters, written in cuneiform script, were discovered at Tell el-
Amarna in Egypt in 1887 and are a valuable commentary on the
political and military climate in Palestine and Syria during the
conquest era. The letters constantly mention the need for military aid from Egypt in order to stop the invasions conducted by
neighboring city-states and groups known as the "Habiru." It is
possible that in some cases the "Habiru" invasions might be a
reference to Israelite military activity, although recent studies

---

[6]For further discussion of this problem and its solution, see John Rea,
loc. cit.

make it clear that the term "Habiru" is not to be equated with "Hebrew" as some have attempted to do.

From a purely human point of view it seems quite strange that a powerful nation such as Egypt would relinquish its iron grip on Palestine especially when it had the resources to maintain that control. But from a Biblical point of view it is quite evident that the Lord was again preparing the way for His people. This radical change in Egyptian foreign policy came just at the time Israel was about to enter Canaan. This meant that Israel would not have to face the mighty armies of Egypt in its conquest of the land, but only the local armies and military coalitions. You will notice that there is no mention of Egyptian resistance anywhere in the Biblical accounts of the conquest. Even when the Egyptians did enter Canaan during this period, it was only to march along the coast in order to contact their enemy to the north, the Hittites. One cannot but thrill at the marvelous way God undertakes for His people in the most difficult circumstances.

The conquest and settlement period has been greatly illuminated by recent archaeological discoveries in Palestine. The Late Bronze period (*ca.* 1500-1200 B.C.) is characterized by the destruction of many cities. This wide-spread series of destructions was due to a number of factors. First, it seems clear that as the Hyksos were driven out of Egypt they settled in certain Palestinian cities, and when the Egyptians observed this, they continued their pursuit of the Hyksos into Palestine, destroying many of their strongholds. Secondly, following the expulsion of the Hyksos, the Egyptians showed renewed interest in Palestine under the Thutmoside rulers and this led to a number of campaigns aimed at bringing Palestinian city-states under Egyptian control again. Finally, the invasion of the Israelites would account for many of the destruction levels.

Palestine in the fifteenth and fourteenth centuries B.C. was a land bustling with activity. In addition to the military activity already described, there was increased interest in trade which resulted in the establishment of new contacts with the Western Mediterranean world. New kinds of pottery which were imported from various parts of the Mediterranean began to make an appearance during this period. This was an age of literary

activity. In addition to the Amarna letters, we have the significant writings of the people of Ugarit (Ras Shamra) located in
the coastal region of Lebanon. These tablets give a rather comprehensive picture of the mythology of these people and significant insight into their religious ideas. It appears that their
gods were the same gods as the Canaanites'. The immoral
character of their deities led the devotees into the most de-
moralizing rites found anywhere in the ancient Near East.
Some of these practices included sacred prostitution of both
sexes, serpent worship and at times the sacrifice of infants. It
is not difficult to see why God issued the command to exterminate the people of the land. The total destruction of the cities
of these idolatrous peoples was to prevent the infiltration of
these practices into Israel.

B. *The Right of Conquest*

That Israel was to have a land of her own is a clear teaching
of Scripture. Over five hundred years before the exodus the
Lord promised Abraham that after a period of affliction his
seed would be freed and have great possessions (Gen. 15:13-
14). In addition to this they would be "given" the land between
"the river of Egypt" and the "river Euphrates" (Gen. 15:
18). Later, special instructions were given to Moses regarding
conquest and settlement of the land (Deut. 7:1-26; 20:1-20).
One should always keep in mind that the directive to conquer
Canaan was not human but divine.

II. THE BIBLICAL RECORD

A. *Introduction to Joshua*

1. *Position in the Canon*

The Hebrew Old Testament is divided into three sections
known as the Law (*torāh*), the Prophets (*nebî'îm*) and the
Writings(*ketubîm*). The Law consists of the five books of Moses.
The Prophets are divided into two sections, the former and
latter prophets (see chart below). The Writings contain the poetical books, the five rolls and some historical books.

Law	Prophets		Writings	
Five Books of Moses	Former Josh. — Kings	Latter Isa. — Mal.	Poetical Five Rolls Historical	(3 Books) (5 Books) (3 Books)

2. The Title of the Book

The book is named after its principal character, Joshua (Heb. *yehošua'*). The name means "Jehovah saves" or "Jehovah is salvation." The title of the book in the Septuagint[7] is *Iesous Naun*, "Joshua the son of Nun."

3. The Author

The liberal-critical view of authorship is that Joshua represents the work of several writers. The two main sources of this book are traced to two supposed documents, J (850 B.C.) and E (750 B.C.). These two documents are assumed to have been re-edited in 650 B.C. and again in 550 B.C. The final form of the book, according to the liberal view, is to be dated to the middle of the sixth century B.C.[8] This view is unnecessary and without real objective proof. Since the book appears as a literary unit, it is better to assume a single author rather than many authors. It is our view that the author of the book was Joshua himself, although some additions were evidently made after his death. The following are the reasons for assuming Joshua as the principal author of the book: (1) The author was an eyewitness to many of the events (Josh. 5:1, 6; 15:4; note the detailed description of the battle for Ai, chaps. 7, 8). The writer speaks of himself as one of those who had crossed over Jordan (5:1) and to whom the land had been promised. (2) Certain parts of the book are said to have been written by

---

[7]Ancient Greek translation of the Old Testament prepared between 250 and 150 B.C.

[8]For a full discussion and evaluation of the Documentary theory of the Pentateuch, see John J. Davis, "The Patriarchs' Knowledge of Jehovah," *Grace Journal*, 1963, Vol. 4, No. 1.

Joshua himself (Josh. 24:26; cf. 8:32). (3) Rahab was still living at the time of writing (6:25). (4) Since the Jebusites are
described as being in control of Jerusalem (15:63), the book
must have been written before the time of David, for David
drove the Jebusites out and took full control of that city (II
Sam. 5:5-9). (5) The Philistines do not appear as a particular
menace in Joshua's time. This would seem to reflect a period
prior to the great Philistine invasion of the southwest coasts of
Palestine in the twelfth century B.C.

4. Purpose of the Book

The purpose of the Book of Joshua is to provide an official
and authoritative account of God's faithfulness in leading His
people into the Promised Land (cf. Josh. 21:43-45). This book
continues the history of Israel begun in the five books of Moses
and is an important link in the chain of God's plan of salvation
for man.

5. Important Themes in the Book

The Book of Joshua contains at least four important theological themes which have practical values for today. First, the
book is a lesson on the covenant faithfulness of Jehovah. The
power of God was not only declared in covenant agreement,
but also demonstrated. Secondly, the book demonstrates the
importance of the written word of God (Josh. 1:8; 8:32-35; 23:
6-16; 24:26-27). There was an authoritative body of written
Scripture in the days of Joshua and this consisted of the books
of Moses. There is no appeal to contemporary customs or oral
tradition. Thirdly, the book points out the utter failure of human effort apart from divine directives. When Joshua and the
children of Israel were faithful to God's word and His will, there
was victory. When they abandoned His will in favor of their
own genius, there was failure and frustration. Finally, the
book is a commentary on God's holiness and His judgment of
sin. The destruction of the cities of Canaan with their inhabitants was not merely to give Israel military control of the area,
but it was, in effect, a judgment of God upon the wickedness of
that land (cf. Gen. 15:16; Deut. 7:5-6).

B. *Outline of the Book*

1. Entering the Land (1:1–5:15)
   a. Joshua's Commission (1:1-9)
   b. Preparations for the Jordon Crossing (1:10–2:24)
   c. Crossing the Jordan River (3:1–5:15)
2. Conquering the Land (6:1–12-24)
   a. The Conquest of Jericho (6:1-27)
   b. The Defeat of Ai (7:1–8:35)
   c. The Southern Campaign (9:1–10:43)
   d. The Northern Campaign (11:1-15)
   e. Summary of the Conquest (11:16–12:24)
3. Dividing the Land (13:1–24:33)
   a. Instructions for Division (13:1-7)
   b. The Division of Transjordan (13:8-33)
   c. The Division of Canaan (14:1–19:51)
   d. The Cities of Refuge (20:1-9)
   e. The Levitical Cities (21:1-45)
   f. The Jordan Altar (22:1-34)
   g. The Last Words of Joshua (23:1–24:33)

III. THE MAN JOSHUA

A. *The Selection of the Man*

While the Bible does not specifically indicate why God chose Joshua for the great responsibility of leading the conquest of Canaan, we do have important information regarding the background and character of the man Joshua which should help us in understanding God's selection. In all probability Joshua was born in the land of Egypt. We know nothing of his parents, but according to Numbers 1:10 and I Chronicles 7:27 his grandfather, Elishama, was a leader of the tribe of Ephraim in the wilderness journey. The first mention of the man Joshua is found in Exodus 17:9, but nothing is given of his background or piety. It is clear from Exodus 33:11 that Joshua was a young man during the time of the wilderness journey. The fact that Moses chose Joshua to lead the Israelite troops against Amalek at Rephidim (Exod. 17:8-13) indicates that he had already distinguished himself in the area of military service. It is possible that Joshua had received some training in Egypt or perhaps had previous experience in military affairs. His later victories in the land of Canaan seem to support this assumption. According to Scripture, Joshua was the only adult Israelite of the exodus, with the exception of Caleb, who survived the forty years of wandering and actually entered Canaan.

Perhaps the outstanding characteristic of the man Joshua was his unqualified courage. This was demonstrated when he and eleven other spies returned from examining the fortified cities of southern Canaan. Joshua and Caleb stood alone in their evaluation of that situation. The ten spies contended that the children of Israel were in fact "like grasshoppers" when compared with the might of the Canaanites (Num. 13:33). The Scripture terms their report an "evil report" (13:32; 14:37). The original for evil has the idea of slanderous report (cf. 14:36). Joshua and Caleb were convinced that in spite of the size of the enemy the Lord was fully capable of giving them victory (Num. 14:9). This was not an easy position to take, for the whole nation turned against them, and God had to bring a severe judgment upon His people (Num. 14:12, 29 ff.). The account, none the less, indicates that Joshua was fully convinced that the Lord was able to care for any situation that might arise. He was not only a man of faith and courage, but he was also a man of unqualified obedience both to Moses his superior and to the Lord (cf. Exod. 17:8-10; 24:13-18 with Exod. 32:15-18; note also Num. 13 and Heb. 11:30). The real success of Joshua, however, probably lies in the fact that he was a Spirit-filled man (Num. 27:18; cf. Deut. 34:9). Joshua's submission to the leadership of the Holy Spirit caused him to have a high respect for the will of God as revealed in the written Word of God. This obedience and respect, of course, led to victory in all areas of his life.

B. *The Preparation of the Man*

It appears from the early chapters of Joshua and certain references in Numbers and Deuteronomy that Joshua was prepared by God in three ways.

1. *Experience*

You can explain to a man the various techniques of swimming, and that man might develop into a thorough scholar of
the theory of buoyancy and stroke techniques. He may have
read all of the books available on various types of competitive
swimming, but if that man has never been in the water, it is
doubtful that he would be much of a swimmer. He must have
experience, not merely theory. Such is the case with Joshua.
Very early in Joshua's career, he was exposed to circumstances
and problems which would help him develop in character and
commitment. He was faced with difficult, if not impossible, military situations. This caused him, at the outset, to trust the Lord
and seek divine guidance from the "captain of the Lord's host."
It has been said many times that experience is a good teacher
but needs a willing pupil. From what we can observe in the
life of Joshua, he was a willing pupil. The second way in which
God prepares a man for His service is by example.

2. *Example*

Joshua had the unique opportunity of serving as "Moses' minister" (Josh. 1:1; Exod. 24:13). This gave Joshua the opportunity to observe the aged statesman of Israel who was over
eighty years old during the time of journeying. He was able to
observe Moses in times of victory and tribulation (e.g., the exodus from Egypt, Exod. 12, 13; the crossing of the Red Sea, Exod.
14). He was also able to witness the reaction and the response
of Moses in times of great frustration and distress (Num. 14:11-
23). Moses had learned the important lessons of prayer and
intercession. When difficulties arose which he could not handle,
he turned to the Lord and sought divine guidance. By being
Moses' minister, Joshua quickly learned what the issues really
were in national leadership. He was taught that the greatest
enemy of Israel was not necessarily the great armies located
in the land of Canaan, but could be the subtle deception of
Satan *within* the nation of Israel. A case in point would be the
tragic description of idolatry recorded in Exodus 32 and 33. On
this occasion, Moses had gone up into the mountain and while
there, the people, supported by Aaron the priest, decided to

make their own gods (Exod. 32:1). They not only made false gods and a molten calf, but they built an altar to these gods and proclaimed special feast days (Exod. 32:5). Joshua was able to witness the broken heart of Moses as he descended from the mountain and saw the people worshiping the very gods which had been proven worthless through the ten plagues in Egypt. According to Exodus 32:17 it was Joshua who heard the noise of the people as they sang and shouted to the false gods. He was also able to witness the anger and holy indignation of Moses as he looked upon the sensuous activity of the Israelites around the golden calf. Joshua certainly must have understood that leadership over this nation would mean standing alone and depending solely on God's power and His word. Joshua not only learned the lesson of obedience from the life of Moses, but he also learned that disobedience would bring the judgment of God. Moses, of course, did not enter the Promised Land because of such disobedience.

The final means by which God prepares a man for His service is through exhortation.

3. *Exhortation*

Joshua was the recipient of considerable special and direct revelation from God. He was not in the dark with regard to what God wanted him to do. He had the exhortations of the Lord as recorded in the five books of Moses. These books were in written form and had full authority. When he was commissioned to take the leadership of the people of Israel, he was reminded that the key to success was meditation in, and complete obedience to, God's revelation (Josh. 1:8).

We should observe at this point that while the program of God is different today, the preparation of the man of God is essentially the same. One learns by experience. The tragedies and the joys of the Christian life cause us to mature in the faith and depend more upon the power of God. The believer learns by the example of others, especially the record of those lives given to us in the Word of God. Observe what the apostle Paul said about the example of Old Testament saints in I Corinthians 10:11, ". . . all these things happened unto them for examples;

and they are written for our admonition upon whom the ends of the world are come" (cf. Rom. 15:4). And finally, the believer learns by exhortations found in the Word of God. He is not without spiritual and practical directives. If he meditates in the Word of God as commanded, he has every right to anticipate progress and victory.

C. *The Success of the Man*

That Joshua was a successful leader cannot be doubted. He took a new generation of Israelites and led them to the east bank of the Jordan. They were confronted with a flooding Jordan River, a well-equipped enemy, rugged and unknown hill country, and well-fortified cities. In spite of this, Joshua was able to accomplish spectacular victories and a very successful conquest of large amounts of territory. This is not due just to the military or tactical genius of Joshua, but it is due to his unqualified obedience to God who brought victory and success. Such obedience is not optional for the believer; it is mandatory. Perhaps one of the reasons believers experience limited success in spiritual warfare today is that their obedience to our Lord is halfhearted. The army of the church occasionally marches slowly and indecisively. In this age of confusion and indecision, the believer needs more than ever to examine the example set by the man Joshua. He needs to return to a recognition of the authority of the Word of God; then he "will prosper and have good success."

2

PREPARING TO CONQUER

After forty years of disillusionment, death, and despair the children of Israel finally reached the eastern banks of the Jordan River. For the first time they could see the Promised Land of which their fathers spoke. To see the land is one thing, but to conquer it another. Such conquest would require inspired leadership, divine help, and personal consecration on the part of every Israelite. Such preparation would in effect be the key to victory for both Israel and Joshua.

This chapter will deal with Israel's *entrance* into the land of Canaan. This subject has two phases: (1) preparations for entrance into the land, and (2) the crossing of the Jordan.

I. JOSHUA'S COMMISSION (1:1-9)

The first verse in the Book of Joshua sets the stage for the events that are to follow. Three important facts are given to us in this verse. We are told that Moses was dead. Moses here is described as "the servant of the Lord." This expression is significant because it gives us further insight into the character and ministry of the man Moses. The expression is used two ways in the Old Testament: (1) to describe a pious Israelite who worshiped the true God (Lev. 25:42, 55; Isa. 41:8; 43:10) and (2) to describe one with a special call or commission (Gen. 26:24; II Sam. 3:18; II Chron. 32:16). Joshua 1:1 informs us that Joshua was the "minister" of Moses. This position included two basic responsibilities: (1) military and (2) religious (cf. Exod. 24:13; Num. 27:18-23; Deut. 1:38; 31:23) Finally, Joshua 1:1 indicates the source of Joshua's commission; namely, Jehovah, the God of Israel (cf. Num. 27:18; Deut. 31:3-7, 23; 34:9).

A. *The Promise of the Land* (1:2-7)

In the following verses, which relate the Lord's promise of the land, three things stand out as significant: (1) *the promise of divine support* (v. 2). Jehovah clearly indicated that He was already in the process or was "about to give" His people the land before them (Heb. *'anoki notēn*). This expression should be compared to a similar one found in verse 3 where the Hebrew is different. It is translated in the Authorized Version ". . . that have I given you" (Heb. *lākem netatîw*). The expression in verse 2 points to the immediate help of the Lord, whereas in verse 3 there is emphasis upon divine finality. As far as God was concerned, the land was already theirs and needed only to be possessed. (2) *The indication of geographic scope* (vv. 3-5). These verses are important because they give to us the general boundaries of Israel's possession. Every part of the land on which they would march the Lord would give to them (cf. Exod. 23:30-31). According to the fourth verse, this would include the area from the wilderness "unto this Lebanon even to the great River Euphrates" (cf. Deut. 11:24). These expressions give us an indication of the northernmost territories of Israel's possession, which possession included "the land of the Hittites." This expression is usually regarded as referring to the land of Syria which, of course, was under Hittite control at certain times.[9] The western boundary of the Promised Land includes all the territory unto "the great sea toward the going down of the sun," a reference to the Mediterranean coast. (3) *Some personal admonitions* (vv. 5-7). The Lord promised Joshua that as He supported and strengthened Moses, so He would strengthen him (Deut. 11:25; also Deut. 7:24; I Sam. 14:6; Rom. 8:31; Heb. 13:5-6). The last expression in verse 5 is interesting. He says there, "I will not fail thee." The Hebrew (*rāpāh*) literally means to be weak. The expression might well be translated, "I will not drop" or "abandon thee." In the light of this promise Joshua was encouraged to be "strong and of good courage" (vv. 6-7; cf. v. 9). Personal courage and consistent obedience to the will of God will secure for Joshua and the children of Israel prosperity, but full prosperity is realized only when there is complete obedience to the Word of God. This leads us to the next point of emphasis in Joshua's commission.

---

[9]This expression is omitted in the LXX and in Deuteronomy 11:24.

B. *The Power of the Word* (1:8)

Many critics today argue that the Scriptures never really appeared in authoritative, written form until after the ninth century B.C. This view, however, is purely speculative and in contradiction to clear statements of Scripture. Verse 8 in this chapter clearly indicates that in the fourteenth century B.C. there was a "book of the law" which was not only recognized as revelatory in nature, but authoritative (cf. Exod. 17:14; 24: 4, 7; Deut. 31:9, 11, 24, 26). Joshua is commanded to meditate day and night in this book and to observe the truths that are taught therein. One should notice also the emphasis upon the word "written" found in this verse. We are talking about a written body of literature which carries with it full divine approval and authority. This verse regards the Word of God as the key to prosperity and success (cf. I Kings 2:3; Ps. 1:1-3). The critical proposition that Scripture is the product of oral tradition surviving many hundreds of years of transmission is not only questionable on historical grounds, but highly improbable from a practical point of view. In addition to this, it should be noted that the Book of Joshua puts specific emphasis on the *written law of Moses* and its importance within the economy of Israel (cf. Josh. 8:32-35; 24:25-27). Our text does not merely require knowledge of the law, but daily meditation in it. Meditation involves mature reflection upon the Word of God and its place in one's life. This practice is the basis of spiritual growth and true progress in practical godliness (cf. Ps. 1:1-3; 119:15, 97).

C. *The Presence of the Lord* (1:9)

When the Lord Jesus sent out His disciples to proclaim the gospel to the ends of the world, one of the things He emphasized was the promise of His personal presence wherever they would go (Matt. 28:19-20). Joshua was also commanded to move out and to conquer in the name of Yahweh. It is therefore significant that he too was promised the special presence of the Lord (cf. Deut. 31:6-8; Josh. 3:7).

II. PREPARATIONS FOR THE JORDAN CROSSING (1:10–2:24)

The actual chronology of events recorded in the first three

chapters of Joshua is somewhat difficult to organize. For example, 1:11 speaks of the possibility of crossing over the Jordan within three days. Then in 2:22 we are told that the spies spent at least three days in the mountains, having made a covenant with Rahab. Finally, in 3:2 we are informed that after three days "the officers went through the host." The question is, "How much time actually transpired between the initial phases of preparation for the Jordan crossing and the actual crossing of the river described in Chapter 3?" Some commentators suggest the following order of events for Chapters 1-3: (1) The spies are sent out (chap. 2); (2) tribal responsibilities are assigned (1:10-18); and (3) preparations are made for the march (3:2 ff.). Other scholars feel that 1:10 and 3:2 are describing synonymous events, and Chapter 2 is really parenthetical. The spy mission is regarded as having begun before the events of 1:10. Either of these views is chronologically possible.

A. *Tribal Responsibilities* (1:10-18)

The immediate problem facing Joshua was the organization of the tribes and preparation of food for the journey to Canaan. Joshua gathered his officers together to give them specific instructions as to how the people should prepare for this journey (vv. 10-11). The expression "officers of the people" (Heb. *šoṭerê haʿām*) literally refers to scribes. In all probability these were scribes of the military roll (muster). Perhaps these are parallel to today's staff officers who issue the administrative orders of a command.[10] Reuben, Gad, and the half tribe of Manasseh were clearly reminded of their military responsibility to the rest of the nation (1:12-18). Moses had earlier given them permission to settle on the east bank of the Jordan River as long as they fulfilled their military responsibility with regard to conquest of the land of Canaan (Num. 32). This obligation was upon them until their brothers had "rest" in the land (v. 15). To this they agreed without qualification (vv. 16-18).

B. *Rahab and the Spies* (2:1-24)

The preparations for, and organization of, a spy mission were

---

[10]On this term, see Exodus 5:6-19; Deuteronomy 1:15; I Chronicles 27:1.

not new to the man Joshua. He had participated in a rather crucial spy mission from Kadesh-barnea (Num. 13-14). Because of that tragic experience in which the spies were permitted to give their report publicly, Joshua decided that this mission should be conducted "secretly" (2:1). He had learned by experience that spy reports should be brought to the leaders only, for the people did not have sufficient orientation or experience to properly evaluate such a report. Because of the proximity of the tribes of Israel to Jericho, it was necessary that this spy mission be carried out with as little commotion as possible. Surely the inhabitants of Jericho were anticipating such a mission. The job given to the spies was not an easy one. Jericho was located in an open valley. It was a walled city, and the people in the city were keenly aware of the danger from without. In addition to these problems we are informed that the Jordan was in the flood stage, overflowing its banks (3:15; 4:18; I Chron. 12:15). This meant the spies probably had to travel some distance north, cross the Jordan, and then come southward, probably entering Jericho from the west side. This would be advantageous for them not only in that they would have the cover of the caves in the mountains to the west of Jericho, but the king of Jericho would least suspect a spy mission from that direction. Upon entering Jericho, they came to the house of Rahab who was described as a harlot (v. 1). Josephus, however, prefers to regard her as an innkeeper.[11] This view, however, even though shared by some modern commentators, does not seem to be the best in the light of the original text and New Testament references.[12]

From the verses and chapters that follow quite a bit can be ascertained about the city of Jericho. For example, we learn, at least by implication, that it was a sinful city (2:1). Secondly, the city had sophisticated political organization, for it had a king (2:2). According to 2:5, 15 it was a walled city with a gate and therefore well fortified. In the fourth place the record indicates that houses were built on and along the wall (2:15).

---

[11]*Ant.* V.8.2, 7.
[12]The Hebrew word is *zonāh;* compare the Greek *pornē* (Heb. 11:31; James 2:25).

This, of course, was customary for houses not only in this period but in the Middle Bronze Age as well. In the fifth place, there is the implication that Jericho had contact with other nations. One of the items discovered at Jericho was a "goodly Babylonish garment" (7:21). This phrase might better be translated "one beautiful mantle from Shinar." This would seem to imply that Jericho had some trade contact with the Tigris-Euphrates cultural milieu. Finally, the text informs us that Jericho had an army (6:2). The size and strength of this army is not indicated in the text, but because of the detailed preparations undertaken by Joshua for this mission, we might assume that the city presented a formidable fighting force.

As the two Israelite spies began questioning Rahab, they immediately became aware of the fact that they had come in contact with one who was knowledgeable of both the history of Israel and the attitude of the Canaanites. For example, she had heard about the crossing of the Red Sea and the great victories accomplished on the east side of the Jordan (v. 10). The Canaanites at this time were very much afraid of the power of Israel and Israel's God. In light of this fear Rahab sought a personal covenant with them that she and her family might be saved when Israel invaded the land (vv. 12 ff.). The spies agreed that if she gave them accurate information and maintained secrecy regarding their mission, she and her family would indeed be rescued, providing they remained in her house at the time of conquest (vv. 18-19). While the spies were speaking with Rahab, the king of Jericho received word of their presence in the city. A contingent of soldiers was sent immediately to the house of Rahab, and they demanded that the spies be turned over to them. In the meantime, Rahab had hidden the spies on the roof of her house (v. 6). To the soldiers she replied that, yes, the spies had come to her, but she did not know where they were (v. 4). This, of course, was a lie, which brings to light a rather interesting problem. Was the lie of Rahab justified? After all, she uttered the lie in defense of two innocent Israelites. If she would have given the truth, would not both of these men have been killed by the king of Jericho? This problem has plagued modern commentators. Modern theologians tend to justify the lie of Rahab by what is commonly called "situational ethics"; that is, in this particular situation the lie was justified. This leads us to another important question, "Does the end really justify the means?" This is not the first time that a lie was uttered in the protection of another. Remember Abraham's lie (Gen. 12, 20). There are other parallel situations in Scripture which indicate that this was a problem to the people of this time.[13] Rahab probably did not see evil in her act. She saw the situation as a choice between two evils — to be morally responsible for betraying the two enemy spies, or to lie and save them. However, it is clear from Scripture that God regards all lies as evil and sinful. For one to lie in this manner is for one to assume that he knows the outcome of a situation which, in fact, he does not. God has control of every situation and therefore it might well be the will of God that the spies should die. It is the job of the believer to represent the truth and allow the Lord to care for that situation.

When the spies returned to Joshua, they brought a rather optimistic report to him. It is clear that they accepted the evaluation of Rahab without question. They were convinced not only of the fear of the Canaanites, but they were also convinced of the Lord's provision for them (vv. 23-24).

III. CROSSING THE JORDAN RIVER (3:1–5:15)

A. *Organization for the Crossing* (3:1-4)

Immediately after the return of the spies, Joshua began preparations for the crossing of the Jordan. The immediacy of Joshua's action is interesting. It indicates that he fully believed in the provision of the Lord. When the time came to actually move toward Jordan, Joshua did not request an extension of time in order to let the Jordan subside. He did not plead for a different route so as to avoid confrontation with the enemy. He did not call for a caucus, a commission, or a committee report in five copies, with this committee to be duly organized and named "The Committee on Crisis in the Contemporary Situation." Without argument and without delay, he prepared to march. The officers went through the tribes, and as they did,

---

[13]Genesis 26; 31:33-35; Exodus 1:15-22; I Samuel 19:14.

they commanded that the ark should be kept in view. There was to be a space between the ark and the people of about 2,000 cubits (v. 4). This would mean that there was a space around the ark of about 3,000 feet. There are probably two reasons why this was done: (1) a desire that all the people might be able to see the ark, and to understand that it was God who was leading them into the land, and not a great military force, and (2) the sacredness of the ark.

B. *Consecration for the Crossing* (3:5-13)

Another indication that the march of Israel was not merely a military exploit, but a spiritual fulfillment, is given in verse 5 of this chapter. The people were not commanded at this point to prepare their swords and shields but to prepare themselves. They were commanded to "sanctify themselves" (3:5; cf. 7:13). This sanctification was not ceremonial but spiritual. They were commanded to set themselves apart for God's program and will. They were ordered to keep their eyes on the Ark of the Covenant for leadership in the march, not the soldiers, the generals, or even Joshua. After Joshua gave the command to march, the Lord again spoke to him and reaffirmed His promise to be with Joshua and give him victory.

C. *The Completion of the Crossing* (3:14-17)

This particular event has given rise to considerable speculation among various Bible commentators. The Scriptures tell us that the priests went down to the waters of the Jordan, which at this time were rushing southward toward the Dead Sea in flood stage. They dipped their feet in the brim of the water (v. 15), and when that happened, the waters were stopped; that is, according to verse 16, they were heaped up in one heap at the city of Adam which is near Zaretan. The Authorized Version at this point is weak. Rather than the translation "very far from the city of Adam" the verse reads "at the city of Adam." This would mean that the waters were stopped at approximately thirteen to fifteen miles north of the Dead Sea. This would, of course, permit a wide expanse for the children of Israel to cross. Adam has generally been identified with Tell el-Damiyeh, about fifteen miles north of the Jericho area. Zaretan has been

The Jordan River.
Matson Photo Service

identified as the site of Tell es-Sa'idiyeh, which is located approximately twelve miles north of Adam.

The nature of this event has been brought in question in recent years. There are at least three views regarding the character of the event as described in Scripture. There are those who
deny the whole event as being purely fictitious. Others assert
that God used a natural phenomenon; that is, an earthquake
actually caused the crumbling of some of the cliffs in the
northern part of the Jordan, thereby blocking the waters and
permitting Israel to cross. There is some precedent for such a
view. On December 8, A.D. 1267, a large section of the west
bank of the river fell into the river, stopping its flow for approximately sixteen hours. Again on July 11, 1927, a landslide
near the ford at Damiyeh was caused by an earthquake, and
the flow was blocked for twenty-one hours. While such events
are possible, one must agree that the timing would have to be a
miracle. Furthermore, these did not occur at the flood season,
whereas the Biblical event did (cf. 3:15; 4:18).

The third view is that the event should be regarded as basically
supernatural in nature; that is, the Lord, by causes unknown
to us, stopped the flow of the Jordan for a sufficient amount of
time to enable the Israelites to cross safely. It is unlikely that
the Lord would employ something as destructive as an earthquake merely to stop the flow of a river. Furthermore, an earthquake in the Jordan Valley would have endangered Israelite
settlements on the east bank (cf. 3:1). It might also be noted
that the Jordan was stopped on two later occasions in order to
permit passage (cf. II Kings 2:8, 14). Are we to assume that
two successive earthquakes occurred merely to permit the prophets to cross? With the facts we have at present, it is the better
part of wisdom not to attempt to provide natural causes for
what appears to be a special act of God in behalf of His people.

D. *The Commemoration of the Crossing* (4:1-24)

The Lord commanded that two memorials be established to
commemorate the miracle of the Jordan crossing. One man from
each of the tribes was to carry a stone out of the Jordan, and
these would be used for a special memorial on the west bank of

this river. In actuality, two memorials were established to commemorate this event. The one which is described in verses 9-18 was actually placed in the Jordan River. The other was situated near or in the camp of Gilgal. This is described in verses 20-24. The memorials were designed to perpetuate the memory of this miraculous crossing. The Lord was concerned that future generations would have an appreciation of God's provision for His people (cf. vv. 21-23). The memorials served not only as a commemoration of God's provision for His own people, but they were evidently designed to be a sign of God's power to the nations around about (v. 24). According to this chapter, all the tribes participated in the crossing. The two-and-a-half tribes sent representative armies with the rest of the nation (vv. 12-13). Verse 13 indicates that 40,000 men of the two-and-a-half tribes actually crossed over the Jordan. It is clear from Numbers 26:7, 18, and 34 that the total potential fighting force of these tribes numbered about 110,580 men. Why, then, did only 40,-000 cross over? The answer is probably found in the situation on the east bank. The conquest might take some time, and the eastern tribes could not afford to leave their cities undefended. We might presume therefore that the remaining parts of their armies stayed on the east side for purposes of local protection.

E. *Circumcision after the Crossing* (5:1-15)

The words found in verse 1 of this chapter are in effect a clear fulfillment of the promises given in Exodus 23:27. They also confirm the evaluation of Rahab recorded in the second chapter of this book. It is appropriate that as the people stand in the new land there should be a renewal of a very important covenant practice. Evidently the practice of circumcision was abandoned during the wilderness journey. Verse 2 describes this as the second circumcision with respect to the exodus. There are two views as to why this important rite was neglected. Some argue that God did not permit them to perform this rite because of their sin (cf. v. 6).[14] According to Numbers 14:29, all Is-

---

[14]Compare John Rea, "Joshua," *The Wycliffe Bible Commentary,* ed. Charles F. Pfeiffer and Everett F. Harrison (Chicago: Moody Press, 1962), p. 211.

raelites twenty years and older were condemned to die in the
wilderness. This was thirty-eight years before they reached the
Jordan River. This means, therefore, that all males under the
age of thirty-eight were uncircumcised, and those between
the ages of thirty-eight and fifty-seven were circumcised before
they left Egypt (cf. v. 5).

Joshua was commanded to make "knives of flint."[15] All Israelites who had not been circumcised were therefore to participate in this important covenant sign, and with participation
should come a renewed commitment to the covenant given to
Abraham (Gen. 15-17). On the fourteenth day of this month,
the children of Israel kept the Passover (v. 10). One day later
they ate of the food of the land, and finally, on the sixteenth
day of that month, the manna which had sustained them the
forty years in the wilderness ceased to be provided (v. 12).

As the Lord appeared to Moses in a special way to prepare
him for leadership (Exod. 3:2), so the Lord appeared to Joshua
in a similar manner (5:13-15). Joshua did not immediately recognize his visitor as a divine being (v. 13); but as the Lord
spoke to him, His identity became clear, and Joshua fell down
and worshiped Him, and that without rebuke (v. 14). This
special appearance of the Lord was not merely to encourage
Joshua, but was to convey important information which he would
need in the conquest of Jericho. It is especially significant that
Joshua was commanded to remove the sandals from off his feet
as Moses had to do in a similar situation (v. 15; cf. Exod. 3:5).
This encounter was designed to give specific instruction for the
conquest of the city of Jericho. It is the view of this author that
the conversation begun in the latter verses of Chapter 5 is continued in 6:2, with verse 1 being a brief parenthetical statement.

One can only imagine the tremendous excitement that must
have characterized the camp of Israel on this occasion. There
was probably activity in every area as the tribes organized, set
up the camps, and as the leaders attempted to plan for the future. Finally, they had reached the shores of the land that had
been promised to their fathers. While there must have been an
air of rejoicing and thanksgiving, there probably was also

---

[15]Hebrew *harḇoṭ ṣurîm* (cf. Exod. 4:25).

considerable concern about the future of this expedition. They had not really encountered the enemy up to this point. Before them lay the walled city of Jericho with its imposing defensive systems. The real tests still lay ahead.

3

THE FIRST ENCOUNTER

Scarcely had the dust from the massive Israelite encampment settled in the Gilgal area when the Israelites realized that the Jordan crossing and the reinstitution of certain covenant practices were merely first steps in the fulfillment of God's promise. To the south of them lay the city of Jericho with its impressive defensive systems. Further to the west lay the great mountains of central Palestine. Before the tribes could even think of settlement in this vast expanse of land, Jericho had to be taken. The following discussion will deal with that problem and the solution that Joshua employed.

I. THE PROMISE OF VICTORY (6:1-2)

A. *Literary Structure*

As indicated in the last chapter, it appears that verse 1 of this chapter is parenthetical and verse 2, in effect, carries on the conversation between Joshua and the "captain of the Lord's host" (5:13-15). The purpose of this parenthetical statement is to explain the immediate situation (6:2-5). So great was their fear of the invading Israelites that the defenders of Jericho shut the gate to the city, not permitting any traffic in or out of the city (v. 1). After the successful visit of the spies, it is easy to understand why such action was taken.

B. *The Certainty of Victory* (6:2)

Jehovah again reminded Joshua that victory was assured because of divine intervention. The expression "I have given" is an exclamation of prophetic certainty (cf. Heb. *nā̱tatî*). The scope of victory is also indicated in this verse. The city, the king, and the army would all fall into the hands of Israel according to God's promise.

II. THE BATTLE PLAN (6:3-7)

A. *The Nature of the Plan*

To say the least, the battle plan revealed to Joshua was most unusual. It was indeed an act of faith on the part of Joshua to propose such a plan to the seasoned generals representing the various tribes. There is no evidence of rebellion to the plan as presented by Joshua, however. This probably indicates the commitment of the military leaders under Joshua to the Lord. The march around the walls was to be characterized by silence (6:10) except for blowing of the rams' horns (6:8). The people were to march around the walls of the city once each day and seven times on the last day at which time the walls would collapse, giving them access to the city of Jericho (6:3-5).

B. *The Purpose of the Plan*

The purpose of such a battle plan was probably twofold. (1) It was designed to test Israel's obedience to the will of God. A march like this would only bring ridicule from the enemy — at least in the early phases. Israel would have to humble herself and remain in complete submission to God's proposals — a very important lesson in this stage of the conquest of Canaan. (2) The plan was obviously designed to strike fear into the heart of the enemy. The defenders of Jericho were already in a state of frustration because of the previous victories of Israel (cf. 2:9-11). The march around the city in military formation, yet without any attempt to attack, must have sent "the Jericho commission on defense" into a number of special late evening sessions! The culmination of this march would be the collapse of Jericho's walls and subsequent destruction of the city (v. 5).

III. THE FALL OF JERICHO (6:8-27)

A. *The March around the Walls* (6:8-19)

This section of Chapter 6 deals with the organization of the march and the manner in which it was carried out over the seven-day period. It is quite clear that the march was not

Air View of the Plain of Jericho. The ancient mound of Jericho (Tell es-Sultan) in the foreground. Modern Jericho lies further distant. The Dead Sea and Mountains of Moab in the background (Joshua 3-6). Matson Photo Service

merely military in nature but religious. The prominent place
given to the priests and the ark indicates that it was God who was
leading them into battle and victory, and not Joshua or the
soldiers of the nation of Israel. A single march around the nine
acre mound area probably took twenty-five to thirty-five minutes. It should not be concluded that every Israelite took part
in this march. Such a feat would not only be impractical,
but would be impossible. It is more probable to assume that
the march was carried out by tribal representation. Such seems
to be the battle procedure even in the conquest to follow. The
order of march is given in verses 7-9, 13. The chart below illustrates the general order of march as indicated in these verses.

ORGANIZATION OF THE MARCH

I	II	III	IV	V
Soldiers	Priests with Rams' Horns	Ark	Soldiers	People
v. 9	vv. 6, 8, 13	vv. 6, 8, 13	v. 9	v. 7

We are not given the details of each day's activities, but can
assume that the early part of the week brought considerable
ridicule from the inhabitants of Jericho. However, as the days
passed, and the army continued to march in confidence, a great
silence probably came over the defenders of that city. When
would Israel attack? What type of strategy were they using?
It was probably not easy for the leaders of Israel to remain silent early in the week when the enemy ridiculed their faith and
their intentions, but as is the case in every generation, when
men act upon the promises of God with complete faith, victory
is theirs.

Joshua instructed the people that the city of Jericho was accursed (vv. 17-18). The Hebrew term translated "accurse" (Heb.

ḥērem) means to "ban, devote, or exterminate." It may also
mean to "seclude from society." This term was applied to capital punishment (Lev. 27:29), to offerings given to God (Num.
18:14; Ezek. 44:29), and with reference to "the utter destruction" of the enemies of God (Deut. 7:26; 20:17; Isa. 34:5). It
is also used spiritually of God's judgment against impenitent
sinners (Mal. 4:6). This expression means, therefore, that Jericho and all of its contents were completely devoted to Jehovah
as the firstfruits of the land, for a sign that the Israelites
would receive all Canaan from Him. Joshua made it clear that no
objects were to be kept by any of the invading Israelites (v. 18).
The exception to this prohibition is found in verse 19. Silver,
gold, and the vessels of bronze and iron were to be kept and consecrated unto the Lord as part of His treasury (v. 19).

B. *The Collapse of the Walls* (6:20-21)

As the people completed their march on that important seventh day, they shouted when the priests gave the signal with
the rams' horns (v. 20). It was at this time that the walls of
Jericho collapsed in place. The literal rendering of the Hebrew is "the wall fell in its place." The question frequently
raised concerning this event is, "Why did the walls of Jericho
fall?" To this question, many answers have been given. For
example, there is the popular view that an earthquake occurred at just the right moment. While this is entirely possible,
it would still require a miracle of timing. Indeed, an earthquake of such magnitude to destroy the walls of an established
city might be one which would bring some destruction to the
encampment of Gilgal located rather near to the city of Jericho.
More bizarre is the viewpoint that sound waves caused the walls
to crumble. One writer suggests that the pitch of the trumpets
and the shout of the individuals caused tremendous vibrations,
thereby bringing about the collapse of the walls. Others have
suggested that the children of Israel marched in step, causing
great shock waves beneath the walls. As a result, the walls
crumbled. Some have suggested that the walls were built on
sandy soil and were already in cracked condition. The vibrations from the shouting, the rams' horns, and the stomping of

feet were the things that caused the walls finally to collapse. Such views, while attractive to the general public, do not really solve any problems. The wall construction at Jericho was not haphazard, as excavations have shown. It is extremely doubtful, in any event, that the pitch of rams' horns or the united voices of the people would really have any effect upon the massive mud brick walls of that ancient city. It is better to assume that God Himself brought about, by supernatural means, the collapse of these walls. Otherwise, we have no way of accounting for the fact that most sections of the wall collapsed except those that surrounded the house of Rahab, for as long as Rahab and her family remained in her house, according to the agreement with the spies (2:17-20), she would be safe from the destruction that was to come to Jericho. This promise was fulfilled as recorded in verse 22 of Chapter 6. While the walls of the city collapsed destroying the houses adjacent to them, the house of Rahab remained intact, thereby preserving her and her family.

C. Archaeology and the Fall of Jericho

The archaeological evidence from Jericho (Tell es-Sultan) is not clear regarding the destruction of this city by Joshua. The excavations conducted at the site, between 1930 and 1936, by John Garstang indicated that the city was extensively occupied down to the year 1550 B.C. This occupation was recorded by Garstang as being that of the Hyksos peoples. Garstang also discovered another city level which he called City IV, and related this to the Late Bronze Age period, or the period of the conquest. He felt that he had discovered the walls of Jericho dating to Joshua's period. The walls were actually two parallel walls. The inner wall measured about twelve feet thick, the outer wall six feet thick with approximately twelve feet between. It appeared to him that these mud brick walls had been destroyed by an earthquake in connection with an intense fire. Between the years 1952 and 1958, the site was again excavated under the leadership of Miss Kathleen Kenyon. Her work at the site indicated that the walls had been misidentified by Garstang. Rather than the walls belonging to the Late Bronze

Age, they represented a much earlier period (Early Bronze) and were not contemporary walls but, in effect, revealed two separate building phases. This does not mean that all of Garstang's evidence has been negated by the later excavations. Dr. Garstang found some 320 Late Bronze Age objects, including two scarabs of Amenhotep III (1410-1372 B.C.) as well as Late Bronze sherds on the mound. After the destruction of the city, about 1550 B.C., the mound lay vacant for about 150 years. Since most of the typically fifteenth century pottery forms are lacking, it is concluded that reoccupation must have taken place about 1410 B.C. or a little earlier. It is entirely possible that the Canaanites occupying the site in Joshua's day reused parts of the Hyksos' fortifications in building their own mud brick walls. The reason that very little Late Bronze Age material is found at the site is that after its destruction by Joshua, the site remained unoccupied for a long period of time. In the light of the completeness of the destruction brought by Joshua (6:21-24) and the fact that the mound was exposed allowing the process of erosion to destroy much of the evidence, we therefore should not expect a great abundance of material from Joshua's period. It is also possible that local inhabitants removed much of the material after the abandonment of the site. It is significant that Jericho is not mentioned in any of the Amarna tablets. This seems to confirm the Biblical record of its total destruction and subsequent abandonment.

D. *The Death of All Living Things*

Upon entering the city, and after a brief battle (cf. Josh. 24:11), the armies of Israel destroyed "all that was in the city, both man and woman, young and old, and ox, and sheep, and ass, with the edge of the sword" (v. 21). This action has been subjected to considerable criticism on the part of many Biblical scholars. For example, James Muilenburg considers this type of treatment to be somewhat below high ethical norms.[16] He regards it as a transitional stage in Israel's evolutionary develop-

---

[16]James Muilenburg, "The History of the Religion of Israel," *The Interpreter's Bible,* ed. George A. Buttrick (New York: Abingdon Press, 1952), p. 310.

ment. Paul Heinisch, on the other hand, regards this event as "one of the imperfections of the Old Testament."[17] Rowley asserts that these practices were in direct conflict with the spirit of New Testament truth.[18] According to his view, we have a contradiction in ethical and moral actions between the Old Testament and the New. W. F. Albright in *From Stone Age to Christianity* argues that this event is no more a moral problem than the massacre of the Armenians by the Turks.[19] He assumes that this was just another national struggle.

Still, the morality of the actions described in this chapter have come under severe scrutiny on the part of modern scholars. Is it true that the Israelites unjustly slaughtered "innocent" Canaanites? There are several facts which should be kept in mind when dealing with this problem. First of all, it should be noted that the destruction of Canaanite cities was based on religious, not political or military considerations (Deut. 7:2-6; 12:2-3; 20:10-18). Secondly, the action taken at Jericho (and also at Ai) was done on the basis of *divine command* (Exod. 17:14; Deut. 7:2; 20:16; Josh. 8:2) and thus involves the moral character of God. If we believe that God is holy and without imperfection, it follows that whatever He commands will be just and right. And, thirdly, it was really *Jehovah* who was destroying these cities and their peoples (Josh. 6:2; 24:8). Israel should merely be regarded as God's instruments of destruction. Fourthly, the *reason* for this command is clearly stated in Scripture and seems to justify the action taken. For example, Deuteronomy 20:18 makes it clear that this demand was designed to preserve the religious purity of the nation of Israel. The destruction of various Canaanite cities should be regarded as a direct judgment from God because of their iniquity (Gen. 15:16-21; cf. Gen. 19). If the Lord thought it necessary to destroy the cities of Sodom and Gomor-

[17]Paul Heinisch, *Theology of the Old Testament* (The Liturgical Press, 1955), p. 214.

[18]H. H. Rowley, *The Rediscovery of the Old Testament* (Philadelphia: The Westminster Press, 1946), p. 32 ff.

[19]W. F. Albright, *From the Stone Age to Christianity* (Baltimore: The Johns Hopkins Press, 1957), p. 280.

rah because of their sin, it is also appropriate that Jericho should be destroyed because of its iniquity. The means that God might use is insignificant in such a case. It might also be observed that the destruction of such cities would serve as a visible illustration of God's view of polytheism. Israel, on several occasions, was warned that if she became like the Canaanites, she too would be punished (Deut. 28:15 ff.; Josh. 6:18; 24:20). Therefore, rather than this command and its fulfillment being in conflict with the New Testament, it is, after all, a complement to the theological and moral principles of Scripture as a whole. God is a holy God. He demands that sin be punished. The Lord reserves the right to punish sin wherever it is found. He may act, then, in the immediate destruction of a city or in the condemnation of the sinner at final judgment. It is only by the mercy and the grace of God that any sinner is permitted to live his life completely. In fact, He could punish sin upon the committing of the first act, take the life of that individual, and still remain a perfectly righteous and holy God.

E. *The Rescue of Rahab* (6:22-25)

The history of Rahab is a remarkable example of the grace of God operative in the Old Testament period. In spite of her past life and the lie that she told, she gave true evidence of her saving faith in God by "having received the spies with peace" (Heb. 11:31; cf. Josh. 6:17, 25). A further evidence of this marvelous grace is the fact that her name appears in the messianic line (Matt. 1:5). The faith of Rahab brought deliverance to her own immediate family as was the case of Noah and Lot.

F. *The Curse on the City* (6:26-27)

The curse pronounced by Joshua involved the *refortification* of Jericho, not mere future habitation. The words "foundation" and "gates" (v. 26) refer to the establishment of a wall around the city. It is evident from Judges 1:16 and 3:13 (cf. Deut. 34:3) that the city was to some degree reinhabited a short time after the destruction. This occupation of the site seems to be very brief and from an archaeological point of view inconsequential.

The first attempt to refortify the city is recorded in I Kings 16: 34. In the days of King Ahab, a man by the name of Hiel attempted to rebuild the walls of Jericho, and in so doing he lost two of his sons in fulfillment of the curse pronounced on the site by Joshua. This curse, therefore, was fulfilled some 500 years after its pronouncement by Joshua. Some have suggested that this curse may have been removed by the intercession of Elisha after the time of Hiel (cf. II Kings 2:18-22).

The quick, spectacular, and decisive victory of the children of Israel at this site caused inhabitants of Canaan to take special notice of their potential. As was the case with victories on the eastern side of the Jordan River, word spread rapidly throughout the land of Canaan regarding the miraculous power of the God of Israel. The secret to success at Jericho was not mere military genius or battle capability. The success of Israel was due to her unconditioned faith in, and obedience to, the revealed will of God.

The Ruins of Ancient Jericho from the East (Joshua 6). Matson Photo Service

4

DEFEAT AND VICTORY

The history recorded in the seventh chapter of the Book of Joshua represents one of Israel's darkest hours. Up to now, everything has gone smoothly, and the armies of Israel have tasted only victory. But now the scene drastically changes. Their progress is suddenly halted. Defeat, sorrow, and loss characterize the camp of Israel. Let us examine the events which brought about this tragic scene.

I. THE TRAGEDY OF DEFEAT (Josh. 7)

A. *The Source of Defeat* (7:1-5, 10-12)

The events recorded in this chapter can be described as both unexpected and unprecedented. This chapter reveals how victory on the part of God's people can be quickly undermined by disobedience and sin on the part of a single individual. The reason for Israel's defeat at the city of Ai is given to us in the first verse of this chapter which asserts that Israel "committed a trespass." The word for trespass in the original is of special importance. It is a technical term referring to the misappropriation of property which was considered in a sacred category (cf. Lev. 5:15). The trespass, according to this text, had reference to the "accursed thing." The Hebrew term used here for accursed thing is the same as that which is used in Joshua 6:18; therefore, we are dealing with open revolt against a clearly revealed prohibition given by God. The effects of the sin of Achan and those who followed him are described in verses 2-5.

In preparation for the next phase of Israel's conquest of Canaan, Joshua sent men from Jericho to the city of Ai which is beside Beth-aven. The city of Ai is generally associated with the ancient site of et-Tell. This site is located in the central hill country of Palestine. From the record it appears that Joshua wasted little time in organizing the spy mission. Notice that the men were sent from Jericho, not Gilgal. Jericho, of course, was the recent place of battle. The men obeyed and went up to the hill country and searched the area surrounding Ai, as well as the city itself, and brought back to Joshua a rather optimistic report regarding their ability to conquer the city. They suggested that only two or three thousand men would be needed to conquer that site (v. 3) since the people of the city were "but a few." Joshua accepted their report as he had done on previous occasions and organized about 3,000 men to take the city. It would appear from the information given in Joshua 8:25 that the spy report was rather accurate. When the city was destroyed, the total slain, including men and women, was 12,000 (8:25). This would seem to indicate an approximate army size of two to four thousand men. The request for 3,000 soldiers, therefore, was not at all unreasonable. However, when the conflict began, the men of Ai had the upper hand from the beginning and were, without a doubt, superior. The Israelite

The Valley of Achor near Jericho (Joshua 7:26). Matson Photo Service

troops panicked and fled toward the rocky cliffs leading down to the Jordan Valley (7:5). Thirty-six men were slain, and the remaining part of the army reached Gilgal in a state of complete humiliation. The hearts of the people "melted and became as water" (v. 5). It is strange indeed that the description which was originally used for the Canaanites about to be defeated now describes the heart of the Israelites (cf. 2:11; 5:1).

B. *The Sorrow of Defeat* (7:6-9)

Joshua, upon hearing this news, "rent his clothes and fell upon the earth" in disappointment and sorrow before the Lord. He and the elders of Israel put dust upon their heads, a common procedure when demonstrating a feeling of deep sorrow and humilitation (cf. Gen. 37:34; I Sam. 4:12; II Sam. 1:2; 13:31). The cry of Joshua recorded in verse 7 is strangely familiar. It raises a question which, in essence, was raised by unbelieving and murmuring Israel during the wilderness journey (cf. Exod. 16:2-3; Num. 14:2-4). Joshua was concerned not only about the destiny of the people but also about the name of his God (v. 9). The Lord responded to Joshua's questions quickly and decisively, and pointed out to him that the reason for Israel's defeat and humiliation was sin (v. 11). He was commanded to get up from his face and immediately care for this problem. Someone had violated the Lord's regulations concerning the "accursed thing," and because of this, Israel had become accursed (v. 12).

C. *The Solution to Defeat* (7:13-26)

1. *Confession of Sin* (7:13-21)

The first step in restoring fellowship with God was for the people to "sanctify themselves" (v. 13). This expression was first noticed in Joshua 3:5. The sanctification mentioned here is not ceremonial, but spiritual. It deals with the commitment of the people to the covenant which they had with their God. It appears that lots were used in determining the guilty party. Notice the expression "the Lord taketh" (v. 14) and similar expressions throughout this section (cf. I Sam. 14:42; Jonah 1:7) which describe lot-casting elsewhere in Scripture. The

first lot fell upon the tribe of Judah (v. 16); the second upon
the clan Zerah (v. 17); the third upon the house of Zabdi (v. 17);
the fourth and final lot fell upon the man Achan (v. 18). This
event was followed by the confession of Achan (vv. 19-21).
The sequence of Achan's temptation and sin, as described in
verse 21, is instructive. His sin involved three crucial steps.
(1) He saw; (2) he coveted; and (3) he took. This is not the
first time that one has been led into sin by this means. Compare,
for example, the experience of Eve in the Garden of Eden
(Gen. 3:6), and the temptation of David (II Sam. 11:2-4).
The objects taken by Achan included a "goodly Babylonish garment" (v. 7; Heb. "beautiful mantle of Shinar"). As previously
noted, the presence of a garment from Shinar might indicate
widespread trade contacts between Jericho and cities to the
north. The stolen treasure also included two hundred shekels
of silver, and a wedge (tongue or ingot) of gold. This wedge
of gold was probably similar to the one unearthed at the city of
Gezer by Macalister. It measured about ten inches, by one inch,
by one-half inch. A similar wedge of gold is also mentioned in
one of the Amarna letters.

2. *The Punishment of Sin* (7:22-26)

According to verse 24, not only Achan but his whole family
was punished for the sin committed. We might assume from
this act that the family had in some way taken part in this
wicked deed. From a purely practical point of view, it is doubtful that Achan could have removed this number of objects and
kept them concealed without some help from his family. The
law of Deuteronomy 13:12-18 was probably in effect in this case.
After he was stoned to death, his body was placed under a
great heap of stones (v. 26). This appears to be a common
method of burying infamous persons (cf. Josh. 8:29; II Sam.
18:17). The fact that all Israel (v. 24) participated in the
punishment of Achan and his family seems to indicate that
they had, indeed, sanctified themselves and were willing to deal
with the sin problem. Once this had been cared for and the
lesson had been learned, God was now ready to give victory to
His people.

II. THE THRILL OF VICTORY (Josh. 8)

A. *The Battle Plan* (8:1-9)

Once again Jehovah encouraged Joshua not to be afraid nor
be discouraged even though Israel had suffered defeat. He was
commanded to take all the people of war and to go up to the
city of Ai. As was the case with Jericho, the Lord promised to
give the people and the city into his hands (v. 1). He was
commanded to utterly destroy the city of Ai as he had done to
the city of Jericho. However, the only difference was that the
Israelites were permitted to take the spoil of Ai, whereas they
were not permitted to do this in the conquest of Jericho (v. 2;
cf. Josh. 6:18-21).

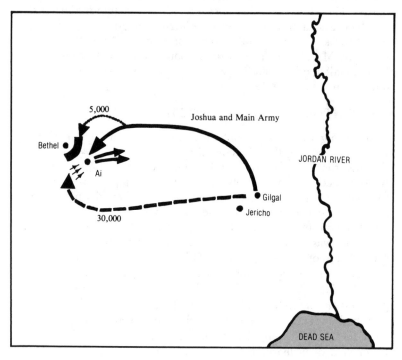

The Battle at Ai (Joshua 8)

The tactical maneuvers that were used in the capture of Ai are most interesting, but not without problems. For example, the numbers recorded in the verses that follow appear to be hopelessly confused; however, when they are studied carefully, they reveal an ingenious plan of attack and are very realistic. Joshua was commanded to select 30,000 men, and send them away by night to make the thirteen-mile journey to Ai, and then to lie in wait on the west side of the city (vv. 3-4). The next day, Joshua took the main army of Israel up to the north side of the city of Ai (v. 11). In addition to that move, another 5,000 were sent to lie in ambush between Bethel and Ai (v. 12). The map (page 56) will illustrate the battle plan as described in this chapter.

The 30,000 troops sent to the west side of Ai during the night were designed to be an attack force prepared to enter the city from that side. The main army of Joshua, encamped to the north, was to be used as a diversionary force to draw the armies of Ai out of the city, thereby leaving the city vulnerable to attack from the west (cf. vv. 13-17). The 5,000 troops, sent to the west side of Ai (v. 12), were deployed as a defensive measure designed to prevent the armies of Bethel from entering the battle or outflanking the 30,000 on the west side of the city of Ai.

B. *The Destruction of Ai* (8:10-29)

The battle plan worked to precision. The arrogant men of Ai were sure that they could again drive the Israelites down into the Jordan Valley. However, when they fled down to the valley in pursuit of the fleeing Israelites, they turned back only to see their city in flames and smoke. The ambush of 30,000 men entered the city, destroying it and killing all in their path. The 5,000 men encountered some resistance from Bethel and apparently were victorious there as well (cf. 8:17). Ultimately, the victory was complete. Over 12,000 men, women, and children were slain in this great battle (v. 25). In obedience to God's will, Joshua burned the city, thus destroying it completely (v. 28; cf. v. 2). Following this, the king of Ai was slain and buried under a great heap of stones (v. 29).

C. Archaeology and the Destruction of Ai

The archaeological situation at the city of Ai is a very complex one as it regards the date of the conquest. Excavations were conducted at the site between 1933 and 1935 under the leadership of Madame Marquet-Krause. These excavations revealed that there was a major occupational gap between approximately 2200 B.C. and 1200 B.C. These data, of course, would not fit anyone's date of the exodus. To shed additional light on the problem and to clarify the earlier excavations, Professor Joseph A. Calloway initiated excavations at the site in May of 1964. The results achieved that year and subsequent years have confirmed the presence of the occupational gap at this site. A number of solutions have been proposed with regard to this problem. There are those who suggest that the site should be located elsewhere in the vicinity. This view is difficult to maintain in the light of recent archaeological work by Dr. Calloway's teams. Many sites have now been eliminated in the vicinity of et-Tell. Some have suggested that the site suffers from major erosion such as was witnessed at Jericho, but this view seems to be unsatisfactory also. A very popular view is that the battle described in Joshua 8 really took place at Bethel and that the story of the battle was transferred to the ruins at Ai. Another writer has suggested that Ai was really a temporary fortress built near the site of Bethel. When this fortress was destroyed with its wall structures, nothing remained. At present, there is no easy or simple solution to the problem. We must await further investigation of both et-Tell and other sites in the central hill country in order to determine a solution to this difficulty.

D. The Covenant Renewal at Mount Ebal (8:30-35)

Following the great victory at Ai, the children of Israel marched northward to Mount Ebal, located about twenty miles north of et-Tell. Excavations conducted at the site of Shechem (Tell Balatah) indicate that there was a substantial occupation at this site about the time of the Israelites' arrival. Even though the site seems to have been fortified at this time, the Bible records no battle at this place. How were the Israelites able to move freely around Mount Gerizim and Mount Ebal without some confrontation from the inhabitants of Shechem? The answer to this problem might be found in several of the Amarna letters which were written about 1380 B.C. or shortly after the conquest period. These letters, written from the king of Jerusalem, and other cities, describe the surrender of the city of Shechem to the invading Habiru. The letters indicate, or at least imply, that the city surrendered without resistance. Is it not possible that the city of Shechem may have also succumbed to Israel in a similar manner? Some writers have suggested that perhaps some descendants of Jacob, who had left Egypt in small numbers before the oppression (cf. I Chron. 7:24), may have been at the site when Israel arrived there.

In any event, Israel moved successfully to the base of Mount Ebal, the mountain which is centrally situated in the land of Canaan. It rises to a height of 3,080 feet. Just to the south of it is the famous Mount Gerizim (2,849 feet). The mountains form a natural amphitheater in which the "cursings and blessings" could be pronounced and heard by those gathered at

Mount Gerizim (Joshua 8:33). Levant Photo Service

the site. Israel came to this site because Moses had specifically
indicated that upon her entrance into the land, sacrifice and
dedication should be made to God in this area (cf. Deut. 11:
26-30; 27:2-8). The first event was the establishment of an altar
and sacrifices (v. 31). Following this, Joshua made a copy of the
law of Moses for all to read (vv. 32-34). The significance of
this occasion cannot be overestimated. After a great victory, it
was now Israel's responsibility to recognize the source of that
victory, and again renew her covenant vows to Jehovah. Public
readings of the law constituted a very important part of
Israelite life and worship in many periods of her history (see
Exod. 24:4, 7; II Kings 23:2; Neh. 8).

III. THE DANGER OF COMPLACENCY (Josh. 9)

After the great events at Mount Ebal, the children of Israel
returned to the Jordan Valley and their center of operations at
Gilgal (cf. 9:6). It was at this place that the southern campaign would really begin. The chapter under consideration
brings to our attention the fact that the kings of the Amorite
city-states, who controlled the southern portions of Canaan, were
desperately trying to form some kind of coalition in order to
survive the invasion by the nation of Israel. Since Egypt showed
no interest in the Palestinian cities at this time, they had no
choice but to depend on one another for mutual defense (cf.
vv. 1-2). The inhabitants of Gibeon, however, were not convinced that such a coalition would really be effective. They
decided that a covenant agreement or a league would, in the
long run, be more effective for them. Thus the Gibeonites,
ingeniously, provide us with what might be termed an "Oscar
winning performance" in deceiving the elders of Israel. The
whole purpose of dressing up in old clothes, taking old sacks,
and wearing old shoes was to convince the elders of Israel and
Joshua that they had, indeed, been on the road for many days
and had come from a "far country" (vv. 6, 9). The question is,
"Why put on such a performance?" The answer to this question
is to be found in two key texts: Deuteronomy 7:1-2 and 20:
10-15. These passages indicate that Israel was permitted to
make peace with the cities that were far off, but not with the

seven Canaanite nations living in close proximity to them. Somehow, the inhabitants of Gibeon found out about this legislation. The Gibeonites were very careful in their approach to the leaders of Israel. Besides clothing, moldy food, and the proclamation that they were from a far country, they even omitted certain events in their discussion of Israel's recent history so as not to give themselves away. Notice that, accordingly, they mention only the exodus from Egypt (v. 9) and the victories on the eastern side of the Jordan River (v. 10). There is no reference to the battle at Jericho or the destruction of the city of Ai. This, indeed, is appropriate, for if they had been on the road for many days — away from contact with cities, as evidenced by their moldy bread — then they should not have knowledge of the very recent battles. They proclaimed to the leaders of Israel that they were, in effect, willing to be "their servants" (vv. 9-10). The use of this expression indicates the desire for a formal treaty or covenant. Such a treaty was drawn up by Joshua and the princes of Israel (9:15). This mistake which was made by Joshua was inexcusable in spite of the fact that the Gibeonites were shrewd in their deception of the elders of Israel. Verse 14 makes note of the fact that the Lord was not sought in the deliberations at hand. The treaty was made, and after three days, the Israelites knew that they had been deceived (v. 16). It is significant that the elders of Israel and Joshua refused to break that covenant even though they had been deceived. The Gibeonites were subjected to a state of servitude (v. 21), but the treaty remained intact. Some have questioned whether there was really any moral obligation on the part of Joshua and the elders to maintain that agreement in the light of the fact that they had been deceived. Others, on the basis of Leviticus 19:12, argue that they had a solemn and sacred responsibility to keep that oath since it was made in the name of the Lord God of Israel (v. 18). The forming of such agreements by the name of Jehovah was not a light matter and therefore they were morally responsible to maintain the agreement which they had made.

The practical lessons from this chapter should be obvious to the child of God. First of all, he should recognize that his enemy is cunning and deceitful. Secondly, he should trust every decision of life into the hands of the Lord who knows the beginning from the end. Thirdly, he should never permit the glow of victory to blind his clear perception of the situations about him, for very quickly, victory can be turned into tragic defeat through complacency and lack of obedience.

5

WHEN THE SUN STOOD STILL

To make a formal oath or covenant in an ancient Near Eastern society was a very important — and in many respects a sacred — event. This was especially true in the case of Israel when, having been deceived, they made a covenant agreement with the Gibeonites in the name of Jehovah. The princes refused to break that oath, realizing that such a breach of agreement would bring wrath upon them (cf. Ezek. 17:12-19). Having made an agreement of peace between the Gibeonites and themselves, the Israelites were responsible not only for the keeping of peace, but for the protection of those people as they lived in servitude to Israel. The keeping of such a covenant agreement was not an easy task, as Chapter 10 demonstrates. In order to provide full protection for the Gibeonites, Joshua was drawn into battle against a major Amorite coalition from southern Canaan.

I. THE SOUTHERN CAMPAIGN (Josh. 10)

A. *The Plot against Gibeon* (10:1-6)

The surrender of the Gibeonites to Joshua and the elders of Israel was viewed as the beginning of a dangerous trend by Adoni-zedec, the king of Jerusalem (v. 1). Gibeon was a great city. In fact, the Bible describes it as one of the "royal cities," and a city that was greater than Ai, having many mighty men (v. 2). If such an important city could surrender peacefully, this might pave the way for other cities in the vicinity of Jerusalem to surrender in like manner, or at least attempt to do so. This, of course, would be a serious threat to the security of Jerusalem. Adoni-zedec was probably a rather powerful king and an influential one in central Palestine. The Amarna letters indicate that Jerusalem was the center of political activity in the fourteenth century B.C. and was always conscious of its own security. The name Adoni-zedec ("lord of righteousness") was probably a common Jebusite dynastic title rather than a personal name.

Gibeon (el-Jib), looking North (Joshua 9-10). Levant Photo Service

It is very similar to Melchizedek (Gen. 14:18), the name of an earlier ruler in Jerusalem. The Jebusites (15:63), who controlled Jerusalem until the time of David when they were driven out, appear to be a racial mixture of Amorites, Hittites, and Hurrians (Ezek. 16:3). According to the Amarna letters, written approximately 1375 B.C., there were only four main independent city-states in southern Palestine (Jerusalem, Shuwardata, Gezer, and Lachish). According to the Book of Joshua, however, there were approximately thirty-one city-states having independent kings (12:9-24). This information appears to place Joshua's conquest prior to the writing of the Amarna letters. The success of Israel brought about the end to many of the independent states, thus leaving only a few self-sufficient political entities in southern Canaan, and also resulted in causing a good deal of confusion among those city-states.[20]

In order to punish the city of Gibeon for its deed, Adoni-zedec contacted other kings in southern Canaan located at Hebron,

---

[20]John Rea, *op. cit.*, p. 217.

Jarmuth, Lachish, and Eglon. The other kings responded positively to Adoni-zedec's plan and moved against Gibeon (v. 5). When the Gibeonites received word of this plan, they immediately sent messengers to Joshua down at Gilgal (v. 6). They reminded Joshua of the covenant agreement that he had with the city of Gibeon and requested protection in fulfillment of that agreement.

B. *Joshua's March to Gibeon* (10:7-9)

Joshua recognized that he did have an obligation to protect the city, and quickly responded to the plea of the Gibeonites. It is clear from verse 8 that all of this was, indeed, in accordance with the Lord's will, for He had given assurance that victory would be theirs. Joshua gathered his forces together, and during that evening they began their march to Gilgal — a journey of approximately twenty-five miles. Such a journey must have been very tiring to the soldiers, epecially since they traveled at night. It is apparent that Jehovah would have to help them if they were to realize the victory promised to them.

C. *The Defeat of the Amorite Coalition* (10:10-27)

1. *The Miracle of Hailstones* (10:10-11)

The battle that is described in the verses that follow is one of the most unusual in Israel's history. In fact, it is one of the most unusual in all recorded history. When the Israelites first confronted the Amorite coalition, the Lord aided their battle plan by discomfiting the enemy. This was accomplished by providing a hailstorm (v. 11). There is no other way to explain this event than to regard it as a miracle, for it appears that the hailstones affected only the enemy and not Israel. It is not characteristic of a purely natural hailstorm to make such a selection! The events described in verses 10 and 11 most likely took place in very early morning. As the day wore on, it became evident to Joshua that he would not be able to complete the battle and gain victory. He also realized that if the enemy were to have the benefit of darkness and rest, it would be most difficult for Israel to confront them again. His troops were tired, but everything at this point was in his favor. The enemy was scattered and frustrated as a result of the hailstorm. He wanted to capitalize on this situation; thus, in verse 12, he appeared before the Lord and brought to the Lord a most unusual request.

2. *The Miracle of Extended Light* (10:12-27)

This portion of Scripture has long been subjected to speculative ideas and interpretations because of the nature of the events herein described. It will not be our purpose to present an exhaustive treatment of the many views offered, but rather a brief summary and evaluation of some of them, followed by the writer's view of this passage.

There are three basic interpretations of the long day of Joshua. (a) *The total eclipse view.* The essence of this view is that God brought darkness rather than light on this occasion. The advocates for this view contend that God actually caused the sun and the moon to stop shining. This was accomplished by the use of clouds, a hailstorm, or perhaps an eclipse of the sun. The arguments for this view are generally based on the Hebrew word *dom*, which usually means "to be silent." It can also have as a secondary meaning, however, the idea of "to cease" or "to desist." The latter translation is suggested by R. D. Wilson, who gave this view prominence in an article written some years ago in *Princeton Theological Review.*[21] It is argued that if the sun could be shaded, it would provide relief for the weary armies of Joshua. While this approach seems plausible at first, careful consideration indicates that it does not fulfill the requirements of the passage. If the sun were to cease shining, thereby providing rest and refreshment for Joshua's soldiers, would this not also be the case for the enemy? In the second place, we might observe that the Scripture describes this as a very unique day. Notice the words of verse 14: "And there was no day like that before it or after it." This seems to be a rather extravagant statement if the event was merely the shading or the eclipsing

---

[21]R. D. Wilson, "What Does 'The Sun Stood Still' Mean?" *Princeton Theological Review,* Vol. 16, 1918.

of the sun. The sun had been darkened before, and we have had many eclipses subsequent to that period of history. The statement, therefore, seems to indicate a day which has no parallel in history. (b) *The poetic interpretation.* According to this view, the account of the battle is nothing more than poetic imagery and should not be taken literally. It is argued that the ideas expressed in these verses were purely subjective, i.e., that it only *seemed* (because of the heat of battle) as if the sun stood still. It is true that verse 13 is a quotation from the book of Jasher and that it is indeed in poetic structure. However, it is not uncommon for literal battles and attending events to be described in poetic language (cf. Judg. 4-5).[22] (c) *The prolongation of light interpretation.* This view, by and large the most popular view of conservative commentators, is that which understands the passage literally. In other words, it assumes that there was an actual extension of light for about a whole day, thereby permitting Joshua to complete the battle. While there is wide agreement among conservative scholars on this general position, there is a great divergence of opinion relative to the method by which this prolongation of light was accomplished.

The following are some representative views on this problem: (1) *The slowing of the earth's rotation.* Many commentators feel that the simplest solution to the extension of light suggested in this chapter is to propose a slowing down of the earth's rotation. There is no question that God was fully capable of such a miracle. At this point, the question is, "Would such a miracle be performed merely to provide assistance to the armies fighting in the area of Beth-horon?" (2) *A comet came near the earth.* Immanuel Velikovsky suggests that the reason the earth's rotation was slowed down was the appearance of a comet near the earth, thus exerting gravitational pull on the earth and disrupting its normal movement. The tail of this comet, he claims, provided the "stones" that dispersed the enemy.[23]

---

[22]For further discussion of this view, see F. R. Fay, *Joshua, Commentary on the Holy Scriptures,* trans. Philip Schaff (Grand Rapids: Zondervan Publishing House, n.d.), p. 96 ff.

[23]Immanuel Velikovsky, *Worlds in Collision* (New York: Macmillan, 1950), pp. 43-44.

This view is typical of those approaches to Scriptures which would attempt to explain miracles by means of natural phenomena or catastrophes. It is very doubtful that a comet with whatever magnetic field it might contain would ever affect the movement of the earth with its great mass, and, of course, it is highly questionable that stones falling from the tail of a comet would strike the enemy and not harm Israel. The most obvious objection to this view is that there is no archaeological or geological evidence of such an event in Palestine. (3) *The tilting of the earth.* George Williams in *The Student's Commentary* suggests that the means that God used to extend light was to tilt the earth on its axis, thus causing the sun to remain above the horizon as it does, for example, in Norway during the summer.[24] Again, this view creates more problems than it solves. Tilting the earth in this manner would be observable in a change of the position of the sun. Also, such tilting would create radical changes in climate. This view, like that of slowing the earth's rotation, assumes that the miracle performed was universal in scope. (4) *The principle of jet propulsion.* In the *Sunday School Times* of August 15, 1942, Hawley O. Taylor proposed that the earth's rotation was indeed slowed down. In order to provide a mechanism for this event, he made the suggestion that a number of volcanic explosions took place, all, of course, facing the east, thus providing a counter-thrust causing the crust of the earth to slow down in rotation. The liquid interior of the earth, however, continued to rotate in its normal pattern. After a period of time the outside crust of the earth resumed rotation along with the inside. This view really does not deserve serious scientific consideration. In the first place, it is impossible that volcanos could ever produce this kind of thrust, and, of course, this view assumes that all the volcanos would be aimed in a certain direction. This would require an immense miracle. The earth has a mass of about six trillion tons and at the equator is moving about a thousand miles an hour. No series of volcanic thrusts could ever produce enough velocity to slow down the rotation of the earth, and even if such eruption occurred, it would

---

[24]George Williams, *The Student's Commentary on the Holy Scriptures* (London: Oliphants Ltd., 1949), p. 114.

bring about mass destruction over large areas of the earth. Views like this do little to help the cause of serious Biblical interpretation.

(5) *The refraction or extension of the sun's rays on a local level.* The best solution to this problem is to regard it as a local miracle performed by God. It is very doubtful that the Lord would have performed a universal miracle involving the whole earth in its relationship to the sun merely to extend light for a relatively brief period in the area of Gibeon. There is an economy of the exercise of God's miraculous power both in the Old and the New Testaments, and in the light of this, a universal miracle involving the whole earth seems rather doubtful. We might note at this point that if such a universal miracle were performed, it would be one of the greatest miracles in Scripture, superseding that of the dividing of the Red Sea or the crossing of the Jordan River. However, there is only one other reference to this event in Scripture, found in Habakkuk 3:11. Furthermore, there was another time when the sun's relationship to the earth was altered in some way. This event, recorded in II Kings 20:10-11, required the shadow on the sundial to go back ten degrees. If we regard this as a literal, universal miracle, it would mean that God would not only have had to slow down the rotation of the earth, but reverse it for the mere purpose of changing the shadow on the sundial of Hezekiah. It is extremely doubtful that such a miracle was performed on that occasion. In fact, the parallel passage found in II Chronicles 32:24-31 seems to imply that it was a local miracle. Verse 24 of this passage indicates that God gave a special sign to Hezekiah. That sign was evidently witnessed only in Palestine, for verse 31 records the fact that ambassadors from Babylon were sent down to Hezekiah to "inquire of the wonder that was done *in the land.*" If the miracle performed in the days of Hezekiah was universal, there would be little need for ambassadors to come all the way from Babylon to inquire of the miracle. The text seems to indicate that this miracle occurred only in the Jerusalem area (cf. v. 31, "in the land"). Eyewitnesses of the event passed the word around Jerusalem, and reports of it ultimately reached the city of Babylon. The astronomers there decided to investigate the matter, thus sending representatives

down to Jerusalem. If the miracle of the sundial was local, then we might assume that the miracle performed for Joshua was also local in scope and did not involve other countries of the world. Somewhat parallel to this event would be the plague of darkness in Egypt (Exod. 10:21-23). There God supernaturally darkened only portions of the land while there was light in the areas occupied by Israel. No one seriously proposes that God darkened the whole earth for the purpose of punishing the people in Egypt. This view is also consistent with the many statements of Scripture which relate to the faithfulness of God's laws regarding day and night (cf. Gen. 1; 8:22; Jer. 33:20 ff.).

The precise method which God used to extend light is really not important at this point. It is clear from Scripture that the extension of light was sufficient to give Joshua and the children of Israel the upper hand in the battle. The kings of the Amorites were forced to flee to the northwest by way of Beth-horon to the Shephelah. From there they continued southwestward along the valleys toward Azekah and finally to Makkedah which was about twenty miles from Gibeon. On the next day the kings were discovered in a cave near Makkedah. They were taken from the cave and ceremonially the officers of Joshua were commanded to put their feet upon the necks of these kings (10:16-24). Such an act was a symbol of the complete subjugation of the defeated enemy. Many times such acts are pictured on monuments of Egyptian and Assyrian kings (cf. I Kings 5:3; Ps. 8:6; 18:38 ff.; Isa. 49:23). Following this the men were slain and their bodies hanged on trees (v. 26; cf. Num. 25:4; Deut. 21:22).

D. *The Conquest of Southern Palestine* (10:28-43)

1. *The Nature of the Campaign*

The battle of Beth-horon was the first step in the southern campaign. The battle continued in days following through Makkedah (v. 28), Libnah (v. 29), Lachish (v. 31), Eglon (v. 34), Hebron (v. 36), and Debir (v. 38). Joshua, at this stage of the campaign, did not seem to be interested in completely destroying each one of the sites, or in occupying them. The nature of his campaign took the form of lightning-like raids against the

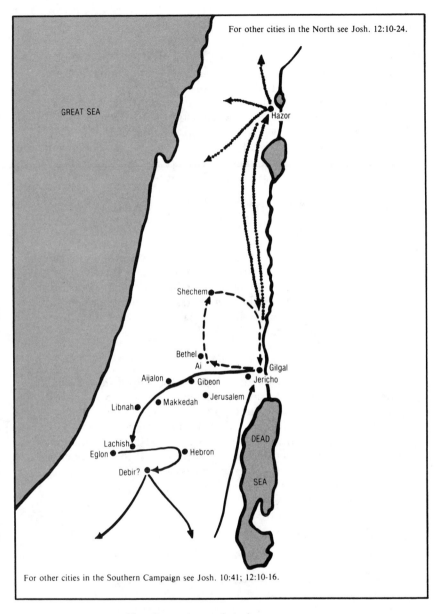

For other cities in the North see Josh. 12:10-24.

GREAT SEA

Hazor

Shechem

Bethel
Ai
Gilgal
Aijalon
Gibeon
Jericho
Libnah
Makkedah
Jerusalem

DEAD

Lachish
Eglon
Hebron
Debir?

SEA

For other cities in the Southern Campaign see Josh. 10:41; 12:10-16.

The Campaigns of Joshua

key military centers in southern Canaan. The purpose of these raids was to destroy the military capacity of the important city-states of this area and not necessarily to occupy the sites immediately after the battle. There is evidence that many of the battles were not even fought within the cities themselves (10: 33; 12:12; 16:10). It would not be practical for Joshua to lay siege to many of these well-fortified cities for such a siege would take a long time. Furthermore, it would not really accomplish the purpose of the campaign at this period.

2. The Purpose of the Campaign

It appears that the purpose of the southern campaign was essentially twofold: (a) to destroy the military capacity of the important city-states, and (b) to strike fear and bring confusion among the other city-states in southern Canaan. There does not seem to be any attempt to occupy or to take complete control of the area, or even to establish garrisons in conquered territory. In fact, there is evidence that several of the sites had to be retaken at a later period (15:13-17).

3. The Results of the Campaign

The latter part of Chapter 10 gives the impression that the campaign was indeed quite successful. In a relatively brief period of time, Joshua was able to secure at least minimal control over the Shephelah and the southern hill country as far south as Lachish. It would now be the responsibility of the individual tribes to conquer the remaining sections of the territory as helped by the Lord. Following the conquest of this territory, Joshua and the armies of Israel returned to the Jordan Valley to their encampment at Gilgal (v. 43).

II. THE NORTHERN CAMPAIGN (Josh. 11)

A. The Coalition of Northern City-States (11:1-5)

When word of Joshua's success reached the kings of the city-states in the areas of Galilee and westward, they decided to take immediate steps to protect their own territory. The leader of this coalition was Jabin, king of Hazor (v. 1). The name Jabin

should be regarded as a dynastic title rather than a personal
name (cf. Judg. 4:2; Ps. 83:9). The city of Hazor was at this
time the head of all the kingdoms in the north (v. 10). It is
understandable why Jabin, therefore, would assume leadership
in this matter. The coalition army that was formed was a rather
impressive one. The main strike force included horses and chariots in great numbers (vv. 4-5).

B. *The Destruction of Hazor* (11:6-23)

As the armies began to mass in great numbers in the northern

Hazor (Tell el-Kedah), the head of the city-states in the North (Joshua
11:10). Matson Photo Service

plains of Palestine, the Lord again appeared to Joshua and comforted him, promising that victory would be given to him again by the Lord's help (v. 6). Joshua was given specific battle instructions by the Lord on this occasion and these included the houghing of the enemies' horses as well as burning their chariots (v. 6). The word "hough" would be better translated "hamstring." The purpose of this act was to prevent Israel from gathering to themselves great military weapons and a large chariot force, for in time they would depend on these things rather than on their God (cf. Deut. 17:16; Ps. 20:7; Isa. 31:1). As in times past, God fulfilled His promise to the people of Israel. A great victory was given to the armies of Israel, allowing them to destroy their enemy, burn the chariots and take the city of Hazor (vv. 9-14). When the city was conquered, it was burned with fire. It, evidently, was the only city so treated in the northern campaign (cf. v. 13). This was no small victory, for archaeology has demonstrated that Hazor was indeed a great city. In the Late Bronze Age it covered an area of about 170 acres, supporting a population of anywhere from thirty to forty thousand people. There is a problem in connection with the archaeological data and Joshua's campaign. According to recent discoveries, the occupation of Hazor continued down through the thirteenth century without apparent major interruption. The answer to this problem might be found in the nature of the destruction and the immediate reoccupation of the site. The site was indeed burned according to Scripture, but if the Canaanites immediately reoccupied it and rebuilt it, as the fourth chapter of Judges seems to indicate, we may have little or no evidence of Joshua's destruction of the city.

The northern campaign of Joshua involved more than the city of Hazor. It included many of the important city-states and smaller towns in the northern hills of Galilee and cities in the lowland (cf. vv. 16-18). The Lord played an important role not only in giving Israel victory but in caring for the attitude of the enemy. According to verse 20, the Lord hardened the hearts of the enemy in order that they would not attempt to make peace with Israel but would face them in battle. This is reminiscent of God's activity with regard to Pharaoh in Egypt (cf. Exod. 4:21; 7:13 ff.; 9:12; 14:17; also Isa. 6:10; John 12:40).

The success of Joshua's campaigns is further illustrated in verses 21-23. The Anakim mentioned in these verses were the gigantic sons of Anak who terrified the spies some forty years before (Num. 13:28, 33; Deut. 9:2). These people were now reduced to a mere remnant living in southwestern Palestine (v. 22). It is significant that the area in which they remained was the very gateway back to Egypt.

III. THE LIST OF DEFEATED KINGS (Josh. 12)

This chapter summarizes the great victories on both the east side of the Jordan and the west side. Verses 1-6 of this chapter describe the conquest of the territories of Sihon and Og under the leadership of Moses. The cities of the west side are listed in verses 7-24. The thirty-one kings defeated by Joshua were local kings having limited power. Verses 9-16 list the kings of southern Canaan, while verses 17-24 make note of the defeated kings in northern Canaan. The list is important because it points out the significant military sites during Joshua's day. Many of the same names appear in the Amarna letters, thus confirming the historicity of our text.

Two important truths stand out in these three chapters which are worthy of special consideration. (1) *The power of God.* When the battle raged in the area of Beth-horon, and Joshua desperately needed additional light, God miraculously provided that light. In the eleventh chapter the power of God was evident in giving victory to Israel in spite of the fact that they were outnumbered and did not have the sophisticated military equipment possessed by the Canaanites. The power of God was also exhibited in 11:20, when He prepared the hearts of the enemy so that they might be defeated in the fulfillment of His own purpose. (2) *The faith of Joshua.* One cannot help but take note of the attitude and unqualified obedience of the man Joshua. He acted not on the basis of the military strength of Israel or on his own genius in the area of tactical maneuvers, but on the promises of God alone. He did not require confirmations or signs, nor did he ask for an extension of time or additional arms. The life of Joshua and the events recorded in these chapters have a very practical bearing upon our own present-

day Christian perspectives. According to Ephesians 6, we are
in a desperate spiritual warfare. God has made adequate provision for us and has given us the promise of His presence. It
is our responsibility to receive these gifts by faith and to act
upon them, anticipating victory.

6

FIRST STEPS IN SETTLEMENT

The significant military victories recorded in the first twelve chapters of the Book of Joshua were only first steps in the settlement of the land. Chapters 13–24 describe in considerable geographical detail the assignment of land made to various tribes. According to the words of Jacob (Gen. 49) and Moses (Deut. 33), the tribes were to anticipate a blessing in the land. The children of Israel at this particular time occupied very little of the land of Canaan. However, Joshua had been successful in removing the significant military threats to Israel's existence. It would now be the responsibility of the tribes to conquer and to colonize their designated territories. The chapters that follow describe the method and the result of land division as assigned to the various tribes. It should be kept in mind that the lists were drawn up before the tribes actually settled the territories and therefore are in some respects idealistic. In reality, most of the tribes did not conquer or control all of their allotted territories (cf. Josh. 15:63; 16:10; 17:12-16; 19-47).

I. DIVIDING THE LAND (13:1–21:45)

A. *The Method of Division* (13:1–14:5)

According to 14:1, three parties were involved in the division of the land: Eleazar the priest, Joshua, and the heads of the fathers of the tribes. The casting of lots before the Lord was the divinely appointed method by which each tribe would receive its share of land (cf. 13:6; 14:2; 18:6).[25] The principal division of territory was between the tribes of Judah and Joseph; the other allotments of land would be contingent upon the area given to these tribes. The allotment of certain territories was not a haphazard procedure. According to 18:4-9, a special group of men was set aside to study the land and to designate border

---

[25]Compare Numbers 26:52 ff.; 33:54; 34:13.

areas. The size of a tribe was also a factor in the assignment of special territories (cf. Num. 26:51-56; 33:54). Various landmarks were used in the delineation of borders. According to Chapter 15, the seas (vv. 2, 4), the rivers (v. 4), the mountains (vv. 8, 10), the desert (v. 1), and towns (v. 21 ff.) were all border indicators. This method of boundary definition is paralleled in a document by Suppiluliuma (a Hittite king of the fourteenth century B.C.), to Niqmadu of Ugarit, Ras Shamra.[26]

Joshua at this time was old and advancing in years (13:1). In spite of his age, however, it was imperative that he continue his leadership over the nation and guide in the allotment of tribal territories. The Lord had instructed him that he was not only to achieve military victory in the land, but was to assume leadership in the division of the inheritance in the land (cf. 1:6).

When the Lord spoke to Joshua regarding his responsibility in the land division, mention was made of the Philistines (13: 2-3). This is the only time the Philistines are mentioned in the Book of Joshua. According to 11:22, it was the Anakim who inhabited Gaza, Gath, and Ashdod. Since the Philistines were not listed among the inhabitants of the land (cf. 12:8), it is apparent that they were still confined to the coastal area of the Negeb (cf. Exod. 13:17). This was the same area in which they appeared during the Patriarchal Age (cf. Gen. 21:32; 26:1). John Rea suggests, "In the light of the foregoing evidence, Joshua 13:3 is perhaps an early scribal notation to inform us that the domain of the five Philistine lords (*seren*, Judges 16:5; I Sam. 5:8) in Joshua's day still belonged to the Canaanites."[27]

The remaining part of Chapter 13 enumerates the tribal allotments with regard to the territory of Transjordan. Reuben (13:15-23) was given the territory which was previously occupied by Moab, just to the east of the Dead Sea. The tribe of Gad (13:24-28) was given territory north of the Arnon River in the original land of Gilead. The territory east of the Sea of Galilee was assigned to one-half the tribe of Manasseh (13:29-33). The other half of the tribe had elected to settle on the west side of the Jordan with the remaining tribes.

[26]See Claude Schaefer, *Le Palais Royal d'Ugarit* IV, 10-18.
[27]John Rea, "Joshua," *The Wycliffe Bible Commentary*, p. 222.

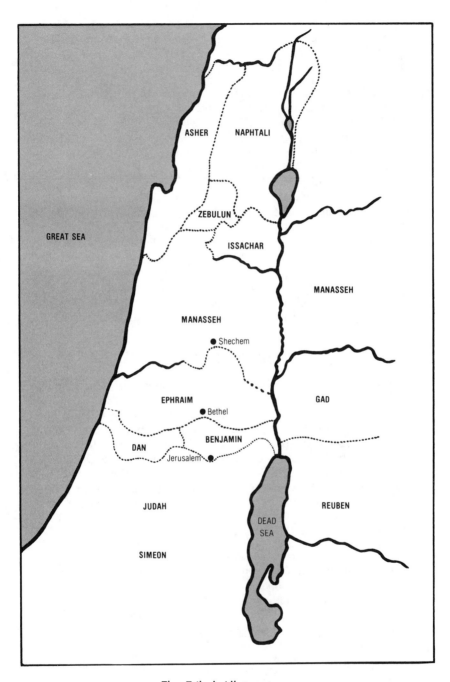

The Tribal Allotments

B. *Caleb's Portion* (14:6-15)

Caleb is one of the outstanding characters in the Joshua narratives. He was a man of faith and courage (cf. Num. 13:30; 14:6). According to Joshua 14:14, he "wholly followed the Lord God of Israel." Because of his faithfulness to his God, and his faithfulness to Joshua in the difficult years of conquest, he was given a special portion of land in the area of Hebron, earlier known as Kirjath-arba (Josh. 14:15). Caleb's statement of age, recorded in Joshua 14:10, is most significant in evaluating the Joshua narratives. The statement gives us a clue to the length of the actual conquest of the land. According to this verse, the main thrust of the conquest would have taken seven years. Caleb pointed out that forty-five years had passed since the giving of the promise to him. That promise was given to him thirty-eight years before the crossing of the Jordan (cf. Num. 14:24). The actual time of conquest was therefore about seven years. According to this verse, Caleb was about forty years old when Moses sent him out as a spy.[28]

C. *The Portion of Judah* (15:1-63)

Judah was the first tribe to receive an inheritance on the west side of the Jordan River. Because of the size of Judah, a considerable portion of land was given to it. This allotment included the territory south of a line extending west from the northern tip of the Dead Sea, bounded on the west by the Mediterranean, on the south by a line from the southern end of the Dead Sea to the River of Egypt (Wadi el-Arish), and on the east by the Dead Sea. Caleb's territory was included in the tribal territory of Judah, as was that of the Simeonites (19:1-9).

D. *The Portion of the Joseph Tribes* (16:1–17:18)

The tribe of Ephraim was located immediately north of Dan and Benjamin (cf. map, page 79). The borders of Ephraim included the Jordan River on the east, the Mediterranean on the west, and the Kanah Valley and eastward on the north. Just

---

[28]Josephus gives the duration of the conquest as five years, *Ant.* V.1.19.

north of Ephraim was the territory of the tribe of Manasseh. The Mediterranean on the west, the Jordan on the east, and the valley of Jezreel on the north constituted the basic borders of the tribe of Manasseh. The tribe of Ephraim, therefore, controlled part of the central hill country, and the tribe of Manasseh controlled the remaining central hill country up to the valley of Jezreel. The Scripture gives us important insights to the success of these tribes in actually occupying their territories. For example, in 16:10, we are informed that the Ephraimites were incapable of driving out the inhabitants of Gezer. In fact, the city of Gezer did not come under full Israelite control until the day of Solomon (cf. I Kings 9:16). This text also provides information with regard to the materialistic attitude of the Ephraimites, for rather than conquering and driving out the Canaanites in their territory, they put them under "tribute," thereby gaining additional wealth. A similar description is given of the efforts of Manasseh in 17:12-13. They, too, were incapable of complete victory and colonization; and like Ephraim, rather than destroying the Canaanites, they put them to tribute (cf. Judg. 1:28). This policy of coalition had disastrous effects in the years that followed.

E. *The Portions of the Remaining Seven Tribes* (18:1–19:51)

The tribal allotments up to this point were conducted in the central camp area at Gilgal. According to 18:1, the center of attention then shifted to Shiloh, which for three hundred years was the center of Israelite political and religious activity. Benjamin was given the territory between Ephraim and Judah. His territory was not very large, but it was centrally located and therefore constituted an important section of land.

North of the valley of Jezreel four more tribes received territory. Zebulun (19:10-16) was given territory north of Mt. Carmel, east of the Mediterranean, and south of the upper Galilean hills. It reached to the east almost to the Sea of Chinneroth. Just south of it, but north of the tribe of Manasseh, was the territory given to Issachar (19:17-23). Asher, on the other hand, settled along the Mediterranean coast, north of the tribe of Zebulun, and west of Naphtali. The Phoenicians were located

Site of Shiloh showing excavation dump to the left in the distance.
Matson Photo Service

on the northern borders of its territory (cf. 19:24-31). The territory of Naphtali is delineated in 19:32-39. It was located to the east of Asher and north of Zebulun (see map, page 79). The final allotment came to the tribe of Dan (19:40-48). The Danites were assigned a parcel of land west of Ephraim and along the Mediterranean coast. The Amorites, who settled portions of the Philistine plain (Judg. 1:34), drove the Danites out of the plains and into the hills. This led to a migration of part of the tribe of Dan northward to Leshem near the northern part of Naphtali (cf. Judg. 17-18). Joshua waited until all territories had been given to the tribes, and at that time he received an inheritance. This portion of land was located in the mountainous district of Ephraim which was his tribe (Josh. 19:49-51).

F. *The Cities of Refuge* (20:1-9)

Because of the widespread practice of blood revenge, God promised a place where the unintentional manslayer might flee (Exod. 21:13). The word "refuge" comes from the Hebrew *qālaṭ* which means "to contract, to draw, to take in, or to receive." The full expression in the Hebrew text is *'ārê hamiqlāṭ*. All of the cities listed in this chapter were Levitical cities, and therefore in a special sense provided divine protection for the unwitting manslayer (cf. Num. 35:9-34; Deut. 4:41ff.; 19:1-13). The Old Testament makes a clear distinction between premeditated murder and unintentional manslaughter (cf. Num. 35:11-16). The taking of a human life in the Old Testament period was viewed as a serious matter, especially in the light of man's relationship to God (cf. Gen. 9:6; see also Exod. 21:12, 14). Where murder had been committed, it was the responsibility of the nearest kinsman or the "avenger of blood" (Heb. *go'ēl hadām*) to punish the guilty party (Deut. 19:12). For the man who unintentionally killed another, there were divine protection and a trial. He was permitted to flee to one of the six cities. There he would be presented at the gate before the ancient law court (cf. Deut. 21:19; 22:15). Later he was brought to stand trial before the congregation of the community nearest the scene of the crime. If he was deemed innocent of premeditated murder, he was returned to the city of refuge until the death of the high priest. Then he could return to his home.[29] The six cities which were set aside for such asylum were located on both the east and the west sides of the Jordan River. The three on the west side were Kedesh in Galilee, and Shechem in the mountains of Ephraim, and Hebron in the mountains of Judah. The three on the east side, described in verse 8, were Bezer in the south, Ramoth in the area of Gilead, and Golan in the territory of Bashan.

G. *The Levitical Cities* (21:1-45)

The Levites were not given any specific allotments of territory. It was God's purpose that they should be scattered throughout the tribes of Israel to act as a spiritual influence and to teach the law (cf. Josh. 13:33; 14:3; 18:7; Deut. 18:1-2). When the leaders of the Levites appeared before Eleazar and Joshua, they requested that their assignment of cities be carried out (21:1 ff.). This was not an unjustified request. God had promised that they would be cared for (Num. 35:1-2). The Levites were assigned forty-eight cities including the pasture lands or "suburbs" around them (Josh. 21:41).

II. PREPARING FOR SETTLEMENT (Josh. 22-24)

A. *The Jordan Altar* (22:1-34)

After the initial conquest of the land and the allotment of territories to the various tribes, Joshua called the Reubenites, the Gadites and the half tribe of Manasseh together. On this occasion, he commended them for their faithfulness to him throughout the difficult years of conquest (22:2; cf. 1:17). Moses originally gave them permission to settle the territory of Transjordan provided that they would join their brethren in the conquest of Canaan (Num. 32:1-42). The two-and-one-half tribes fulfilled this responsibility and as a consequence were praised by Joshua. While their military commitments had been fulfilled Joshua reminded them that they had spiritual commitments which

---

[29]John Rea, "Joshua," p. 227.

would continue. These are expressed in verse 5 of this chapter. The six infinitives are employed to emphasize their responsibility to the Word of God and to His will. The admonitions given were very important in the light of the fact that these tribes would be separated from their brothers. The Jordan Valley was indeed a significant barrier to continuous contact with the tribes located in Canaan. As a result of successful conquest and faithfulness in responding to military needs, the two-and-one-half tribes returned with silver, gold, cattle, bronze, and iron (v. 8).

The events in this chapter raise an important question as to the right of the two-and-one-half tribes to settle the area of Transjordan. Many have argued that their presence in Transjordan was in opposition to the will of God. They argue that the reason for settlement on the east side of the Jordan was purely selfish. It is their feeling that the events recorded in Numbers 32 indicate the self-centered interest of the two-and-one-half tribes. Moses merely accommodated himself to their wishes. However, one does not gain this impression with a careful study of Joshua 22 or related portions. It appears, in the first place, that the eastern boundary of the Promised Land was not the Jordan Valley, but the mountain range of Gilead. Secondly, Joshua blessed the tribes and indicated that they indeed did have a right to settlement in Transjordan. Thirdly, the fact that God delivered the land of Sihon and Og to Israel seems to imply that someone was to possess it (Josh. 24:8).

Following the counsels of Joshua, the two-and-one-half tribes proceeded to make their way back across the Jordan to their families and homeland. On the way, they erected an altar on the west bank of the Jordan River (cf. v. 10). When the other tribes saw this altar, they were convinced that the eastern tribes were attempting to set up an altar in opposition to the one at Shiloh. They gathered themselves together at Shiloh and prepared for war (v. 12). Phinehas, the son of Eleazar the priest, stepped in and offered to arbitrate in order to ascertain the nature of the case (v. 13 ff.). In verses 16 ff., the charge against the two-and-one-half tribes takes the form of three kinds of sin. In verse 16, reference is made to a trespass (Heb. *ma'al*). The word for trespass as used in this verse is the same one employed in 7:1, in connection with the sin of Achan. The sin of the two-and-one-half tribes was also likened to the "iniquity of Peor" (v. 17). The iniquity of Peor had as an essential element idolatry and open disobedience to God's will with regard to worship (cf. Num. 25). Finally, their sin is described as an act of rebellion (vv. 18-19).

The defense of the two-and-one-half tribes is recorded in verses 21-29. Their response was that of innocence to the charges placed against them. Their principal concern was that their children would have equal rights to worship and movement throughout the land on the west side of the Jordan. They saw the Jordan Valley as a natural barrier to continued fellowship between the tribes. In order to care for the possibility of this problem arising in the future, they felt that a ceremonial altar should be erected as a sign of their right to worship in Shiloh. This altar, according to them, was not designed for sacrifice but merely as a witness (Heb. 'ēd) between them and the future generations living on the west banks of the Jordan (vv. 26-27). It is entirely possible that the altar which was erected was patterned after the one at Shiloh and perhaps this is the reason that the other tribes reacted as they did. In verse 28, reference is made to the "pattern of the altar of Jehovah." The Hebrew word for "pattern" is tabnît which literally means a "form, model, replica, or pattern." This might mean that their altar was patterned after the one at Shiloh and therefore, at least from outward appearance, would be designed for sacrifice. When the explanation was given, Phinehas and the princes were satisfied that the motives of the two-and-one-half tribes were indeed pure.

Even though a war was averted at this time, it became clear that there would be a problem of unity between the tribes settled on the east side of the Jordan and those in Canaan. Strictly speaking, the action of the two-and-one-half tribes was both needless and presumptuous. According to the law, all Israelite males were to appear before the Lord at the tabernacle three times a year (Exod. 23:17). God had not given instructions for the building of any other monument. Furthermore, it was God's plan that through faithful worship at Shiloh, all the tribes would remain together in unity. The action taken by the two-and-one-half tribes was merely the first in a series of independent

acts on the part of various tribes which would lead to later fragmentation of the tribes of Israel. Building other altars was, in
fact, a departure from God's plan for centralized worship. The
unifying factor in ancient Israel was not her culture, architecture,
economy, or even military objectives. The long-range unifying
factor was her worship of Jehovah. When the central sanctuary
was abandoned as the true place of worship, the tribes then
developed independent sanctuaries, thus alienating themselves
from other tribes and weakening their military potential. The
effects of this trend are fully seen in the period of the judges.

B. *The Last Words of Joshua* (23–24)

   Near the end of Joshua's life, he appeared before the tribes
with final warnings with regard to God's will for them in the
land. He was at this time rather old. We would assume that
he was between the age of 100 and 110 years (23:1; cf. 24:
29). Joshua reminded them that their successful conquest of
the land was dependent upon God's work in their behalf. They
were to recognize that successful occupation and colonization
of the land would require no less. Two principal requirements
were laid before Israel with regard to future occupation of their
territory. The first was unqualified obedience to the Word of
God (vv. 1-6). As in the first chapter of this book, so we are
again reminded of the authority of the written Word of God.
The principles for godly activity were not to be found in the
land of Canaan, but were clearly revealed in the book of the
law of Moses (v. 6). The second qualification for prosperity of
the land involved separation (vv. 7-16). That separation had
both a negative and a positive aspect. Israel was to be separated
from the gods of the land (v. 7; cf. Exod. 23:13; Deut. 12:3).
They were also to remain separate from the peoples of the
nations (v. 7). The positive aspect of their separation is described in the eighth verse. They were separated not only from
the world about them but *unto* their God.
   Joshua did not merely settle for a series of public admonitions
in order to guide Israel after his death. The twenty-fourth
chapter describes a formal covenant renewal enacted at the

site of Shechem for the purpose of getting a binding commitment
on the part of the people of Israel to the written Word of God.
In the light of the events of Joshua 8, it is significant that this
gathering should be called to the site of Shechem. Modern
critical scholars argue that this chapter records the real beginning
of the "nation" of Israel. They refer to Israel as here forming an
amphictyony — an association of neighboring tribes around a
common religious center. As one writer puts it, "The ceremony
represents the inauguration of a twelve-tribe confederacy . . . ."[30]
Such a theory does not deserve detailed refutation, for at its
basis is a denial of all historicity to Biblical narratives and in
many cases it ignores positive archeological evidence supporting
the claims of Scripture. Joshua 23:16 indicates that a formal
covenant *was already in existence*. This covenant, of course,
was established at Sinai shortly after the exodus from Egypt.
Therefore, what we have in Chapter 24 is a *covenant renewal*,
not the establishment of a new covenant.

The literary form of Chapter 24 is parallel to the well-known
suzerainty treaties of the Middle East dating from this period
of time. In such a treaty, a monarch obligated his vassals to
serve him in faithfulness and obedience. Such treaties are common in the international agreements between the Hittite empire
and its vassal states (1450-1200 B.C.).[31] Verses 1 and 2 constitute the preamble to the covenant renewal. In it we have
the identification of the God of Israel and the parties involved
in the treaty agreement. Verses 2-13 describe the historical
prologue; that is, the provision made by the king for his people.
In this section Joshua reviewed God's blessing upon His nation
from the time that Abraham was called from the land of
Mesopotamia up until their conquest of the land of Canaan.
In every case, God provided for the military and economic
needs of Israel.

Verse 12 of this section graphically describes the Lord's sending of a "hornet" before them. This expression has given rise

---

[30]Bernhard W. Anderson, "The Place of Shechem in the Bible," *The
Biblical Archaeologist*, Vol. 20, No. 1 (Feb., 1957), p. 14.

[31]See George E. Mendenhall, *Law and Covenant in Israel and the Near
East* (Pittsburgh: The Biblical Colloquium, 1955).

to considerable speculation as to what the "hornet" must have been. Two principal views have emerged. First, John Garstang understood it as a veiled reference to the Egyptian armies that had defeated the Hyksos and other peoples in Palestine shortly before the conquest. He supported his contention by noting that the bee (or hornet) was considered as a sacred symbol of the Pharaohs.[32] There are two principal objections to this view. First, the sending of the "hornet" was still future on the eve of the conquest (Deut. 7:20). Second, there is no evidence that the Egyptians had a serious interest in the region of Transjordan at this time. The Amorites may have been defeated in Transjordan, but they were still a major threat in the land of Canaan.

The other view is preferable, for it regards the expression as figurative, referring to the panic-producing power of God which overcame both Sihon and Og. This suggestion is supported by Exodus 23:27-30; Deuteronomy 2:25 and 7:20. The prophecy of the "hornet" in Exodus 23:27-28 seems to further support this view, for the two verses are in synonymous parallelism. The expressions "terror" and "hornet" appear to refer to the same idea. That this view is historically correct can be argued from Joshua 2:9, 11 and Joshua 5:1. Rahab clearly testified to the panic produced by the fear that the Canaanites had of Israel.

The stipulations of this covenant renewal are recorded in verses 14-24. They include the obligations imposed upon, and accepted by, the vassal. The heart of the matter is observed in verse 14. Two things are required of Israel: (1) to fear Jehovah, and (2) to serve Him. Joshua was careful to define what the nature of that service was to be. First of all, it should be sincere, and then it should be founded on truth. It is not enough for one merely to serve God in sincerity. If the service is not founded on, and conditioned by, the truth of Scripture, it is worthless activity. True service also involves separation; thus the children of Israel were commanded to put away the gods which were among them (cf. v. 15 ff.). The people agreed

---

[32]John Garstang, *Joshua-Judges: The Foundations of Bible History* (New York: Richard R. Smith, Inc., 1931), p. 259.

to these stipulations, and Joshua reminded them of the tremendous obligation that was theirs in the light of this commitment.

The final portion of the covenant renewal involved the writing down of the agreement and depositing that covenant in a place where it could be observed and read (vv. 25-28).

The death of Joshua is described in the remaining verses of this chapter. At the age of 110, he passed off the scene of Israelite history. He was buried in his inheritance in the mountains of Ephraim. During his lifetime, the children of Israel remained faithful to the Lord (v. 31). A fitting conclusion to the story of Joshua would be the words of Psalm 44:1-3, "We have heard with our ears, O God, our fathers have told us, what work thou didst in their days, in the times of old. How thou didst drive out the heathen with thy hand, and plantedst them; how thou didst afflict the people, and cast them out. For they got not the land in possession by their own sword, neither did their own arm save them: but thy right hand, and thine arm, and the light of thy countenance, because thou hadst a favor unto them."

JUDGES

7

FAILURE AND ITS CAUSES

In the Book of Joshua the *survival* and the *success* of the nation of Israel during the years of conquest are the dominant themes. The Book of Judges, on the other hand, emphasizes the religious and military struggles of this nation during its long period of settlement in the land.

I. INTRODUCTION

A. *The Title of the Book*

The Hebrew title of the book is *šopeṭim* ("judges"). This title is based on the type of leadership Israel experienced between the days of the elders who ruled after Joshua and the rise of King Saul. The establishment of the office of judge was first mentioned by Moses (Deut. 16:18; 17:9; 19:17). A *šopēṭ* was to stand by the side of the high priest as the supreme judge or leader in Israel. The function of the office of judge included more than mere civil service activities. In many cases their responsibilities included leadership in both military and religious affairs. Generally they were summoned directly to their work by divine appointment (cf. 3:15; 4:6; 6:12; etc.). The majority of judges functioned more in the role of "deliverer" from foreign oppression than as a civil judge. After deliverance was accomplished, the judge became a civil leader.

B. *Authorship and Date*

According to the Babylonian Talmud, Samuel was the author of the book. But there is no specific or conclusive evidence to support this claim. On the basis of the nature of the content of this book and its chronological notices, it is possible to say that Samuel may have written portions of the book with final additions by one of his students. Liberal criticism considers this book to be Deuteronomic in its present form (i.e., about 550 B.C. it supposedly received its final revision).

The date of composition was probably sometime in the early days of the United Monarchy. The frequent expression, "In those days there was no king in Israel" (17:6; 18:1; 19:1; 21: 25), indicates that the book was written after the establishment of the monarchy under Saul. According to 1:21 the Jebusites still controlled Jerusalem. This would place the time of writing before David's capture of the city about 990 B.Ć. (cf. II Sam. 5:6 ff.; I Chron. 11:4-9). When the book was written, the Canaanites were still in control of Gezer. (1:29). This would place the writing sometime before Solomon's reign, for the Egyptians captured the city and Pharaoh gave it to Solomon as a wedding gift (I Kings 9:16). Furthermore, it should be observed at this point that some portions of the book present material which seems to antedate the time of David. For example, Sidon rather than Tyre was regarded as the chief city of Phoenicia. This points to a time before the twelfth century B.C. With all evidence in view, it appears that the Book of Judges was most likely written sometime in the latter days of Saul or in the early days of David.

C. *Major Themes*

The principal theme of the Book of Judges is "Failure through Compromise" which is in contrast to the main theme in the Book of Joshua which was "Victory through Faith." The Book of Judges is a commentary on the nature and characteristics of spiritual apostasy. The writer not only presents the theological trends involved in apostasy, but vividly describes the practical consequences of apostasy in everyday life. The covenant failures of Israel are contrasted with the covenant faithfulness of Jehovah. The key verse of the Book of Judges is 17:6 which says, "In those days there was no king in Israel, but every man did that which was right in his own eyes" (cf. 21:25). Moral and spiritual relativism led to anarchy in those days.

D. *Historical Setting*

The events described in the Book of Judges cover a period which begins about 1380 B.C. and lasts until the rise of Saul in 1043 B.C. (see chart, p. 16). During the reign of the elders, and

in the early period of the judges (Othniel's judgeship and the
oppression under Eglon of Moab), Egypt remained weak under
the leadership of Akhenaton, Tutankhamun and Ay (*ca.* 1377-
1345 B.C.). Horemheb was able to consolidate some of Egypt's
forces, but real military revival took place during the Nineteenth Dynasty (*ca.* 1318-1222 B.C.). During the Ramesside age
there was renewed interest in Palestine. The Pharaohs of this
period increased and improved Egyptian military garrisons in
Palestine. The victory stele of Merneptah (*ca.* 1234-1222 B.C.)
records a successful campaign and among the defeated peoples
he lists Israel. The stele reads, "Israel is laid waste, his seed is
not."[33]

There are two other Egyptian documents that shed interesting
light on this period. The first is a satirical letter describing
the journey of an Egyptian envoy through Syria and Palestine.
The document is generally dated in the second half of the
thirteenth century B.C. It describes the roads of Palestine as
being overgrown with cypresses, oaks and cedars that were very
tall, thereby making travel rather difficult. It makes mention of
the fact that lions were numerous, thus confirming some of the
details of the Samson story (Judg. 14:5; cf. also I Sam. 17:34).
The envoy twice encountered thieves, indicating the difficulty of
unhindered travel (cf. Judg. 5:6-7). One night they stole
his horse and clothing, and on another occasion, his bow, sheath
knife, and quiver. The story reveals that the writer had considerable knowledge of Palestinian geography. Most significant
among the details of the document, however, are the many reflections of the unsettled conditions in the land and the problem
with robbers and thieves. This story reflects the same situation
described in Judges. "Every man did that which was right in
his own eyes."

The other document of interest to us is known as the story of
Wenamon. Wenamon was a temple official sent to Byblos, a
Phoenician port city, to purchase cedar for the bark of Amen.
He received his orders from Heri-Hor, a priest-king residing in

---

[33]James B. Pritchard (ed.), *Ancient Near Eastern Texts*, "Hymn of Victory of Mer-ne-Ptah," trans. John A. Wilson (Princeton: Princeton University Press, 1955), p. 378 (herafter referred to as *ANET*).

Thebes. When he reached the Palestinian coast, he was robbed before reaching his destination. He received no cooperation from the local kings he encountered. In fact, he was humiliated on many occasions. All this probably indicates the growing independence of Syrian and Palestinian monarchs. Egypt at this time was suffering from internal struggles and did not have the prestige it formerly enjoyed in Palestine. The date generally assigned to this document is the first half of the eleventh century B.C. Again this sheds light on the general political conditions of the Judges period.[34]

One of the archenemies of Egypt during this time was the Hittite empire (ca. 1400-ca. 1200 B.C.). After a series of struggles the two countries concluded a peace treaty.[35] Not many years after this treaty, the Hittite empire, like other lands, fell to the "Sea Peoples." The Egyptians, under the reign of Ramses III (1190 B.C.-1164 B.C.), repulsed an attempted invasion of the Delta area by these "Sea Peoples" among whom the Philistines were numbered. After their defeat in Egypt, many settled along the southwest coast of Palestine, thus joining the earlier Minoan settlers of the area (the "Philistines" of Abraham's day).

The power of Egypt as well as other surrounding nations was used by God to awaken Israel out of the deep sleep of apostasy which set in many times during the Judges period. The apostasies of Israel paved the way for her powerful enemies to oppress her. When Israel repented, leaders were raised up and the nation was delivered from the oppression.

E. *The Literary Structure of the Book*

The chapters of the Book of Judges are not arranged in strict chronological sequence. Chapters 1 and 2 contain the introduction to the period. Chapters 3 through 16 describe the period of judgeships and oppressions. The last five chapters are an appendix to the book and describe events which occurred before or during the judgeship of Othniel. The reason for plac-

---

[34]See *ANET*, "The Journey of Wen-Amon to Phoenicia," trans. John A. Wilson, p. 25 ff.

[35]*ANET*, "Treaty Between Hattusilis and Ramses II, trans. Albrecht Goetze, p. 201ff.

ing these events before those of Chapter 4 will be discussed later.[36] The following chart will help in understanding the literary structure of the book.

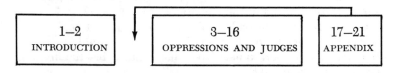

1–2	3–16	17–21
INTRODUCTION	OPPRESSIONS AND JUDGES	APPENDIX

F. Basic Outline

1. The Record of Incomplete Conquest (1:1–3:4)
2. The Oppressions and the Judges (3:5–16:31)
3. Appendix: The Period of Tribal Disorder (17:1–21:25)

II. THE RECORD OF INCOMPLETE CONQUEST (1:1–3:4)

A. The Political-Military Situation (Judg. 1)

1. Judah and the Kenites (1:1-20)

The Book of Judges begins the same way the Book of Joshua does; namely, with the death of a great leader. In Joshua 1:1 the death of Moses marked the end of the wilderness journey and the beginning of the conquest era. Judges 1:1 records the death of Joshua and therefore marks the period of tribal settlement in the land. The first phase of the conquest had been completed under Joshua; now the phase of settlement and colonization would begin. This marked the beginning of a very long, slow process covering a period of about 350 years. The question raised in verse 1 reflects the principal concern of the tribes at this time, ". . . who shall go up for us against the Canaanites?" The term "Canaanites" here is used in a broad, inclusive sense involving all the ethnic groups of Canaan. The selection of Judah (v. 2) is appropriate since it was the largest of the tribes and occupied one of the largest territories. Simeon joined with Judah in the settlement of the South as would be

---

[36]Infra, p. 147.

expected since Simeon's allotment was with that of Judah (Josh. 19:1).

The initial efforts of Judah and Simeon were successful as indicated by verses 4-7. One important battle was fought at the site of Bezek located in the vicinity of Jerusalem (cf. v. 7). The armies of Bezek were badly defeated, losing 10,000 men (v. 4). Adoni-Bezek, leader of the Canaanite forces, was able to escape but only for a short time. Upon his capture his thumbs and great toes were cut off (v. 6), a practice designed to render one useless for military service. The principle of *Lex Talionis* was employed in this case and Adoni-Bezek recognized this (v. 7). Following this, Judah captured Jerusalem (v. 8) but did not maintain control of the city (cf. v. 21). The city was regarded as a foreign city in 19:11-12. It was not until the time of David that the city came under permanent Israelite control. The military victories of the Kenites are enumerated in verses 11-16. Many of the events described in this chapter must have taken place before the death of Joshua (cf. Josh. 15:13-20). The Kenites were dwelling in the Jericho area according to verse 16. The expression "city of palm trees" is either a reference to Jericho itself or areas immediately adjacent to it (cf. 3:13 with Deut. 34:3 and II Chron. 28:15). It will be remembered that the curse Joshua placed upon Jericho applied to refortification of the city, not mere habitation.

Judah was successful in achieving most of its initial goals, which included the hill country around Hebron (v. 9; Heb. *hāhār*), the steppe areas to the desert in the south (Heb. *hanegeb*; v. 9) and the foothills leading toward the coast to the west (v. 9; Heb. *hašepēlāh*). Due to the effective deployment of iron-reinforced chariots by the Canaanites (v. 19; cf. 4:3; Josh. 17:16; I Sam. 13:19), they were unable to conquer the larger valleys.

2. Benjamin (1:21)

While Benjamin probably occupied most of its allotted territory, it was unable to gain control of Jerusalem which was under strong Jebusite control (v. 21). The expression "unto this day" reveals that the account was penned before David's capture of the city.

3. *Manasseh and Ephraim* (1:22-29)

The failures of Ephraim and Manasseh were largely due to their disobedience in not destroying Canaanite settlements in their territory. Rather than total destruction as God had commanded, they enslaved the Canaanites and put them to "tribute," better translated "taskwork or labor gangs" (Heb. *mas;* note v. 28). Gezer, according to verse 29, remained in the hands of the Canaanites. This was evidently the case until a Pharaoh of Solomon's day captured it and gave it to him as a wedding gift (I Kings 9:16).

4. *The Remaining Tribes* (1:30-36)

Many of the other tribes adopted the same policies as the tribe of Manasseh in that they did not destroy their enemy, but used him to increase their wealth (cf. vv. 30, 33). The tribe of Asher merely moved in among the Canaanites without attempting to control their area (cf. v. 32). Because of the strength of the Amorites in the valleys to the west, the Danites were restricted to the mountains (v. 34). This led to eventual frustration and the search for new territory in the north (18: 1-31).

B. *The Religious Situation* (2:1–3:4)

1. *The Reasons for Failure* (2:1-15)

a. *Religious Life in the Days of Joshua* (2:1-9)

Chapter 2 presents an interesting comparison in Israelite religious life during the days of Joshua and after the death of Joshua when a new generation had control of the nation. In the days of Joshua, divine rebuke met with a spirit of repentance (2:1-6), resulting in service to Jehovah (v. 7). The people of Joshua's day had witnessed the miraculous workings of their God and had constant reminders of their covenant responsibilities (Josh. 8:30-35; 18:1-7; 23:1–24:28).

When the angel of the Lord spoke to the people at Bochim (v. 1, a site probably located in the vicinity of Shiloh), there was a clear emphasis upon Jehovah's covenant faithfulness and the obvious disobedience of the nation (v. 2). Israel remained faithful to Jehovah during the days of Joshua and the period when the elders ruled after Joshua (v. 7). This does not mean that there were no times of failure and apostasy for this is quite clearly the case as intimated in Joshua's farewell address to the nation (Josh. 24:24 ff.).

b. *Religious Life after the Days of Joshua and the Elders* (2:10-15)

After the death of Joshua and the elders which followed him, a new generation arose which had been exposed to Canaanite culture from birth. This generation had not witnessed the great miracles performed by God for His people in the initial conquest (v. 10). Their parents did not evidently exercise a very strong godly influence on this generation, for it had turned aside to the worship of "Baalim" (v. 11). The term "Baalim" was probably used to describe all the false deities of the land and would therefore be synonymous with the expression "other gods." The principal gods of Canaan which this new generation worshiped are named in verse 13. Baal was one of the most popular gods in the Canaanite pantheon. This is attested by both Ugaritic and Biblical literature. Baal was the fertility god who rode upon the clouds and was responsible for the rains which brought life to the parched soil of Canaan. In Ugaritic mythology he was called the "son of Dagon" (cf. Judg. 16:23; I Sam. 5:1-7).[37]

Ashtoreth appears as Athtart in Ugaritic literature. In the Old Testament the name appears in both singular and plural forms (sing. Ashtoreth, pl. Ashtaroth; cf. I Kings 11:5; also I Sam. 31:10). She entered the Greek world by way of Cyprus and later became known as Astarte (Aphrodite of classical mythology). She was the Canaanite goddess of generation and fertility. She was also considered as a goddess of war. Ishtar was her Assyro-Babylonian counterpart.

The Canaanite cultic practices relating to the worship of Baal and Ashtoreth are well known to us through recent dis-coveries. Their system included animal sacrifices, in many cases

---

[37]*ANET*, "Poems about Baal and Anath," trans. H. G. Ginsberg, pp. 130, 142.

Baal-Hadad (Jupiter-Helios) from ruins of Baalbek in Lebanon. Levant
Photo Service

using the same animals as Israel did in her sacrifices.[38] Temple
prostitution was a widespread practice and one that was thoroughly degrading. Moses was careful to warn against such a
practice (Deut. 23:17). Fertility rites using libations of wine,
oil, and so on, were common in attempting to assure fertility
of the land. In some places human sacrifice was practiced.
The more one studies the activities involved in the worship of
Baal, the clearer it becomes as to why Jehovah demanded
complete destruction of this religious system and its followers.

The question that needs to be raised at this point is, "Why did
Israel fall prey to this sensuous form of worship when she had
such a lofty revelation of the true God and clear standards of
moral conduct?" Several answers may be given to this question.
First, the gradual fragmentation of the tribes contributed to an
abandonment of Shiloh as the only center of worship. As previously noted, the principal unifying factor in Israel was her religion and commitment to one place of worship. As the tribes
moved into new territories, rather than defeating their enemy,
they sought ways to establish peaceful coexistence with them.
This was probably the case as tribes moved down into the valleys where Canaanite religious and cultural influence was the
greatest. Secondly, Baalism may have had a pragmatic appeal.
The Israelites who attempted to farm in the hill country must
have experienced some frustration and looked with envy on the
beautiful crops of their Canaanite neighbors in the fertile valleys.
The temptation to look to Baal to increase fertility was always
there and many fell to it. In this connection notice the words
of Jeremiah (44:17-19). Thirdly, the sensuous appeal of temple
prostitution would have allured some into Canaanite practices.
Finally, the quest for political compatibility led many to recognize the gods of Canaan through formal treaties. Intermarriage
also led to formal recognition of the gods and gradual infiltration of pagan ideas into the community of Israel. Religious syncretism was slow, subtle, and disastrous.

2. The Remedy for Failure (2:16)

In order to provide spiritual and military leadership for Is-

---

[38]Ibid., "Keret," A.II.60 ff., 143.

rael, the Lord raised up judges. This provision, however, was in many cases rejected or ignored by apostate Israel (v. 17).

3. The Response of Israel (2:17-19)

The recognition and worship of other gods continued in spite of divine warning and admonition. Verse 17 describes the activity of unbelieving Israel as "whoring after other gods." In the light of the nature of Canaanite temple worship, this expression is most appropriate. In effect, the tender mercy of God and His gracious provisions were trampled down in highhanded rebellion. This was indeed a dark hour in the history of Israel. From the *triumphal conquest* of Joshua we are now brought face to face with the *tragic crisis* in the days of the judges.

4. The Rebuke from Jehovah (2:20—3:4)

Because Israel had broken her covenant with Jehovah (v. 20), the Lord promised that He would no longer drive out the nations before her as He had done before (v. 21). The nations would remain there to test Israel (v. 22; 3:1, 4). This new generation would learn of war because of this (3:2). Among the main enemies of Israel were the five "lords" of the Philistines (v. 3). The Hebrew word for "lord" (*seren*) is always used in connection with the Philistines with one exception. Most scholars feel that this is a Philistine loan word.

C. Practical Considerations

Someone once said, "If I could just see a miracle performed by God I know my faith would be established and never waver." This sounds like a reasonable statement at first, but after careful examination, it will be seen to be faulty. If visible miracles were really the solution to weak faith, then Israel should have been an unshakable nation spiritually. No other people on the face of the earth have ever witnessed more miracles and yet they were led astray. Remember that during the days of Christ here on earth, men witnessed many miracles but they still refused to believe. We are reminded of the words of Hebrews 11:1, "Faith is the substance of things hoped for, the evidence of things not seen. . . ."

A second lesson to be learned from these opening chapters is that spiritual and theological apostasy is a subtle process. Merely being in possession of a correct theology does not guarantee freedom from crisis. There must be a consistent application of divine truth in the life of the believer in order to be assured of a job well done and a battle well fought (II Tim. 4:7).

8

GAINS AND LOSSES

Whatever glory the people of Israel experienced in the days
of Joshua, and the days of the elders which followed, quickly
disappeared under the crushing defeats brought about by Israel's apostasy. Judges 3–9 are an enlightening commentary
on the fortunes of Israel during the fourteenth and thirteenth
centuries B.C. This period was characterized by recurring cycles
of spiritual apostasy, oppression from foreign nations, repentance
on the part of the people, and deliverance achieved through
the leadership of divinely appointed judges. A bird's-eye view
of the situation can be gained by study of the following chart.

Chart of the Oppressions

Nation	Time	Delivering Judge
Mesopotamia, under Chushan-rishathaim	Eight years	Othniel
Moab, under King Eglon	Eighteen years	Ehud
Philistines	?	Shamgar
Canaanites, under Jabin of Hazor	Twenty years	Deborah and Barak
Midian	Seven years	Gideon
?	?	Tola
?	?	Jair
Ammonites	Eighteen years	Jephthah
?	?	Ibzan
?	?	Elon
?	?	Abdon
Philistines	Forty years	Samson

I. OTHNIEL – THE FIRST JUDGE (3:5-11)

A. *Oppression from the Northeast* (3:5-8)

One of the factors leading to national apostasy was the widespread intermarriage between the Israelites and the Canaanites

105

in the land. One of the results of such intermarriage was a recognition of the gods of the Canaanites (v. 6). This apostasy
led Israel to abandon their worship of Jehovah and serve Baalim
and the "groves." The true meaning of the original Hebrew
word is not fully conveyed by the translation "groves," for
the Bible describes "groves" as being carried out of the
house of the Lord (see II Kings 23:6). The Hebrew expression
'ašērāh apparently refers to some kind of a wooden pole or perhaps a tree trunk which would have been set up beside a heathen
altar and used as an object of worship. It is probable that such
an object was regarded as the dwelling place of a deity (cf.
Deut. 16:21 and II Kings 17:10). Evidently the father of Gideon
had such an object in his sanctuary (Judg. 6:26). Others were
located in Samaria, Jerusalem, and Bethel (II Kings 13:6; 23:
6, 15). The tablets discovered at Ugarit (Ras Shamra) reveal
the fact that one of the popular Canaanite goddesses was given
this same name. This goddess was represented as a mother of
the gods and frequently had the title "Lady of the Sea."

In order to bring this idolatry to an end, the Lord permitted
a king by the name of Chushan-rishathaim from Mesopotamia to
oppress Israel for eight years (v. 8). The king's name literally
means "doubly wicked Chushan." It is felt by many that this
is an epithet assigned to him by his enemies. It is also possible,
however, that the word "rishathaim" is a Hebraized form of a
foreign word, perhaps a place-name.[39]

B. *A Deliverer Appointed* (3:9-11)

After eight years of servitude under Chushan-rishathaim, the
children of Israel again looked to their God (v. 9). The Lord
heard their cry and raised up a deliverer by the name Othniel,
the son-in-law of Caleb. Othniel was a good choice because
he had wide experience in warfare, having shared in the conquest of Canaan. He was previously known for his heroism at
Kirjath-sepher (Josh. 15:15-20 and Judg. 1:12 ff.). He was
from the tribe of Judah and therefore would have gained rather
wide support for his campaigns.

[39]Charles F. Pfeiffer, "Judges," *The Wycliffe Bible Commentary* (Chicago: Moody Press, 1962), p. 239.

The preparations for the office of judge and the functions of that office are clearly delineated in verse 10. In spite of the wide military experience of Othniel, he still needed additional divine help for the tremendous task at hand. In order to prepare him adequately, the Spirit of God empowered him in a special way for the task. This ministry of the Spirit should not be confused with regeneration which is permanent in nature and brings a change in life and character. The empowerment in these cases was for a special task and did not necessarily produce any moral transformation in the individual (cf. I Sam. 16:14 with Ps. 51:11). The responsibilities of the office of judge were basically twofold: (1) a civil responsibility involving the "judging" of Israel, and (2) a military responsibility; that is, to lead Israel against the enemy which had oppressed them (v. 10). The efforts of Othniel were successful and Israel was freed from the oppressing hand of Chushan-rishathaim. Following this deliverance Israel enjoyed forty years of rest (v. 11).

II. EHUD — A GIFTED BENJAMITE (3:12-30)

After forty years of freedom from foreign domination, however, Israel again forgot the penalty for idolatry. According to verse 12, they repeated the apostasy for which they had been punished earlier, and the Lord, therefore, raised up another oppressor in the person of Eglon, king of Moab. Approximately 1335 B.C., the Moabites conducted a successful campaign in the area of Transjordan. Presumably they defeated portions of the eastern tribes and then were able to move down into the Jordan Valley and establish a provincial capital at Jericho, described in verse 13 as the "city of palm trees." The Moabites were not alone in this conquest. According to verse 13, Eglon allied himself with the Ammonites (whose kingdom lay to the north of Moab) and with the Amalekites, who were migrant nomads to the south. For eighteen years Eglon, king of Moab, enjoyed military supremacy on the east bank of the Jordan and in the Jordan Valley. After eighteen years, Israel began to realize the helplessness of their situation. Again they were forced to cry unto their God for deliverance. Even though they had betrayed His trust once, God, in His mercy, listened to their cry and raised up a deliverer, this time, however, from the tribe of Benjamin rather than from the large tribe of Judah. The tribe of Benjamin had probably suffered the greatest at the hands of the Moabites. It was, therefore, appropriate that the leader should come from that tribe.

Another detail is given to us about Ehud in verse 15; namely, that he was left-handed. This seems to be a characteristic of the Benjamites as noted in Judges 20:16. In I Chronicles 12:2 they are described as being ambidextrous. Being left-handed would be an advantage for Ehud in the situation in which he found himself, for a left-handed person would bind his dagger on the opposite side to that on which it was usually carried, a distinct aid in concealing the weapon. The pretext which he used to gain access to Eglon, king of Moab, was the delivering of the yearly tribute described in verse 15 as a "present." In preparation for the trip, Ehud made a dagger which had two edges and measured a cubit in length (v. 16). The Hebrew word for "cubit" here is unique and not used elsewhere in the Old Testament. It is the word gomed. Some judge this dagger to have been about one foot long. King Eglon is described in this chapter as a "very fat man" (v. 17). It is not usual for the Bible to indulge in personal descriptions; however, such a description is necessary to the understanding of the events that follow; namely, verse 22. Ehud went down through Gilgal to Jericho, and there came in contact with Eglon, who was at that time sitting in "a summer parlor" (v. 20). This summer parlor was probably an upper room of the building which would provide some fresh air. Ehud announced that he had "a message from God." The importance of this statement was immediately realized by Eglon, and the Bible says that he arose out of his seat, which for him may have been quite a chore. Following this, Ehud removed the dagger and thrust it into the corpulent king — a most unusual employment of visual aids announcing the "message from God" (v. 20)! Considerable time elapsed before the servants discovered the assassination, and certainly much too late, for Ehud had escaped, returned to his territory, and had given a call to arms (v. 27). The children of Israel took advantage of this situation, and as a result, under the leadership

of Ehud, brought about eighty years of freedom from foreign oppression (v. 30).

III. SHAMGAR – OUTSTANDING WARRIOR (3:31)

Shamgar is described as "the son of Anath." This is somewhat
problematic, since Anath was the name of the Canaanite goddess of sex and war, and the sister of Baal. However, in the light
of the idiomatic use of the expression "son of" the description
may be interpreted to mean "the warrior." Shamgar lived in
the latter days of Ehud and the early days of Deborah and
Barak (cf. 5:6). He lived in a time when the highways were
unoccupied, and the travelers had to walk through narrow side
paths because of the dangers throughout the land. His exploits
were directed principally against the Philistines of whom he
slew 600 with an ox goad. This number may represent a lifelong total rather than a single battle. The ox goad which was
employed in such fighting was an instrument used for urging
oxen forward, and measured as much as eight feet long.
It was normally pointed at one end with a metal tip and it
had a chisel-shaped blade on the other end for scraping a plow
share. Such goads could be used effectively in the place of a
spear. It was a humble weapon indeed, but then God many
times uses humble things to accomplish His purpose.

IV. DEBORAH AND BARAK – PARTNERS IN VICTORY
(Chapters 4 and 5)

A. *The Military Strength of Jabin* (4:1-3)

After eighty years of peace, Israel again grew careless in their
spiritual commitments and forsook the Lord their God. As a result, the Lord allowed Jabin, described as the king of Canaan
reigning in Hazor, to overrun the northern territories of Israel
and to bring the nation again under foreign domination. The
name "Jabin" was probably not a personal name, but a dynastic title (cf. Josh. 11:1 and Ps. 83:9). According to the records
in Joshua 11 the Israelites conquered the city of Hazor and killed
Jabin, king of that city. However, it seems that the Israelites,
even though gaining victory in the area, were not able to con-

solidate their position, and the Canaanites had quickly retaken
and rebuilt the city. During the time of Joshua, Hazor was the
head of the kingdoms in that area (Josh. 11:10). It is not impossible that Hazor achieved a similar position in the time of
the judges under the leadership of Jabin and his general, Sisera.
Sisera is described as having dwelt in Harosheth of the Gentiles
(4:2). This site is generally identified with modern Tell
Amar located at the place where the Kishon River passes
through a narrow gorge to enter the Plain of Acre. It is about
ten miles northwest of the important city of Megiddo. The
military strength of the Canaanites was very impressive. In addition to thousands of foot soldiers, Sisera had under his control about 900 iron-reinforced chariots (cf. vv. 3, 13). This
number of chariots is not out of proportion for that part of the
country. Thutmoses III boasted of having captured 924 chariots
among the spoils of the battle of Megiddo.[40]

B. *Preparations for Battle* (4:4-13)

Following the twenty years of oppression, the Lord raised up
a prophetess and judge by the name of Deborah. Verse 5
indicates that she sat in judgment at a site somewhere between
Ramah and Bethel in Mount Ephraim. The time came when battle preparations should be made and an attack should be prepared against Jabin and Sisera. She called on Barak, an experienced general from the tribe of Naphtali (v. 6). Using 10,000
men from the tribes of Naphtali and Zebulun (v. 6) and other
tribes (5:14-15), he was to go to the area of the river Kishon
and there meet Sisera and the Canaanite armies (v. 7). Barak
refused to go without a prophetic complement; namely, the
presence of Deborah. Barak should not be judged as lacking
faith at this point. He merely wanted the one who could give
divine guidance and help for such an important occasion. He
was quickly reminded by Deborah that the victory which God
would give would not come as a result of his genius, but in effect would be a victory brought by the Lord.

---

[40]*ANET*, "The Asiatic Campaigns of Thut-mose III," trans. John A.
Wilson, p. 237.

The ultimate downfall of Sisera, according to verse 9, would be at the hand of a woman — not Deborah, but Jael (vv. 18-21).

C. Encounter and Victory (4:14–5:31)

1. The Nature of the Battle (4:14-16)

The battle followed and the Scripture tells us that the Lord discomfited Sisera and his chariots (v. 15). At this point we are not given any details as to what method God used in immobilizing the chariot force of Sisera. However, in the victory hymn of Deborah and Barak, recorded in Chapter 5 of this book, an additional clue is given. In verse 21 we are informed that the river Kishon "swept them away." We might suppose from this that the Lord brought rains, thereby flooding parts of the valley floor and causing the chariots to be immobilized. Recent history has given us additional light on the nature of such an event. Torrents of water contributed to the defeat of the Turks in this very area in April of 1799 when numbers of their fleeing troops were swept away and drowned. During World War I, English troops found that fifteen minutes of rain on the clay soil rendered cavalry maneuvers almost impossible.

2. The Flight of Sisera (4:17-24)

As the battle continued, Sisera recognized the hopelessness of his situation. When his chariot was no longer able to move, he fled away on foot (v. 17). On his way northward, he came to the tent dwelling of Jael, the wife of Heber the Kenite. He fully expected protection from this small clan of Kenites, for they had joined peaceably with the Canaanites in that area. Remember that the Kenites originally were settled in the area of Hebron along with Caleb (Josh. 14:10-15; 15:15-20; Judg. 1:16). Evidently Jael was not in agreement with the coalition made by her husband and others with the Canaanites and used this occasion to express her dissatisfaction. She invited Sisera to her tent for refreshment and rest, as would be the normal custom in the ancient Near East. But, once he was asleep, she took a tent peg and a mallet and brought his life to an end (v. 21). The great victory accomplished on that day was not due to the

genius of Barak, nor to the aggressiveness of Jael, but — according
to verse 23 — the power of God. This victory brought peace
and prosperity to Israel for about forty years (4:24; 5:31).

3. The Song of Praise (5:1-31)

The song of victory recorded in this chapter was, in all
probability, written by Deborah. It is a song expressing praise
to God for His intervention in behalf of His people. It recognizes His great patience in the light of Israel's infidelity. Even
though written in highly poetic style utilizing very difficult
archaic Hebrew words, it none the less is a song of beauty and
one that provides us with very interesting details about Israel's
past history. For example, in verse 4 it describes the Lord bringing rains during the days of the wilderness wandering. This
information sheds important light on Israel's survival during
this period. Living conditions in the days of Shamgar and
Jael are also described in verse 6. The highways were unoccupied because the enemy controlled them. This was a time of
open idolatry, for Israel "chose new gods" (v. 8). This was also
a time of tribal independence, for not all the tribes participated
in the war against Sisera. Verses 15-17 list Reuben, Gilead, Dan,
and Asher as those who refused to join in this battle. The reference to Dan as remaining in ships (v. 17) is interesting and
enlightening. It implies that the migration of the Danites recorded in Judges 18 had taken place prior to the time of Deborah
and that the Danites had experienced some degree of amalgama-
tion with the seafaring Phoenicians to the northwest. After a
brief description of the battle in poetic form (vv. 19-27), the
writer then gives us a look into the household of Sisera. The
feminine touch is obviously present here as the emotions and
the reactions of the mother of Sisera are viewed. It is the
feeling of many that this indeed represents the hand of Deborah.

V. GIDEON — MAN OF VALOR (6:1–9:57)

A. The Midianite Oppression (6:1-10)

As a result of Israelite apostasy (v. 1) and open disobedi-

ence to God's commands (v. 10), they were delivered into the
hands of the Midianites and the "sons of the east" (v. 3) who
came from the eastern desert regions. These nomadic peoples
ranged from the southern part of the Sinai peninsula (Exod.
3:1) northward to the gulf of Aqabah (I Kings 11:18) and as
far as the plains east of Moab (Gen. 36:35; Num. 22:4; 25:1, 6;
Josh. 13:21). The Midianites were related to the Hebrews in so
much as Midian was a son of Abraham by his second wife,
Keturah (Gen. 25:1-6). Joining the Midianites in their raids
from the east were the Amalekites and the "children of the
east" (v. 3). Since the "children of the east" were probably nomads from a Syrian desert, it was appropriate that these people
should employ camels for their military needs rather than horses
and chariots (cf. v. 5). It appears that the Midianite invaders
destroyed many of the crops of Israel, and for seven years Israel
did not realize full productivity (cf. vv. 6-7). The result of
seven years of frustration and even starvation was that Israel
again cried to their God (v. 7). In response, the Lord sent a
prophet who issued a severe warning and rebuke to the people
of Israel (vv. 8-10). While there is the expression of Jehovah's
extreme hatred for sin in the earlier verses of this chapter, we
are also reminded of Jehovah's great love for the sinner in the
fact that He provided a prophet and a judge to bring deliverance.

B. *The Call of Gideon* (6:11-40)

The character and the actions of Gideon are not always subject to easy analysis as is evident from the various views regarding this man. Some consider him a weak, insecure man and
therefore lacking real faith. Others consider him a great champion of faith. Only a careful analysis of the verses that follow
will help to solve this problem. Gideon, like most Israelites at
that time, lived in fear as evidenced by the fact that he threshed
his wheat beside the winepress in order to avoid detection by
the Midianites. It was there that he encountered the angel of
the Lord (Heb. *mal'ak yahweh*). This expression is best understood as describing a theophany. It represents the same
type of encounter recorded in 2:1-5. The first thing pointed
out to Gideon was that the Lord was with him (v. 12). This

statement, however, presented a theological problem to Gideon, for he asked, "If the Lord be with us, why then is all this befallen us?" (v. 13). In other words, "If God is on our side, why have we experienced seven years of tragedy?" Of course, the answer to this should have been obvious to Gideon. It was the wickedness of his people that brought destruction and despair. The Lord then challenged Gideon to be Israel's new leader. Like Moses (Exod. 4:1, 10), Gideon found excuses as to why he did not qualify for the responsibility. Gideon was probably nearing middle age at this time since he had a son in his teens (8:20). He also pointed out that his family was "poor in Manasseh" (v. 15), which probably referred to the military weakness which characterized the tribe of Manasseh. In addition to that, he was the least — that is, the youngest — in his father's house. Gideon was then given a sign as a confirmation of God's claim upon his life (cf. Exod. 4:2-9).

While we might agree that Gideon was weak in faith at this point, we should not consider him a man of no faith whatsoever. The sign which God provided for him required that he bring certain things before the angel of the Lord. These objects included valuable food stuffs (cf. v. 19), and during a time of famine, it would indeed take an act of faith on the part of Gideon to use such material. This faith on the part of Gideon was honored by God in that fire consumed the offering brought on that occasion (v. 21). Gideon immediately recognized that the visitor to whom he had been speaking was the Lord Himself (v. 22), and he had great fear because to see God would probably mean certain death (Exod. 33:20). The real test of Gideon was yet to follow. The fact that he did make a definite commitment to his God is evidenced in his going to his father's own house and destroying the altars of Baal along with the grove that was built beside it (v. 25). This portion of Scripture is also a sad commentary on the tribe of Manasseh, for here was located a private sanctuary dedicated to Baal and Asherah. Perhaps most disheartening is the reaction of the men who lived in that town, for when they discovered that the sanctuary dedicated to Baal had been destroyed, they sought the life of Gideon. It is ironic indeed that the Israelites were willing to take the life of a man who destroyed a pagan altar (v. 30). Even though

Gideon's father was probably a worshiper of Baal previously, it appears that he joined Gideon in his stand for the true faith (v. 31). His arguments in behalf of Gideon are effective. He charged that if Baal were really a god, let him defend himself. Why should a man have to save his god? It ought to be the other way around; namely, the god saving individual man. With this responsibility cared for, Gideon now had to face the principal task at hand; that is, the threat of the Midianites and the Amalekites.

Gideon, like Othniel (3:10), was prepared by the Holy Spirit in a special way for the task at hand (v. 34). The original text at this point, however, is different from that which describes the experience of Othniel. Here the Hebrew word for "come upon" is *lābesāh*. This verb literally means "to clothe"; in other words, the Spirit of God clothed Gideon. With this strength he began to marshal the armies of Israel. But, again, Gideon wanted divine assurance that he was within the will of God and had clearly understood God's directives. Therefore, he required another sign. He suggested that a fleece be placed on the stone threshing floor, and if the dew remained only on the fleece and the earth was dry around it, he would consider this as a sign from God (vv. 36-37). When this was fulfilled, he considered the matter again and realized that it was not unnatural for the dew to remain on the fleece, whereas the ground would quickly dry up in the sun. For this reason, he requested a second sign or confirmation of God's will. This time the process was reversed, and the fleece was dry and the ground around it remained wet with the dew after the sunrise (v. 39). With these signs Gideon was assured of God's directives in the matter of warfare.

C. *Selecting the Troops* (7:1-15)

Along the foothills of Mount Gilboa, Gideon began to marshal the troops together. When his army was organized, he had 32,000 men, which was a small number compared to the Midianite coalition which numbered 135,000 (8:10). Gideon's faith was again tested, for the Lord told him that he had too many soldiers. He was commanded to urge those who were afraid to return home from the camp at Gilead. When the message was given to the people, 22,000 returned home, leaving him with an army of only 10,000 men (v. 3). Again the Lord spoke to him, and indicated that the army was still too large and that it had to be reduced even further. This reduction took place at the site where the men would drink their water. Those who bowed on their knees to drink were dismissed, whereas those who lapped with their tongues "as a dog lappeth" (v. 5) were kept in the army of Gideon. Those who were kept appear to be the ones who stood upright while drinking the water from their hands, thus prepared for a sudden attack. Josephus, however, interpreted the passage in a different way. Rather than selecting the men who were most fit from a military point of view for the battle, he argues that the Lord chose the least fit from a military point of view in order that the miracle might be greater.[41] After the army was organized, a third sign was given to Gideon to confirm the forthcoming victory (vv. 13-14). Gideon expressed his thankfulness for the sign in the form of worship (v. 15).

D. *The Victory over Midian* (7:16–8:21)

The army was divided into three companies of 100 each (cf. I Sam. 11:11). They were to carry torches covered by a clay pot or juglet of some kind. In the beginning of the middle watch (v. 19), that is, a little before midnight, they were to blow the trumpets and the pitchers were to be broken, thus exposing the torches and producing great light. This surprise maneuver was very effective, for the camels were probably frightened and the men were turned one against the other (vv. 21-22). The Lord used this to give Gideon the initial victory over these armies in spite of the overwhelming odds. Once the Midianite coalition was on the run, Gideon called additional help from the other tribes to complete the battle. The narrative actually ends with 7:24 and is not resumed until 8:4. There the battles in the Jordan Valley and the area to the east are described. The intervening verses record the dissatisfaction of the tribe of Ephraim in not being called during the initial stages of the battle (8:1-3). Gideon responded to this dissatisfaction by

---

[41]*Ant.* V.6.3.

commending them on their valor. Jephthah was not so kind, however, when the arrogant tribe of Ephraim later expressed similar dissatisfaction (cf. 12:1-15). Perhaps the tribe of Ephraim was not accustomed to taking second place in battle plans, especially since Joshua was an Ephraimite and was a great leader in Israel. The remaining portion of Chapter 8 describes the successful pursuit of the Midianite alliance toward the east and their ultimate defeat. Gideon did not receive cooperation from the eastern tribes however. They were afraid that the victory of Gideon was merely temporary and if they joined him, they would later be severely defeated by a reorganized army from the east (8:4-21). The result of Gideon's great victory was that the people of Israel wanted him to become king (v. 22). This he refused, for he considered God to be their King.

E. *The Last Days of Gideon* (8:22-35)

Unfortunately, the latter days of Gideon were marked by failure and apostasy. Gideon, along with the other Israelites who engaged in the battle, had access to tremendous quantities of riches taken from the Midianites (vv. 25-26). As a result of this, Gideon was led into cultic idolatry as evidenced by his making an ephod an object of worship (v. 27). He evidently was also involved in polygamous practices (cf. vv. 30-31). The last days of Gideon and the time shortly after his death were times of national decay according to verse 33. The decay and apostasy that characterized Israel's history at this time were also characteristic of the family of Gideon. This is reflected in the rebellion of one of his sons, recorded in Chapter 9.

F. *The Rebellion of Abimelech* (9:1-57)

Gideon's polygamous practices brought great sorrow to his family after his death. Gideon's son by a concubine (8:31) decided that kingship was a legitimate thing and that he was the best candidate. Evidently Abimelech's mother was from Shechem, for he returned to that site in order to gain popular support for his proposed reign over Israel (9:2-3). Such support he did receive both from the inhabitants and from the priest of the local shrine at Shechem (v. 4). The designs of Abimelech for the city of Shechem and the tribes in that area

brought about the death of his brothers, with one exception (v.
5). In spite of the warning given to Shechem by Jotham, the
youngest son of Gideon, the city made Abimelech king and for
three years he reigned over that city (v. 22). It is doubtful
that the reign of Abimelech gained recognition anywhere else
than in the Shechem area, and even this was short-lived. A
spirit of arrogance and suspicion overtook both Abimelech and
the men of Shechem. The life of Abimelech came to an end
very much like that of the great general Sisera — at the hand of a
woman. According to verse 53, a certain woman cast the upper
part of a millstone upon Abimelech's head. This did not bring
immediate death and in order to save face, Abimelech called
for his armorbearer to draw the sword and to slay him (cf. the
death of Saul, I Sam. 31:3-4).

G. *Practical Considerations*

The story of Gideon is a study in contrast. It is an excellent
example of what God can do with a man when he acts in faith.
Military might, prestige, and wealth are not able to frustrate
God's purposes for men. In spite of the impressive numbers and
the military strength of the Midianites, Gideon was given victory. A second lesson worth noting in this story is the danger of
failure in spite of initial victories. Gideon had enjoyed unparalleled success in military matters; however, the victory
brought to him access to tremendous wealth, and this in turn
led him astray spiritually. He turned to cultic practices and the
taking of many wives. The result was a major rebellion in Israel
under Abimelech, one of his sons. The implications of this
story should be obvious to the believer. Even though he might
enjoy significant success in spiritual things, he should be aware
of the fact that he is human and open to the subtle temptations
of Satan. If a great man such as Gideon could be tempted and
could fall, how much more should we take care that we stand
in full obedience to the Word of God.

9

JEPHTHAH'S VOW

After the turbulent reign of Abimelech over the city of Shechem, there was a period of relative peace under the leadership
of two judges about whom we are told very little. The forty-
five years following Abimelech's rebellion were probably peaceful ones for the most part. There is evidence however, in 10:1,
that some deliverance was necessary from outside oppression.

I. PROSPERITY AND PEACE (10:1-5)

A. *The Judgeship of Tola* (10:1-2)

Following the reign of Abimelech, Tola the son of Puah assumed leadership in Israel. Tola and his father were of the
tribe of Issachar and were named after two of the sons of Issachar (cf. Gen. 46:13; Num. 26:23). During the days of David,
the Tola clan was known for its men of valor (I Chron. 7:1-2).
So far as we know, Issachar was the only tribe to furnish a
judge during this period. While we know little of the ministry
of Tola, it is clear from verse 1 that he was raised up by God
"to save" Israel (Heb. *lehošia'*). His judgeship lasted for a
period of twenty-three years after which he died and was buried
in Shamir (v. 2).

B. *The Judgeship of Jair* (10:3-5)

The judgeship of Jair began about 1131 B.C. and lasted for
twenty-two years (v. 3). This judge is described as a Gileadite
(v. 3). Since his name was the same as that of one of Manasseh's
sons (Num. 32:41), it is fair to assume that he came from that
tribe. He was a man of considerable wealth and prosperity. He,
like other of the judges, engaged in polygamy, for he is described
as having thirty sons (v. 4). The evidence of his rank and
prominence in the land is further indicated by the fact that his
sons rode thirty ass colts (v. 4). The ass was highly esteemed
as a riding beast and many times carried with it special recog-

nition (Judg. 1:14; I Sam. 25:20). The judgeship of Jair was probably limited to the area of Gilead primarily. After his death, he was buried in Camon (v. 5).

II. APOSTASY AND OPPRESSION (10:6-18)

A. *The Nature of Israel's Sin* (10:6)

While Jair was probably a successful and prosperous judge, there is no evidence that he exerted any strong spiritual influence among the eastern tribes. The same can be said for Tola who probably exercised his greatest power in the central hill country on the west banks of the Jordan River. With an obvious absence of strong, vital, spiritual leadership, Israel again began to turn to the gods of Canaan which included the Baalim and Ashtaroth (v. 6). The apostasy of this time included much more than the mere recognition of Canaanite deities. According to verse 6, the gods of Syria (Aram) were worshiped. These would have included Hadad, Baal, Mot, and Anath. The gods of Zidon would be basically those of Syria. In Moab, Chemosh was a prominent deity (I Kings 11:33); while in Ammon, Molech seems to have been popular (I Kings 11:7, 33). The Philistines looked toward Dagon and Baal as well as other Canaanite deities for fertility and guidance. The spiritual trends observed in Israel at this time did not merely reflect syncretism, but in many cases involved the total abandonment of the worship of Jehovah in favor of other national deities.

B. *The Consequences of Israel's Sin* (10:7-12)

While idolatry seemed attractive at first, after eighteen years of oppression and warfare, the Israelites were forced to consider the liabilities of such commitments. Their affections, which had been directed to other gods, caused the anger of the Lord to be stirred against Israel, and as a result, God permitted them to be subject to two foreign nations: the Philistines to the southwest, and the Ammonites to the east. The awesome power of Ammon is expressed in verses 8-9: it is stated that their victory marches had led them through Reuben's territory to the east of the Jordan and up into the central hill country where they encountered the armies of Judah, Benjamin and Ephraim. Presumably, these tribes were not able to successfully stop the Ammonite penetration into central Israel. Military and spiritual frustration led Israel to cry once again to her God. With her self-confidence gone, illusive dreams of pleasure vanished, the people finally turned to the God who had been faithful to them all the time. They suddenly realized that idolatry had betrayed them and that heathen idols were entirely impotent to help them in the time of crisis. However, a mere recognition of sin was not enough this time (cf. v. 10). God wanted repentance and a total, unqualified commitment from His people that they would again obey the law.

C. *The Challenge of Jehovah* (10:13-14)

Before the Lord responded to their need, He gave them a very significant challenge. Since Israel had turned to the gods of Canaan and Syria and Moab and Zidon, why in times of crisis did they not look to those gods for deliverance? Verse 14 records the awesome words of God, "Go and cry unto the gods which ye have chosen; let them deliver you in the time of your tribulation." These words could not help but pierce to the very hearts of the wicked Israelites. They realized that prayers to the deities about them were of no avail at this stage. In their utter helplessness and sorrow of heart, they again turned heavenward and cried to their God.

D. *The Compassion of Jehovah* (10:15-18)

The greatness of Jehovah and His intense love for His people is nowhere more evident than in this particular situation. The inspired writer records the fact that as Israel cried out to their God "his soul was grieved for the misery of Israel" (v. 16). Human passion and concern would long since have been exhausted had they encountered the kind of rebellion that Jehovah witnessed. However, God is infinite in His mercy and love, and in Israel's great distress He was grieved. His people, moreover, would not go without deliverance. Chapter 11 will introduce us to one of the most interesting of the judges and, we might add, one of the more problematic. The complete frustration of Israel's leaders is in evidence in verses 17-18. As the Ammonites began to regroup their forces and to gain control of most of Gilead, the princes looked one to another and found that they had no one to lead them effectively (v. 18).

III. DELIVERANCE AND FREEDOM (11:1 – 12:15)

A. *The Call of Jephthah* (11:1-11)

In the year 1089 B.C. a man appeared who seemed to have the qualifications to meet the Ammonite challenge. He was a man of strange background – a Gileadite – a man recognized for his military strength and skill, and yet rejected by his own brothers because he was a son of a harlot (v. 1). The bitterness of his brothers was so great that he was driven out of their territory, and had to dwell in the land of Tob. While in Tob, he gathered about him a small band of men and fought a number of small battles. They were in a sense soldiers of fortune, probably making their living by hiring out as mercenaries or scouts. When the elders of Israel were searching for one to lead their armies, he was requested by the elders to become their captain and their leader (vv. 5-6). This opportunity came as somewhat of a surprise to Jephthah in the light of the previous treatment accorded him (v. 7). The elders, however, were not concerned about his background or even his morality. They were interested in one thing and that was a man with military capability (v. 8). Jephthah was willing to accept this responsibility only on the condition that after a victory was achieved he would not be driven out of the land again. With this, Jephthah and the elders met together before the Lord in Mizpeh, and the agreement was concluded (vv. 9-11).

B. *Negotiations with Ammon* (11:12-29)

Jephthah's first act was not to marshal the armies of Israel together and confront the Ammonites, who at this time were enjoying unparalleled success, but rather to negotiate for peace. Messengers were sent to the king of Ammon to ask what the issues really were in the conflict with Israel (v. 12). According to the king of Ammon, Israel had no legitimate right to the territory which they occupied on the east bank of Jordan. He evi-

dently knew something of the history of Israel's conquest of the
land, for he made reference to their exodus out of Egypt, and
their settlement in Transjordan. His request was a simple
one: Restore those lands without reservation (v. 13). Jephthah
replied to the king of Ammon by pointing out that he too knew
Old Testament history. He reminded the arrogant king that when
Israel marched up through Edom into Moab the territory at
that time was under the control of Sihon who was the king of
the Amorites (vv. 16-19). Sihon refused peaceful passage
through the territory, and the area was conquered by Israel.

Beginning with verse 21, Jephthah postulated four arguments
in answer to the charge of the king of Ammon. First of all he
pointed out that the land which Israel possessed was originally
in the hands of the Amorites, not the Ammonites (cf. Num.
21:21-30; Josh. 13:21). The second argument of Jephthah was a
religious argument stating that the God of Israel gave that land
to Israel. Even the pagans recognized that when victory was
given by a deity, the victors had full right to possess that territory. Notice verse 24, "Wilt not thou possess that which
Chemosh thy god giveth thee to possess?" By way of note, we
might add that Chemosh was generally regarded as the god of
the Moabites, whereas Milcom was the god of Ammon (cf. I
Kings 11:5, 33). This is not an error on the part of Jephthah. He
was far too familiar with the cultures east of the Jordan to make
such an obvious error. The territory to which the king of Ammon was referring in this discussion was really territory originally
belonging to both the Amorites and the Moabites; therefore, it
was appropriate to refer to the god of that territory as Chemosh. In the famous Moabite Stone inscription the king of Moab
mentioned in II Kings 3:4-5 ascribes all Moabite victories to
the good will of Chemosh and all defeats to his anger. The
third argument of Jephthah was one based on political precedent. He raised the question that if Balak, an earlier king of
Moab, did not fight against Israel on the grounds of land rights,
why then should the king of Ammon do so this late in history?
It is true that Balak resisted Israel in that territory, but only
because of his personal hatred of the nation, not because he was
attempting to make formal claim on that territory. The final argument of Jephthah in the negotiations was a time argument.

The information provided by Jephthah in verse 26 is most instructive. He pointed out that the king of Ammon had, in effect, waited too long to make claim to that territory, for 300 years had passed since Israel settled in Heshbon on the east side of the Jordan. If the land did not really belong to Israel by right of conquest, then why was not the claim made to it much earlier? As noted in the introduction (cf. page 18), this statement by Jephthah is most important. It indicates that the period of the judges must cover approximately 350 years. If 144 years, representing the time from the second year of Jephthah to the fourth year of Solomon, and thirty-eight years from the exodus to Heshbon should be added to 300 years, the total would be approximately 482 years, which is in general agreement with the statement made in I Kings 6:1 that there were 480 years between the exodus and the fourth year of Solomon.

The impressive arguments of Jephthah, however, were of no avail. The children of Ammon refused to end their aggression. As in the case of past judges, the Spirit of the Lord came upon Jephthah in order to give him the necessary strength and wisdom for the challenge that lay ahead (v. 29).

C. *Jephthah's Vow* (11:30-40)

1. *The Reason for the Vow*

The situation which Jephthah faced was a serious and a critical one. He realized that apart from divine intervention, an engagement with the powerful Ammonite armies might spell disaster for Israel. Surrounded by tension and concern, Jephthah uttered a vow unto the Lord (v. 30). This vow required a divine response which would guarantee victory over the Ammonites.

2. *The Nature of the Vow*

Scholars are not quite sure just how to interpret or evaluate the vow made by Jephthah. Some understand it as an act of deep piety before God. Others feel that it was rash and unfortunate. Until the Middle Ages the interpretation of this vow seems to have been fairly consistent. It was generally regarded as involving human sacrifice. Josephus, for example, says that Jephthah "sacrificed his daughter as a burnt offering; offering such an oblation as was neither conformable to the law, nor acceptable to God, not weighing with himself what opinion the hearers would have of such a practice."[42]

In recent days, however, interpreters have presented an alternative to that view. Many feel that the vow involved mere dedication to temple service rather than sacrifice. There are, therefore, today, two prevailing interpretations of this portion of Chapter 11. The first is that he did not kill his daughter. This view is suggested by a number of conservative writers.[43] The arguments for this view are as follows: (1) Jephthah was too well acquainted with the law to be ignorant of God's condemnation of human sacrifices (cf. 11:15-27). (2) He must have known that a human being would come out of the home. Furthermore, an animal would have been too small a sacrifice for such a victory. (3) Jephthah must have been a godly man, or his name would not have appeared in Hebrews 11. (4) If his daughter were to be slain, there would be no point in emphasizing her virginity (vv. 37-39). (5) Jephthah could not have done this especially after the Spirit of God came upon him (v. 29). (6) There were women at this time who gave their lives to serving the Lord in the tabernacle at Shiloh (I Sam. 2:22; cf. Exod. 38:8). Thus, Jephthah could have vowed that in case of victory, he would dedicate to God for tabernacle service one member of his household. The fact that it turned out to be his daughter was tragic for him. Indeed, she was his only child; he could never expect to' see grandchildren; and he would seldom, if ever, see her again. (7) It is argued that the conjunction which appears in the vow in verse 31 should be translated "or" rather than "and." In other words, Jephthah is thought to have said, "Whatever comes from the doors of my home to meet me as I return shall be devoted to the Lord's service if it is human, or if it is a clean animal, I will offer it up as a whole burnt

[42]*Ant.* V.7.10.

[43]C. F. Keil and F. Delitzsch, *Biblical Commentary on the Old Testament; Joshua, Judges, Ruth* (Grand Rapids: Wm. B. Eerdmans Publishing Co., 1950), p. 388 ff.

Gleason Archer, *A Survey of Old Testament Introduction* (Chicago: Moody Press, 1964), p. 266 ff.

offering." (8) It is argued by those holding this view that the expression "to lament" in verse 40 should be translated "to talk to," indicating that the daughter remained alive.

Briefly let us evaluate the arguments that are presented in support of this view. First of all, even though Jephthah was acquainted with the Pentateuch, that would by no means guarantee that he would not violate the law. We should recall that David knew the law well, and yet committed adultery. The fact that Jephthah's name appears in Hebrews 11 is not an effective argument for the idea that he did not commit sin. In Hebrews 11, the names of Rahab and Samson also appear, and both are known to have committed evil deeds. It is true that the Spirit of the Lord came upon Jephthah, but we cannot be sure that this event immediately preceded the vow which he made unto the Lord, for it appears in verse 29 that there was a considerable amount of travel between that event and the time when he made a vow unto the Lord. Furthermore, the fact that the Spirit of the Lord came upon him does not guarantee that all of his future acts would be without sin. Remember again that Samson received the Spirit, and many of his acts were wicked. Recall also that David was probably filled with the Spirit for kingship, and he committed adultery. The argument that there was a group of virgins at this time serving the Lord at the tabernacle at Shiloh is an extremely weak one. The women referred to in I Samuel 2:22 and Exodus 38:8 are not clearly associated with the tabernacle as *permanent residents*. Also, there is no evidence in this text, or any other text in the Old Testament, of an ancient equivalent of the modern-day nun. Perpetual virginity and childlessness were looked upon as the greatest of misfortunes. There is no law or custom in the Old Testament that intimates that a single woman was looked upon as more holy than a married one. We might point out that Deborah and Huldah were both prophetesses and were both married. The final argument offered by the advocates of this view is that the conjunction in verse 31 used in Jephthah's vow should be translated "or" rather than "and." While it is true that the Hebrew conjunction *waw* can be used disjunctively or conjunctively, it is extremely doubtful that the disjunctive use ("or") is used here. It is also extremely doubtful that Jephthah had an animal sacrifice in mind at all, for such a formal vow was quite unnecessary to bring an animal sacrifice after a great victory.

The second view with regard to Jephthah's vow and its fulfillment is that he did offer his daughter as a human sacrifice. Again this view is supported by many well-known writers.[44] The arguments for this view are as follows: (1) The Hebrew word for burnt offering is 'olāh which always has the idea of a burnt sacrifice in the Old Testament. Of particular significance is the fact that the Hebrew of 11:31 is essentially the same as that used to describe God's command to Abraham regarding the sacrifice of Isaac (Gen. 22:2). One would think that if Jephthah had dedication in mind, he would have used language similar to that which Hannah employed in the dedication of Samuel (I Sam. 1:11, 22, 25, 28). (2) Jephthah was the son of a common heathen prostitute (Zonah) and spent a great deal of time with various peoples on the east side of the Jordan (11:1-3). Furthermore, it should be observed that later individuals engaged in such human sacrifice. II Kings 3:26-27 records the action of the king of Moab in offering his eldest son for a burnt offering on the wall of his city. II Chronicles 28:3 tells of Ahaz's burning of his children, and II Kings 21:6 tells of Manasseh's sacrifice of his son. If such practices were followed by leaders in Israel at a later period, it is not impossible that they could have been introduced at this earlier period. (3) The fact that Jephthah was a judge of Israel does not remove the possibility of his making a rash vow. The dominant philosophy of this day was a moral and spiritual relativism in which "every man did that which was right in his own eyes" (Judg. 21:25). Many of Israel's leaders were affected by this attitude. Recall that Gideon made a golden ephod which led Israel to idolatry, and Samson engaged in activities that were obviously in opposition to the law of Moses. (4) If Jephthah could lead in the slaughter of 42,000 Israelites (Judg. 12), he would cer-

---

[44]J. Barton Payne, *The Theology of the Older Testament* (Grand Rapids: Zondervan Publishing House, 1962), p. 388.

John Rea, "Jephthah," *The New Bible Dictionary*, ed. J. D. Douglas (Grand Rapids: Wm. B. Eerdmans Publishing Co., 1962), p. 605.

F. F. Bruce, "Judges," *The New Bible Commentary*, ed. F. Davidson (Grand Rapids: Wm. B. Eerdmans Publishing Co., 1954), p. 250.

tainly be capable of this vow and its fulfillment. (5) The fact that her virginity is bewailed in verses 36-40 seems to imply that there was no hope for children in the future because of her impending death. Her lamentation "is probably mentioned to give greater force to the sacrifice, as it would leave him without issue, which in the east was considered a special misfortune."[45] Finally, the argument based upon the Hebrew word for "lament" in verse 40 by those holding the dedication view is rather tenuous. The verb *tanah* occurs only once elsewhere in the Hebrew Bible (Judg. 5:11). The best translation of this form appears to be "to recount."[46]

When all the evidence is weighed, it appears that the latter viewpoint is preferable, even though it is not appealing.

One question might be raised here with regard to this view, however, and that is, "If he made clear that he was going to sacrifice a human being, would God have honored that vow?" There is no doubt that Jephthah did achieve victory over the Ammonites. Space will not permit a discussion of this particular problem, but it is one which the student should consider.

D. *The Ephraimite War* (12:1-15)

1. *The Pride of Ephraim* (12:1-4)

When the Ephraimites appealed to Gideon with regard to being passed over in national affairs, they encountered a sympathetic ear (Judg. 8:1-3). However, the case was different with Jephthah. They again complained that they had not been called in the battle against the Ammonites, a claim which Jephthah refused to accept (cf. v. 2). They even threatened to destroy his house with fire (v. 1). According to Jephthah, the lack of support on the part of Ephraim put his very life in danger (v. 3). As a result, Jephthah gathered together the men of Gilead

---

[45]Merrill F. Unger, *Unger's Bible Dictionary* (Chicago: Moody Press, 1957), p. 569.

[46]Francis Brown, S. R. Driver, and Charles Briggs, *A Hebrew and English Lexicon of the Old Testament* (Oxford: The Clarendon Press, Corrected Impression, 1952), p. 1072.

and fought with the Ephraimites. The cause of warfare, however, was much greater than a personal feud between Jephthah and the men of Ephraim. Verse 4 indicates that the Gileadites had developed a hatred for the Ephraimites and the Manassites living on the west side of the Jordan. Why a jealousy arose between the Manassites on the east of the Jordan and those on the west is not given to us in the text. But this attitude, coupled with the impatience of Jephthah, led to the intertribal war which spelled disaster for the tribe of Ephraim.

2. *Encounter and Defeat* (12:5-7)

When the war broke out between Ephraim and the Gileadites, the Gileadites secured positions along the Jordan River, thereby preventing the escape of the Ephraimites back to the west. Anyone who attempted to cross the Jordan at this time would have been stopped by the Gileadite soldiers and asked to pronounce a special password. The word that was required was "shibboleth." Evidently some type of dialectical differences had developed between the Gileadites and the tribes on the west bank. The Ephraimite pronunciation of this word might constitute what was commonly called an isogloss (a linguistic phenomenon characteristic of a given area). It is rather strange that the Ephraimites were incapable of pronouncing a sibilant which was common to all west Semitic languages. E. A. Speiser suggests that the Gileadites may have pronounced the word *tubbultu* after a cognate Aramaic form.[47] In any event, according to the Hebrew text the Ephraimites were required to pronounce the word "shibboleth," but if they were from the west bank they would say "sibboleth," for they were not capable of pronouncing it after the Gileadite fashion. This screening process resulted in the death of 42,000 men (v. 6). After this war, the life of Jephthah came to an end, concluding a judgeship of six years. He was buried in one of the cities of Gilead (v. 7). Thus the Biblical description of one of the most unusual judges ends. His life was one of mystery and contradiction.

---

[47]E. A. Speiser, "The Shibboleth Incident, Judges 12:6," *Bulletin of the American Schools of Oriental Research*, No. 85 (Feb., 1942).

E. *Jephthah's Successors* (12:8-15)

1. *The Judgeship of Ibzan* (12:8-10)

This judge ruled in Israel for a period of seven years (v. 9). The place of his birth and residence is not clear. It is described as Bethlehem. This might have been Bethlehem of Judah, or it might have reference to the Bethlehem in the tribe of Zebulun, the present *Beit-laḥm*, seven miles northwest of Nazareth (cf. Josh. 19:15-16). He probably began his judgeship about 1081 B.C. and this would have lasted until approximately 1075 B.C. He undoubtedly engaged in polygamous practices and it appears that it was his policy to create marriage relationships with families throughout Israel. This was probably done to improve civil and political influence in various areas.

2. *The Judgeship of Elon* (12:11-12)

Following the rule of Ibzan, Elon the Zebulunite judged Israel. According to verse 11, the judgeship lasted for ten years (1075 B.C.-1065 B.C.). Nothing else is known of this judge other than the fact that he was buried in Aijalon in the territory of Zebulun.

3. *The Judgeship of Abdon* (12:13-15)

It was in the year 1065 B.C. that Adbon became the principal judge in Israel. He remained judge for approximately eight years (v. 14). According to the information in verse 15, he probably was an Ephraimite. He evidently had achieved wide acclaim for his rather large family which included forty sons and thirty grandsons, all of whom rode on ass colts — a sign of prestige and authority (cf. 10:4). According to verse 15, he was buried in Pirathon in the land of Ephraim, which evidently was occupied by the Amalekites during this period of time.

IV. PRACTICAL CONSIDERATIONS

This portion of Scripture gives us interesting insights into the character and power of God as well as the weakness and failures of men. God is seen as sensitive and compassionate with

regard to the needs of His people in spite of their constant
rebellion against Him (10:16). One cannot help but be impressed with the infinite patience of God. Time and time again
Israel turned her back on the very Lord who had provided for
her and redeemed her. These Scriptures re-emphasize the fact
that while Jehovah has a deep hatred for sin, He at the same
time has an unending compassion for the sinner.

The power of God is also a dominant theme in this section of
Scripture. Not only was the Lord sensitive and compassionate
to the needs of Israel, but He had the necessary power at His
disposal to meet those needs, even if it meant utilizing weak
and frail men. The men described in this section of Judges were
indeed weak and in many cases undependable. Certainly the
victory and the freedom brought to Israel during this period
was not the result of human achievement alone. God delivered
His people in spite of the weakness of the leaders He had to use.
This indeed is an encouragement. It reminds us that the purposes
of God cannot be frustrated either by the designs of Satan or
the weaknesses of men. The believer is again reminded that
nothing short of a thorough knowledge of the Word of God and
obedience to it will suffice in the conflicts which he will encounter.

10 (Judges 13–16)

SAMSON — MAN OF STRENGTH

It was in the twelfth century that the Philistines began to play a dominant role in politics and the military affairs of the land of Canaan. This was no accident in history, for Judges 13 records the fact that Israel again did evil in the sight of the Lord. We might assume that there was a return to the kind of idolatry described in the previous chapters. Because of this situation, God permitted the Philistines to strengthen themselves and for forty years to dominate Israel (13:1).

Prior to the time of Samson, the Philistines had played a small, but significant, role in the historical developments of southern Palestine (cf. 3:31; 10:7-11). When Ramses III turned back the invasion of sea peoples in 1194 B.C., this caused many Philistines to settle the coast lands of southwest Palestine. They joined the earlier Minoan settlers and became a significant military force in the years that followed. The judgeship of Samson began about 1069 B.C. and continued until about 1049 B.C. The historical information provided by the monuments of Ramses III helps to provide the cultural and military background for the events in the time of Samson.

I. THE BIRTH OF SAMSON (13:2-25)

A. *His Family* (13:2)

The parents of Samson resided in a border city (Zorah) between Dan and Judah, approximately seventeen miles west of Jerusalem. Manoah and his wife had not been blessed with a child. This was considered a great calamity to a Hebrew woman. The same tragedy was inflicted on Sarai (Gen. 16:1), Rebekah (Gen. 25:21), Hannah (I Sam. 1:2), and Elizabeth (Luke 1:7). God, in His providence and omniscience, looked to the day when Israel would require deliverance and an outstanding leader. Manoah and his wife were to be part of God's plan.

132

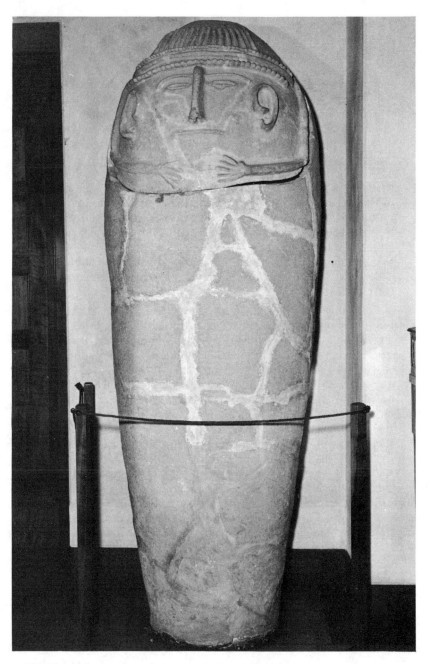

Philistine Anthropoid Coffin. Levant Photo Service

B. *The Announcement of His Birth* (13:3-23)

The announcement of the birth of a child is not without parallel elsewhere in Scripture. Isaac's birth was announced as was John the Baptist's and the Lord Jesus'. The announcement of the birth was brought by the angel of Jehovah, who had appeared previously to Gideon and others during the period of the judges. The initial appearance of the angel of the Lord was only to the wife of Manoah. On that occasion, she was informed that she would conceive and bear a son (v. 3). In addition to that, it was made clear that this child was to be a Nazarite unto God (v. 5). According to Numbers 6:1-6, the Nazarite had three restrictions placed upon him: (1) He was to abstain from wine (Num. 6:3-4). (2) He was to allow the hair of his head to go untouched by a razor (Num. 6:5). (3) He was not to touch a dead body in order that he might prevent defilement (Num. 6:6).

Following this conversation, the wife of Manoah came to him and brought the news which had been given to her by the angel of the Lord. Manoah's response is most impressive and instructive. He did not question the message brought to his wife, but sought further instructions. He requested another appearance of the man of God in order to receive instruction on rearing the child. That prayer was answered by God (v. 9). Once again the man of God appeared — this time to both of them — and Manoah's principal concerns were repeated. They took the form of two questions. The first one literally translated is, "What shall be the ordering of the child?"; that is, "What shall be the rule of life for this child?" He then asked, "What shall be his work?" (v. 12). Manoah was searching for confirmation of the original message given to his wife and additional instruction as to their responsibility in rearing the child. Up to this point Manoah did not realize that he stood face to face with the angel of the Lord (v. 16). He inquired further of the identity of this visitor by asking his name (v. 17). The angel responded by saying, "Why askest thou thus after my name, seeing it is secret?" (v. 18). The last word of this sentence might better be translated "wonderful" (Heb. *peli'y*). This is the same word that occurs in Isaiah 9:6 and is rendered "wonderful" (cf. 13:19, "wondrously"). After a special offering was miraculously consumed by fire and the angel of the Lord ascended in the flame heavenward, Manoah immediately knew that it was the angel of the Lord (v. 21). He, like Gideon, was struck by great fear because he thought he had seen God and would therefore die (cf. Judg. 6:23; Exod. 33:20). His wife assured him that he would not die for this was certainly not God's will in this case (v. 23).

C. *His Birth* (13:24-25)

In the fullness of time, Samson was born and the Lord blessed him (v. 24). There has been some speculation as to what the name of Samson means. It most likely comes from the Hebrew Šemeš which means "sun." Some suggest, on this basis, that it has the idea of "brightness." We are not informed as to what happened in the childhood days of Samson. Verse 25 merely indicates that the Spirit of Jehovah moved him at times in the camp of Dan between Zorah and Eshtaol.

II. THE MARRIAGE OF SAMSON (14:1-20)

A. *The Woman in Timnath* (14:1-4)

Because of the proximity of the tribe of Dan to the center of Philistine influence, it was not surprising that Samson came in contact with a number of the young ladies from Philistia. According to verses 1-4, he was very much attracted to one of the women among the daughters of the Philistines. In order to make arrangements for his marriage he came to his mother and father. His parents, of course, knowing the law and having a commitment to the spiritual future of Samson, immediately objected to this kind of arrangement. The ultimate concerns of Samson in this case were not spiritual, but personal; "Get her *for me; for she pleaseth me well*" (v. 3). The parents of Samson did not realize that even this evil act on the part of their son was included in God's perfect plan and would be utilized by Him. The writer of the text looked back over the history of Samson and saw in his movements, and even in his weaknesses, the hand of God. The marriage between Samson and a Philistine woman ultimately resulted in the destruction of many of Israel's enemies. Verse 4 points to the fact that "he sought an occasion against the Philistines." The antecedent of "he" is probably Jehovah, although grammatically it could refer to Samson as well. In view of the theological nature of the first statement of this verse, it appears that Jehovah is meant, rather than Samson.

B. *The Lion and the Riddle* (14:5-20)

Evidently, Samson persisted in his demands to take the young girl from Timnath as his wife. His father and mother proceeded to Timnath to make the necessary arrangements for the marriage (v. 5). Later Samson made the trip in that direction and on the way he was encountered by a young lion, one in the prime of life (Heb. *kepîr*). The Spirit of the Lord came upon him (v. 6), giving him the necessary strength and skill to slay that lion. After having visited his prospective wife, he went back to his home (v. 7). Later he returned to Timnath to "take her" (v. 8), and on the way he noticed the dry, clean carcass (skeleton?) of the lion which he had slain. A swarm of bees had produced honey in that carcass so he stopped to eat and enjoy it. Bees, of course, avoid any kind of decomposition. We probably should assume here that birds and time had cleared away all of the decayed material, leaving a skeleton. Again, Samson kept this event a secret (v. 9). After the wedding a feast was prepared for Samson and his bride (v. 10). The Hebrew of this verse is very important, for this was no mere "feast." The Hebrew indicates that this was a "drinking feast" (Heb. *mišteh*). Thus, in a short period of time Samson had violated two of the requirements for the Nazarite. He had contaminated himself ceremonially by touching the carcass of the lion, and he had participated in a drinking feast.

His future was further complicated when, in accord with local customs, he told a riddle (v. 12). The pride of those gathered there would not permit them to admit they could not analyze the riddle or interpret it. Finally, on the seventh day of the feast week, they came to Samson's wife and demanded the answer to the riddle, on the threat that they would burn her house (v. 15). The men were able to go back to Samson and explain the riddle to him (v. 18). He recognized the source of their information, but nonetheless paid off the obligation he had to these men.

It might be noted, however, that he paid off his debt at their expense. Again, the Spirit of the Lord came upon him (v. 19), and he went down to Ashkelon, an important Philistine city. There he slew thirty men, and took their garments to pay off the men who had explained the riddle. In the meantime, however, the father-in-law was convinced that Samson was irresponsible and really unconcerned about the young girl from Timnath; thus, in the process of time she was given to the best man. This complicated the life of Samson even further (v. 20), but not without divine purpose (cf. 14:4).

III. SAMSON AND THE PHILISTINES (15:1–16:31)

A. *The Rise of Samson to Power* (15:1-20)

A short time after the wedding feast, Samson returned to Timnath to get his wife. He evidently did not see his wife after he went to Ashkelon and now it was the time of the wheat harvest, or about the middle of May. His father-in-law had already taken steps to find another husband for his daughter (vv. 1-2). He did, however, offer Samson his younger daughter who he claimed was even fairer than she (v. 2). This proposition, interestingly enough, has a familiar ring to it (cf. Gen. 29:17 ff.). Samson, very displeased with this situation, again turned against the Philistines, resulting in the destruction of many of their crops. He caught some three hundred jackals (v. 4), tied torches between their tails, and set them free in the grain fields of the Philistines (v. 5). When the Philistines witnessed this mass destruction of their crops, they revenged this act by burning the house of Samson's father-in-law (v. 6). It is ironic that this house should be destroyed by fire, for earlier the wife of Samson attempted to save the house from such a fate by betraying the trust of Samson (14:15). This act on the part of the Philistines enraged Samson further. According to the principle of *Lex Talionis* Samson dealt with the Philistines in violence once again. This time "he smote them hip and thigh with a great slaughter" (v. 8). The idiom "hip and thigh" is simply a proverbial expression for "completely" or "entirely." The Philistines then responded to this by going up into Judah in order to take Samson

captive (v. 9). The men of Judah at this time were very weak
and not in a position to resist the Philistines or to reject their demands. Three thousand men of Judah went to Samson, an indication of their great respect for his strength (v. 11). When they
inquired of Samson why he had acted the way he did in increasing the belligerency of the Philistines, he merely responded that
he had treated them just as they had treated him (v. 11). The
men of Judah bound Samson with two "new cords" (v. 13), but
these were not to last, for the Spirit of God came upon him again
(v. 14), and the cords were broken. On this occasion he slaughtered one thousand Philistines (v. 15). This he did with a
fresh or moist jawbone of an ass. It is not impossible that Samson
was assisted by the men of Judah on this occasion, although he
took full credit for the victory (v. 16). His arrogance and self-
sufficiency were not overlooked by the Lord. In physical thirst
and weakness, he was forced to call on the Lord. The Lord
heard that cry and strengthened him (vv. 18-20).

B. *The Fall of Samson into Sin* (16:1-22)

1. *Samson at Gaza* (16:1-3)

While Samson had control of his great power, he unfortunately
did not have the same control over his passions. At Gaza he spent
time with a harlot and this situation again brought him into
great danger. The men of the city heard of his presence there
and surrounded the city, waiting for morning to come when they
could initiate a detailed search to locate him (v. 2). However,
when Samson rose at midnight and prepared to leave the city,
he found that all the gates were shut tight. This, of course, was
no problem to a man of Samson's strength. He merely tore
the gates from their posts and carried them toward Hebron!
Since Hebron is approximately thirty miles from Gaza, it is
doubtful that he carried them all the way to the city. The Hebrew seems to imply that he carried them to the foothills which
are before Hebron.

2. *Samson and Delilah* (16:4-22)

Sometime after his escape from Gaza, he found a woman in
the valley of Sorek. Samson had spent much of his life in this

valley — now known as Wadi es-Surar — which starts about fifteen miles west of Jerusalem and runs toward the coastal plain. The town of Zorah, Samson's home, was situated in this valley. The name of the woman whom he loved was Delilah. No other information is given about her in the Scriptures. Many have supposed she was a Philistine, but this is merely an assumption. It is not clearly indicated as to whether she became his wife or not. In all probability, she did not, in the light of his previous activities as described in verses 1 through 3. In any event, the lords of the Philistine Pentapolis (Heb. *sarnê* *pelištîm*) offered 5,500 pieces of silver for the secret of Samson's strength (v. 5).

Delilah then set out to discover that secret. Samson responded to her questions in an arrogant, playful attitude. He first told her that if he were bound with seven green (Heb. "moist") ropes or bow strings that were never dried, he would be as another man (v. 7). This she did, and then called in Philistine soldiers to take him prisoner. Using his strength, he broke these and presumably killed the men. This, of course, displeased Delilah greatly (v. 10), and why should it not? Five thousand five hundred pieces of silver were at stake here! Again she pressed him for the secret of his strength, and again he gave her false information. This time he suggested "new ropes" should be used and he would then be as any other man (v. 11). She then called the Philistine soldiers, and again the cords were broken (v. 12). This situation was becoming costly to the Philistine lords and embarrassing to Delilah. She reprimanded Samson for his deceit and mockery, and once again sought the secret of his strength (v. 13). In arrogant pride he continued to play the game with her. He suggested that if seven locks of his hair were woven into a web, he would be helpless; so she began to weave the hair, and when he had fallen asleep, she called for the Philistine soldiers. Once again he tore loose from the weaver's beam and presumably slew the men waiting to take him prisoner (v. 14). This was indeed a frustration for Delilah. The silver was so close and yet so far! But she did not end her search at this point. Verse 16 informs us that she pressed him daily, questioning and taunting him concerning his strength, until finally he revealed his secret. He pointed to the fact that he was dedicated as a Nazarite to God and if he were shaven, his strength would leave him (vv. 16-17). There was no doubt in Delilah's mind this time that he had spoken the truth (v. 18).

The scene that follows is tragic and one of the darkest moments in the history of the judges. Delilah called for the Philistine lords and instructed them to bring the silver which they had promised (v. 18). After Samson had fallen asleep, his head was shaven, and when awakened, he was unable to defend himself as he had in the past (vv. 18-20). It was not the mere loss of hair that brought Samson into humiliation; it was his disobedience to God and the complete violation of the Nazarite vow. The pride and insensitivity of Samson are clearly viewed in verse 20. He assumed that he would go out as before and tend to the threat of the Philistines, but he did not know that Jehovah — that is, the strength of Jehovah — had departed from him. Like many believers, Samson was asleep when he lost his strength. To add to the humiliation, the Philistines took him captive, put out his eyes, and took him down to Gaza, the city which he had left so arrogantly by destroying their gates. They bound him with fetters of bronze and took him to the prison house where he worked as an animal (v. 21). The downfall of Samson was not due to a failure on God's part, but it was due to Samson's uncontrolled pride and sinful passion.

C. *The Death of Samson* (16:23-31)

The humiliation of Samson did not end with his imprisonment or the removal of his eyes. Later he was taken to the temple dedicated to the Philistine god, Dagon (vv. 23-24). The term "Dagon" has been traced to two Hebrew roots. One suggestion is that it comes from *dāg,* meaning "fish." Supporting this theory are a number of coins found at Ashkelon, having an image of a deity that was half man and half fish. A preferred view, however, traces the term to *dāgān,* which means "grain." If this is the case, Dagon would be a fertility god. In Ugaritic literature Baal is referred to as the "son of Dagon." This deity was evidently recognized widely in the land of Canaan, especially along the coast. The capture and humiliation of Samson was the cause of great rejoicing in the cities of Philistia (vv. 23-24). In order to make the most of their capture of Samson, they brought him to the temple of Dagon, where, now blind and in chains, he was the object of laughter and scorn. This was also an occasion of praise and thanksgiving to the gods of the Philistines (v. 24).

This temple must have been of considerable size. It probably had a long main hall with adjacent rooms. The complex was capable of supporting approximately three thousand men and women on the roof as well as a large number inside the temple proper (v. 27). While voices were lifted in praise to Dagon, Samson also lifted his voice. For the first time in years, he realized he had to throw himself on the mercy of God and depend on His help. In utter simplicity Samson prayed to his God. The essence of his prayer is wrapped up in two key words: "Remember me" (v. 28). This kind of prayer is indicative of a soul in need. Two other times in Biblical history a similar prayer was offered. Hannah, in a state of despair and frustration, came to the tabernacle and lifted up her voice in prayer to her God. In bitterness of soul she cried to heaven, "Remember me" (I Sam. 1: 11). The Lord recognized the sincerity of this prayer and answered it by giving her a child, Samuel. Many years later, a similar prayer was offered. This time it was at Calvary. One of the malefactors who was hanged with Jesus looked at Him with faith and said, "Lord, *remember me* when thou comest into thy kingdom" (Luke 23:42). Again, the Lord recognized the sincerity and simplicity of that request. To it He replied, "Today shalt thou be with me in paradise" (Luke 23:43). The Lord likewise recognized the sincerity of Samson's plea and answered his prayer, giving to him strength, enough strength to destroy the temple of the Philistines and those gathered inside (vv. 29-31). This last heroic act brought an end to his life.

IV. PRACTICAL CONSIDERATIONS

The life of Samson is a study in contrasts. There was the godliness and sensitiveness of his parents. In contrast to this was the arrogance and self-sufficiency of Samson. Samson was a man of great gifts, and yet a man who failed to utilize them to the greatest degree in bringing glory to his God. Samson realized many victories and yet suffered many losses. While Samson was able to defeat the strongest of men, he was defeated and humiliated by the weakest of women.

The life of Samson is both a lesson and a warning. The believer needs to be diligent concerning the gifts that God has given to him. Nothing can be taken for granted. At every point Satan will attempt to rob the believer of his very source of strength. Whenever the believer fails because of his own arrogance and pride, the forces of evil rejoice and men's hearts are gratified in their rejection of the Lord. After a judgeship of twenty years, Samson's life passed from the scene of Israelite history. The memory of him is not forgotten, however, for in Hebrews 11:32 we are reminded that he was indeed a man of heroic faith. Even though blind and helpless he was able to destroy an important temple of the Philistines and slay over three thousand people gathered at that site, one of the greatest single victories realized.

Samson's life is also a reminder that men can fall either as a result of *uncontrolled power, false pride or evil passion.* All of these must come under the control of the Spirit of God. The apostle Paul reminded us that he had to keep his body under subjection (I Cor. 9:27). While we may not possess the same physical strength as Samson, we nonetheless are confronted with the same temptations and are equally liable to fall. We, therefore, need to turn to the Lord and rest in His strength and wisdom, and not in our own. In this we find victory.

11
(Judges 17–21)

CONFUSION AND CONFLICT

The last five chapters of this book represent the author's supplement or appendix to the history of the Judges period. The author intended to provide further insight into the issues which gave rise to the conflicts of this and later periods. The history of this period is dealt with in the local sense as it related to families and clans and, of course, as related to Israel as a nation. As was the case in the earlier chapters of the Book of Judges, these chapters deal with the subject of spiritual apostasy and its effects upon the nation of Israel.

I. THE DANITE MIGRATION (17:1–18:31)

A. *The Idolatry of Micah* (17:1-13)

A careful reader of this chapter will find important instruction with regard to the nature and effects of apostasy as it is viewed in the life of one individual and his family. The apostasy of the Judges period, according to this chapter, was characterized by three observable trends.

1. *Religious Syncretism* (17:1-5)

Religious syncretism involves the blending together of different religious attitudes and ideas into one system. This trend was observable in the lives of Micah and his family as they were affected by the popular trends of their day. According to verse 1, Micah was an Ephraimite. This fact is significant because the tabernacle was set up at Shiloh which is in Ephraimite territory. However, as we study the story of Micah, it becomes clear that Shiloh had lost its spiritual influence among many of the families and clans within the tribe of Ephraim. If this were the case for the tribe of Ephraim, how much less influence must the sanctuary at Shiloh have had among the other tribes located in more distant regions? In spite of the significance of Micah's name ("who is as Jehovah?") it is clear that he was very much caught up with the spirit of his generation. He had gone so far as to

143

steal from his mother. According to verse 2, he had taken eleven hundred shekels of silver. This, as we learn from 16:5, was no small amount. When the money was taken, his mother had evidently put a curse upon the thief, and as time went on, Micah found himself unable to use the silver because of the curse. He therefore returned the money to his mother and she responded with praise (v. 2). This theft on the part of Micah was probably characteristic of his age. When the law was abandoned and its principles forsaken, dishonesty and thievery probably characterized everyday life in Israel (cf. 18:14-19). Following the return of the money, the mother indicated that she had "wholly dedicated this silver to Jehovah" (v. 3).

Again it appears we have a healthy religious situation. However, two hundred shekels of silver were used by that mother and Micah to make a "graven image" and "molten image" (v. 4). The religious syncretism of this period is clearly illustrated in these verses. Money which was "dedicated to Jehovah" was, in effect, to be employed for the making of idols. It is entirely possible that these idols were in some way used in the worship of Jehovah, thus reflecting the blending together of Canaanite cultic practices and traditional worship of Jehovah. It is not clear from verse 4 whether one or two images were made from the allotted amount of silver. Some feel the second expression is merely an explanation or further description of the first. However, in 18:17, the two words are separated in such a manner as to indicate the existence of two idols. The making of the two idols was not the beginning of idolatry in Micah's household. According to verse 5, he already had a "house of gods" (Heb. bêṯ 'elohîm). In addition to this he made an ephod and used it for cultic purposes (cf. Judg. 8:27). The teraphim mentioned in verse 5 are usually interpreted as referring to household idols (Gen. 31:19, 34). They were, on occasion, used as oracular instruments (Ezek. 21:21; Zech. 10:2). It appears that some of the teraphim were rather large, perhaps having human form (cf. I Sam. 19:13-17). Worship at this site was conducted by one of Micah's sons who became "his priest" (v. 5).

2. Moral Relativism (17:6)

The writer again reminds us that we are in the pre-monarchial

period, for there was no "king in Israel" (cf. 18:1; 19:1; 21:25).
When men began to reject the law of Moses as the standard of
conduct, there was only one other way in which moral activity
could be conducted and that was on the basis of subjective
norms; that is, every man established principles of righteousness
on the basis of his own evaluation. This type of philosophy led
to confusion and spiritual conflict among the tribes.

3. *Extreme Materialism* (17:7-13)

Another individual entered the scene at this point of the story.
He is described as being a Levite from Bethlehem-judah (v. 7).
His journey northward was intended to provide for him "a place"
(i.e., a place of service, v. 8). Evidently this Levite was un-
employed and had no place of permanent service. During his
travels northward he encountered Micah who asked of him the
reason for such a journey (v. 9). The Levite responded by indicating that he sought a place of service. The very fact that
the Levite wandered, seeking a means of support, might indicate
that the apostasy had left the Levites without tribal support.
In any event, Micah extended to this young priest an official
"call" to his local shrine. This included a salary of ten skekels
of silver, a suit of apparel, and food (v. 10). The introduction
of the Levite into this story is important because it indicates
that apostasy had not only influenced the thinking of the Israelites generally, but also of the Levites and the spiritual leaders
in Israel. The Levite was content to accept such a position
(v. 11) in spite of what he knew of the law of Moses and its
prohibitions with regard to idolatry. He was consecrated by
Micah and then served as a private priest in this household (v.
12). The sinfulness of the Levite contributed to the deepening of
Micah's apostasy. Now Micah became arrogant and self-sufficient
in spiritual attitude for he proclaimed, "Now know I that the
Lord will do me good, seeing I have a Levite to my priest"
(v. 13).

B. *Danite Unrest* (18:1-29)

In spite of the fact that the tribe of Dan had a military potential of 64,000 men (Num. 26:43), they were unable to occupy

the territory that was allotted to them. The reason for their frustration and their interest in other territory (v. 1) is given in 1:34 of this book. According to the historian's observation, the Amorites had forced the Danites up into the mountains, not permitting them to occupy the larger valleys.

Preparations for a Move (18:1-26)

Because of the problems the Danites faced they sent a spy contingent northward to search out new territories in which they could dwell safely. In the process of their journey they encountered the young Levite. According to verse 3, they knew him. Perhaps they knew him before their journey or they may have recognized him as a Levite by his dress. In any event, they sought special counsel from this Levite (v. 5) which he gladly gave them (v. 6). He endorsed their plan and encouraged them to seek new territory. The five men then traveled northward to a site named Laish (v. 7), elsewhere called Leshem (Josh. 19: 47). The spies noted that Laish was a peaceful town and far enough removed from the Phoenicians and Sidon as not to face another military threat. After they returned back to Philistine territory, 600 warriors with their families joined in the migration northward (vv. 11-14). Once again they passed the sanctuary of Micah, and on that day they helped themselves to the images and idols that were inside the sanctuary (v. 14). As previously noted, robbery was very common during this period (cf. 17:2-3). In addition to taking the idols of the sanctuary, they decided to give another "call" to this young priest. This time they encouraged him that his ministry would be far more effective among a whole tribe than just to a small family (v. 19). The young Levite found this offer very attractive and, therefore, joined the Danites on their trip northward. Again we are able to see the materialistic attitude of the Levite during this time.

When Micah returned home, he was much disturbed by the absence of both the objects of the sanctuary and his private "pastor." He, along with some others, pursued the Danites in an attempt to rescue his gods and his priest. When he caught up with the Danites, he explained why he had made such a journey.

His words are very enlightening, for they reflect the theological thinking of this man. First of all, in verse 24 he indicated the gods which he had made had been taken. It is rather sad that an Israelite should assume he could actually make a god. Furthermore, it was quite strange that a man should have to rescue his god. It ought to be the other way around; namely, his god providing deliverance for him. The apostasy of Micah is further illustrated by his total frustration in the light of these events, for with his idols gone and his priest gone, he said, "What have I more?" (v. 24). The Danites were not impressed by the arguments or the pleas of Micah. He was therefore forced to return home without the things which he had lost. The Danites and the young Levite priest continued their way northward to Laish and occupied that site (vv. 27-29). At that time the name of the city was changed from Laish to Dan (v. 29). Since the site is called Dan in 5:17, it is probable that the events here described occurred before the war with Sisera.

C. *Danite Idolatry* (18:30-31)

After Laish was conquered, the Danites established a sanctuary for the idols. Jonathan became the high priest at that place (v. 30). According to this verse, he was a descendant of Manasseh. It is clear from the original text that this expression should be read "the son of Moses" rather than "the son of Manasseh." A scribe evidently tried to remove the name of Moses from being associated with idolatrous practices. This verse indicates that the events described in Chapters 17 and 18 actually occurred early in the Judges period, for Jonathan is a near descendant of Moses. The "captivity of the land" referred to in this verse has been variously interpreted. Some feel it refers to the deportation of northern peoples by Tiglath-pileser (II Kings 15:29). Others feel it describes the exile of the ark from Shiloh (I Sam. 4:11) — the time of Philistine domination (1 Sam. 4). The latter view seems more probable in the light of the fact that the house of God at Shiloh was destroyed by the Philistines (cf. v. 31 with I Sam. 4:4). From this time onward, the city of Dan became a center of idolatry. Some years later, Jeroboam set up golden calves at Bethel and Dan (I Kings 12:29).

II. THE BENJAMITE WAR (19:1–21:25)

A. *The Reason for the War* (19:1–20:14)

Chapters 17 and 18 gave us insight into the effects of apostasy as it related to a family and a tribe. The chapter that lies before us will be a detailed analysis of the effects of apostasy among the whole nation of Israel. Perhaps most significant is the influence of idolatry and moral relativism on the tribe of Benjamin.

1. *The Crime at Gibeah* (19:1-28)

The historian begins his narrative by providing historical context for the events that are to follow. The period is the pre-monarchial era. The story again revolves around a Levite who had taken a concubine from Bethlehem-judah as a wife. In the process of time, she had become unfaithful to him. The result was a separation and her return to her father's house (vv. 1-2). The Levite then made a journey to the home of the concubine in order to restore his relationship with her. After abiding in the father-in-law's house for three days, he decided to return home, but the father-in-law insisted that he remain one more day, and this he did (vv. 5-7). On the fifth day, a similar request was made by the concubine's father, but the Levite and his wife began their journey (vv. 7-9).

Their journey northward was an eventful one. They were not able to stay in Jerusalem because it was still in the hands of the enemy (v. 12). The name of Jerusalem at that time was Jebus (v. 10), apparently named after the people who ruled it, the Jebusites (cf. Josh. 18:16, 28; Judg. 1:21; I Chron. 11:4). Because it was not safe to stay in Jerusalem, it was decided to continue northward either to Gibeah or to Ramah (v. 13). They ultimately reached Gibeah which was located in the tribal territory of Benjamin (v. 14). After entering the gate, they remained in the public square just inside the gate, hoping to receive an invitation for lodging (v. 15), but such an invitation did not come. The absence of hospitality on the part of the Benjamites should be regarded as an outward sign of apostasy, for in the Old Testament a godly man, among other things, was one who extended hospitality to those in need (cf. Job 31:32).

Finally, an Ephraimite, who was sojourning in Gibeah, gave them a place to stay. During the evening certain "sons of Belial" came to the house, desiring carnal relations with the Levite (v. 22).

The use of the expression "sons of Belial" is significant. This term is reserved for those who have no regard for law or morality. The term literally translated means "sons of no profit" or "sons of worthlessness." Elsewhere in the Old Testament this expression is used to describe those involved in idolatry (Deut. 13:13), rebellion (I Sam. 2:12), and drunkenness (I Sam. 1:16; here the expression is "daughter of Belial"). In this chapter it has reference to lewd and sensuous men (cf. 20:13). The story recorded here is reminiscent of the one in Genesis 19. In similar fashion, the master of the house gave to these men not the guest, but the concubine (vv. 24-25). The concubine of the Levite was then taken and abused all evening. As a result, she died (vv. 27-28). When the Levite witnessed this, he took her body home and dismembered it into twelve parts. One part of her body was sent to each tribe as a challenge and warning (vv. 29-30). The purpose of this act was to awaken Israel from its state of moral lethargy and to marshal the tribes together to face up to their responsibility. A similar deed was performed by King Saul some years later, probably to achieve the same effect (I Sam. 11:7). This act on the part of the Levite was designed to get action and it worked.

2. Responses to the Crime (19:29–20:48)

a. The Levite (19:29-30)

The response of the Levite is described in the last two verses of Chapter 19. His response was one of indignation because of the open sin of the wicked men of Gibeah. The Levite felt that nothing short of immediate judgment and punishment would be satisfactory.

b. The Tribes (20:1-48)

When word was received regarding the crime that had been committed in Gibeah, the tribes gathered together and their armies made ready. They numbered 400,000 (v. 2). For the

first time in many years the tribes were gathered together in
singleness of purpose (cf. vv. 8, 11). They all agreed that the
guilty parties at Gibeah should be punished. Lots were cast in
order to determine who should care for the food supplies for the
armies (v. 10). A select group of men then went through the
territory of Benjamin demanding the punishment of the guilty
parties at Gibeah. The death penalty for this crime was clearly
in mind (v. 13). Because of the apostasy of the tribe of Benjamin, rather than turning the guilty men over for punishment,
they protected them (v. 13). They elected to go to war with the
other tribes rather than have the evil men punished. Besides
the 700 men from the town of Gibeah, they marshaled together
26,000 soldiers (v. 15). Among the 26,000 there were 700 left-
handed men who were experts with the sling-shot (v. 16; cf.
3:15). The tension which developed during this time was probably paralleled only during the tribal conflict recorded in Joshua
22.

That the decision to fight Benjamin was not an easy one is
indicated by their journey to the house of God in search of
God's will (v. 18). The Lord required that Judah should go into
battle first (cf. 1:3 ff.). Judah was most likely selected because
of its size and fighting capability. The first battle was fought
at Gibeah (v. 20) and resulted in the loss of 22,000 Israelites
(v. 21). Again the leaders of Israel came before the Lord in
search of His will (v. 23). The second day the tribes went to
battle, and as in the previous encounter the Benjamites were
successful. Eighteen thousand Israelites were slain in that
battle (v. 25). This caused the tribes to again appear before God
in humility and concern (vv. 26-27). Phinehas, the son of Eleazar, took the responsibility of giving guidance (v. 28). Phinehas,
of course, is well known from the days of Joshua. It was he who
mediated the tribal conflict described in Joshua 22. The mention
of his name in this account indicates that the events here recorded must have occurred early in the Judges period.

The third battle fought between Benjamin and the other
tribes was quite different from the first two. This time Israel
set an ambush much like the one used by Joshua in the battle
of Ai (Josh. 8:4-29). The arrogant Benjamites were drawn
away from the city and then those lying in wait on the other

side of the city entered the city, destroying all. This was the beginning of what was almost total annihilation for the tribe of Benjamin. When the dust of battle had settled, only 600 Benjamite males remained. These had fled to the rock of Rimmon about four miles east of Bethel (vv. 34-47).

It might be asked at this point, "Why didn't Jehovah give victory to the armies of Israel in the first two battles? Why did they suffer the loss of over 40,000 men before they realized victory?" This question, of course, is difficult to answer. It is apparent that the setbacks did have a healthy effect on the spiritual outlook of the tribes. They were driven to fasting and prayer with an earnest attempt to find the will of God.

B. *The Results of the War* (21:1-25)

The tragedy of the Benjamite war was not only in the fact that this tribe had been nearly annihilated, but that the other tribes had taken an oath not to permit the marriage of any of their daughters to a Benjamite (v. 1). The results of their victory, coupled with the oath that they had taken, meant that Benjamin might not survive as a tribe in Israel (v. 3). The only hope for the survival of the tribe of Benjamin would be to find wives for the 600 men who remained. A search of the war records indicated that the men from Jabesh-gilead did not participate in the recent battles, and it was decided that the city should be judged (vv. 8-9). Twelve thousand soldiers were sent from the tribes to go against the city of Jabesh-gilead with the instructions to kill every man, woman, and child with the exception of the virgins (vv. 10-12). The 400 virgins were given to the surviving Benjamites, leaving only 200 without wives (v. 12). Some of the Benjamites most likely returned to Jabesh-gilead to settle down. This probably had something to do with later action on the part of Saul (a Benjamite) on behalf of that city (I Sam. 11:1 ff.). The tribes apparently felt that the provision of 400 wives was not sufficient to guarantee the survival of Benjamin. The remaining 200 Benjamites were encouraged to "take" wives from among the maidens who danced during the festivals at Shiloh (vv. 19-21). If any of the relatives objected to this procedure, they were reminded that elders had agreed that the

Benjamites should have wives. Also, they had not, in effect, "given" these girls in marriage to the Benjamites; hence there was no violation of their oath (v. 22).

The Book of Judges concludes with a fitting evaluation of that age. The statement in verse 25 indicates both the political and moral status of Israel during that time.

Conclusion

The study of the books of Joshua and Judges is a study in contrasts. Joshua portrays the excitement of conquest and the thrill of victory. The people of God were sensitive to their covenant relationship and attempted to remain faithful to it. After the death of Joshua, the political and spiritual trends in Israel changed. The tribes became more interested in material wealth and political compatibility than obedience to the law. Through intermarriage and religious syncretism, the strength of Israel began to decline. Tribes became independent and many sanctuaries were built in addition to the one at Shiloh. Rather than progression and victory, the Book of Judges portrays the sad story of retrogression and failure.

The Book of Judges serves as both a challenge and a warning. It is a challenge because it illustrates the fact that God can and will work in behalf of men when they turn to Him. It is a warning to all, that God will not tolerate sin.

The books of Joshua and Judges are also books of action. They involve conquest and conflict. In the light of the situations, the admonition given to Joshua on the eve of march is significant and with important application today: "This book of the law shall not depart out of thy mouth; thou shalt meditate therein day and night, that thou mayest observe to do all that is written therein: for then thou shalt make thy way prosperous and then thou shalt have good success" (Josh. 1:8).

RUTH

12

SOJOURN IN MOAB

Treasures are many times discovered in the most unlikely places. Once while walking across the dry, barren hills of Judah, I looked down amidst the stones and saw a small coin. This discovery changed my view of that immediate area. Whereas I had considered the area as never having been occupied and therefore of little importance, it now took on a new character. The Book of Ruth is, in some respects, like that coin. Out of the gloom and decadence of the period of the judges comes this refreshing, wholesome love story which is an excellent illustration of the grace of God at work in the Old Testament era. The period of the judges was marked by sensuousness and shallow passions. Remember the attitudes and acts of Samson which failed to rise above the trends of his day. In striking contrast to this is the story of Ruth, the Moabitess. Her story is one of godly faithfulness and true love. It is the story of sacrifice rather than self-centered interests.

I. INTRODUCTION

A. *The Title of the Book*

This book derives its title from the principal character of the book, Ruth, the Moabitess. It constitutes one of two books in the Old Testament which were named after a woman — Esther being the other. The derivation and meaning of the name Ruth are uncertain. It is felt by some that it is related to the Hebrew verb *rā'āh* which has the idea of "associating with someone." Others are inclined to regard it as a contraction of the Hebrew word *re'ut* which means "friendship."[48] In both cases the central idea would be "friendship" or "friend." In the English Bible the book constitutes an appropriate appendix to the Book of Judges and serves as an introduction to the historical looks of Samuel.

---

[48]C. F. Keil and F. Delitzsch, *op. cit.*, p. 466.

B. *Authorship of the Book*

The author of the book is unknown. The historical setting of the book is the times of the judges (1:1). Since David's name is mentioned in the book (4:22), but not Solomon's, it is probable that it was written during the reign of David. Some have suggested that Samuel may have been the author, but this cannot be verified. Critics generally date the book in the post-exilic period. They suggest that it was written in the time of Ezra and Nehemiah as a protest against their stringent laws prohibiting marriage between Jews and non-Jews. Several Aramaisms are cited as further proof of its late composition. However, these arguments are not conclusive and rest on questionable presuppositions. The fact that King David is mentioned and not Solomon seems to be an argument in favor of a rather early date of composition. A later writer would surely have made some mention of Solomon in this book.

C. *Position in the Canon*

In the Hebrew Bible this book is listed with the *ketubîm*, the third division; it appears fifth, though, according to the Talmud, it must have been first at one time in that division. It is one of five books included in the *megilloth*. The *megilloth* consisted of five books which were read in the synagogue on five special occasions or festivals during the year. In printed editions of the Hebrew Old Testament these books are usually arranged as follows: Canticles, Ruth, Lamentations, Ecclesiastes and Esther. Ruth is placed in the second position because it was read at the feast of weeks, later known as Pentecost, the second of five special festivals. Greek translators of the Old Testament Scriptures considered the book an appendix to the Book of Judges and therefore gave it no special title of its own. Later editions of the Septuagint, however, inserted the expression *telos ton kriton* ("the end of the judges") to indicate the break between Judges and Ruth.

D. *Purposes of the Book*

Some see only one purpose in the book, which is "to provide a genealogical link between Judah and David." However, a care-

ful study of the book from all perspectives indicates that there
are at least four purposes for the writing of this book: (1) To ex-
hibit faith and godliness in the time of apostasy. (2) To illustrate
a concept of a kinsman redeemer. (3) To show that the scope
of God's grace in the Old Testament included the Gentiles.
(4) To trace the ancestry of David back to Judah. This last
point is recognized by almost all writers. For example, Keil and
Delitzsch make the following observation:

> In this conclusion the meaning and tendency of the whole nar-
> rative is brought clearly to light. The genealogical proof of the
> descent of David from Perez through Boaz and the Moabitess
> Ruth (chap. 4:18-22) forms not only the end, but the starting
> point, of the history contained in the book.[49]

The data supplied by the Book of Ruth are essential to the
reconstruction of the messianic line in the Old Testament. The
genealogical information in Ruth is employed by both Matthew
and Luke (Matt. 1:3-6; Luke 3:32-33). Of special interest in
these genealogies is the fact that the names of four women are
included. This is unique simply because genealogical lists are
usually based on male descendants. Also of interest in this regard
is the character of the women named. In addition to Ruth the
following women appear in these genealogies connected with
the line of Christ: Tamar (Gen. 38), Rahab (Josh. 6), and
Bathsheba (II Sam. 11).

E. Historical Background

According to 1:1, the historical context of the Book of Ruth
is the days of the judges. While none of the judges are named
in the Book of Ruth, many feel these events fall in the days of
Gideon, due to the fact that a famine is mentioned during this
period (cf. Judg. 6:3-4).

The early part of the story takes place in the land of Moab.
The Bible gives us a rather complete picture of the origin and
development of the nation of Moabites. According to Genesis
19:37, Moab was the son of Lot by an incestuous union with his

---

[49]*Ibid.*

elder daughter. The development of the nation of Moab from
the offspring of Lot is not described in Scripture. It is not until
the exodus period that we read about Moabite activity to any
great degree. Evidently, the Amorites had taken control of
Moabite territory at the time of Israel's movement through their
land. Balak, king of Moab, did not attempt to stop Israel
militarily. He employed the services of Balaam, from Mesopotamia. In spite of the enmity that existed between Israel and
Moab, God forbade Israel to fight with Moab for possession of
that land (Deut. 2:9). The Moabites were later the chief source
of Israel's agony. For eighteen years under the leadership of
Eglon they oppressed Israel (Judg. 3). The sojourn of Elimelech
and his family in the land of Moab probably took place after the
defeat of the Moabite peoples. Some years later, King Saul was
forced to defeat the Moabites (I Sam. 14:47). It appears that
during the early days of David, however, friendly conditions
existed, for David was able to leave his parents under Moabite
protection (I Sam. 22:3-4). The chief deity of the Moabites
was Chemosh (Num. 21:29), who seems to have been propitiated
by human sacrifices (see II Kings 3:26-27). The famous Moabite
Stone, discovered at Dibon, gives us further information about
the conflict between Moab and the dynasty of Omri.

F. *Basic Outline*

1. *The Journey of Ruth* (1:1-22)
2. *The Gleaning of Ruth* (2:1-23)
3. *The Appeal of Ruth* (3:1-18)
4. *The Marriage of Ruth* (4:1-22)

II. THE JOURNEY OF RUTH (1:1-22)

A. *Ten Years of Tragedy* (1:1-5)

As already noted, verse 1 provides the immediate historical
background for the events that follow. The move of Elimelech
and his family from Bethlehem to Moab was brought about by a
serious famine in the land. Since this event is placed during
the time of the judges, it is fair to conclude that this famine

was a special judgment of God upon His people (cf. Lev. 26: 14, 16; Deut. 11:16-17). The sojourn of Elimelech and his family is reminiscent of similar events that occurred during the patriarchal period. Abraham (Gen. 12:10), Isaac (Gen. 26:1), and Jacob (Gen. 42:1-5) all sought aid in other lands during similar famines. It is also significant to observe that problems usually attended such migrations on the part of God's people.

The names of the individuals involved in this story are significant in the light of the events that take place. Elimelech literally means "my God is King" and might reflect his faith in Jehovah. Naomi can be translated "my sweetness" or "delight" or "the sweet one." The meaning of the names of the two sons is more difficult to ascertain. Mahlon probably means "weakly" and comes from the Hebrew root ḥālāh meaning "to be sick." The name of the other son, Chilion, is more difficult to interpret. It is generally regarded as meaning "wasting" or "pining." After living in Moab for some period of time, Elimelech died, leaving Naomi and her two sons. Following the death of their father, the two boys married Moabite girls whose names are given as Orpah and Ruth (v. 4). The two sons, with their wives and their mother, remained in the land of Moab about ten years. During this time both the sons died, leaving three widows (v. 5).

The marriage of the two sons to Moabite girls has raised a number of questions. Some scholars feel that the marriage was legitimate since Moab was not specifically mentioned in Deuteronomy 7:13. However, since both Ezra (Ezra 9:1) and Nehemiah (Neh. 13:23) apply this law to the Moabites, it should be regarded as including this nation. It is obvious from the study of Deuteronomy 7 that not every nation is mentioned, only the outstanding political enemies that controlled Canaan at that time. Jewish commentators have generally regarded that the death of the two sons was an evidence of divine judgment for such intermarriage.

B. *The Journey to Bethlehem* (1:6-22)

1. *A Search for Alternatives* (1:6-15)

With her sons and husband dead, Naomi decided to return to Bethlehem where relatives still lived. She had received word that the famine had ended and the Lord again was blessing His people (v. 6). This statement in verse 6 indicates that the famine in verse 1 was regarded as a judgment from God. As they began their journey home, Naomi realized that the land of Israel offered little for these girls. She encouraged them to return to their mother's house (v. 8). The expression "mother's house" is somewhat unique. Normally we should expect her to refer to their "father's house." A number of explanations have been offered for this unusual statement. Some have felt that the father of these girls was dead. Another possibility is that Naomi felt the greatest comfort at this time could be found in the presence of their mother. In any event, she encouraged their return and offered a blessing to them. Her reference to their kindness to their husbands indicated that the girls had been responsible wives and had perhaps adopted the faith of their husbands. She indicated that she hoped that they would find rest in the house of their husbands (v. 9). Naomi's use of "rest" here is probably synonymous with the idea of marriage (cf. 3:1). The girls responded that they would return with her to Bethlehem (v. 10). As they continued their journey toward Bethlehem, Naomi again implored them to return to their own people, for she was too old to bear sons and she had no husband (vv. 11-12). She could offer them no hope and, therefore, she felt that their hope at this time lay in Moab.

It is interesting that Naomi reflected upon her experiences from a theological point of view, for she saw the hand of God in her circumstance (v. 13). This observation included both blessing (v. 6) and judgment (vv. 13, 21). When Orpah heard the words of Naomi, she again wept along with Ruth, but this time she returned to her people and to her gods (v. 15). When Naomi challenged Ruth to do the same, it was clear that Naomi's test was not only a practical and emotional one, but a theological one as well. The only hope for these Moabite girls in Israel would be that they should completely forsake their people and their gods. According to Mosaic law an Ammonite and a Moabite were not to enter the congregation of Israel (Deut. 23:3). If the faith of Ruth were really genuine, she would not be tempted to return to the gods of Moab.

2. A Daring Decision (1:16-18)

The response of Ruth to Naomi, recorded in verses 16-17, contains some of the most beautiful language in all the Old Testament. It is one of the highest expressions of faith to be found in the Bible. The words of Ruth are a good example of what Christ had in mind when He uttered the words recorded in Matthew 19:27-30. Ruth concluded her testimony and her commitment of faith with the well-known oath, "The Lord do so to me, and more also, if ought but death part thee and me" (v. 17). In effect, she invoked the punishment of God if she should let anything less than death part her from Naomi. The same formula appears in I Samuel 3:17 where Eli invoked God's punishment against Samuel if he should hide from him anything that God had revealed to him. It also appears in I Samuel 25:22 where David used the formula as an oath that he would destroy Nabal and all those belonging to his household. David once again used the formula in his oath to make Amasa captain of the armies (II Sam. 19:13). When Naomi saw that the faith of Ruth was unshakable and unchangeable, she encouraged Ruth to continue with her to Bethlehem. The journey they made was not an easy one. It would have covered approximately seventy-five miles, assuming they were abiding in the Moabite tableland. The descent from the mountains of Moab to the Jordan Valley would have been 4,500 feet, and the journey would have also required an ascent to Bethlehem of 3,750 feet through the hills of Judah.

3. Theological Perspectives (1:19-22)

As they entered the city, they were undoubtedly greeted by some of the women of the town, for the verb used in verse 19 is a feminine plural (Heb. to'marnāh). The question they asked was, "Is this Naomi?" Naomi's response to them is interesting. She said, "Call me not Naomi [which means 'sweetness'], call me Mara [which means 'bitterness']." Naomi recognized that she had gone out full and rich, while she had returned empty and poor. She again recognized the hand of God in the history of her life and this time she made reference to šaday. This name of God is associated with His power and His might. Such expressions on the lips of a believer are significant, for they recognize that all things work together for good to all those who are called according to the purpose of God (cf. Rom. 8:28). It was probably very difficult for Naomi to face many of her friends, but her frank testimony is a credit to her godly character. According to verse 22, they returned at the beginning of the barley harvest, thus placing the event in the month of April.

III. THE GLEANING OF RUTH (2:1-23)

A. *Ruth Meets Boaz* (2:1-18)

Boaz, according to verse 1, was a "friend" or "acquaintance" (Heb. *moyda'*) of Naomi's husband. He is also described as a "mighty man of valor" (Heb. *gibor ḥayil*), here better translated a "man of wealth" or a "man of property." Ruth then requested that she be permitted to go to the fields to glean grain after the reapers. Ruth evidently had knowledge of the law of Moses which indicated that those owning fields were to permit gleaners to gather grain after the reapers. This was done in order that the poor might have adequate provision made for their needs (cf. Lev. 19:9; 23:22; Deut. 24:19). The fact that Naomi did not join in the gleaning probably indicates that she was either weary from the journey or incapable of such activity because of age. Not all farmers would have permitted the poor to do this in their fields, and this is why Ruth said that she would search after the one "in whose sight I shall find grace" (v. 2). The very fact that Boaz permitted her in the fields was an indication of his godly character. As Ruth prepared to enter the fields, we are told, "chance her chanced" or "it happened" that she came on a part of the field belonging to Boaz (v. 3). What was chance from a human point of view was a perfect plan from a divine point of view. Boaz again gave evidence of his godly character as he walked through the fields. The relationship between himself and the reapers was an ideal one. His greeting was, "The Lord be with you"; and they answered him, "The Lord bless you" (v. 4). If the laborer-management situation were conditioned by such theology, perhaps many of the problems would be solved in a shorter period of time. In any event, as Boaz

Reaping in the Fields East of Bethlehem (cf. Ruth 2:4). Matson Photo Service

went through the fields, Ruth caught his eye. He asked, "Whose damsel is this?" (Heb. *na'arāh*, v. 5). Those in the field identified her as the young lady who had returned with Naomi from the land of Moab (v. 6). Ruth was a good worker. According to verse 7, she spent very little time resting. Boaz was probably impressed with her faithfulness and her love for her mother-in-law. He went out of his way to show kindness and love toward her (cf. vv. 12-16). At the end of the day she had gathered approximately thirty pounds of barley (v. 17). After this, she returned to her mother-in-law and reported the events of the day.

B. *Ruth Reports to Naomi* (2:19-23)

The meeting that evening must have been an interesting one. Naomi, very anxious to hear of the events of the day, inquired of Ruth as to where she worked and how she fared. When the name of Boaz was mentioned, she immediately praised the Lord (vv. 19-20). Naomi identified Boaz as a *go'ēl;* that is, a near kinsman or a kinsman redeemer. Ruth evidently had freedom to glean all during the barley harvest. They had returned from Moab at the beginning of the barley harvest (1:22) and Ruth continued to glean until the end of the barley harvest (2:23). During that time the faithfulness and the love of Ruth probably impressed Boaz all the more.

The story of Ruth through the first two chapters is a thrilling one. It is one of simplicity and tragedy, but out of this tragedy the Lord began to work, and His sovereign power was displayed and His will accomplished. Far too often believers surrender to situations of life simply because of loss or death, when, in effect, they have not given God the full opportunity to exercise His power and to display His glory. Again we are reminded by the apostle Paul that "all things work together for good to them that love God, to them who are the called according to his purpose."

13

RUTH AND BOAZ

When Naomi discovered the acquaintance that Ruth had made with Boaz, she immediately took steps to encourage this relationship. Naomi was faced with two critical problems. First, how could the name of Elimelech be maintained among the tribes of Israel, when he and his sons were dead? Secondly, what steps should be taken to protect the inheritance, which Elimelech had evidently left in Naomi's trust? The marriage of Ruth and Boaz could care for both of these problems. Chapter 3 describes the arrangement and procedures adopted by Naomi and Ruth in an attempt to solve the problems.

I. THE APPEAL OF RUTH (3:1-18)

A. *Naomi's Plan* (3:1-6)

When Naomi recognized Boaz as a near kinsman and realized that he had a special interest in Ruth, she immediately took steps to encourage the marriage of these two. Ruth 3:1 reflects that interest, for she made mention of the fact that she should seek "rest" for Ruth. The use of the word "rest" here has reference to marriage and a home (cf. 1:9). Ruth was instructed to go to the threshing floor in the evening (v. 2). The early evening was one of the best times for winnowing because of the breezes which would come up from the Mediterranean coast. It is also possible that this was a time of danger, making it necessary for owners to remain with the grain at the threshing floors. Ruth was instructed to make note of the place where he should rest that evening. She was to go there and "uncover his feet" and lie down with him (v. 4). In the eyes of many observers, this represents an immoral act. However, when the customs of Israel are taken into view, rather than a scene of immorality, we have one of legal appeal. Verse 6 informs us that Ruth obeyed her mother-in-law, which again appears to be an evidence of the faith and obedience of Ruth.

B. *Ruth's Performance* (3:7-18)

1. *The Morality of the Act* (3:7-11)

The question which naturally arises at this point regards the condition or the state of Boaz on this occasion. Verse 7 has led some interpreters to feel that Boaz was drunk at this time, for the text describes him as having eaten "and drunk and his heart was merry." It is true that on occasion "to make the heart merry" can refer to the excessive use of wine and therefore drunkenness. However, this is not necessarily always the case. Many times the expression "merry" or "happy heart" merely refers to satisfaction after good eating. (cf. Judg. 19:6-9; I Kings 21:7). Most probably, the word "merry" suggests that Boaz was happy and had a sense of well-being since, following the years of famine (1:1), he now had an abundant harvest.[50] One Targum interprets this expression by the following reading: "He (Boaz) blessed the name of Jehovah."[51]

The morality of this situation has also been questioned by virtue of the fact that Ruth "uncovered his feet" and lay down with him (v. 7). Verse 9 records the request of Ruth for Boaz to cover her with his "skirt" (Heb. *kānāp;* cf. 2:12). In their fullest historical and cultural context, the events described in these verses take on a note of ethical and moral beauty. According to Hebrew law, Ruth "was entitled to call upon her nearest of kin to fulfill the various duties of a responsible kinsman."[52] Ruth's actions were, therefore, in accord with previous revelation and well-known customs. Pfeiffer remarks, "The custom of a man's placing a corner of his garment over a maiden as a token of marriage is known among the Arabs."[53] The situation described in Ruth 3 perhaps parallels this modern Arabic custom. Ruth probably lay crosswise at the feet of Boaz and covered herself with the corners of his garment, thus requesting Boaz to become the kinsman redeemer (cf. v. 9). Boaz fully

---

[50]Francis D. Nichol (ed.), *Seventh-day Adventist Commentary*, Vol. II (Washington D.C.: Review and Herald Publishing Assoc., 1954), p. 438.

[51]James Morrison, *Ruth, The Pulpit Commentary*, ed. Joseph S. Exell and H. D. M. Spence, Vol. 8 (Grand Rapids: Wm. B. Eerdmans Publishing Co., 1950), p. 48.

[52]*Ibid.*

[53]Charles Pfeiffer, *op. cit.*, p. 271.

understood the request as evidenced in verses 10 through 12. It is interesting to observe that in verse 11 the moral character of Ruth was reaffirmed by Boaz in the expression, "Thou art a virtuous woman" (Heb. *'ēšet ḥayil 'āt*). This description of Ruth, along with the expressions applied to her in Chapter 2, vindicates her moral character and behavior. There was an obvious concern on the part of Boaz to maintain that pure image before the village (vv. 11-13).

2. The Legality of the Situation (3:12-18)

Boaz, having received the request of Ruth, pointed out that he was not legally able to assume kinsman responsibilities at this stage, for there was a kinsman nearer than himself. Boaz was only a nephew of Elimelech, whereas a brother was probably still living. According to Hebrew law, the brother of Elimelech bore first responsibility as kinsman redeemer (Heb. *go'ēl*). Ruth remained at his feet until morning and rose up "before one could know another" (v. 14). The verb translated "know" in this text is not the one which has reference to sexual intercourse, but another verb having the idea "to discern or recognize" (Heb. *yakîr*). Before leaving the threshing floor, Boaz gave her six measures of barley to take back to Naomi (v. 15). When she came to the home of her mother-in-law, she was asked, "Who art thou, my daughter?" (v. 16). The question of Naomi can be interpreted two ways. It might mean it was so dark that she could recognize her visitor only as a woman and therefore asked for further identification. Or, perhaps the question has the idea of "How did you fare, my daughter?" (RSV). The last command of Boaz is suggested in verse 18. Ruth was requested to remain at home (sit still) until the legal problems of the matter had been cared for.

II. THE MARRIAGE OF RUTH (4:1-22)

A. The Legal Process (4:1-13)

In order to clear up the legal complications that hindered the marriage, Boaz organized a hearing at the gate of the city (v. 1). The area inside the gates was commonly used as a place of legal transaction in Hebrew cities (cf. Deut. 21:19-21). The

nearer kinsman was informed of the hearing, and ten elders of
the city of Bethlehem were selected to hear the case (v. 2).
Evidently ten was the necessary quorum for this type of case.
The problems of the case at hand were immediately brought
before the ten elders and the nearest kinsman. The first problem dealt with by Boaz involved the inheritance of Elimelech;
namely, a parcel of land. Naomi was about to sell this land
(v. 3). The verb which occurs in this verse — "selleth" — is a
perfect form, normally translated as a past ("sold"; Heb.
mākerāh). However, it is better translated "about to sell" here
because of the information supplied in verses 5 and 9 (". . .
of the hand of Naomi"), indicating that she had not yet
disposed of the land. Evidently, Naomi intended to sell
the rights for use of the land until the time of Jubilee. The
responsibility of the nearest kinsman was to purchase that property in order that it should not fall into the hands of strangers,
but remain in the family of Elimelech (v. 4). Redemption of
the deceased brother's property was one of three responsibilities
ascribed to the *go'el* in the Old Testament (Lev. 25:25). The
other two involved the avenging of the blood of a deceased
brother (Deut. 19) and levirate marriage (Deut. 25:5).

The offer of Boaz was attractive at first to the nearest kinsman, for if he could bring this parcel of land under his control,
even though it might cost him a high price, the productivity of
the land would more than pay him for his effort. However,
Boaz did not leave the issue at that point. He further stated
that if the nearest kinsman were going to be a *go'el* and assume
the responsibility of land redemption, then he was also responsible to raise up a name for the deceased brother; that is, to
fulfill the requirement of levirate marriage (v. 5). Boaz, at
this point, used some legal skill, for strictly speaking, the kinsman redeemer was not responsible to fulfill every legal obligation of the *go'el*. Boaz, however, connected the two and made
one contingent upon the other. As the nearer kinsman contemplated this situation, the offer of the purchase of land became
less attractive.

> He must have reasoned that in order to buy Naomi's land he
> would have to invest a part of the value of his own estate, or
> inheritance. Then should he father a child of Ruth's that son

would in Mahlon's name, not his own, become the heir of land
which he bought with money from his own estate. He seemed
willing to redeem Naomi's property if it should not hurt him
financially, or if he might possibly gain by it, but he could
not accept the responsibility if it should eventuate in a diminu-
tion of his own resources and a consequent injustice to his own
heirs.[54]

With this official refusal, Boaz was free both to redeem the
property and to marry Ruth. The transfer of kinsman responsibility was symbolized by the nearest kinsman's removing his
sandal and giving it to Boaz. This custom is well known, not
only from the Book of Ruth, but also from Deuteronomy 25:9.
It has been further attested in the Nuzi Documents.[55] This
marriage had as its first aim raising up the name of the deceased
upon his inheritance (v. 10). In this sense, the marriage of
Boaz to Ruth was similar to a levirate marriage, but due to the
fact that Boaz was not a near kinsman to Elimelech, it differs
from levirate marriage which is described in the Mosaic law.[56]

B. The Divine Blessing (4:14-22)

The marriage of Ruth and Boaz was blessed by the Lord in
the birth of a son (v. 13). It is interesting that the women of
the town of Bethlehem praised Naomi for this event, for the
name of her husband would not be blotted out in the land of
Israel (v. 14). The great affection of Naomi for the child is
evidenced by the fact that she nursed it when it was quite
young (v. 16). Notice also that the women of the village described the son as that which was born to Naomi (v. 17), and
they gave him the name Obed which simply means "servant."

---

[54]S. Herbert Bess, Systems of Land Tenure in Ancient Israel (Unpublished Ph.D. dissertation, University of Michigan, 1963), p. 78.

[55]See E. A. Speiser, "Of Shoes and Shekels," Bulletin of the American
Schools of Oriental Research, No. 77 (Feb., 1940), p. 17.

Ernest R. Lacheman, "Notes on Ruth 4:7-8," Journal of Biblical Literature LXI (1937), pp. 53-56.

[56]For an excellent discussion of the legal aspects of this marriage see
H. H. Rowley, The Servant of the Lord (Oxford: Basil Blackwell, second
edition, revised, 1965), pp. 171 ff.

The Book of Ruth concludes with the genealogy from Pharez to King David (vv. 18-22). The chart below will help to illustrate this important line.

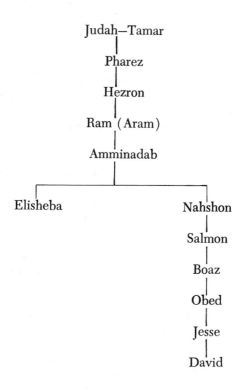

It is very fitting that our story of the Judges period should end on this note. The story of Ruth is one of tragedy and triumph. What seemed like a hopeless situation turned out to be one in which the Lord was fully glorified and His purposes accomplished. The love of Boaz and Ruth along with their sensitiveness to the laws of Israel is refreshing in a time when those about them had abandoned the truth of Scripture. Among the rugged, dry barrenness of the Judges Period, the Book of Ruth is indeed a precious gem to behold.

Part Two

THE BIRTH
OF A KINGDOM

Studies in I-II Samuel and I Kings 1-11

John J. Davis

I-II SAMUEL

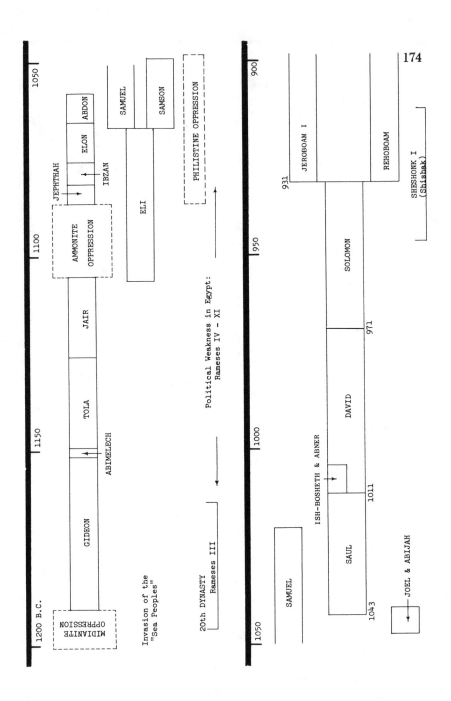

174

14
INTRODUCTION

Triumph and tragedy are the two words which best describe the content of the books of Samuel. Some of Israel's greatest moments of glory and darkest hours of defeat are retold with simplicity and candor. The stories retold in these books are of significant value didactically for this present age. The faith and the failures of both great and small are viewed in the light of sovereign grace. Historically the books are masterpieces of national record.

The campaigns of Joshua conducted about 1400 B.C. enabled the children of Israel to occupy the hill country and certain sections of the lowlands. However, with that occupancy came the gradual infiltration of Canaanitic social and religious practices. These had a tremendous negative effect on the progress of Israelite colonization. Due to the subtle infiltration of Baalism, the spiritual life of Israel very quickly degenerated into a state of apostasy.[1] The rise of divinely appointed judges during this period provided mainly for military needs. Under many of the judges there was a noticeable spiritual decline, and in many cases, this was either initiated or permitted by the judges themselves.[2] In addition to the internal strife and spiritual weakness there was increasing military pressure upon Israel from the outside. It was in this context that the prophet Samuel made his appearance, and a most important one it was. He was a very capable physician coming to the aid of Israel at a time when her fever was at the highest.

Before entering upon a study of the text of Samuel, it is imperative that the historical and cultural framework of the period of the United Monarchy be clearly established. The discussion that follows, therefore, will be devoted to a broad view of the na-

---

[1]For a full discussion of this era see Chapter 7, "Failure and Its Causes," pp. 93-104.

[2]E.g., Gideon (Judg. 8:27-32), Jephthah (Judg. 11:30-40), and Samson (Judg. 14:1–16:31).

tion of Israel and her place in the ancient Near East during the days of Samuel, Saul, David, and Solomon.

I. HISTORICAL SETTING

A. *The Biblical Data*

The historical framework for the books of Samuel is the eleventh and tenth centuries B.C. The chronology for this period is established upon the date for the death of Solomon in 931/30 B.C.[3] The beginning of Solomon's reign would therefore fall in the year 971/70 B.C. since he reigned for forty years (I Kings 11:42). According to I Kings 6:1 the construction of Solomon's temple began in the fourth year of his reign (i.e., 967/66 B.C.). II Samuel 5:4 states that David reigned for a period of forty years, thus placing his coronation date in the year 1011 B.C. The exact date for the beginning of Saul's reign is not so easily established. The only information available to us is found in Acts 13:21. There it is stated that Saul's reign lasted for a period of forty years, thus placing the beginning of his reign in 1050 B.C. It is possible, however, that this figure includes the total duration of his dynasty rather than his specific rule. If this were the case, his reign would have begun in 1043 B.C., for Ish-bo-sheth lived seven years after the death of Saul and reigned part of that time (cf. II Sam. 2:10-11).

The ministry of Samuel spanned the latter days of Samson, Elon, and Abdon, and continued through most of the reign of Saul (see chart, page 174).

B. *Egypt and Palestine*

1. *Egypt: The Twentieth Dynasty*

The last significant king of the Nineteenth Dynasty was Merneptah (1234-1222 B.C.) who was already an old man when he came to the throne in 1234 B.C. His reign was marked by a number of major invasions, the most notable of which was that attempted by the Libyans. He claimed to have successfully re-

---

[3]Edwin J. Thiele, *The Mysterious Numbers of the Hebrew Kings* (Grand Rapids: William B. Eerdmans Publishing Co., Revised edition, 1965), p. 53.

sisted this invasion and to have captured 9,000 prisoners.[4] The most interesting inscription attributed to the time of Merneptah is his famous victory stela in which Israel is mentioned. The account of his victories in Canaan reads as follows:

> The princes are saying: Mercy;
> No one raises his head among the nine bows.
> Desolation is for Tehenu; Hatti is pacified;
> Plundered is the Canaan with every evil;
> Carried off is Ashkelon; seized upon is Gezer;
> Yanoam is made as that which does not exist;
> Israel is laid waste, his seed is not.[5]

That Israel was already in Palestine and had expanded its landholdings toward the west is implied by this inscription. The death of Merneptah initiated a period of political chaos in Egypt which lasted for some twenty years. During this time a number of usurpers succeeded in getting the throne, one of them even being a Syrian. The restoration of order and national unity was not achieved until Setnakht (1197-1195 B.C.) took the throne. This began the Twentieth Dynasty in Egypt. His son Ramses III (1195-1164 B.C.) was a strong and energetic king. During his reign the Libyans again made their presence felt and successfully infiltrated portions of the fertile Delta region. This clearly was a serious internal threat to the security of the rest of the country. In the fifth year of Ramses III a very bloody battle was conducted with the Libyans resulting in victory of this Pharaoh. With this victory the troubles of Ramses III had not ended, however. From the north there were ominous signs of another major power invasion by a people known in Egyptian documents as the "Sea Peoples" or "Peoples of the Sea." These too were defeated by Ramses III in a great battle, and this prevented the overthrow of the Delta region from the north. A very

---

[4]Francis D. Nichol, ed., "The Ancient World from c. 1400 to 586 B.C.," *The Seventh-day Adventist Bible Commentary* (Review and Herald Publishing Assoc., 1954), II, p. 26.

[5]James B. Pritchard, ed., *Ancient Near Eastern Texts,* "Hymn of Victory of Mer-ne-Ptah," trans. John A. Wilson (Princeton: Princeton University Press, 1955), p. 378 (hereafter referred to as *ANET*).

vivid representation of this battle is found in the temple at Medinet Habu.

Following the reign of Ramses III, Egypt once again went into a period of decline under Ramses IV through XI. The high priests of Amun were gaining significant political and economic power in Egypt. At the end of the Twentieth Dynasty (ca. 1085 B.C.) Egypt was at its lowest point. The Twenty-first Dynasty in Egypt was also a period of considerable confusion and weakness. Kings came from families of the high priests at Karnak, and princes of Tanis. One of the results of this period of weakness and internal strife was the loss of prestige in Palestine. This phenomenon is reflected in the story of Wen-Amon and his journey to Byblos as an Egyptian envoy.[6]

2. Palestine

The materials which best reflect the historical-cultural context of the United Monarchy come to us from two archaeological periods known as Iron Age I (1200-900 B.C.) and Iron Age II (900-550 B.C.). The Iron Age I period was politically dominated by the presence of the Philistines along the coast lands and in portions of the Esdraelon Valley, and as far east as the Jordan Valley.[7] Their power was centered, however, in five cities in southwestern Palestine. These were Ashkelon, Ashdod, Ekron, Gaza, and Gath (I Sam. 6:17). Each city was ruled by a "lord" (Heb. *seren*). One of the secrets to Philistine military success was their effective use of iron. About 1200 B.C. the Philistines introduced it to Palestine for common use. Prior to this time the Hittites used iron quite widely in Asia Minor. The monopoly of the iron smelting process was a decided advantage to the Philistines in keeping Israel weak and on the defensive militarily (cf. I Sam. 13:19-22). It was not until the time of David that this monopoly was successfully broken, and Israel achieved the military strength necessary to occupy portions of the Philistines' territory. The Iron I period was also character-

---

[6]*ANET*, "The Journey of Wen-Amon to Phoenicia," trans. John A. Wilson, pp. 25-29.

[7]G. Ernest Wright, "Fresh Evidence for the Philistine Story," *The Biblical Archaeologist*, XXIX, 3, (Sept., 1966), p. 74.

Clay Lamp from Iron Age I (1200-900 B.C.). Levant Photo Service

ized by an absence of Israelite sanctuaries. According to Albright, very few amulets dating to this period have been discovered in Israelite cities.[8] Philistine burial customs are known to us from the discovery of a number of anthropoid clay coffins.[9] The pottery of the Philistines was quite distinctive. Most characteristic of the decorations were metopes enclosing stylized birds, very often with the head turned back (see illus., p. 185). These motifs show affinity with typical patterns found on pottery from the Aegean area. Philistine jugs were usually provided with a strainer spout, probably intended to drain out the barley husk from beer.[10] The clay lamps from the Iron Age I period became a little more shallow. The rims on the outside were flat

[8]William F. Albright, *The Archaeology of Palestine* (Baltimore: Penguin Books, 1961), p. 120.

[9]G. Ernest Wright, "Philistine Coffins and Mercenaries," *The Biblical Archaeologist*, XXII, 3, (Sept., 1959).

[10]William F. Albright, *op. cit.*, p. 115.

or flared at the back, and the pinching effect in the front was far
more pronounced and deeper (see illus., p. 179). The city walls
of this period were generally constructed after the casemate pattern. Casemate walls were double walls with a space in between and supported by a series of buttresses at regular intervals.
The Iron Age II period (900-550 B.C.) includes the period of
the Divided Monarchy. Many very significant written documents have come to us from this period, such as the famous
Gezer calendar discovered in 1908.[11] Also included in this important body of written documents are the Samaria Ostraca,[12]
the Lachish Ostraca,[13] and the Siloam inscription.[14] Objects
from this period tend to be standardized to a high degree perhaps due to the development of mass production techniques.
Vast amounts of information have come to us from Samaria,
Megiddo, Lachish, Tell Beit Mirsim, Tell en-Nasbeh, Tell el-
Far'ah, and Hazor regarding the material culture of this period.
In 1968 work was begun at the important site of Tekoa, and one
rather large tomb excavated under the supervision of the author
yielded a fine selection of pottery from this period. The wall
and gate systems of important cities are now well documented.
More recent studies have shed light on water systems from this
period.[15]

C. *Other Nations*

One of the more serious threats to Israel's expansion policy

[11]*ANET*, "The Gezer Calendar," trans. W. F. Albright, p. 320.

[12]D. Winton Thomas, *Documents from Old Testament Times* (New
York: Harper & Brothers, 1961), pp. 204-208.

[13]*Ibid.*, pp. 212-217. Also of importance is the fine collection of ostraca
found at Tell Arad. "During five seasons of excavation, over 200 ostraca
were found, nearly half Aramaic (from approximately 400 B.C.) and the
rest Hebrew, from the time of the monarchy" — Yohanan Aharoni. "Arad:
Its Inscriptions and Temple," *The Biblical Archaeologist*, XXXI, 1 (Feb.,
1968), p. 9. See also Y. Aharoni, "Hebrew Ostraca from Tel Arad,"
Israel Exploration Journal, XVI, 1 (1966), pp. 1-7.

[14]D. Winton Thomas, *op. cit.*, pp. 209-211.

[15]Yigael Yadin, "The Fifth Season of Excavations at Hazor," *The
Biblical Archaeologist*, XXXII, 3 (1969), pp. 63 ff., and William G. Dever,
"The Water Systems at Hazor and Gezer," *ibid.*

under her early kings came from a territory to the north known as Aram (AV, "Syria"). In the century or so before the rise of the Hebrew monarchy, these people gradually gained control of the territory from Haran in northern Mesopotamia, west to the Lebanon Mountains, to the Taurus Mountains in the north, and beyond Damascus on the south. One of the most significant of the Aramean states was known as Zobah, located north of Damascus (cf. II Sam. 8:3-9).[16]

The Hittite empire between 1400 and 1200 B.C. was of considerable significance as evidenced in both Hittite and Egyptian literature. However, about 1200 B.C. the Hittite empire came to a catastrophic and immediate end. This was most likely caused by the mass movement of "Sea Peoples" known to us from Egyptian documents and Palestinian archaeology. Also important to the history of this period was the rise and decline of Assyria. Complete independence came under Ashur-uballit I (1375-1340 B.C.). Prior to this time Assyria appears to have been subject to Mitanni. One of the more significant kings of this period of Assyrian rise was Tiglath-pileser I (1115-1102 B.C.). His reign was characterized by consistent, ruthless campaigning. He successfully campaigned to the Black Sea in the north and the Mediterranean on the west. Only a Babylonian revolt saved Palestine from Assyrian aggression at this time. After the death of Tiglath-pileser I, Assyria went into a period of general decline, thus preventing any major encounter with the rising empire of King David.

The only other enemies that existed during this period of time consisted of smaller nations to the east and the south of Israel. These were the Edomites, Amalekites, Moabites, and Ammonites. In many cases these nations were defeated by Saul, but it was not until the time of David that their territories were occupied and successfully controlled on a long-term basis. Generally speaking, therefore, the stage was set and prepared for the rise of the Hebrew monarchy.

---

[16]For a more complete discussion of this subject, see Merrill F. Unger, *Israel and the Aramaeans of Damascus* (London: James Clarke & Co., LTD, 1951).

II. THE BIBLICAL RECORD

A. *The Title of the Books*

The two books of Samuel were originally one. It was not until the third century B.C. that the translators of the Septuagint divided the book into two portions. The Vulgate followed this division, and it has been adopted in almost all translations since. The translators of the Septuagint called I and II Samuel the first and second books of the Kingdoms; the two books of Kings were then known as the third and fourth books of the Kingdoms. This two-fold division of the books of Samuel was first introduced into the Hebrew text by the Venetian printer Daniel Bomberg in his first edition of the Hebrew Bible, dated 1516.

The books get their title from the prophet Samuel, the principal character of the opening chapters. In view of the fact that he was the last of the judges, one of the greatest prophets, founder of the schools of the prophets, and the one who anointed both Saul and David, it is not inappropriate that these books bear his name.

B. *Position in the Canon*

The Hebrew Old Testament is divided into three sections known as the Law (*tôrāh*), the Prophets (*Neḇî'im*), and the Writings (*keṭūḇîm*). The Law consists of the five books of Moses. The Prophets are divided into two sections — the former and the latter (see chart below). The books of Samuel are included in that section known as the Former Prophets. The Writings contain the poetical books, the five rolls, and some historical books.

Law	Prophets		Writings	
Five Books of Moses	Former Josh. — Kings	Latter Isa. — Mal.	Poetical Five Rolls Historical	(3 Books) (5 Books) (3 Books)

C. *Authorship*

Most liberal critics hold one of two views with regard to the sources of the books of Samuel. Many follow Robert Pfeiffer in citing two principal sources for these books: J and E. Others follow Eissfeldt who specifies three sources: L, J, and E. Some parts of the books of Samuel are held to be Solomonic while other parts are considered to be later editions (dating about 550 B.C.) by a redactor of the Deuteronomic school. Both of these theories of composition, however, have been shown to be inadequate and in most cases improbable.[17]

According to the Talmud, Samuel was the author of Judges, Ruth, and the first part of Samuel. The remainder of I Samuel and II Samuel were supposedly composed by Nathan and Gad (I Chron. 29:29). This view, however, was questioned by Jewish commentators at a very early date. There are indications that large portions of the books must have been written after the death of Samuel (cf. I Sam. 25:1 and 28:3), and even after the division of the kingdom (I Sam. 27:6). The author of the books as we have them today is, therefore, unknown. In all probability a prophet, most likely from Judah, who lived after the division of the kingdom, composed these books incorporating earlier materials. The author would have made use of existing books such as the "Book of Jasher" (II Sam. 1:18) and the records of the "acts of David" (I Chron. 29:29).

D. *Literary Quality and Text*

Regardless of authorship, the narratives contained in the books of Samuel are masterpieces of historical writing. They represent the maximum achievement in the area of ancient historiography, for both the principal and the minor individuals are included in the narratives. These books present us with a gallery of historical portraits that are incomparable. Nowhere else in contem-

---

[17]See R. K. Harrison, *Introduction to the Old Testament* (Grand Rapids: William B. Eerdmans Publishing Co., 1969), pp. 696-709, and Gleason L. Archer, *A Survey of Old Testament Introduction* (Chicago: Moody Press, 1964), p. 272.

porary ancient Near Eastern literature do we have such personal profiles as those contained in the books of Samuel.

The text of these books, however, comes to us in a state of comparatively poor preservation. The exact reason for this is not known to us at this point. Some of the problems with regard to the transmission of the text have been solved by study of the Dead Sea Scrolls. Other problems are still beyond solution at this point,[18] but none are of such a serious nature as to impair the basic theme and flow of the narrative.

E. *Purpose and Major Themes*

The principal purpose of these books is to provide an official account of the ministry of Samuel along with the rise and development of the monarchy through the days of King David. The transition from a theocracy to a monarchy is a crucial one in Hebrew history; therefore, these books merit careful study. The books of Samuel also emphasize several important theological themes which should be noted. (1) There is the rejection of the theocracy and its consequences, politically and spiritually. (2) These books provide us with a unique study of the ministry of the Holy Spirit within the framework of monarchial rule. (3) The books also give insight into sin and its effects in the human heart. (4) The development of the prophetic office and the phenomenon of prophetism are described in many ways.

III. BASIC OUTLINE: I AND II SAMUEL

A. *Samuel: Judge and Prophet* (I Sam. 1:1–7:17)
1. The Birth of Samuel (1:1–2:11)
2. The Childhood of Samuel (2:12–3:21)
3. The Capture and Return of the Ark (4:1–7:17)
B. *The Reign of Saul* (I Sam. 8:1–14:52)
1. Israel's Demand for a King (chap. 8)
2. Saul's Appointment and Anointing (9:1–10:27)
3. Victory at Jabesh-gilead (11:1-15)

---

[18]Further discussion of these problems and suggested solutions can be found in R. K. Harrison, *op. cit.*, p. 697 ff., and G. L. Archer, *op. cit.*, p. 273.

    4. Samuel's Address (12:1-25)
    5. War with the Philistines (13:1—14:52)
C. *The Decline of Saul and Rise of David* (I Sam. 15:1—31:13)
    1. Disobedience (15:1-35)
    2. David Chosen and Anointed (16:1-23)
    3. War with the Philistines and Its Consequences (17:1-58)
    4. Saul's Attempts on David's Life (18:1—20:42)
    5. David as a Fugitive (21:1—31:13)
D. *David's Rule over Judah* (II Sam. 1:1—4:12)
    1. The Lamentation of David (1:1-27)
    2. The Crowning of David (2:1-32)
    3. Abner and David (3:1-39)
    4. The Murder of Ish-bosheth (4:1-12)
E. *David's Rule over All Israel* (II Sam. 5:1—24:25)
    1. David's Early Reign in Power and Prosperity (5:1—10:19)
    2. David's Sin and Troubles (11:1—21:22)
    3. Appendix (22:1—24:25)

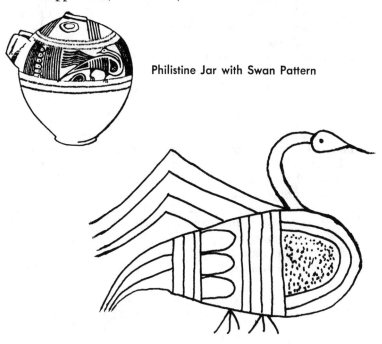

Philistine Jar with Swan Pattern

A Bird, as Painted on a Philistine Jar

15

SAMUEL: JUDGE AND PROPHET

Out of the confusion and turmoil of the period of the judges arises one of the great figures of Old Testament history, the prophet Samuel. His appearance in this time of religious degeneracy and political distress was no accident of history. With the death of Samson, the country was disunited and leaderless. The Philistines were achieving greater strength and realizing significant victories as they directed their campaigns to the east. Corruption in the priesthood and moral scandals in connection with tabernacle worship (I Sam. 2:22) rendered the nation of Israel weak and impotent. This was also a time of very limited prophetic influence (I Sam. 3:1).

It was at this point that a ray of hope appeared through the ominous black clouds of disaster. God placed His hand on a young lady who was without children and heartbroken. It was the faith and the prayers of this inconspicuous figure that brought about a turning point in the events described above.

I. THE BIRTH OF SAMUEL (1:1–2:11)

A. *His Family Background* (1:1-9)

The father of Samuel is introduced in I Samuel 1:1. He is identified as Elkanah from Ramathaim-zophim in the mountains of Ephraim. The name Ramathaim-zophim literally means "two high places of the watchman," or "twin heights of the Zuphites." The exact location of Ramathaim-zophim is not known for sure. Three sites have been suggested: (1) *Beit Rima*, about twelve miles west of Shiloh in the mountains of Ephraim; (2) *Er-Ram*, about five miles north of Jerusalem in Benjamite territory; (3) Ramallah, in the mountains of Ephraim approximately eight miles north of Jerusalem.[19] Elkanah, like Gideon (Judg. 8:30-

---

[19]See Francis D. Nichol, *op. cit.*, p. 548 ff., for a discussion of these sites and their value as candidates for the site of ancient Ramathaim-zophim.

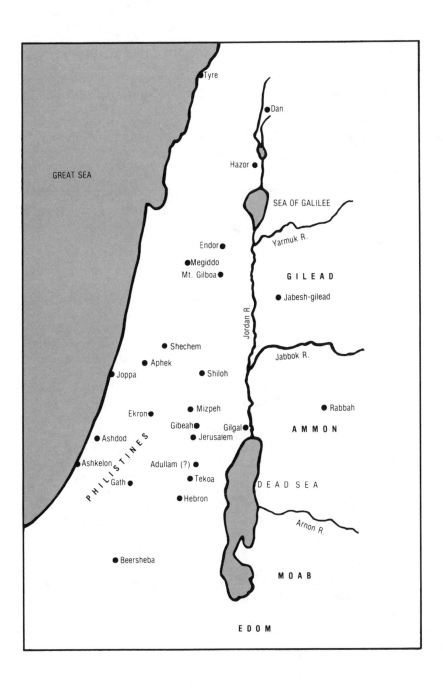

31) and Jair (Judg. 10:3-4), was a polygamist. With polygamy came trouble as was always the case in Biblical history. The one wife, Peninnah, bore him several children, but Hannah was barren despite her devotion to God (vv. 2, 5, 6). It was Elkanah's custom to go to Shiloh annually to worship the Lord at the tabernacle. Pilgrimages to Shiloh were required at least three times yearly according to Exodus 23:14-17 and Deuteronomy 16:16. Each year Hannah was given a "worthy portion" (v. 5), better translated "a double portion" (Heb. *mānāh 'aḥaṯ 'apāyim*). The great sorrow of Hannah is reflected in the tragic words of verse 8, which depicts her experiences at Shiloh as characterized by weeping, fasting, and heaviness of heart.[20]

B. *Hannah's Vow* (1:10-23)

In great bitterness of soul (v. 10; cf. II Kings 4:27) she prayed to the Lord and the essence of this prayer is wrapped up in two words found in verse 11, "remember me." These words have a familiar ring to them. They represent the prayer of a soul in desperate need. One is reminded of the simplicity of Samson's prayer recorded in Judges 16:28. In blindness and helplessness he cried out to his God and asked to be "remembered." This prayer was also found on the lips of a man being crucified at Calvary. One of the malefactors who was hanged with Jesus looked to Him with faith and said, "Lord, *remember me* when thou comest into thy kingdom" (Luke 23:42). The sincerity and the simplicity of this plea were quickly recognized by the Lord, and He replied, "To day shalt thou be with me in paradise" (Luke 23:43). Hannah vowed that if a son were given to her, she would dedicate him as a lifelong Nazarite (v. 11). Only two other lifelong Nazarites are mentioned in Scripture: Samson (Judg. 13-14) and John the Baptist (Luke 1:15). The requirements for a Nazarite were threefold: (1) the abstinence from wine (Num. 6:3-4); (2) letting the hair grow untouched by a razor (Num. 6:5); (3) refraining from ceremonial defilement by touching a dead body (Num. 6:6). A fragment from

---

[20]The expression "better than ten sons" was evidently a common idiom meaning "large family" (cf. Ruth 4:15).

the book of Samuel found in the fourth cave at Khirbet Qumran
specifically states that Samuel was a Nazarite.

Eli, the priest, mistook Hannah for one who was drunk with
wine, in that she moved her lips but did not make audible
sounds (cf. v. 12 ff.). She quickly denied the charge that she
was a drunkard and pled that she should not be counted as a
"daughter of Belial" (v. 16, Heb. *bat belîyāʻal*). To be regarded
in this manner was to be given an extremely low and degraded
position. The expression, "the sons of Belial," is commonly found
in the Old Testament and is associated with idolatry (Deut. 13:
13), rebellion (I Sam. 2:12), lewd and sensuous acts (Judg. 19:
22; 20:13), arrogance and stupidity (I Sam. 25:17), and murder
(I Kings 21:13). The Hebrew expression "Belial" literally means
"without profit or value." Upon hearing Hannah's explanation,
Eli assured her of blessing and sent her away in peace (v. 17).
Notice the composing influence of prayer in the life of this individual. Whereas she was unable to eat previously (v. 8), she
now was able to eat and her countenance was changed (v. 18).
As a result of her faith and obedience, the Lord "remembered
her" (v. 19). In due time a child was born and was given the
name Samuel, which has been variously interpreted to mean
"name of God" (Heb. *šēm* +*'ēl*), "his name is God" (Heb. *šemo*
+*'ēl*), "heard of God" (Heb. *šemûaʻ*+*'ēl*)

C. *Hannah's Obedience* (1:24-28)

After the child was weaned, that is, after about two or possibly three years,[21] he was taken to the tabernacle at Shiloh
and, after appropriate sacrifices were offered (vv. 24-25), dedicated to the service of the Lord.

D. *Hannah's Praise* (2:1-11)

This chapter stands in contrast to the events recorded in Chapter 1. There Hannah appeared on the scene in the deepest of
grief and with a broken heart (1:8). In this chapter, however,
she stands high with a heart that rejoices and praises her God

---

[21]Cf. II Macc. 7:27.

because of victory (2:1). The prayer itself is in contrast to the
prayer of Chapter 1. There she prayed in bitterness and wept
(1:10). In this chapter her voice is that of a victor rejoicing in
God's blessing (2:1). Four stanzas, or themes, are apparent in
this short prayer. The first is characterized by thanksgiving and
praise (vv. 1-2). The second (v. 3) is a severe warning to those
who are arrogant and proud. The third includes verses 4 through
8 and speaks about the humiliation of those who are lofty and
the elevation of those who are humble and lowly. The final
stanza is an expression of confidence as she looked toward the
future (2:9-10). The prayer of Hannah exhibits considerable
theological insight and knowledge of the Pentateuch. For example, the *holiness* of God is emphasized in verse 2, and the
knowledge of God in verse 3. In the remaining verses the *power*
of God is quite evident. Especially interesting is the expression
in verse 10, "and he shall give strength unto his king, and exalt
the horn of his anointed." Even though Israel did not have a
king at this time, such was anticipated, for Moses had prophesied
of a king (Deut. 17:14). The expression "anointed" could be
applied to priests (Lev. 4:3) and prophets (I Kings 19:16), as
well as to kings. It might well, however, point to the future
Messiah who would be the King of kings. Hannah's song recorded
in this chapter appears to be the basis of Mary's *Magnificat*,
found in Luke 1:46-55.

II. THE CHILDHOOD OF SAMUEL (2:12–3:21)

A. *Corruption in the Priesthood* (2:12-36)

The real tragedy of those days cannot be fully appreciated until one carefully studies the verses that follow. The sons of Eli
are described as "sons of Belial" (cf. 2:12). The sons of Eli
clearly reflected the conditions of the times in which they lived.
They were very much a part of the apostasy of the age of the
judges. They, in fact, were openly stealing from God (vv. 13-
17). The priest was allowed to take only the breast and right
thigh as his share of the sacrifice (Lev. 7:34). He was not to take
this share until the meat had been properly offered to God. In
the light of these facts, it should be observed that the sin of

Hophni and Phinehas was threefold: (a) They took any part of
the meat they wished to have (2:13-14). (b) They took the
meat before it had been offered to the Lord (2:14-15). (c)
They took it by force (2:16). In contrast to this dark and discouraging situation were the faith and obedience of Elkanah and
his family (vv. 18-21). They returned to Shiloh faithfully to worship their God, and the Lord honored this faith by giving to
Hannah additional children (v. 21).

The writer then turns our attention again to the sons of Eli
who, in addition to destroying proper sacrificial procedures, also
brought shame and immorality to the central sanctuary (v. 22).
These actions, at least for Phinehas, may have meant open adultery (cf. 4:19). The moral and spiritual effects of these acts
were widespread in Israel (2:24), resulting in more sin and corruption among the leaders (4:3; 8:1-5). Another result was a
breakdown in the people's faithfulness to the law of Moses (cf.
I Sam. 14:32). Eli's sons had become so hardened in their
deeds that they completely refused counsel and rebuke from
their father (v. 25). Such rebuke, however, may have been very
mild and perhaps very late in life (cf. 3:13). The lack of pater-
nal restraint is quite clearly one of the causes of delinquency of
these young men. A prophet was sent to the sanctuary to bring
warning to Eli and to prophesy the death of his sons (vv. 27-
36). The death of Hophni and Phinehas was a sign of God's
displeasure and judgment upon Eli's household (v. 34). But the
Lord promised to raise up a "faithful priest" who would follow
His ways and walk in accordance with His revealed will.

B. *The Identity of the Faithful Priest* (2:35)

The precise interpretation of this verse has been subject to
considerable discussion on the part of scholars throughout the
years. The promise of a perpetual priesthood was first given to
Aaron, a descendant of Levi, the son of Jacob (Exod. 28:43; 29:
9). This promise was, of course, made to Aaron and his house
generally. It was because of the sacrilegious acts of Nadab and
Abihu in offering "strange fire" (Lev. 10:1-2; Num. 3:4) that
they "died before Jehovah." They had no children; so Eleazar,
the third son of Aaron, and his younger brother, Ithamar, oc-

cupied a more important position, for they "ministered in the
priest's office in the presence of Aaron their father" (Num. 3:4;
I Chron. 24:1-2).

When Aaron died, Eleazar, the oldest living son, became the
high priest (Num. 20:22-29). Later the priesthood was given to
Phinehas, the son of Eleazar, "because he was zealous for his God,
and made atonement for the children of Israel" (Num. 25:11-
13). Due to some unexplained cause, the high priesthood was
transferred from the line of Eleazar to that of Ithamar in the
person of Eli. The book of Samuel begins with Eli as high priest,
and there is no hint that Eli's claim to the priesthood was a false
one or that he usurped the office in an improper manner.

The context at hand indicates that with the death of Hophni
and Phinehas a faithful priest would arise who would fulfill the
will of God (vv. 34-35). A number of views are held by commentators with regard to the identity of this faithful priest. Some
feel that this prophecy was fulfilled in the "whole house of
Aaron."[22] Spence, on the other hand, argued that Samuel fulfilled the requirements of that verse.[23] Renwick asserts that the
"faithful priest" was completely fulfilled only in Christ, although
it had a partial reference to Samuel.[24] The preferable view
seems to be that which considers the prophecy as fulfilled in the
accession of the priest Zadok and his family to the office in the
time of Solomon. When I Kings 2:26-27 is examined in the light
of I Samuel 14:3 and 22:20, it is clear that the house of Eli continued until the days of Solomon. Then God transferred the high
priesthood back to the line of Eleazar, in the person of Zadok,
who remained faithful to David at the time of Adonijah's rebellion (I Kings 1:7-8). This prophecy also indicates that there
will never lack a descendant of Zadok to walk before God's

[22]C. F. Keil and F. Delitzsch, *Biblical Commentary on the Books of Samuel,* trans. James Martin (Grand Rapids: William B. Eerdmans Publishing Co., 1950), pp. 40-43.

[23]H. D. M. Spence, "I Samuel," *Ellicott's Commentary on the Whole Bible,* Charles Ellicott, ed. (Grand Rapids: Zondervan Publishing House,
n.d.), p. 303.

[24]A. M. Renwick, "I and II Samuel," *The New Bible Commentary,* F. Davidson, A. M. Stibbs, and E. F. Kevan, eds. (Grand Rapids: William B.
Eerdmans Publishing Co., 1953), p. 265.

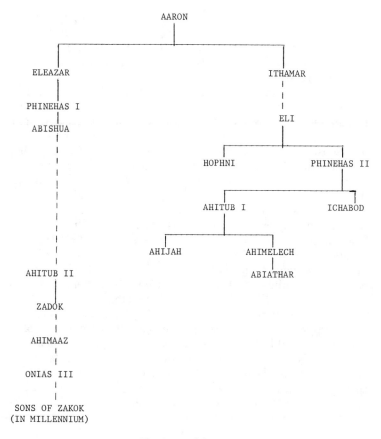

The Line of Aaron

anointed kings. Zadok himself walked before David and Solomon, and the sons of Zadok will walk before Christ in the millennial temple (Ezek. 44:15; 48:11; cf. Jer. 33:21).

C. *Encounter with the Lord* (3:1-21)

The call of Samuel recorded in this chapter is rather unique. Apostasy and prophetic inactivity characterized those days. Literally translated, the latter part of verse 1 reads, "The word

of the Lord was scarce in those days; vision was not common."
There were evidently very few men who were willing to follow
the Lord and proclaim His revelation. A notable exception is
recorded in 2:27 ff. Eli at this time was very old (v. 2), and his
sons were extremely corrupt. It appeared that there was little
hope for religious revival in Israel under those conditions. It
was during the early morning hours that the Lord spoke audibly
to Samuel (cf. v. 3).[25] The audible call of Samuel was somewhat unique in reference to prophetic revelation (cf. Num. 12:
6). Because of the inability of Eli to see (v. 2), Samuel perhaps
assumed that it was he who was calling in order to get some
help. After several occurrences of this experience, Eli recognized
that the voice was that of the Lord, and recommended that Samuel respond accordingly (v. 9). The first charge given to Samuel
was not an easy one to carry out. It was one which would make
"the ears of everyone that hear it tingle" (v. 11; cf. II Kings 21:
12 and Jer. 19:3). He had to bring to Eli the sad tidings of
divine judgment upon his household (vv. 13-14). This, indeed,
was a most difficult task for Samuel who had spent many precious years with Eli. The tension of the situation is revealed in
verse 15. This was, indeed, the first great test for Samuel. He,
however, weighed the issues and realized the importance of his
message and told all to Eli in obedience to God's command (vv.
18 ff.). This valor and commitment brought blessing to the life
of Samuel as it always does to the man of God who faithfully
conveys God's message, whether it is of judgment or blessing.
In fact, one of the marks of a true prophet was that he was not
ashamed or afraid to reveal the essential needs of God's people
(Mic. 3:7-8).

III. DEFEAT AND SHAME (4:1–7:17)

After the death of Samson (about the middle of the eleventh
century B.C.), the Philistines were able to regroup their military

---

[25]The "lamp of God" is a reference to the candlestick in the tabernacle.
The seven lamps were lighted every evening and burned until the oil was
consumed the next morning (Exod. 27:20-21; Lev. 24:2; II Chron. 13:11).
The reference, therefore, is to the period just before the morning dawn.

units and once again attempt penetration into Israelite-controlled territory. The Philistines not only played an important military role with respect to Palestine at this time, but as previously noted they encountered Merneptah and Ramses III in the Delta region of Egypt. The Philistines were, in fact, one of a number of tribes known in Egyptian sources as "Peoples of the Sea," which was a collective name for eight tribes which participated in the invasion of Egypt. The migration of Sea Peoples from Crete and the Aegean was not a new phenomenon. In the Pentateuch we read of "Philistines" who had settled along the southwest coast of Palestine (see Gen. 21:34; 26:1; Exod. 13:17-18). That Minoan settlers who had been in Palestine for centuries never achieved independent military strength is proved by the treaties they sought with Abraham and Isaac (Gen. 21:22-32; 26:26-33). However, when the Philistines and other tribes among the Peoples of the Sea joined these Minoan settlements, they formed a rather strong political and military organization. The Philistines were, therefore, the greatest menace to Israelite security during the days of Samuel.

The Philistines saw this time as a golden opportunity for invasion. Israel was badly divided and lacked religious and military leadership. A major battle took place in the area of Aphek (4:1), where the Philistines were decisive victors, as indicated by the death of 4,000 Israelite troops (v. 2). When the Israelites assessed the situation, they concluded that the reason for failure was the absence of the Ark of the Covenant in their midst (v. 3). They had evidently assumed that their successful crossing of the Jordan (Josh. 3:11) and the victory at Jericho (Josh. 6:7, 8, 13) were due to the presence of the Ark. Their view of the Ark at this point appears to be somewhat superstitious, if not idolatrous. The two sons of Eli fully agreed to the plan to take the Ark to the camp of the Hebrews, which resulted in great rejoicing among the troops (vv. 5-6). The next battle was even more disastrous for Israel than the previous one, for again the Philistines were victorious and slew 30,000 footmen among the children of Israel (v. 10). But that was not the only tragedy on that occasion. The two sons of Eli were slain, and the precious Ark of the Covenant was taken into captivity (v. 11). The news of the death of Hophni and Phinehas, along

with the capture of the Ark, was too much for Eli and resulted
in his death (v. 18). At that time Phinehas' wife gave birth to a
child who was given the name I-chabod. Some translate this
name as meaning "Where is the glory?" However, a better rendering of the Hebrew 'ikāḇod would be "no glory." The first
element in the compound name ('i) is an ancient negative par-
ticle used in a number of names. The departure of the Ark meant
the absence of glory from Israel (v. 22).

The journey of the Ark of the Covenant is a most interesting
one (see map). The Ark was first taken to the city of Ashdod
which appears to have been a rather important commercial
center in the Iron Age period.[26] The mound has some twenty
occupational levels ranging from the Early Bronze Age
to the Byzantine period. Tablets from the city of Ugarit men-

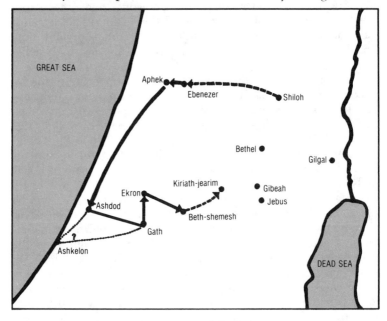

The Journey of the Ark

[26]See David N. Freedman, "The Second Season at Ancient Ashdod," *The
Biblical Archaeologist*, XXVI, 4 (Dec., 1963), p. 134 ff.

tion the fact that shipments of linen came from Ashdod. Some of the walls from the Philistine period still stand to a height of seven feet. It is clear, therefore, that Ashdod was an important city to the Philistines. The Biblical account confirms this observation in mentioning the presence of a temple dedicated to one of the principal Philistine deities, Dagon. The term "Dagon" has been traced to two Hebrew roots. One suggestion is that it comes from *dāg* meaning "fish." Supporting this theory are a number of coins found at Ashkelon, having an image of a deity that was apparently half man and half fish. A better view, however, traces the term to *dāgān* which means "grain." Evidently this deity was an important fertility god among the Philistines and perhaps among the peoples of Ugarit. In Ugaritic literature, Baal is referred to as the "son of Dagon."[27] From the information gathered in Chapters 5 and 6 it appears that the Philistines had developed a rather sophisticated religious system including a temple (5:2), a priesthood (6:2), religious "diviners" (6:2), and some concept of an "offering" (6:3-4).

When the Ark reached Ashdod, it was an object of tremendous attention. To capture the most sacred object of the enemy was, indeed, a great achievement. However, the Ark brought to Ashdod and its temple shame and humiliation along with a serious plague. According to 5:6, the Lord plagued the people of Ashdod with emrods (Heb. *'apōlîm* — "boils"). Many feel that this is one of the first references to "the black death," or bubonic plague. This is inferred from the mention of tumors and mice (possibly rats) that "marred the land" (cf. 5:6; 6:4-5). The exhibition of the Ark at Ashdod was hardly a credit or an asset to that city. With considerable dispatch and speed it was moved to the city of Gath (v. 8) where a similar tragedy occurred. From there the Ark was taken to Ekron and the plague followed it there.

After seven months (6:1) the Philistines realized the cause of their humiliation and sickness. The priests and the diviners suggested that the Ark be immediately returned to Israel and that it

---

[27]*ANET*, "Poems about Baal and Anath," trans. H. L. Ginsberg, C (I) III ABB, p. 130; h. IAB, p. 140; IV ABIII, p. 142, and "The Legend of King Keret," KRT A (ii), p. 143.

should be accompanied with a "trespass offering" (v. 3). The
"golden mice" mentioned in 6:4 demonstrates that the Philistines
believed in what is commonly known as "sympathetic magic,"
that is, the removal of evil or disaster via models. The Ark was
returned to the Israelite city of Beth-shemesh (v. 9) and here
another tragedy befell the men of that city. This was occasioned
by their disobedience and mishandling of the Ark. The men of
Beth-shemesh were really without excuse in their presumptuous
sin of looking into the Ark. In the first place, Beth-shemesh was
a priestly city (Josh. 21:16) and certainly had proper orientation
as to the handling of the Ark. Second, there were Levites present on this occasion who certainly knew the penalty of mishandling the Ark. God had given clear instructions on this matter to
Moses (Num. 4:5-6, 15-20).

It is doubtful that the number "50,000" belongs in the text. In
the first place, the syntax is irregular in that there is an absence
of the conjunction and the small number comes first. Second,
three reputable manuscripts omit that number. Third, it is highly improbable that 50,000 people lived in that small community.
Fourth, Josephus states that 70 died and does not mention the
50,000 (Antiquities 6.1.4).[28]

After the judgment at Beth-shemesh the Ark was then taken
to Kirjath-jearim (7:2) where it remained for a considerable period of time. There are a number of explanations offered as to
why the Ark was returned here and not to Shiloh. Some suggest
it was a sign of the apostasy of the period. Others feel that the
carrying away of the Ark and its removal from Shiloh was, in effect, a judgment and the people were not permitted to return it.
The best explanation, however, comes from archaeological data.
A Danish expedition excavated the site of Shiloh between 1923
and 1931 and demonstrated that Shiloh, while occupied from the
thirteenth to the eleventh centuries B.C., was probably destroyed
approximately 1050 B.C.[29]

Following these events, Samuel gathered all Israel together at

---

[28]For further discussion of this problem see John J. Davis, *Biblical Numerology* (Grand Rapids: Baker Book House, 1968), pp. 87-89.
[29]See Millar Burrows, *What Mean These Stones?* (New York: Meridian
Books, 1957), p. 80.

Mizpeh (Tell en-Nasbeh), located about seven miles north of Jerusalem. The people, who had now put away their strange gods, were ready to listen to the spiritual counsel of Samuel (cf. vv. 3-5). Samuel promised to pray for the people (v. 5), a practice for which he was well known (cf. 8:6; 12:19, 23). Samuel preached at Mizpeh and the people confessed their sin. The Philistines noted this return to unity and spiritual commitment and considered it a serious threat to their own security (v. 7). Samuel assured the people of Israel that victory would be theirs if they would trust in their God for power. When the Israelites encountered the Philistine armies for the third major battle, they were given victory which was rather decisive (cf. vv. 13-14).

One would expect a continued revival and spiritual growth among the people who had experienced such a reversal in political and military trends; however, such was not the case. As the Philistines and Ammonites began to apply additional pressure on the borders of Israel, the children of Israel, rather than turning to God, sought out a human leader to provide military victory.

16 (I Samuel 8–12)

SAUL: RUSTIC WARRIOR AND KING

Frustration and despair have a way of distorting human perspectives to such a degree that rash and ofttimes hasty decisions are made, which are later regretted. In the days of Samuel the nation had gone through many moments of military and social anguish. The shame of national defeat was more than Israel could continue to bear. It was out of these conditions that Israel decided that the solution to her problem was the establishment of a monarchy.

I. ISRAEL'S DEMAND FOR A KING (8:1-10)

As Samuel grew older he placed his sons in important positions of legal authority (vv. 1-2). His sons, like the sons of Eli, did not follow his ways. These young men were easily turned aside by bribes, thus perverting and distorting the basic elements of proper judgment (v. 3). The corruption of the priesthood, the lack of honest deportment among the judges and the advanced age of Samuel caused the elders of Israel to approach Samuel at Ramah (v. 4) and demand a king. At least three reasons were given by the elders for their decision on this matter: (1) They wanted to prevent further military losses (cf. 8:20;

Ramah (Er Ram), the home town of the prophet Samuel (I Sam. 1:19; 2:11; 7:17). Matson Photo Service

12:12). In previous battles with the Philistines over 34,000 men lost their lives (4:2, 10). In addition to this, two sons of the high priest were slain and the Ark had been taken by the Philistines and kept for seven months. (2) There was corruption among Israel's leaders (cf. 2:12-17; 8:3, 5). The sons of Eli and the sons of Samuel were complete failures and merely compounded the frustration of Israel rather than giving hope for the future. The leaders perhaps felt that a tribal confederacy under the leadership of divinely appointed judges was not the best answer to their immediate problems. They, perhaps, looked back on the three hundred years that had gone by with various degrees of success and failure. In all probability, they looked at the failures during the times of the judges and attributed those failures to the political organization rather than to national apostasy. (3) They wanted to be like the other nations (8:5, 20). This viewpoint reflected a serious problem in the spiritual and moral consciousness of the nation. It completely reversed God's design for His people who were chosen to be holy and separate (Lev. 20:26). Through the series of miracles in Egypt, God intended to make a clear difference between Israel and Egypt (cf. Exod. 11:7). Because Israel had failed in the total conquest of Canaan, she now took the direction of political compatibility and assumed that this would solve the problems of oppression and military failure.

While these were the formal reasons given to Samuel to establish a monarchy, a careful study of Israel's attitudes during this period of time indicates that there were other underlying motives: (1) The Israelites rejected the theocracy, as God recognized immediately (cf. 8:7). (2) They had serious interests in materialistic success. This is indicated in the first chapter of Judges. When the tribes had the ability to drive out the enemy, they instead put them to task work in order to improve their own economic status (cf. Judg. 1:28, 30, 33). It is also possible that the people of Isreal wanted security without moral and spiritual responsibility. The following observation is interesting at this point:

> So then, the people claimed and exercised what in these days is called "the right of self-determination." The change-over from theocracy to monarchy was of themselves. God gave them a

king and constituted a kingship. The fact would seem to be
that Israel had wearied of a theocratic form of government
which made their well-being dependent on their right conduct.
Perhaps they vaguely supposed that a government under a human king would relieve them somewhat of this responsibility,
inasmuch as their well-being would rest more with the character
of the government and the qualities of the king himself.[30]

The request of the elders was a blow to Samuel. He regarded
this as a personal rejection. When Samuel appeared before the
Lord, he was reassured that the rejection was not of his rule, but
of divine rule (v. 7). Following this prayer to the Lord, Samuel
returned to the people. Then, as the Lord had instructed, he
"protested" their intentions and warned them of the problems of
monarchial rule (v. 9).

II. THE PRICE OF KINGSHIP (8:11-22)

Liberal scholarship usually attributes this portion of Scripture
to late sources (Deuteronomic) and argues that it represents
strong anti-monarchial attitudes of a much later period than the
days of Saul and David.[31]

The warnings issued by Samuel were not merely the idle ram-
blings of a disappointed prophet, but they accurately reflected
some of the more serious problems related to monarchial rule as
known to us from the ancient Near East at that time. A great
deal of light has been shed on Samuel's protest of kingship from
the documents of Alalakh and Ugarit.[32] In the context of verses
11 through 18, five serious problems are cited by Samuel. They
are as follows: (1) A military draft would be established (vv.
11-12). (2) The people of the land would be put in servitude
(v. 13). (3) There would be widespread land confiscation (v.

---

[30]J. Sidlow Baxter, "Judges to Esther," *Explore the Book* (Grand Rapids:
Zondervan Publishing House, 1960), II, p. 55.

[31]See E. J. Young, *My Servants the Prophets* (Grand Rapids: William
B. Eerdmans Publishing Co., 1955), p. 80.

[32]I. Mendelson, "Samuel's Denunciation of Kingship in the Light of the
Akkadian Documents from Ugarit," *Bulletin of the American Schools of
Oriental Research*, No. 143 (Oct., 1956), p. 17.

14). Such land confiscation was common among kings of the ancient Near East. These lands were many times given to successful warriors for their own private use. (4) There would be taxes (v. 15). (5) There would be the loss of personal liberty (vv. 16-17). Samuel warned the people that whatever success might be achieved by the appointment of a king at this point would be purely temporary, and the day would come when the people would cry out for freedom from such rule (v. 18).

The warnings of Samuel went completely unheeded, however. The people at this point were not interested in the facts of monarchial rule, for their minds were made up, and again they repeated their demand to establish a king over them (v. 19). The cry of the Hebrew nation at this stage of their history is interesting. Note that two principal crisis points in Jewish history revolve around the establishment and the rejection of a king. Here the voices of Israel demand a king, but at Calvary Israel rejected their king. Observe the words of John 19:15, "We have no king." The people persisted in their demands, desiring political compatibility and jurisprudence which would be similar to that of their neighbors. They also wanted a warrior who would lead them against the encroachments of the Ammonites to the east (v. 20; cf. 12:12). Samuel was commanded to listen to the voice of the people and to give them a king (v. 22).

While it might appear at this point that the purposes of God were not being completely fulfilled, let it be noted that God in His sovereignty takes into account even the evil deeds of men and these accomplish His will (cf. the treatment of Joseph, Gen. 50:20). Israel, in its moment of wrath and sin, was, in effect, accomplishing God's purpose from the beginning — the preparation of a kingdom for His Son (Gen. 49:10; Num. 24:17).[33] Even the selection of Saul accomplished the purposes of God, for through his evil David was selected. The rule of Saul, by the very nature of the case, had to be temporary in the light of Genesis 49:10, for there the writer tells us that the scepter belonged in Judah. Therefore, even if Saul had accomplished good, his rule would have to come to an end in the light of God's prophetic plan for His Son's kingdom.

---

[33]In this connection see Ps. 76:10.

The truths of this passage call our attention to some important theological dimensions; namely, the sovereignty of God. This doctrine is often neglected and in our day the character of God is generally humanized by liberal scholarship to the point that He has no transcendent meaning to the believer. The only ultimate hope that the believer has is the fact that God is sovereign and that all things are under His control — even the evil deeds of men. As noted above, Joseph recognized this truth and was comforted by it (Gen. 50:20). This was an important element in Moses' teaching as well (cf. Exod. 7:3-5; also Rom. 9: 17). The rise and fall of kings and nations is not outside the scope of God's sovereign plan as indicated in Daniel 4:25-37.

III. THE PRIVATE APPOINTMENT OF SAUL (9:1–10:16)

Saul was the son of a Benjamite by the name of Kish and described as a "man of wealth" (Heb. *gibbôr ḥāyil* — cf. Ruth 2:1; II Kings 15:20). Saul possessed a number of qualities which would have commended him as a military leader. In verse 2 he is described as a "choice young man" (Heb. *bāḥûr*). This expression refers to a man in the prime of life. He is also described as "goodly" (Heb. *toḇ*). This term ". . . describes Saul's stature, not his looks as is evident from the second half of the verse."[34]

While looking for his father's lost animals, Saul came in contact with Samuel (9:3ff.). Samuel is described in a significant manner in verses 6 and 9. He is called a "man of God" (cf. Deut. 33:1; II Kings 4:9). He is also presented as an "honorable man" whose predictions always came to pass. This latter characteristic was essential for a prophet in the light of Deuteronomy 13 and 18:22. The expressions found in verse 9 have produced a wide variety of opinions among scholars as to their precise meaning. Samuel is referred to as a "prophet" (Heb. *nābî'*), whereas the earlier term was "seer" (Heb. *rō 'eh*). Some have attempted to argue for clear distinctions between these two terms, often concluding that they represented two entirely different functions

---

[34]S. Goldman, "Samuel," *Soncino Books of the Bible* (London: Soncino Press, 1951), p. 45.

or offices. This view has been generally rejected or modified by conservative writers.[35]

When Saul met Samuel he was informed that he would be king over Israel. Saul's immediate response was that of surprise and bewilderment, for he came from the smallest of the tribes of Israel (9:21). After a time of conversation and eating, Samuel sent the servants of Saul away and privately anointed him a "captain" (Heb. *nāgîd*) over Israel (cf. 9:22–10:1). From the standpoint of physical strength and mental capacity, Saul appears to have been a good choice. He was striking in appearance, had initiative, was brave and patriotic. Like Moses[36] and Gideon,[37] Saul was given signs to confirm the will of God in this matter. The first was an encounter with two men who would tell of the finding of the lost animals of his father (10:2). The second sign would be an encounter with men going to Bethel, carrying three kids, three loaves of bread, and a bottle of wine (10:3-4). The final sign would be Saul's meeting a company of prophets coming down from a high place, singing prophetic messages (10:5ff.). Samuel promised that when he encountered the prophets the Spirit of the Lord would come upon him and he would "be turned into another man" (10:6). He was also commanded to wait for Samuel at Gilgal for a period of seven days, which, as will be noted later, he failed to do. When he left Samuel, the Scripture indicates that "God gave him another heart" (10:9). This expression should not be regarded as the act of regeneration, but rather a work of the Spirit of God by which he was prepared for kingship. Regarding this change É. J. Young notes the following:

> It would, however, be a change of degree rather than of kind. Saul was to become a different man, in that he would now have the ability to act as a king should act. He would have a

---

[35]Helpful discussions of this problem can be found in E. J. Young, *op. cit.*, pp. 61-66; Hobart E. Freeman, *An Introduction to the Old Testament Prophets* (Chicago: Moody Press, 1968), p. 40; and James Smith, "The Life and Thought of the Pre-Literary Prophets," *The Seminary Review*, XIII, 4 (Summer, 1967), p. 94.

[36]Exod. 4:3-9.

[37]Judg. 6:36-39.

wider vision of the duties that were required of a king, and he
would receive the capacity to carry out those duties.[38]

When the Spirit of God did descend upon him (perhaps in the
same manner that He came upon the earlier judges), he took the
part of a prophet and became as one of those who came down
from the high place (10:10).[39]

IV. THE PUBLIC APPOINTMENT OF SAUL (10:17-27)

Appropriately, Samuel called all the people of Israel together
at Mizpeh, the location of a previous revival (cf. I Sam. 7:5-8).
On this occasion Samuel again warned the people with regard
to their spiritual attitude which, in effect, involved a rejection of
God (v. 19). He required that the people present themselves
by their tribes and by their "thousands" (Heb. 'alpîm — families).
Lots were evidently used on this occasion officially to select Saul.
This is indicated by the verb "taken" in verse 20. The procedure followed here was probably similar to the one Joshua followed in the case of Achan's sin (cf. Josh. 7:16-18). The king
was then brought before the people and declared their leader.
His appointment was accepted (v. 24). These matters were
recorded in writing (v. 25). Saul's troubles, however, had already begun, for at this time an opposition party was formed
consisting mainly of the "sons of Belial" (Heb. benê belîya 'al
— v. 27; cf. I Sam. 1:16; 2:12).

V. CONFIRMATION OF SAUL'S KINGSHIP (11:1—12:25)

The Ammonites, descendants of Lot (Gen. 19:38), continued
their belligerency toward the tribes settled in the eastern territories of Israel. It was the Ammonite military threat under the
leadership of Nahash, among other things, that caused Israel to
demand a king (cf. I Sam. 12:12). Nahash gave the people of
Jabesh-gilead seven days to agree to his terms of surrender

---

[38]*Op. cit.*, p. 87.
[39]Cf. Judg. 3:10; 6:34; 11:29; 14:6, 19; 15:14. Also see E. J. Young,
op. cit., p. 87 ff.

which involved the thrusting out of the right eye of the inhabitants of that city (11:2-3). The savagery of these peoples is elsewhere seen in Amos 1:13. The loss of the right eye had military implications, for it would disable the men of that city for military duty since the left eye was usually covered by the shield in battle and the right eye used to spot the enemy. This practice has also been attested in Ugaritic literature. Cyrus Gordon observes the following:

> As an illustration we may note, in both the Bible and Ugaritic literature, the idea of punishing or humiliating a city by blinding its inhabitants in one eye. This barbaric usage, which is what Saul saved the people of Jabesh-gilead from (I Sam. 11:2), is now attested in Ugaritic (AQHT: 65-168). . . .[40]

The Ammonites were apparently sure of victory as evidenced by the nature of their proposal. The elders of Jabesh-gilead asked for a seven-day delay in order to formulate an official reply. Nahash responded affirmatively to this request. This concession illustrated the contemptuous regard which he had for the fighting strength of Israel.

Messengers were immediately sent from Jabesh-gilead to Saul's headquarters located at Gibeah (11:4). This site has been identified with Tell el-Ful, located just north of Jerusalem. Tell el-Ful has been excavated and has provided interesting insights into the nature of Saul's headquarters. William F. Albright, who first excavated the site, describes Saul's Gibeah as follows:

> Though strongly constructed, the fortress walls were built of hammer-dressed masonry, and its contents were extremely simple. It is probable that the fortress was originally constructed by the Philistines as one of a chain (I Sam. 10:5) and was adapted by Saul for his own purpose.[41]

---

[40]*Ugaritic Literature* (Rome: Pontifical Bible Institute, 1949), p. 5. Also see his *World of the Old Testament* (London: Phoenix House, 1960), p. 158.

[41]*The Biblical Period from Abraham to Ezra* (New York: Harper & Row Publishers, 1949), p. 50. Cf. also Lawrence A. Sinclair, "An Archaeological Study of Gibeah (Tell el-Ful)," *The Biblical Archaeologist*, XXVII, 2 (May, 1964), pp. 52-64.

Tell el-Ful (Gibeah of Saul, I Sam. 11:4; 15:34), the location of the fortress of Saul. Levant Photo Service

It is also enlightening to observe that Saul was, at this time, back in the field, working as a farmer (11:5). The question has been rightly asked, "Why was he working with oxen rather than assuming the duties of a king?" Two answers have been given to this question: (1) Some feel that he returned to his former occupation until a special occasion should arise that would call him to higher responsibility. (2) Others argue that since his selection had been opposed by some (10:27), he decided to refrain from exercising monarchial rights until such opposition should subside. Either of these views is a legitimate possibility, or perhaps both are true.

Saul's anger was aroused not only because of the bodily mutilation threatened against the inhabitants of Jabesh-gilead, but more specifically, he may have had a special concern for Benjamites living in the city. It should be remembered that in the tragic Benjamite war (Judg. 20—21) 400 women from Jabesh-gilead were given in marriage to the Benjamites who survived

that conflict (Judg. 21:8-12). In all probability, many of the
Benjamites returned with the women to Jabesh-gilead after their
marriage. If this were the case, then Saul's concern for the defense of the city had tribal implications. The first thing Saul did
in preparation for war was to take a census to determine the
military capacity of the nation. Verse 8 indicates that a political
distinction had already arisen between Israel and Judah. Perhaps it was men from Judah who opposed the original appointment of Saul as king (10:27). This distinction is noted two other
times in the book of I Samuel (15:4; 17:52). The messengers
returned with a firm commitment of defense from Saul, which
certainly must have brought great relief to that city. The elders
of Jabesh-gilead contacted Nahash and indicated that the answer
he sought would be delivered the next day (11:10). This, of
course, was an effective delaying tactic which would lull Nahash
into a false sense of security and provide Saul and his men adequate time to reach the site. Saul used this time wisely to organize his forces into three companies, perhaps following the same
procedures used by Gideon at an earlier time (cf. Judg. 7:16).
The attack came in the morning watch, which was the last of
three watches (cf. Lam. 2:19; Judg. 7:19; Exod. 14:24-27). After
a complete victory, the people of Israel reaffirmed their commitment to their king at Gilgal (11:13-15).

The confirmation ceremonies at Gilgal were concluded by a
message from Samuel. The first twelve verses of Chapter 12 are
a review of the history of this period and Samuel's ministry
among the people. Samuel wanted to establish his innocence and
his fidelity to the people, but in so doing indirectly admitted
that his sons were failures (12:2-5).

The judges listed in verse 11 present special difficulties. Jerubbaal is, of course, identified with Gideon (Judg. 6:25-32). The
name "Bedan" is problematic because this name does not appear
in the Book of Judges. It has been supposed by some that this is
a reference to a lesser judge whose deeds were not officially recorded. This view, however, appears to be unlikely in view of
the nature of Samuel's argument. The others listed are rather
imposing personalities connected with specific and important
events. What purpose would the name of an unknown judge
serve in the argument? Perhaps the best explanation for the ap-

pearance of this name is that it represents a copyist's error in the text for the name Barak. The Syriac, Septuagint and Arabic versions have all adopted the latter name.

The remaining section of Chapter 12 (vv. 13-25) is a severe warning to Israel with regard to their faithfulness to the Lord. If Israel and her king were obedient to Jehovah, there would be blessing and prosperity (vv. 14-15). If, however, they forsook the Lord, judgment would fall. A special sign was given to confirm the validity of this message. Thunder and rain came during the time of the wheat harvest, which was most unusual since the wheat harvest came about the end of May and early June, long after the latter rain. Again one is reminded of the spiritual depth of Samuel's ministry. His achievements were not due to mere human ingenuity, but to a sincere and consistent prayer life. This fact was clearly recognized by the people (cf. v. 19). Samuel's view of prayer and its importance in the life of the people is most instructive (v. 23; cf. 7:5; 8:6). He did not consider prayer an option to be exercised at convenient moments, but essential to an effective prophetic ministry. One wonders whether the lack of power and impact, so evident in many pulpits, is not due to the absence of fervent, continuous prayer as exemplified in the life of Samuel (and in the life of our Lord).

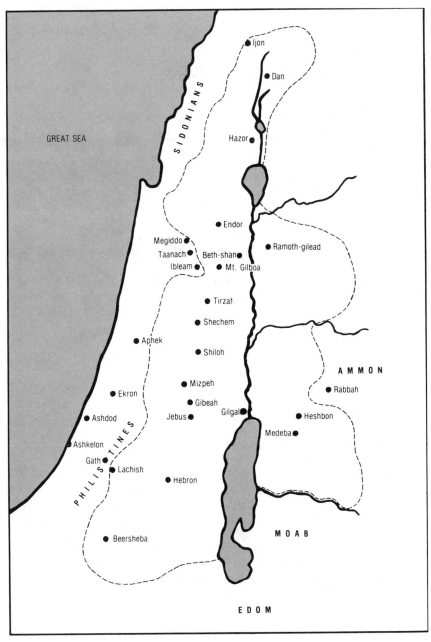

GREAT SEA

SIDONIANS

● Ijon

● Dan

● Hazor

● Endor

Megiddo ●

Taanach ●   Beth-shan ●   ● Ramoth-gilead

Ibleam ●   ● Mt. Gilboa

● Tirzah

● Shechem

● Aphek

● Shiloh

AMMON

● Mizpeh

● Ekron

● Gibeah   ● Rabbah

Ashdod ●   Jebus ●   Gilgal ●   ● Heshbon

Ashkelon ●   Medeba ●

Gath ●
● Lachish

PHILISTINES

● Hebron

MOAB

● Beersheba

EDOM

The Kingdom of Saul

17

SAUL: A REJECTED KING

With Saul's decisive victory over the Ammonites in the east his popularity rose to unprecedented heights. When word of this victory reached the Philistine pentapolis, it became apparent that they would have to move quickly before the whole nation of Israel was militarily solidified and strengthened under monarchial leadership. In Chapters 13 to 15 of I Samuel, two of Saul's important campaigns are recorded, one directed against the Philistines in the west and the other against the Amalekites to the south. While both of these efforts produced victories, there were also some very serious discouragements because of some of Saul's personal deeds. It is entirely possible that the Ammonite victory gave Saul a false sense of self-sufficiency, for at least on two occasions he made decisions without consulting the Lord. Both cases resulted in divine rejection and judgment.

I. THE PHILISTINE WAR (13:1–14:52)

A. *Saul's Presumptuous Act at Gilgal* (13:1-23)

1. *Jonathan's Victory at Geba* (13:1-7)

The initial verse of this chapter presents a serious textual problem. A literal translation of the text would be "the son of (one) year was Saul when he began to reign and he reigned two years over Israel." It is obvious that both statements in this verse are impossible. He could not reign when he was one year old, and it is not possible to fit all the events of Saul's life into two years. Early editions of the Septuagint avoided the difficulty by omitting the verse entirely. The Syriac rendered the verse ". . . when Saul had reigned one or two years. . . ." The Targums paraphrased the verse to read "Saul was as innocent as a one year old child when he began to reign." Modern commentaries are generally agreed that the present form of the Hebrew text suffers from an omission of numbers that were originally there. The verse apparently contains two omissions and should read as follows: "Saul

was . . . years old when he began to reign, and he ruled . . . and
two years over Israel."[42]

Saul, at this time, was organizing a series of defenses in the
central hill country. It does not appear that he intended to confront the Philistines in full force at this particular time. He had
mobilized only 3,000 troops according to verse 2. The remaining
elements of the army had returned to their homes. Jonathan,
however, felt that the time to strike was now, before the Philistines could establish themselves in the hill country. Jonathan,
therefore, struck at the Philistine garrison in Geba. The bravery
and aggressiveness of Jonathan on this occasion inspired Saul
and others of the Hebrew warriors. Saul then marshaled additional troops and attempted to rally the forces at Gilgal. The
fact that Saul chose Gilgal as a rallying point probably indicates
that large sections of the hill country were under Philistine control. That the Philistines had a very low regard for Israel is indicated by the expression, "Israel also was had in abomination"
(v. 4). This is better translated from the original, "and that Israel made himself odious with the Philistines." The verb used
here is the same one used in Exodus 16:20, 24 to describe manna
that had been left overnight.

The staging area selected by the Philistines was the site of
Michmash (v. 5). It is extremely doubtful, however, that the
total number of chariots employed on this occasion numbered
30,000 as the text presently reads. The town of Michmash was
located in the hill country of central Palestine, which would
render such a large chariot force useless. In addition to this, the
number is many times in excess of other records of chariot divi-
sions in a single encounter. Pharaoh, for example, had only 600
chariots when he pursued the Israelites (Exod. 14:7); Sisera,
900 (Judg. 4:13); and Zera, the Ethiopian, 300 (II Chron. 14:
9). In the great battle of Qarqar (853 B.C.), the coalition that
met Shalmaneser III had only about 4,000 chariots.[43]

When word regarding the size of the chariot force reached the
Israelites at Gilgal, many of them fled across the Jordan to the

---

[42]See John J. Davis, *Biblical Numerology*, p. 86.
[43]*Ibid.*, p. 84. Note that the number 30,000 is reduced to 3,000 in the
Lucian edition of the LXX text and the Syriac.

Gorge at Michmash (I Sam. 14:4-14). Matson Photo Service

hills of Moab (v. 7). Saul at this point found himself in a most difficult position. Not only were the Philistines well equipped and prepared for a major engagement in the central hill country, but the people of Israel were badly scattered and afraid (v. 6). It was in this context that Saul took a most disastrous step in disobeying a specific command of Samuel.

2. Saul's Disobedience and Rejection (13:8-23)

Rather than waiting for Samuel, as previously instructed (10: 8), Saul took it upon himself to offer a burnt offering in an attempt to unify the people and perhaps to seek God's will. We do not know why Samuel was late in arriving at Gilgal, unless perhaps to test Saul's faith. In any event, when Samuel did arrive, the actions of Saul were openly challenged and rebuked by Samuel. There has been considerable discussion as to the nature of Samuel's rebuke. Was it only because Saul offered a sacrifice? This is doubtful because Solomon later offered sacrifices and apparently without rebuke (I Kings 3:4, 15). It seems that Samuel's rebuke was directed at Saul's impatience and his disobedience in not waiting for prophetic guidance. In an attempt to justify himself, Saul offered three excuses for his action. These are recorded in verse 11. They are as follows: (1) "the people were scattered," (2) "thou camest not within the days appointed," and (3) "the Philistines gathered themselves together at Michmash." Notice that Saul did not claim that he misunderstood the instructions previously given to him. They were quite clear. His disobedience was in impetuously moving ahead without prophetic counsel. Samuel did not accept the proposition that the end justified the means, and regarded Saul's actions as being foolish (v. 13). As a result of this act the Lord promised that the kingdom of Saul would not continue and the Lord would seek another man who would be more sensitive to His will (v. 14). Following the prophetic rebuke, Saul found himself with only 600 men (v. 15).

The remaining part of Chapter 13 describes the tremendous power the Philistines exercised over Israel during this period of time. Not only did the Philistines have an impressive chariot force, but also maintained their monopoly over the use of iron

(v. 19). This monopoly continued with some success until the time of David when Israel began to produce iron objects rather freely (cf. I Chron. 22:3). The reading of verse 21 is made very difficult in the Authorized Version because the translators did not understand the Hebrew text. The phrase translated "yet they had a file" is now better translated "and the price was a pim" or "the charge was a pim." In recent years small weights have been discovered at Lachish, Jerusalem, Gezer and Tell En-Nasbeh with the Hebrew letters *pîm* inscribed on them. The *pîm* weight represented two-thirds of a shekel. The actual weight was about one-quarter of an ounce.

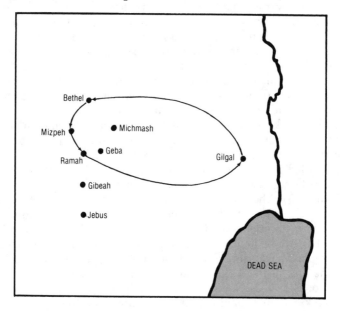

The Cities of Samuel

B. *The Battle of Michmash* (14:1-23)

The major battle took place at the town of Michmash (v. 5). The account of the battle is an exciting one and gives significant insight into the character and heroism of Jonathan, as well as providing extremely accurate topographical information concerning that area. Note, for example, Jonathan's confidence as ex-

pressed in verse 6, "It may be that the Lord will work for us: for
there is no restraint to the Lord to save by many or by few."
Jonathan was perhaps recalling the historical events surrounding
Gideon's defeat of the Midianites (Judg. 7:4 ff.). By means of a
careful strategy and a great earthquake provided by God (vv.
15, 20, 23) a crucial victory was achieved in this initial engagement. The nation was badly depressed and scattered. This heroic act on Jonathan's part provided the inspired leadership
necessary to rally the forces again. Hebrews who had hidden
themselves in caves were now prepared to join the battle in pursuit of the Philistines westward to Beth-aven (v. 23). Many of
the Hebrews were fighting as allies with the Philistines at this
time (v. 21). Some scholars feel that these individuals were
probably slaves captured from Israel in previous raids; however,
it seems more likely that they were professional soldiers or mercenaries who had sold themselves into military service. When the
Israelites were victorious, they changed their allegiance and
fought with Saul.

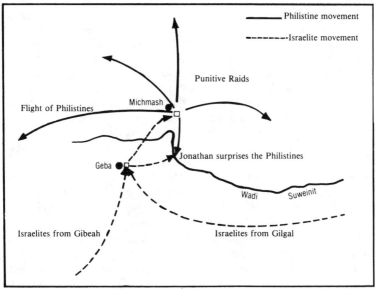

The Battle of Michmash

C. *A Rash Oath* (14:24-45)

Rather than immediately pursuing the enemy to complete the defeat of their forces, as one would expect, Saul took this occasion to exercise his authority, evidently for its own sake. He proclaimed a decree that no one was to eat food until the evening in order that "I may be avenged on mine enemies" (v. 24). It is obvious from Saul's statement that he had lost true perspective of the situation. This was not his war, nor were they particularly "his" enemies; they were the Lord's (v. 23). There may be a number of reasons why Saul issued the decree at this time. Perhaps he was trying to reinstate himself in the eyes of the people, having been humbled by the previous rebuke at the hands of Samuel. It is also likely that he feared the growing popularity of Jonathan, who at this point was regarded as a military hero. The people, however, were not in a position effectively to maintain a continuous pursuit because "they were faint" (v. 28). Jonathan obviously disagreed with this decree and its implications (v. 29). He knew that this would destroy the strength and morale of the Israelite army which was on the verge of victory. As the Israelite armies marched westward down to the valley of Ajalon, a distance of some twenty miles from Michmash, they became extremely hungry and were very weak (v. 31). When they came upon the spoil of the enemy, they took of the cattle and sheep, slew them, and ate the meat with the blood (v. 32). This, of course, was in direct violation of the law of Leviticus 19:26. Saul had not only weakened the fighting potential of Israel with his rash oath, but he had also caused the people to sin. Recognizing the seriousness of this situation with respect to possible immediate divine punishment, he commanded that a large stone be brought to him in order that the animals could be slain on it, thus allowing the blood to run off. Shortly after this Saul erected an altar in an attempt to acquire divine counsel, but without avail (v. 37).

Jonathan, not knowing of his father's decree (v. 27), had eaten some honey. Saul became violently angry when word reached him that his decree had been publicly violated. He demanded the death of Jonathan his son (vv. 39-44). The people, however, would not permit this to happen and went to the aid of Jonathan

(v. 45). Could it be that the political honeymoon was coming
to an end?

D. Summary of Saul's Reign (14:46-52)

The verse which concludes this chapter represents a summary
of Saul's military activity. During his reign he fought the enemies on every side and secured the central hill country and much
of the steppe lands for Israel, although most of his battles were
defensive in nature. The principal enemy throughout his reign
was Philistia according to verse 52. While Saul enjoyed some
limited success in battle against them, they were still a serious
threat at the end of Saul's reign.

II. THE AMALEKITE WAR (15:1-35)

South of Israel in the Negeb, large areas were occupied by a
people well known for their vicious fighting ability. Shortly after
Israel's exodus from Egypt it was the Amalekites who attempted
to prevent Israel from moving into the Sinai Peninsula (cf. Exod.
17). The Lord had not forgotten that encounter and it was
promised on that occasion that Amalek and his descendants
would be utterly destroyed (Exod. 17:14). When Joshua entered
Canaan, either the Amalekites were not near the areas defeated
by Joshua or he consciously avoided contact with them, for we
do not read of any major confrontation with these peoples. In
any event, by this time they had grown to considerable size and
had developed an impressive fighting force. Judah and Simeon,
therefore, must have been under constant threat from these peoples. In view of this situation and previous history, God, through
Samuel, commanded their total destruction (Heb. *ḥerem*). Such
a command was not an encouragement to the barbaric slaughter
of "innocent people" as some have argued, but represents a fully
justified act on the part of a holy God who reserves the right to
judge sin at any point in history (cf. v. 18). So Sodom and
Gomorrah fell under God's judgment (Gen. 19), as did Jericho
(Josh. 6) and Ai (Josh. 8). Destructions of this kind were not
based on mere political or military considerations, but especially
on religious grounds (cf. Deut. 7:2-6; 12:2-3; 20:10-18). More-

over, simply because this command came from God, it, *a priori,* is just, by virtue of the perfect character of God. For a full discussion of the application of the *ḥerem* principle in the Old Testament, see Part One, "Conquest and Crisis."[44]

Since this battle was to be fought in the open spaces of the desert, Saul used an army of much larger proportion than previously employed in the hill country (v. 4). The initial encounter with the enemy resulted in victory for Saul and his forces. However, Saul made the fatal mistake of not completely obeying the instruction of Samuel in applying the total "ban" (Heb. *ḥerem*) upon the people. Allowing King Agag to live was clearly in violation of God's original command. In all probability others were permitted to live as well, for it was not many years later that they attacked and destroyed Ziklag, the residence of David (I Sam. 30). Animals belonging to the Amalekites were also kept alive as booty, presumably to be used for sacrifices (v. 21). This disobedience on the part of Saul brought "repentance" to the heart of Jehovah (vv. 11, 35). The "repentance" of God should not be regarded as remorse because of an error in judgment, but deep sorrow in the light of man's failure in spite of divine provision (cf. Gen. 6:6). God's laws and decrees do not change (cf. 15:29); but as men change, different laws operate.

The next morning Samuel paid a visit to Saul to discuss the results of the campaign. As he approached Gilgal, he was greeted by Saul who very proudly said, "I have performed the commandment of the Lord" (v. 13). Note the emphasis on the pronoun "I." But Samuel raised a rather embarrassing question, for he heard the sound of many sheep and other animals which had been brought back from the battle. The shift in pronouns on the part of Saul is interesting. Saul replied to Samuel's penetrating question by saying, "*They* have brought them from the Amalekites (v. 15). He concluded his response, asserting, "... the rest *we* have utterly destroyed" (v. 15). The shift in pronouns is an obvious example of the ancient (and modern) art of "passing the buck." Saul attempted to justify the deeds of the people on the grounds that their intentions were good. In other words, the end had fully justified the means. He assumed that any sacri-

---

[44]pp. 48-49.

fice, whether prepared in disobedience or obedience, would be
acceptable to God. How far he had missed the point! The rebuke of Samuel for this philosophy was quick and decisive. Samuel rightly observed that the Lord delighted more in genuine
obedience than the mere slaughter of an animal (even though
that was important too; cf. v. 22). The response of Samuel should
not be interpreted as an "anti-priestly polemic" as some have
asserted. Samuel was merely pointing out a basic truth that sacrifices *in themselves* were not the final answer to man's need in
restoring fellowship with his God. A true sacrifice was to be a
genuine sign of faith and obedience. If sacrifices were offered in
apostasy and unbelief, they were as worthless as the sacrifices of
the Canaanites in the sight of a holy God (cf. Isa. 1:11; 66:3; Jer.
6:20; Hos. 6:6; and Mic. 6:6-8). Following the rebuke of Samuel,
Saul confessed his sin (v. 24). One wonders how genuine this
confession really was (cf. the words of Pharaoh, Exod. 9:27). The
result of this disobedience on the part of Saul led to his final rejection as king of Israel (vv. 23, 26).

In the presence of Saul and the soldiers, Agag, king of the defeated Amalekites, was put to death by Samuel (v. 33). Samuel
then returned to his home in Ramah, and Saul went to Gibeah in
Benjamin. The sin of Saul not only led to rejection and separation with respect to God, but to Samuel as well (v. 35).

What tremendous changes had taken place in the monarchial
situation of Israel and in the life of Saul. Saul had all the qualities of greatness, but his independent spirit and pride had
stripped him of the glory that could have been his. His early
career was characterized by initiative and aggressiveness which
resulted in victories (cf. 11:7), but this later degenerated into
mere personal ambition (20:31). What was originally outstanding bravery (13:3) turned into a form of recklessness (14:24).
Like Samson, he was a man of talent and ability, but these were
an asset to his leadership only as they were committed to God
and brought into conformity to His will.

The experiences of Saul are an unmistakable lesson to believers of all ages. The possession of physical attractiveness, talent
and popularity does not guarantee divine blessing or success in
one's pursuits.

18

A VALIANT SHEPHERD

Following divine rejection of Saul's kingship, and the personal separation of Samuel from Saul, the Biblical narrative now shifts its emphasis from Saul to David. The utter failure of Saul and his gross disobedience to God's will led to heartbreak on the part of Samuel. As Samuel sat in his hometown, Ramah, and contemplated the political future of Israel, he probably saw nothing but ominous clouds of despair and confusion. This led him to great searching of soul and mourning (16:1). That situation was about to be changed, however. The silence of the heavens was broken, and Samuel was commanded to cease his mourning and move ahead in pursuit of new prospects and new opportunities for the deliverance of Israel.

I. DAVID CHOSEN AND ANOINTED (16:1-13)

Samuel was commanded to fill his horn with oil and prepare to go to Bethlehem to anoint the new king of Israel. This request, however, brought fear to Samuel, for he calculated that if Saul should hear of such a deed, his life would be brought to an end (v. 2). The Lord cared for this situation by requiring that he take a heifer with him for the purpose of sacrifice to Jehovah. It was not in the best public interest at this time to conduct a public anointing of David. It must always be remembered that the will of God has three dimensions: the man, the place, and the time. When all these factors are brought together in conformity to God's will, there is success and accomplishment. Samuel, as he had done in the past, obeyed the Lord even though it meant jeopardizing his own life. When he arrived in Bethlehem, the elders of the town were greatly afraid at his presence. Perhaps they expected the pronouncement of judgment, or perhaps the presence of the prophet at this time of the year was most unusual

(v. 4). In any event, they were assured that his presence there
was for peaceful reasons. They were commanded to "sanctify
themselves" in preparation for the sacrifice (v. 5). The sanctification referred to here was basically ceremonial, relating to the
washings and legal purifications which accompanied a sacrifice
(cf. Exod. 19:10, 14, 22).

When Jesse and his sons came to Samuel, Samuel was instructed not to regard their outward appearance in considering the
next king, but the total man. The Israelites had already made the
mistake of selecting a king on the basis of physical qualities
alone. Samuel was reminded that the Lord looks on the heart
while man looks on the physical appearance (v. 7). The original
text of this verse is very expressive. It literally reads, "Man sees
the eyes, but Jehovah sees the heart." The Hebrew term 'ênay-
im ("eyes") refers to the visible outward appearance of man,
the physical qualities, while the Hebrew term lēḇāḇ ("heart") refers to the innermost spiritual and psychological qualities of man.
It was natural for Jesse to expect the eldest of the sons to be selected, but as is the case with God's elective plan, many times
the younger is selected above the elder (cf. Rom. 9:11-13).
When David appeared before Samuel, it was clear that he was
God's choice. David is described as being "ruddy" (Heb. 'admônî
— "reddish"). This expression is usually considered to refer to
the color of his hair ". . . which was regarded as a mark of beauty
in southern lands, where the hair is generally black."[45] The other
expressions in verse 12 lead us to believe that David was a very
attractive young man. At the Lord's command, Samuel took the
oil and anointed him in the presence of his brothers and his father. On this occasion, the Spirit of the Lord came upon David
(as He came upon the judges before him), thus enabling him to
fulfill the specific tasks which God assigned to him (cf. I Sam.
10:6, 10). This anointing was the first of three anointings. The
second occurred when he was made king over Judah at Hebron
(II Sam. 2:4), and the third when he was chosen king over all
the nation of Israel (II Sam. 5:3).

---

[45] C. F. Keil and F. Delitzsch, op. cit., p. 169; also S. Goldman, op. cit.,
p. 95.

II. A MEETING WITH THE KING (16:14-23)

A. *The Departure of the Spirit* (16:14-17)

When the Spirit came upon David in the anointing ceremony, the Spirit of God departed from Saul; that is, the gifts for kingship were taken from Saul. The difficulty in verse 14 is the interpretation of the last clause which says, ". . . an evil spirit from the Lord troubled him."

1. *The Nature of This Event*

There are various viewpoints as to the meaning of the expression "evil spirit from the Lord" and what precisely happened when the spirit "troubled him." The following are some representative views: (a) Saul was demon possessed. The following discussion is perhaps most representative of this viewpoint:

> The "evil spirit from Jehovah" which came into Saul in the place of the Spirit of Jehovah, was not merely an inward feeling of depression at the rejection announced to him, which grew into melancholy, and occasionally broke out in passing fits of insanity, but a higher evil power, which took possession of him, and not only deprived him of his peace of mind, but stirred up the feelings, ideas, imagination, and thoughts of his soul to such an extent that at times it drove him even into madness. This demon is called "an evil spirit (coming) from Jehovah" because Jehovah sent it as a punishment. . . .[46]

(b) Some have suggested that this evil spirit was an evil messenger, perhaps analogous to the situation in I Kings 22:20-23. (c) The evil spirit was, in effect, "a spirit of discontent" created by God in the heart of Saul. This view draws on the analogy of Judges 9:23 where it is stated that God "sent an evil spirit between Abimelech and the men of Shechem. . . ."

2. *The Effects of This Event*

Most commentators who hold the above views are agreed that the effects of the evil spirit working in Saul's life were mental and psychological.

---

[46]C. F. Keil and F. Delitzsch, *op. cit.*, p. 170.

> Saul is afflicted by a form of insanity which manifested itself in sudden fits of terror, unreasoning rages and on occasions homicidal violence. The symptoms suggest manic depressive psychosis.[47]

The ancient historian Josephus describes the situation as follows:

> But as for Saul, some strange and demonical disorders came upon him, and brought upon him such suffocations as were ready to choke him. . . .[48]

Whatever this malady was, it was a serious one which brought great concern to Saul's servants. They recognized that a solution to the problem was the playing of music (v. 16). When this evil spirit was upon him, he evidently went into a frenzied condition in which he lost control of his emotions and his actions (cf. 18:1-11). When a man was sought out to provide the necessary music for Saul's comfort, Davids' name was suggested. This, of course, was no accident, and is reminiscent of the rise of Joseph in the Egyptian royal court. When David played upon the lyre, Saul returned to psychological normalcy (cf. v. 23—Heb. *rāwah lesā'ûl* — "Saul's spirit revived"; "Saul was refreshed").

B. A Perspective on David (16:18-23)

There can be no doubt in one's mind as to the attractiveness of David. He was a man of many skills which included the playing of an instrument as well as courage in times of danger. The expressions, "mighty valiant man," and "a man of war" (v. 18), need not refer to military combat alone, but also to his conflicts with lions and bears (cf. 17:34-35). Perhaps the outstanding quality of David was the fact that "the Lord was with him" (v. 18). Even at this point in his career, this fact must have been evident to those associated with him. David's skill and his graciousness endeared him to Saul (v. 21).

---

[47]S. Goldman, *op. cit.*, p. 96.
[48]*Antiquities* VI.8.2 (hereafter referred to as *Ant.*).

III. DAVID AND GOLIATH (17:1-58)

A. *The Philistine Challenge* (17:1-14)

The Philistines who had been badly beaten at Michmash (14: 4 ff.) had regrouped themselves for another encounter with Israel. The stage was set approximately seventeen miles southwest of Jerusalem between Shochoh and Azekah. Because of their severe losses at Michmash and elsewhere, they decided to confront the Israelites by means of representative combat, a common practice in the ancient Near East by which one individual would represent an army. The man chosen for this task was Goliath of Gath (v. 4). He stood about nine feet, six inches, tall. Many feel that he was a descendant of the gigantic sons of Anak, who, according to Joshua 11:22, were still resident in the southwest corner of Palestine. The details regarding the armor of Goliath are of interest. Most of his defensive equipment was made of bronze, whereas the weapons of attack were made of iron.[49] Not only was the armor of Goliath impressive, but his claims were as well. He was obviously a very arrogant man, and one who had not suffered defeat in the past. He called himself "the Philistine" (v. 8 — Heb. *happelišti*).

B. *A Shepherd's Courage* (17:15-58)

The acts of David recorded in the remaining verses of Chapter 17 not only reflect his great courage, but also indicate that he was a man of great faith. In the past he had been confronted by wild beasts which, humanly speaking, would have created a situation of disaster; but because the Lord intervened in his behalf, such was not the case (vv. 34-37). David was confident that as God's anointed he would be protected.

When David was to face Goliath, he prepared for the situation by taking five stones and his sling which he had great skill in using. The sling used in David's day consisted of two long cords with a leather or wooden pocket fastened to them. After the

---

[49] The Hebrew word *neḥošet* should be translated "bronze," which is an alloy of copper and tin, rather than "brass," a compound metal made of copper and zinc. Brass was not used until a later period.

stone was placed in the pocket, the sling was whirled around the head, and one string released, thus casting the stone with terrific force. The stones used were generally rather large (two or three inches in diameter) and composed of flint or limestone. Apparently the Israelites had developed considerable skill in the use of such slings (cf. Judg. 20:16). The presence of David was considered a complete insult to Goliath, and he immediately held

Shepherd Boy with Sling. Matson Photo Service

David in the highest of contempt. He asked David if he considered him to be a dog (v. 43); that is, the lowest of animal creatures in the land. The dialogue between David and Goliath is an interesting comparison of attitudes and beliefs. In a brief period of time the victory was David's. Not only was Goliath slain at the hand of this humble shepherd, but his head was cut off and kept. Verse 54 indicates that David brought the head to Jerusalem as a war trophy for all to see, but the armor of Goliath was

kept for himself. This verse also presents a problem since it is
known that the Jebusites were still in control of the city (II Sam.
5:6). Two explanations are possible here. One would be that the
account anticipates the conquest of Jerusalem by David and the
ultimate placing of the head at Jerusalem as a war trophy. The
other would be that the city had been temporarily conquered
by the Israelites, as was the case in the past, but was not permanently held by them (cf. Judg. 1:8, 21).

Saul's questions recorded in verses 55 through 58 create a
rather difficult problem in the light of 16:18, 23 and 17:37-38.
It would appear from the previous account that Saul had already
been introduced to David and knew him well; however, the text
at hand gives the impression that Saul did not know him and
was inquiring as to his identity. Three explanations are usually
offered as a solution to the problem at hand. (a) The evil spirit
that came upon Saul (16:14) brought a mental malady that affected his memory. Some argue that only in fits of madness
had Saul seen David; when sane he did not recognize him
(cf. 16:23); however the account in Chapter 16 (vv. 21-23)
implies that David was a regular member of Saul's retinue,
and thefore was in his presence quite regularly, not merely
to play music. (b) Some argue that a considerable length
of time had elapsed since David's last visit to the court,
and as he was then in very early manhood, he had, so to
speak, grown, in a comparatively short length of time, out
of Saul's memory. However, it is doubtful that a great period
of time had elapsed between the events in Chapter 16 and
those in Chapter 17. (c) Saul was not inquiring about David,
but about his father's worth and social condition in order
that he might know the parentage of his future son-in-law,
or perhaps he had some other similar end in view.[50]

David's victory over Goliath was a turning point in his life. It
not only gave to Israel renewed opportunity to strengthen themselves with respect to Philistine incursion but it, in fact, confirmed David's anointing to the kingship. David's victory over

---

[50]See C. F. Keil and F. Delitzsch, *op. cit.*, p. 186. Discussion of this
problem can also be found in H. D. M. Spence, *op. cit.*, p. 369.

this giant is also an excellent example of the divine principles of operation as explained by the apostle Paul in I Corinthians 1:27-28.

IV. LIFE IN THE ROYAL COURT (18:1–20:42)

A. *Jonathan and David* (18:1-5)

The very warm and human relationship sustained by Jonathan and David is one of the bright spots in the narratives of I Samuel. In contrast to the cold rebellion of Saul is the very warm sensitivity of his son and heir to the throne, Jonathan. The covenant of friendship established between Jonathan and David (v. 3) was something that Jonathan probably longed for, for he could not find it with his father because of his father's lack of spiritual insight. The evidence of Jonathan's genuine love for David is witnessed in verse 4. The precious gifts given to David were not only a ratification of their pact, but coming from the heir apparent to the throne, this was a public mark of honor. Further evidence of the Holy Spirit's ministry in David's life is seen in verse 5. In every assignment given to him by King Saul, David "behaved himself wisely," and as a result he was one of the military leaders in Israel.

B. *The Jealousy of Saul* (18:6–19:11)

1. *The Reasons for His Jealousy* (18:6-8)

The success of David in warfare, and his growing popularity, became a matter of great concern to Saul. To compound the problem the number one folk song of that era was "Saul has slain his thousands, but David his ten thousands" (v. 7). This song was not only well known to the Israelites, but apparently the Philistines had heard it and reflected this knowledge on two occasions (I Sam. 21:11; 29:5). There were, therefore, two fundamental reasons for Saul's deep jealousy regarding David's success. The first was the fact that David had captivated the imagination of the Israelites throughout the land, and had risen so rapidly in popularity. The folk song was quite clearly a thorn in Saul's side (v. 8). The other reason for Saul's jealousy is detected in verse

12, and that was Saul's great fear of David. It was quite evident to Saul that David was, indeed, especially blessed of God, and at the same time he was probably cognizant of the fact that the Spirit of God had departed from him, thus leaving him without the skills and abilities necessary for successful rulership.

2. The Results of His Jealousy (18:9–19:11)

Needless to say, one of the clear evidences of Saul's jealousy was his open hatred and anger toward David (v. 8). His deep fear of David's rise to power was also one of the products of his deep jealousy (18:12). Perhaps the other obvious result of his disposition of jealousy was the numbered attempts on David's life, the first of which is recorded in this chapter. Apparently on two occasions Saul threatened the life of David (vv. 10-11), but on both occasions David was able to escape. There is some question as to whether the javelin was thrown on both occasions or on just one. In any event, David demonstrated his graciousness and his patience in returning to the presence of Saul in spite of the obvious attempts on his life. Most of us would not have been inclined to subject ourselves to this type of treatment a second time. In the light of Saul's attempts with the javelin, something might be said concerning David's skill and maneuverability, for not only on this occasion was he able to escape, but evidently on subsequent occasions as well (cf. 19:10). One wonders what the palace wall must have looked like in view of Saul's fruitless attempts with the javelin! Where these personal attempts of taking the life of David had failed, Saul attempted more subtle means. By putting David in the forefront of Philistine confrontation, Saul hoped that his life would be taken, and in this way he would not be directly responsible for his death (cf. vv. 17, 25). Saul used his two daughters to try to accomplish this, the one named Merab, and the other, Michal. David, of course, was not aware of these subtle attempts at this time; and much to Saul's distress, David was successful in his conquest of the Philistines, thus fulfilling the requirements for receiving Michal as his wife (cf. vv. 25-28).[51]

---

[51] Is it possible that David got his plan for Uriah's death from these experiences (cf. II Sam. 11:15)?

Jonathan became rather concerned over the growing rift between Saul and David. In an attempt to patch up a crumbling relationship, Jonathan spoke well of David before his father and encouraged his father not to attempt to take the life of David (19:4-5). To this admonition Saul agreed and swore that David would not be slain (v. 6). With this encouragement, David returned to the royal court of Saul, and tried to soothe the savage soul of Saul when the evil spirit came upon him by playing his lyre as he had done on previous occasions. While David played the lyre, Saul sought for the third time to slay him with the javelin, and once again David was successful in fleeing this attempt.[52] From this point onward, David became a fugitive and an outcast with regard to the royal court.

C. David's Escape (19:12—20:42)

After David left the royal court, he returned to his house and to his wife, Michal, who, upon hearing of Saul's attempts on his life, made provision for David's escape. David was let down through a window; this made possible his flight from the city (19:12). It is entirely possible that David's house was situated along the outer city wall, much like the location of Rahab's house (Josh. 2:15). To help cover his escape and to gain more time, Michal took "the image" (Heb. hatterāpîm) and placed it in the bed (19:13). This is a rather unique usage of the term "teraphim," for this expression usually refers to rather small household deities. In addition to the image, or "the teraphim," she put a "quilt of goats' hair" in the bed either to cover the complete image or to give the appearance of hair on the image placed in the bed. The translators of the Septuagint confused the Hebrew kebîr ("quilt") with kābēd ("liver") and translated the expression as a "goat's liver." Josephus adopted this interpretation, and in his Antiquities of the Jews suggested that a palpitating liver was placed in the bed to give the impression of life.[53]

---

[52]Perhaps David made the mistake of playing the popular folk tune mentioned in 18:7; 21:1; and 29:5!

[53]VI.11.4. See also S. Goldman, op. cit., p. 118; and C. F. Keil and F. Delitzsch, op cit., p. 195.

From here David fled to Ramah, the hometown of Samuel (19:
18). Perhaps David needed counsel in these times of great distress. When Saul heard of David's presence in Ramah, he sent
three contingents of messengers to attempt to take David, which
attempts were rendered useless because of the ministry of the
Spirit of God. On all three occasions, the Spirit came upon the
messengers and they prophesied (19:20-21). In utter frustration
Saul decided to go to Ramah himself and capture David, only
to experience the same thing, namely, the descent of the Spirit
of God causing him to prophesy and to strip off clothing in a
manner that would cause others to ask, "Is Saul also among the
prophets?" (19:22-24). When David heard of Saul's presence in
the city, he was forced to flee once again, and this time he came
to Jonathan and pled his case before his closest friend. In rather
amazing words, Jonathan told David, ". . . my father will do nothing" (20:2). Had Jonathan so quickly forgotten the events described in Chapter 19, or is it possible that he fully believed his
father's oath recorded in 19:6? Jonathan made a valiant attempt
to reconcile Saul and David for the second time. A very elaborate
procedure was formulated by which Jonathan could determine
the will of his father and try as best he could to influence that
will in favor of David; however, it became very apparent to Jonathan that any attempt at reconciliation at this stage would be
impossible. In fact, the attempt of Jonathan to reconcile the two
sent his father into a rage which almost ended up in the slaying
of Jonathan himself (20:33).

The stories of Saul and David recorded in these chapters are
most instructive. They give insight into what happens to a
man whose programs and prospects are conditioned only by his
own will and interest. In contrast, David's attitudes reflect a heart
which is controlled by the Spirit of God. His conduct at this
point exemplifies the highest ideals of a spiritual life. He showed
patience, love, discretion, and spiritual insight. These are the
very qualities that bring success.

19

THE ADVENTURES OF A FUGITIVE

Widespread popularity and permanent security were not often the lot of godly people in the Old Testament era. This was especially true with David during these tragic years of separation from the royal court. Perhaps one of the greatest frustrations experienced by David was the fact that his persecutors came from within Israel as well as without. These chapters in the book of I Samuel are most important if one is to understand properly the background and circumstances of many of the Psalms. One learns quite a bit about David the Psalmist in these chapters, as well as about David the fugitive. Out of his rich and varied experiences come some of the most eloquent expressions of praise as well as petition to his God. The highest of human joys as well as the deepest of personal sorrows are given fullest expression.

I. TRAGEDY AT NOB (21:1–22:23)

A. *A Visit to the Sanctuary* (21:1-9)

After David parted company with his friend Jonathan (20:42), he came to the town of Nob which was located between Anathoth and Jerusalem according to Isaiah 10:30, 32. This is the first reference in Scripture to this site. It is mentioned a total of six times in the entire Old Testament, four of which occur in Chapters 21 and 22. At the site of Nob, David came in contact with Ahimelech the priest. It is apparent that the tabernacle was now located at Nob rather than at Shiloh. As noted earlier, this was due to the fact that Shiloh had been destroyed by the Philistines. The Ark of the Covenant, however, was still in the house of Abinadab in Kirjath-jearim (cf. 7:2 with II Sam. 6:2-3). Ahimelech was the son of Ahitub (22:9) and therefore a great-grandson of Eli (14:3). The chart on page 193 illustrates the relationship of Ahimelech to the family of Eli. David was afraid of the strong allegiance of Ahimelech to Saul and therefore decided

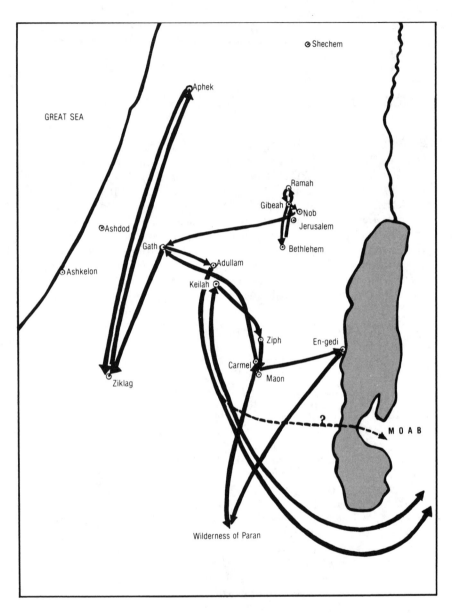

David's Wanderings (I Sam. 19—30)

that the only way to get help was to lie regarding his business in the area. He did this by deceiving Ahimelech into believing that he was there on official business from the royal court of Saul. This was the second lie told by David in a short period of time (cf. 20:6). David evidently adopted what is commonly known today as a "situational ethic." He assumed that the situation was of such a nature that the greatest good could be accomplished by getting food for his men at the cost of truth. This perhaps was the same feeling shared by Abraham in deceiving the king in Egypt (Gen. 12:13). Recall also the lies of Rahab (Josh. 2:4) and David's wife, Michal (I Sam. 19:14). The concept of a situational ethic, therefore, is not a new one. The very fact that these sins were recorded are an evidence of divine inspiration of Scripture since they involve some of the great heroes of the Old Testament. As is the case with many lies, they seem to meet the immediate need of a given situation, but have ultimate effects which perhaps were not foreseen by the one lying. Such was the case in David's experience, for this lie led to the ultimate destruction of the city (cf. 22:17 ff.).

David's need at this point was food for himself and those with him. The pitiful condition of the priesthood of this time is evidenced by the fact that there was no common bread available to them (21:4). The only bread that Ahimelech could make available to David was the loaves kept on the table of shewbread, which bread was hallowed (v. 6). According to the law, the old bread was to be eaten by the priest and only in the holy place (Lev. 24:9); however, an exception was made in this situation. The whole transaction was not carried out in secret, and was openly witnessed by a man who would ultimately bring destruction to the city of Nob. This man is identified as Doeg, an Edomite. The question has been raised as to why an Edomite would be present at a place like this, and holding the position of "chiefest of the herdmen that belonged to Saul" (v. 7). Three views have been suggested in solving this problem. The first is that Doeg was a proselyte and therefore had won acceptance in the royal court of Saul as a religious functionary. Another view is that the term "Edomite" is used only as geographical designation and Doeg was, in effect, an Israelite who had lived in Edom.

The final suggestion is that Doeg was one of many captives brought back as a result of Saul's campaign recorded in 14:47.

Recognizing the need for armor in the light of the military pressure upon him, David requested that the sword of Goliath the Philistine be given to him. It was evidently kept in a prominent place in the tabernacle behind the ephod (v. 9). David, of course, had some claim to this since he had killed Goliath and it was with this sword that Goliath's head was cut off (17:50-51).

B. *Encounter with Achish* (21:10-15)

After David's conversation with Jonathan it became apparent that to remain in Israel at this point would be most precarious Saul's hatred and malice had reached such an intense level that David's life and the life of his friends would be in severe danger if he remained in the reach of Saul. He fled southwest to the country of the Philistines and came to the city of Gath which was ruled by Achish. In Psalm 34, Achish is given the name Abimelech, which was probably the standing title of Philistine princes at Gath. Another explanation of the two names is that the Philistine name was Achish and the Semitic form of the name was Abimelech. The journey from Nob to Gath would have been a distance of about thirty miles. It is very doubtful that Saul would think of looking for David in a Philistine city. Also, David was rather well acquainted with the countryside, for it was there he had obtained the dowry for his wife by a victory over the Philistines. In certain respects, it seems rather strange that David would go to the city of Gath, the hometown of Goliath (17:4). Perhaps he felt that he would not be recognized, for some time had elapsed since his victory over Goliath; however, if he carried the sword of Goliath with him, this certainly would have given him away. In addition to that, he must have been identified by some of the people, for they remembered the popular folk tune so well known in Israel that "Saul has slain his thousands, and David his ten thousands" (v. 11; cf. 29:5). When David saw that he had been identified, his only hope was to act out insanity, and that he did with an "Oscar winning" dramatic performance. This act must have been rather convincing, for he was released. In this very narrow escape, David was preserved for future kingship.

C. *From Adullam to Mizpeh* (22:1-5)

After escaping from the city of Gath, David went eastward into the hill country of Judah to the cave of Adullam, which, according to Josephus, was located near the city of Adullam.[54] Others feel that the cave of Adullam is located in the neighborhood of Bethlehem as implied in II Samuel 23:13-14. The cave must have been one of considerable size, for he had with him ap-

---

[54]*Ant.* VI.12.3.

View of the Judean Wilderness from the main entrance of the Cave of Adullam. It was here that David gathered to himself 400 men (I Sam. 22:1-2). Levant Photo Service

proximately 400 men (vv. 1-2), which number would soon be
increased to 600 (cf. 23:13). Because of the unchanging belligerency of Saul, David feared for the safety of his parents. In order
to afford them protection, he went further eastward to Mizpeh
of Moab, and there placed his father and mother in the custody
of the king. Mizpeh was probably a small fortress or watchtow-
er in the mountain country. The Moabites probably viewed David as an enemy of Saul, and therefore were willing to care for
his parents, perhaps in exchange for a favor on his part. In this
hour of flight and confusion, David was approached by the
prophet Gad, who must have been a welcome sight. It is entirely possible that Samuel had sent this prophet to join David
and to give him spiritual counsel. This prophet had a long career
with David (II Sam. 24:11, 19), and along with Nathan, the
prophet, was one of the compilers of David's biography (I Chron.
29:29). The prophet's advice to David was not to remain in Mizpeh, but to return to Judah to the forest of Hareth (v. 5) which
was located northwest of Hebron on the edge of the mountain
district.

D. The Destruction of Nob (22:6-23)

Word came to Saul by way of his watchmen that David had
returned to the hills of Judah, but he probably did not know his
precise location. Saul called together his servants and his standing army, which evidently was made up of men from his own
tribe (v. 7). The persecution complex from which Saul suffered was very much in evidence in his speech to the Benjamites
recorded in verse 8. Listening to that speech was Doeg, the
Edomite, who at this point saw a perfect opportunity for political advantage and further advancement. He was already "set
over the servants of Saul" (v. 9) and perhaps took this opportunity to advance himself even further in the royal court. He
informed Saul of David's encounter with Ahimelech at the city
of Nob, and the fact that Ahimelech inquired of the Lord for David, gave him food, and gave to him the sword of Goliath, the
Philistine (v. 10). Saul initiated an immediate inquiry into the
matter (v. 11). When Ahimelech appeared before the king, he
admitted to helping David but was not aware of the fact that Da-

vid was the enemy of Saul and that he was turning against the crown in giving David aid (vv. 14-15). The explanation was not satisfactory to Saul, however, and he pronounced condemnation upon Ahimelech and those who associated with him (v. 16).

Saul then called together his footmen (Heb. *rāṣîm* — "runners") and commanded them to go to the city of Nob and slay all the priests at that city as well as other inhabitants including men, women, and children (v. 19). The Hebrew term translated "footmen" in the Authorized Version is sometimes used of the royal bodyguard, which appears to be the usage here. Samuel probably had this position in mind when he warned Israel that a king would take their sons and use them "to run before his chariots" (8:11). One wonders what must have gone through the minds of these Israelite soldiers as they heard the command of Saul to slay the priests of the Lord. They normally followed all orders of Saul, but this was too much and they refused to slay the priests of the Lord. Saul did have a friend in Doeg, the Edomite, who was looking for this very opportunity to gain additional favor in the sight of the king. He followed out Saul's command and slew eighty-five priests of the city of Nob, and in addition to that, men, women, children, and animals. Evidently, Saul put the city under the ban (Heb. *ḥerem*). One young priest, Abiathar, was able to escape and he came to David. When David heard of the tragedy of Nob, he began to look back to the causes of that tragedy. He probably remembered his lie, and now viewed it in a completely different perspective. He assumed full responsibility for that slaughter. "I have occasioned the death of all the persons of thy father's house" (v. 22). If David were interviewed following that news, he probably would have had a different view on the propriety of telling a lie for the sake of a single situation. The modern proponents of situational ethics fail to look beyond a given situation. Very rarely is a single situation of life an end unto itself. For this reason, the teaching that a deed is right or wrong in the light of that situation alone is most tragic and misleading. The Bible always exhorts the individual to truth, and this should be the practice of all believers in all ages, turning over all situations to God for the disposition of His will.

It is interesting to note that on an earlier occasion, Saul kept Agag, king of the Amalekites, and many sheep alive as an evidence of his religious fervor, but now he lowered himself to the mass slaughter of Israelite priests. One wonders whether or not some of the men of Israel did not have second thoughts about the monarchy at this point. Samuel had clearly warned the people that the day would come when the young men would be appointed "runners" before the king, and now they were commanded not only to be runners before the king, but to participate in the mass slaughter of their own people.

The presence of Abiathar with David must have been of considerable comfort at this time, for now he had the ephod and the Urim and the Thummim (23:6). In spite of the destruction and devastation at Nob, God had made provision for David. This, indeed, was an act of mercy and grace. Abiathar remained with David for a long period of time, and after David's time as an outlaw was appointed high priest. He held the office until Solomon banished him for his share in Adonijah's attempt at seizing the throne (I Kings 2:26ff.).

II. A HERO WITHOUT A HOME (23:1–26:25)

A. *The Rescue of Keilah* (23:1-13)

While in the Hebron area, word came to David that the Philistines were planning a campaign in the Shephelah against the city of Keilah which was located northwest of Hebron, about thirteen miles east of the Philistines' stronghold of Gath. This raid was to take place in the early summer, since they planned to "rob the threshingfloors" (v. 1). The spiritual maturity and sensitivity of David were evident in the fact that he immediately inquired of the Lord before undertaking this war in spite of the fact that such defense would have been perfectly legitimate. The Lord's answer was positive, and David was commanded to go and to protect the inhabitants of Keilah. The 600 men who were with David, however, were very apprehensive about this plan, for they feared reprisal from the men in Judah. It is evident from the third verse that the great majority of the people were still faithful to the crown and would help Saul against David. Again David inquired of the Lord (v. 4) and the answer remained the same with the assurance that victory would come because of the Lord's help. He encountered the Philistines

and won a decisive victory, even capturing cattle which belonged to the Philistines (v. 5). Following the battle, Abiathar,
the priest, joined David and brought with him the sacred ephod
(vv. 6-9). Even though David had saved the city, he was not
able to remain there because of the loyalty of many of its inhabitants to Saul (vv. 11-12). David then departed with his men
and abode in the wilderness of Ziph (v. 14).

B. *From the Wilderness to En-gedi* (23:14–24:22)

The rugged mountains in the wilderness of Ziph just south of
Hebron provided a good hiding place for David, whose life was
in danger every day as a result of Saul's pursuit (23:14). In this
time of emotional and physical crisis, the Lord once again provided for David's needs. Jonathan, Saul's son, went to David in
that rugged territory and assured him that he would not be slain
at the hand of Saul (v. 17). Even more important was the recognition on Jonathan's part that David would be king over Israel
and Jonathan would be below him. To seal this agreement, a
covenant was made (v. 18).

The inhabitants of the wilderness of Ziph were loyal to Saul,
and went to him to inform the king of David's travels in that
countryside. The king requested that they come back with a
more specific location, which they did. And Saul went down to
the wilderness of Ziph only to find that David had gone further
southward to the wilderness of Maon (v. 24). Saul and his men,
probably numbering approximately 3,000, were able to surround
David, and it appeared that the situation was very dark for this
man who had been promised the kingdom; however, providentially, the Lord stepped in, for a messenger came to Saul with
the news that the Philistines had invaded the land (v. 27). Evidently the Philistines had heard of Saul's interest in David in
the wilderness, and took this opportunity to invade the central
portion of Palestine. Saul had no alternative but to return to
the north and confront the Philistines, which decision, of course,
permitted David to escape once again. And once again we are
impressed with the unique and unending providential care of
God for His anointed.

From here David fled eastward to the wilderness of En-gedi

(see map, p. 234). After Saul's encounter with the Philistines, he received word of David's move to En-gedi, and immediately dispatched troops numbering 3,000 to go to that site. Saul, while wandering through the wilderness of that area, went into a cave to "cover his feet."[55] What Saul did not know was that David and some of his men were in the cave. Some of David's servants encouraged him to put an end to Saul's life, which David refused to do; but he did cut off part of the outer skirt of Saul (24:4). This act brought no great joy to David, for his heart "smote him" in that he had mistreated God's anointed (cf. v. 5). David recognized that this deed was of his own bidding and not that which was commanded by God. In addition to that fact, David was very sensitive to the sanctity of the throne. As far as David was concerned, Saul was still God's anointed. Nowhere had the Lord indicated that it was his time to assume the throne. In the light of these facts, David considered his act most inappropriate. When Saul was awakened, David reminded him of the opportunity that he had to take his life (v. 10), and David pleaded with Saul to discontinue the constant search for his life. David even attempted to put the behavior of the king in full perspective when he asked him, ". . . after whom dost thou pursue? after a dead dog, after a flea?" (v. 14). Dogs, especially of the wild variety, roamed through the streets as scavengers and were generally considered the lowest of creatures in a Palestinian town. One can only imagine what the value of a dead dog might be (cf. II Sam. 9:8). David also likened himself to a flea. This, of course, was done to show the ridiculousness of Saul's pursuit. For a king of Israel to pursue one with no more standing than a flea would indeed involve a complete waste of time (cf. I Sam. 26:20).

When David completed his argument, Saul was overcome with emotion and lifted up his voice and wept. Even with his arrogant, belligerent attitude, Saul recognized the mercy of David (vv. 17-19). In the light of this he asked for a covenant that David would swear not to slay his household when he became

---

[55]A euphemism for "to relieve himself" or "to have bowel movement" (cf. Judg. 3:24).

king (vv. 20-21). To this David agreed, and the two evidently
parted with those words.

C. David and Nabal (25:1-44)

1. The Death of Samuel (25:1)

Samuel's death must have occurred sometime after the events
at En-gedi, and for that reason is included in the narrative at
this point. The fact that "all the Israelites" were gathered together and lamented for him indicates that he was very popular and
well accepted in all Israel. He was buried in his house at Ramah,
perhaps in the courtyard of his house, or possibly in a special
burial chamber constructed for him.

2. David at Carmel (25:2-44)

The town of Carmel is located about three miles south of Hebron in the territory of Maon. Living in that city was a man by
the name of Nabal whose name in Hebrew means "fool." He is
described in verse 3 as a "churlish" man (Heb. qāšeh — "hard,
severe") and evil in his ways. Nabal was evidently a man of
considerable means, for David sent ten of his young men to his
house to ask for help. When the men arrived there, they were
given something less than a royal welcome. The sarcasm and the
insults of Nabal were quickly relayed to David (cf. vv. 8-12).
When David heard these things, his immediate response was to
arm his men and go up and take that which they wanted by
force (v. 13). While David exhibited some impatience at this
point, he learned an important lesson and later exhibited great
patience (cf. II Sam. 16:11-12). The servants of Nabal were
very frustrated by their master's lack of insight. They immediately went to Abigail, Nabal's wife, and reported the events of
that day to her. The lack of respect on the part of the servants is
evident in their description of their master, for they classify him
as a "son of Belial" (v. 17). Abigail immediately made preparations to intervene and to mediate what appeared to be a disastrous situation. Her arguments and her wisdom were most impressive to David, so much so that after the death of Nabal,
David took her to become his wife (vv. 39-42). He probably did
this due to the fact that Michal, Saul's daughter, had been given

to another man (cf. v. 44); however, that David's practices involved polygamy is made quite clear by the information found in verse 43.

D. Saul's Life Again Spared (26:1-25)

Because of the similarities between this chapter and Chapter 24, many critics regard the two stories as duplicate versions of the same incident. It should be pointed out, however, that the differences outweigh the resemblances, and the difficulty of reconciling the narratives, if they refer to the same occurrence, is far greater than that of supposing that somewhat similar events happened twice.

For the second time the Ziphites were the informers as to David's location (v. 1; cf. 23:19). Saul took 3,000 men with him and sought David in the wilderness of Ziph (v. 2). David heard of Saul's move and sent out his own spies in an attempt to locate Saul and to observe his movements. Among the soldiers of David was a certain Ahimelech, a Hittite. The presence of a Hittite among David's men indicates that he had a number of foreign mercenaries serving in his band of 600. David was able to locate Saul in the camp of Israel by virtue of the fact that Saul had a spear "stuck in the ground at his bolster." A better translation of this phrase would be "his spear stuck in the ground at his head." The spear was the symbol of authority in place of the scepter. This is the reason that the spear ("javelin" — A.V.) was at hand in the royal court of Saul (cf. I Sam. 18:8ff.; 19:9). This traditional sign of authority still exists among some bedouin Arabs today. A spear stuck in the ground outside the entrance distinguishes the tent of the sheikh. Abishai considered this the opportune time to take the life of Saul (v. 8). But again, David was very sensitive to the fact that Saul was still God's anointed, and to attempt assassination would be out of the will of God (v. 9). Perhaps David had the law of Exodus 22:28 in mind, "You shall not revile God, nor curse a ruler of your people" (RSV). David's patience, spiritual insight, and deep sense of faithfulness to the crown are unparalleled in ancient history. Perhaps David fully recognized that if assassination were carried out here, he would have no guarantee that it would not become a practice when he took the throne.

In order to demonstrate how close Saul came to death, a spear and a water container were taken from Saul's side (v. 11). This was all made possible because a deep sleep from the Lord had fallen upon Saul and his servants (v. 12). After they were a good distance away, David called out to Abner, who was the king's personal guard that night (v. 14; cf. v. 5). David's chiding of Abner's inability to guard the king awakened Saul (cf. vv. 15-16). A dialogue then began between Saul and David, and once again David reminded Saul of the opportunities he had to take his life. David also pointed out to Saul the great inconvenience which he had suffered as a result of Saul's attitude. His own countrymen had made him a man without a country, and in driving him from Israel, they left him only with the alternative "to serve other gods" (v. 19). Perhaps the people suggested this because once someone left Israel and the sanctuary, they felt the only way he could worship would be to worship god of foreign lands. Once again David likened himself to a flea, and tried to impress Saul with the futility of his searches (v. 20). David also likened Saul's pursuit to a partridge hunt in the mountains It is appropriate that the illustration used here made reference to the partridge hunt in Palestine. The nature of the hunt paralleled quite accurately the situation of David. The common species of partridge in the Holy Land attempts to save itself by running rather than by flight. The bird is continually chased until it is fatigued; then it is knocked down with sticks thrown along the ground. This, in a very vivid way, reflects the nature of Saul's pursuit. Even more interesting is the fact that David compared Saul's actions to a partridge hunt *in the mountains*, a very unlikely place. Who would hunt a single partridge which had flown into the mountains or had run there, when these birds can be found in large coveys in the fields below?

David's respect for the throne of Israel is further in evidence in the fact that he returned the king's spear. This spear, of course, was a sign of authority, and even though David had been anointed to the throne, again it was not the right time. David was fully committed to the will of God, and refused to usurp the throne that had been promised to him.

III. RETURN TO PHILISTIA (27:1-12)

The faith of David at this stage in his career reached a very
low point. He had given up any hope of reconciliation with the
royal court (v. 1). The only option that he saw open was to return to the land of the enemy, for there perhaps he could find a
place of rest. Thus, David with his band of 600 fighting men
returned to the city of Gath. This seems to be a rather unusual
decision on his part since he had been previously turned away
from that site (v. 2; cf. 21:10-15), but some time had elapsed
and David's status as an outlaw or a fugitive had been well established in Philistia as well as in the hills of Judah, thus making
it possible to offer "allegiance" to, and request protection of,
Achish, the king of Gath. Achish, of course, was more than happy
to accommodate David, for he knew of David's skill as a warrior
and was convinced that David could be a great help in his attempts to conquer Israelite territory.

David was suspicious of permanently residing near or in the
royal court of Achish and requested a territory of his own in the
countryside (v. 5). This he did so he would be free from the
constant surveillance to which he would be exposed in the capital city. Also, David probably wanted freedom to observe his
own religious rites. David's decision also may have involved his
attempt to protect his followers from assimilation with Philistine religious ideas and customs. The fact that David was accepted by the Philistines probably indicates that he was similar
to the typical *Habiru* of Canaan. Also, it is entirely probable that
Achish was in desperate need of reinforcements following his
encounter with King Saul (cf. 23:27-28).

The year and four months (v. 7) that David dwelt among the
Philistines provided him with many opportunities to help his
countrymen in Judah. David took this opportunity to destroy
some of the enemies of Judah; and such victories, by their very
nature, had to be complete in order that survivors could not inform the king of Gath regarding the nature of David's raids (cf.
vv. 9-12).

David's experiences among the Philistines would have further
consequences, however. When he would become king, he would
have considerable knowledge of Philistine geography and mili-

tary tactics, which would be a decided advantage in planning attacks and conquering their territory. Again we have an excellent example of God's providential preparation of a man. In many respects, David's time in Philistia was parallel to Moses' days in Egypt. While Saul's pursuit of David was fully intended for evil, God meant it for good (cf. Gen. 50:20).

20

A VOICE FROM THE DEAD

Saul's preoccupation with the pursuit of David through the hills of Judah could not but result in military complications for Israel. In all probability Saul gave little attention to the growing Philistine threat since his concentration was centered on David and his men. Word certainly reached Achish, king of Gath, and other kings of Philistia relative to the mental and spiritual problems in Saul's life. Achish was convinced that with David and his men numbered among his forces he had a decided advantage in planning an attack against Israel. He was sure that David was now the enemy of Israel (27:12) and would seize upon an opportunity to gain revenge against Saul. From the standpoint of Israel's strength, prospects were dark indeed. Saul had become a man of unpredictable temperament and preoccupied with the preservation of his personal dignity. This caused him to neglect crucial problems within the borders of Israel. In addition to that, one of his more capable warriors, David, was now fighting with the enemy. Perhaps even more frustrating to Saul was his inability to get divine help.

Chapter 28 of the book of I Samuel records one of the darkest hours of Saul's reign. This chapter is a startling contrast with the earlier chapters of I Samuel where a young, energetic, heroic king is described. The vitality and strength of Saul had been stripped away by divine judgment (16:14). As the Philistine army units began to mobilize in preparation for an encounter with Israel, Saul trembled perhaps as he had never trembled before. It was this situation that led Saul to seek help from a "witch" (necromancer) located in the north at En-dor.

I. THE PLIGHT OF SAUL (28:1-6)

A. *The Philistine Menace* (28:1-5)

As the Philistines mobilized their troops for warfare, Achish gave David the order that he was to join him in battle (v. 1).

This situation was indeed most awkward for David, for it meant he would have to fight his own people. In the light of David's past performances with regard to Saul, it is quite clear that he would not actually fight against Israel. For if he refused to take the life of Saul, it follows that he would not participate in a battle which would bring the death of his fellow countrymen. However, it was not possible for David to refuse outright the command of this king, for in so doing he would not only jeopardize his own life, but the lives of his men; therefore, with intentional ambiguity he responded by saying, "Surely thou shalt know what thy servant can do" (v. 2). Achish was satisfied with the answer and promised to give David a special position in his court. In this situation David had no alternative but to rely on divine intervention for a way of escape. Somewhat parenthetically, the writer inserted two important facts necessary to our understanding of the rest of the chapter. First, he noted that Samuel was dead and, as a matter of fact, had been dead for some time (25:1). Second, Saul had put out of the country those who had "familiar spirits."

The Philistines continued to organize their armies and moved northward to the site of Shunem (v. 4). This site is now known as Solem, about three miles north of Jezreel at the southern base of the hill of Moreh across the valley from Mt. Gilboa. The very fact that the Philistines could move freely to such a location and occupy the site indicates something of Saul's neglect with regard to the defense of Israel's borders. Certainly the presence of the Philistines in that area was a serious threat to the tribes of Issachar, Zebulun and Asher. David evidently remained with the Philistines during this period of time and probably hoped for an opportunity to remove himself from the battle or, if that failed, to turn on the Philistines and become an ally of the Israelites. In all probability Saul, by means of his scouts, had received word that David was with the Philistine forces encamped in the north. This, and the absence of Samuel, probably accounted for Saul's desperate move recorded in the remaining part of this chapter.

B. *The Silence of God* (28:6)

With a major confrontation with the Philistines drawing near, Saul "enquired of the Lord." The heavens, however, were silent at this time. Some might regard this as a harsh or unjust act on the part of God, but it should be remembered that in the past Saul had many opportunities to discover the will of God. He had openly disobeyed prophetic commands (I Sam. 10:8) and had murdered the priests of the sanctuary at Nob (22:9-23). Since Saul had voluntarily chosen to follow his own counsel, God permitted him to reap the fruit of such sowing (cf. Gal. 6:7).

Some have suggested that there is a contradiction between this verse and I Chronicles 10:14. The latter text suggests that Saul "enquired not of the Lord," whereas the Samuel passage states that he did inquire of the Lord. In the Samuel passage we are given no hint as to the means that Saul used for such inquiry or the attitude that existed at the time of inquiry. The passage in I Chronicles appears to be a divine interpretation of the situation. In a real sense Saul did not inquire of the Lord with a repentant heart, and therefore the inquiry was not a legitimate one.

The three means by which the will of God was discerned during this period were: (1) dreams, (2) Urim and (3) prophetic revelation. Dreams were often used by God as a means of special communication (cf. Gen. 20:6; 37:5-10; 41:1-32; I Kings 3:5; Dan 2:3-45; 4:5-19; Matt. 1:20). Dreams were apparently common to the Mosaic era and those interpreting dreams had to be carefully screened (cf. Deut. 13:1, 3, 5).

The second means of divine communication involved the Urim (Heb. 'urim — "lights"). A complete identification of the function of the Urim and Thummim (Heb. tummîm — "perfection") is difficult because of the limited number of references to them and their use. They were associated with the breastplate of the high priest (cf. Exod. 28:30; Lev. 8:8). During times of national crisis the high priest was called and judgment was sought by means of the Urim (Num. 27:21). The Urim and Thummim were commonly used in the Mosaic period and the early days of the United Monarchy. The use of these objects seems to have declined or ceased until the post-exilic period when they are again mentioned.[56] There is a wide variety of views as to the particu-

---

[56]Hosea 3:4 may be a possible exception.

lar form or identity of the Urim and Thummim. Josephus identified them with the twelve stones in the breastplate of the high
priest. He suggested that the stones were illuminated thus giving
divine information prior to the time of battle.[57] A Talmudic explanation suggests that certain letters appeared on the stone in
the breastplate and were illuminated at the moment of revelation, thus giving the high priest an indication of God's will.
Other scholars feel that there was nothing in the objects themselves that revealed the divine will, but they were merely symbols of God's revelation. When a problem was presented to the
high priest, he merely laid the matter before God in prayer and
by means of inspiration received the answer. More recent discussion on the subject attempts to identify the Urim and Thummim
as two flat objects (stones). On one side of each was the word
Urim, derived from the Hebrew root *'ārar* — "to curse"; the other side was marked Thummim ("perfect" = "yes"). When both
Urim sides appeared, the answer was negative, and when both
the Thummim sides appeared, the answer was positive. The
identification of the Urim and Thummim with the sacred lots
appears to have some possibilities, but there are serious difficulties with this view due to the fact that the answers ascribed to the
Urim and Thummim are not always the equivalent to a yes or no
answer (cf. Judg. 1:2; 20:18; I Sam. 22:10; II Sam. 5:23; 21:1).[58]
Regardless of the precise nature of the Urim and Thummim it is
clear that Saul did not have access to the original objects at this
time, for since the slaughter of the priests at Nob, the high priest,
Abiathar, with the ephod had been in David's camp (cf. 22:20ff.;
23:6; 30:7). It is, of course, not impossible that Saul appointed a
new priest and made a new ephod with Urim and Thummim.
If this were the case, it would further explain why God refused to
respond to Saul's inquiry.

---

[57]*Ant.* III.8.9.
[58]For further discussion of the problem see J. A. Motyer, "Urim and
Thummim," *The New Bible Dictionary,* J. D. Douglas, ed. (Grand Rapids:
William B. Eerdmans Publishing Company, 1962), p. 1306; and Nathan
Isaacs, "Urim and Thummim," *The International Standard Bible Encyclopedia,* James Orr, ed. (Grand Rapids: William B. Eerdmans Publishing Co., 1960), V, p. 3040.

Village of Endor. Matson Photo Service

II. SAUL AND THE WITCH OF EN-DOR (28:7-25)

A. Witchcraft in the Ancient Near East

The concept that information from a deity could be gained by means of outward signs was not uncommon in ancient Greece, Egypt, Babylon, and Palestine. The Old Testament makes reference to at least six forms of divination. All these, however, were clearly condemned as inappropriate to the search for God's will. They are as follows: (1) Hepatoscopy, which was the process of divining from the liver of a sacrificed animal (cf. Ezek. 21:21). That this was a common practice not only in Babylon, but also in Palestine, is evident from the discovery of clay models of livers found at Megiddo and elsewhere. (2) Hydromancy, or divination by water. Many feel that this is referred to in the Joseph story (Gen. 44:5). (3) Rhabdomancy. This refers to the use of a divining rod or the casting of arrows (cf. Ezek. 21:21; Hos. 4: 12). (4) Teraphim. The use of teraphim or household images was quite common among the peoples of Mesopotamia and Palestine. They were a sign of authority and land ownership, but were also used for purposes of divination (cf. Ezek. 21:21; Zech. 10:2). (5) Astrology. The study of the stars rests upon the belief that the heavenly bodies are in fact deities or are controlled by deities and influence the destiny of men. Those who study the stars and their various patterns claim to understand the future of individuals. Such a practice was very common to Babylon and appeared to be a problem in the days of the prophets (Isa. 47:13; Jer. 10:2). (6) Necromancy. Necromancy includes two ideas. One involves the worship of ancestors and the other is that the dead may be consulted for purposes of determining the future. The practice of necromancy is uniformly forbidden in the Old Testament (see Lev. 19:31; Deut. 18:11; Isa. 8:19; 19:3). While Saul had apparently driven out many who practiced consultation with the dead (cf. I Sam. 28:3), some individuals continued to live and practice their craft within the borders of Israel.

B. The Woman with a Familiar Spirit (28:7-11)

In his desperation to seek an omen for the future, Saul commanded that a woman be sought out who could consult the dead.

The Hebrew text describes such a woman as follows: *'es̆at ba-'alat 'ôb*. "The Hebrew word *'ôb* may refer to a 'skin-bottle' or a necromancer."[59] Its usage in this context is quite clearly a reference to departed spirits or subterranean spirits. A woman practicing such witchcraft was discovered at the site of En-dor, south of Mt. Tabor, about eight miles from where Saul was staying with his forces on Mt. Gilboa. Saul disguised himself as a common Israelite and contacted the woman at night, the only time that necromancy could be practiced because of Saul's previous action (v. 8; cf. v. 3). When the woman expressed apprehension in fullfilling Saul's request, he swore that the whole thing would be kept secret and her safety would be assured (v. 10). The request of Saul was that Samuel the prophet be brought back from the dead in order that communication might be established (v. 11).

C. *The Appearance of Samuel* (28:12-19)

The appearance of Samuel on this occasion has created a great deal of discussion among Bible scholars and has produced a number of viewpoints with regard to the precise nature of this event. They are as follows: (1) The appearance of Samuel was not a literal one, but merely the product of psychological impressions. According to this view the woman had permitted herself to become emotionally involved and psychologically identified with the prophet so that she was convinced that he had actually appeared when called. Daniel Erdmann describes this approach as follows:

> This can be explained psychologically only as by an inner vision, the occasion for which was given by Saul's request to bring up Samuel, and the psychological foundation of which was her inward excitement, in connection with her lively recollection of Samuel's form, which was well known to her from his earthly life, and stood before her mind in vividest distinctness.[60]

---

[59]Francis Brown, S. R. Driver, and Charles Briggs, *A Hebrew and English Lexicon of the Old Testament* (Oxford: The Clarendon Press, Corrected Impression, 1952), p. 15.

[60]"The Books of Samuel," *Lange's Commentary*, Philip Schaff, ed. (Grand Rapids: Zondervan Publishing House, 1960), V, p. 336.

Two objections can be raised against this view. The first is derived from verse 12 which indicates that when Samuel did appear the medium cried out with a loud voice, apparently surprised or startled by his appearance. Such would not be the case if she were merely seeking a vision produced by "psychological excitement." Second, the general reading of the text leads one to the conclusion that not only did the woman speak with Samuel, but Saul spoke with him as well (cf. v. 15).

(2) A demon or Satan impersonated Samuel. Those holding this view argue for the idea that a visible form of Samuel himself appeared, but that it was in reality merely an impersonation of him.[61] Many who defend this view argue that God would not permit a woman of this type to actually disturb the rest of a godly man. The whole affair is therefore considered a satanic or demonic deception of Saul. The advocates of this view remind us that Satan can appear as "an angel of light" (II Cor. 11:14) and, therefore, has the ability to carry out such deceptions. In evaluating this view, it should be pointed out that the basic reading of the Biblical text leads one to the conclusion that this was actually Samuel and not an impersonation. While it is true that Satan can perform such deception, it is highly doubtful that he has the prophetic knowledge necessary to reveal that which was given to Saul in this chapter. Furthermore, if this were a demon or an evil spirit, it is improbable that he would have given the prediction found in this passage. More likely, in the light of the godly character of David and the wickedness of Saul, the demonic power would have flattered Saul with a positive prophecy.

(3) The whole thing was a deliberate imposture practiced upon Saul. The witch really did not see Samuel, but fooled Saul into believing that her voice or that of someone else was that of Samuel. Those maintaining this view point out that only the woman saw Samuel and reported his words. Saul heard and saw nothing. The following is a representative argument for this view:

---

[61]Merrill F. Unger, *Biblical Demonology* (Wheaton: Van Kampen Press, Inc., 1952), p. 150. Cf. also Matthew Henry, *Commentary on the Holy Bible*, II, p. 767.

The more reasonable view is that the whole transaction was a
feigning on the part of the woman. The LXX uses the word
eggastrimuthos (a ventriloquist) to describe the woman and
those who exercise kindred arts (v. 9). Though pretending ignorance (v. 12) the woman doubtless recognizes Saul from the
first. It was she who saw Samuel, and reported his words; the
king himself saw and heard nothing. It required no great skill
in a practical diviner to forecast the general issue of the battle
about to take place, and the disaster which would overtake Saul
and his sons; while if the forecast had proved untrue, the narrative would never have been written. Saul, in fact, was not
slain, but killed himself. The incident, therefore, may best be
ranked in the same category as the feats of modern medium-
ship.[62]

A number of objections may be raised against this view. In the
first place, the Bible does not specifically say that the woman reported Samuel's words; on the contrary, it makes it clear that
Samuel spoke directly to Saul. Orr's statement that the king "saw
and heard nothing" is in direct conflict with the obvious reading
of the text (cf. v. 15ff.). It is also highly doubtful that she was
in a position to predict the outcome of the battle and specifically
forecast the death of Saul's sons. It is also unlikely, from a practical point of view, that she would give such a forecast to a man
obviously aligned with the Israelite camp.

(4) The most popular view and that which is maintained by
most orthodox commentators is that this was a genuine appearance of Samuel brought about by God Himself. In favor of this
proposal is the Septuagint reading of I Chronicles 10:13 which
is as follows: "Saul asked counsel of her that had a familiar
spirit to inquire of her, and Samuel made answer to him." Furthermore, the fact that she cried out when she saw Samuel indicates that she did not bring up Samuel and did not expect him
to appear in this manner. The fact that Saul bowed himself to
the ground and did obeisance is a further indication that this was
a real appearance of Samuel. It is doubtful that he would have
reacted merely on the grounds of a verbal description or a false

---

[62]James Orr, "Witch of Endor," *The International Standard Bible Encyclopedia*, II, p. 944.

impression. Samuel's statement to Saul in verse 15 should not be regarded as a proof of the idea that the witch of En-dor or Saul brought him back from the dead.[63]

What, then, was the purpose of God in bringing Samuel back for this appearance? This unusual act on the part of God was certainly designed to emphasize the doom of Saul and God's displeasure for his coming to a necromancer. Robert Jamieson suggests three additional reasons: (1) To make Saul's crime an instrument of his punishment, (2) to show the heathen world God's superiority in prophecy, and (3) to confirm a belief in a future state after death.[64]

Two other men who made an appearance on the earth after death were Moses and Elijah at the transfiguration of Christ (Matt. 17:3; Luke 9:30-31). They, however, appeared in glory," but Samuel appeared in the mantle which he had worn while on earth. Therefore, in a real sense the appearance of Samuel after death was a completely unique event.

Since occultism and necromancy are again enjoying popular acceptance, it might be well to sound a note of warning at this point. There are many well-meaning persons who are being led into a very subtle trap regarding these practices. It is clear from Scripture that the believer is not to participate in any practice of this kind (Lev. 19:31; Deut. 18:10-14). Basically, physical death involves the separation of the soul from the body. That soul is then committed into the hands of a sovereign God and remains either in the presence of Christ or in the confines of Hades. The Bible makes it clear that the next major event involving that individual is the judgment (Heb. 9:27). The Bible nowhere hints that individuals on earth can contact or communicate with those who have departed. It is also clear that believers in the intermediate state are in a condition of "rest" or "comfort." This could hardly be said if they were capable of being called to return to the earth by mediums (cf. Luke 16:25; Rev. 6:11).

[63]On this point see Christian Wordsworth, *The Holy Bible with Notes* (London: Revington's, 1873), II, Part II, p. 63.

[64]"I Samuel," *Commentary on the Whole Bible*, Jamieson, Fausset and Brown, eds. (Grand Rapids: William B. Eerdmans Publishing Co., 1948), II, p. 211.

It is even more doubtful that God would permit such individuals, whether in His presence or in Hades, to be called back to earth for the superficial reasons which are usually given for such communication.

The account of Lazarus and the rich man provides some important information on this subject. It is asserted that between the believer and unbeliever is a great "gulf" fixed which cannot be crossed (Luke 16:26). It is also evident from the story that those who have departed are not able to return to earth for any reason (cf. Luke 16:28-31). It would be a tragic thing indeed if the souls of believers could be brought back from the presence of Christ by an unbelieving medium here on earth for the mere purpose of attending to the sentimentality of a relative.

D. Saul's Sorrow (28:20-25)

The stern condemnation of Samuel was all too clear to Saul, and the future was now apparent to him. He wanted to know the disposition of events in the immediate future — now he knew them. He also knew well the divine reason for disapproval (28: 18). The scene before us is a tragic and pitiful one indeed, for on the ground lies a man once known for his heroic deeds as a soldier, one who had been filled with the Spirit of God, one who had a bright future ahead of him. All of this now was lost because of rebellion against and contempt for God's will. The woman tried to console Saul as best she could. A meal was provided for Saul and his servants, but he refused to eat until he was compelled (v. 23). Food and physical comfort now seemed insignificant to Saul, for on the horizon he could see the ominous, black clouds of death beginning to gather. His hours and days were numbered; the end was not far away.

21

THE END OF AN ERA

The final chapters of the book of I Samuel describe one of the saddest stories of ancient Hebrew history. Approximately forty years earlier a young man from the tribe of Benjamin was chosen and anointed by Samuel as Israel's first king. He was a man with physical strength and military capability. The legal, spiritual and military fortunes of Israel were placed upon his shoulders; but one thing was not taken into account on the part of Israel in those early days of optimism. Samuel sounded a warning concerning the danger of putting trust in human capacity alone. The real success of Israel did not lie in her production of capable men, but in her faith in Jehovah, as well as complete obedience to His revelation. The tragic events recorded in the concluding chapters of the book of I Samuel are in direct contrast to the optimism and enthusiasm of the tribes recorded in I Samuel 10. When Saul was selected king and publicly recognized as such at Mizpeh, the future indeed looked bright, at least from a human point of view. Saul appeared to be the man of the hour, a man with the promise of a bright future. As the book of I Samuel concludes, however, Saul is viewed in a heap, wounded and bleeding on Mt. Gilboa. Disobedience and constant insensitivity to the will of God led to this tragic end.

The final chapters of this interesting book are not exclusively devoted to a pessimistic outlook for Israel. One is able to see the providential deliverance of David from a rather awkward and delicate situation, thus vindicating the promise of God that David would be the next king.

I. DAVID AND ACHISH (29:1-11)

A. *The Mobilization of the Philistines* (29:1-5)

The historical narrative found in this chapter continues that which was begun in 28:2. The march of the Philistine armies led them northward to Aphek which has not been definitely located, for there are a number of towns with this name. The Israelite armies located their camp by a fountain which was in Jezreel. That fountain is usually identified with the present Ain-Jalud located at the foot of Gilboa. Battle preparations were carried out by the Philistines by organizing their forces into companies of hundreds and thousands (v. 2). The principal leaders of the organization were the "lords of the Philistines" (v. 2 – Heb. *sarnê pelistîm*; cf. Josh. 13:3 and I Sam. 6:16). David, along with Achish, formed the rear guard.

As military organization continued, the "princes of the Philistines" (Heb. *sārê pelistîm*) noticed that Hebrews were among the Philistine forces. The princes mentioned in verse 3 are to be distinguished from the principal leaders of the march mentioned in verse 2. Evidently the princes were company leaders who immediately recognized the presence of David and his men. Their use of the term "Hebrew" to identify an Israelite is in agreement with other uses in the Old Testament. The term "Hebrew" was used commonly by foreigners to identify an Israelite. Achish was very quick to defend the presence of David and his men by reminding the princes that David had been with him for a long time and had served him faithfully. The argument of Achish was less than convincing, however, and the military leaders demanded that David return. Their concern is expressed in the latter part of verse 4. The original text is of some interest here. The commanders were concerned that in the heat of battle David, rather than being an ally, would turn on them and become an "adversary." The Hebrew term for adversary is *śātān* ("satan"). The use of the term *śātān* in this context is enlightening, for it gives important insight into the character and deceitfulness of the adversary of the believer. An adversary, as described in this context, would be one who would make out to be an ally, but at a crucial time would turn and bring disaster. This is precisely the apostle Paul's characterization of Satan, the adversary of the believer (cf. II Cor. 11:14; I Tim. 5:14). The princes remembered well the exploits of David and, in particular, his defeat of Goliath. They also remembered the popular folk tune which was well known not only to the Israelites, but evidently to the Philistines as well (v. 5; cf. 18:7; 21:11).

B. *The Return of David* (29:6-11)

Achish realized that the military leaders were serious in their demands. Since he could not afford to risk his political future for the sake of David and his men, he told David to return to his hometown. The words of Achish as recorded in Scripture are somewhat problematic, for in his attempt to emphasize the innocence of David, he employed the expression "as the Lord liveth." This appears to be a strange statement coming from the lips of a heathen king. Scholars have tended to interpret this expression in three different ways: (1) Some feel that Achish may have been attracted to Israel's religion through his association with David and, therefore, would have used the expression quite naturally. (2) Others feel that Achish actually used a different expression, but the writer used a substitution in preparing the final record of these events. (3) The most probable view, proposed by S. Goldman, is that Achish used this expression basically to impress David with his sincerity.[65] The very fact that Achish had found no deceit in David gives some indication of David's skill as both a warrior and politician while living in the land of the enemy. The raids which he conducted gave every appearance of being favorable to Philistine interest, but in essence were in defense of the land of Judah.

David was very diplomatic in his response to the words of Achish, for quickly to agree with Achish's command would be to raise questions concerning his loyalty to the Philistine cause. But to object to it too vigorously might lead to engagement in the Philistine battle with Israel, which would place him in a most awkward position indeed! Thus, very diplomatically, David reacted with surprise and indignation that his loyalty should be questioned. Inwardly he certainly must have rejoiced at the deliverance from the dilemma in which he found himself (v. 8). The mild reaction of David satisfied Achish that David was truly an ally, but he continued to remind David that while he was a man without guilt he still could not participate in the Philistine battle. It appears that Achish was rather knowledgeable of Israelite customs and literary idioms, for in describing the inno-

----

[65]*Op. cit.*, p. 174.

cence of David he referred to him as "an angel of God." This
seems to have been a common Hebrew expression of this period
(cf. II Sam. 14:17; 19:27).

The words of Achish recorded in verse 10 have been somewhat
perplexing to expositors, for it seems that David is described as
a subject of Saul rather than a vassal-servant of the Philistines.
The expression "thy master's servants" (Heb. 'aḇdê 'aḏōnèkā) is
better translated "the servants of your lord," a clear reference to
King Saul. Why would Achish refer to David and his men in this
manner? Several suggestions have been offered in solution to
the problem. H. D. M. Spence's explanation is as follows:

> It is hardly the expression we should expect Achish to use of
> David's followers. All Israelites were, of course, "subjects of
> Saul," but the term would hardly be used except of one hostile
> to David, as Nabal was: he once (25:10) made use of an insult-
> ing term of a like nature to David. Achish, we know, seemed
> ever kindly disposed to the outlaw son of Jesse. A probable
> suggestion has, however, been lately made, that the reference
> here is to those tribes of Manasseh (cf. I Chron. 12:19-21) who
> had only lately come over to David. Was it not also possible
> that these very Manassites, who had only very recently deserted
> the king's cause for David's, were known to some of the Philis-
> tines as Saul's soldiers, and that their suspicion had been awak-
> ened in the first place by finding them marching under David's
> standard in the division of Gath?[66]

Another writer suggests that ". . . the use of these terms may
suggest that Achish did not consider David his vassal any longer, but delicately intimated that David was at liberty to leave
Philistia if he so desired."[67] It is entirely possible, of course, that
Achish used the expression in a purely non-political sense, referring, perhaps, to David's ethnic relationship, rather than his political commitments.

II. THE DESTRUCTION OF ZIKLAG (30:1-31)

Three days after David left Achish he and his men approached

---

[66]Op. cit., p. 421.
[67]Francis D. Nichol, op. cit., p. 591.

the small town of Ziklag where they had resided. Rather than being received warmly by his friends and family, he discovered mass destruction and sorrow. The Amalekites, who wandered in the Negev district in great numbers, had taken advantage of David's absence to avenge themselves on his previous invasions and plundering (cf. 27:8). It will be remembered that Saul defeated these people in a major battle earlier, but failed to destroy them completely as commanded by God (I Sam. 15:2 ff.). The Amalekites, in addition to destroying the city, had taken the women captives, probably to sell them in the Egyptian slave market. Those captured included David's two wives, Ahinoam the Jezreelitess and Abigail (v. 5). Adding to David's sorrow over this tragedy was the wrath of the people who evidently considered David's absence the cause of the disaster. Such public indignation was not new in Israel's history, for Moses experienced a similar reaction (cf. Exod. 17:4).

It seemed that in the darkest hours of tragedy and confusion David's spiritual countenance shone the brightest. Verse 6 indicates that in this hour of sorrow David "encouraged himself in the Lord his God." The Hebrew text is far more vivid at this point than is reflected in the Authorized Version. The translation should read, "but David strengthened himself in the Lord his God." David had complete confidence in the sovereignty of his God and immediately turned to the Lord for consolation and wisdom. The evidence of his faith is also observed in the procedure described in verse 7. David immediately called for Abiathar, the priest who had been with him since the massacre at Nob (cf. I Sam. 22:9-23; 23:9). As the high priest, of course, Abiathar had the sacred ephod. This meant that inquiry by means of Urim and Thummim would be possible. It is interesting that David inquired of the Lord at all regarding this problem. It certainly gives rich insight into his spiritual sensitivity to the will of God. The most natural inclination would have been to take revenge on those who had destroyed the city, but David recognized that warfare included more than mere retaliatory acts. He did not want to jeopardize the lives of those who remained. The Lord assured David that he would be given a complete victory and instructed him to pursue the Amalekites (cf. vv. 8-10).

On the way south David encountered an Egyptian who described himself as a servant of an Amalekite (cf. vv. 11-13). The
fact that an Egyptian was a slave to an Amalekite is very enlightening. It appears that the arrogant Amalekites had raided
parts of Egypt and had taken slaves from there as well. The
young Egyptian servant was ill and of no value to the master; so
he had been left to die in the desert. David agreed to spare the
life of this young man if he would reveal the location of the Amalekite forces. When David and his men reached the Amalekite
camp, they found them spread across the desert, eating, drinking
and dancing in celebration of their victory over the towns in Judah (cf. v. 16). This extravagant victory celebration is reminiscent of one which was carried out in a later period of history by
Benhadad I in the days of Ahab (cf. I Kings 20:15-20). David
took advantage of this situation and his men rushed upon the
Amalekites who were in no position to defend themselves. The
victory was complete, allowing David to recover all that the
Amalekites had taken from Ziklag (v. 18). The only ones to escape the destruction of David were four hundred young men
who fled on camels (v. 17). Camels were evidently the principal
method of mobilization used by the desert fighters throughout
this period of time. One is reminded of the mobilized forces of
the Midianites who also employed the camel for military use
(cf. Judg. 6:5).

On the return back to Ziklag David was confronted with another very delicate problem. The men who actually participated
in the battle numbered only four hundred. Two hundred of his
men had to remain behind, perhaps because of exhaustion in the
forced march southward (v. 9). Certain men among the four
hundred felt that only those who actually fought in the battle
should be the recipients of the spoil which they had recovered
(v. 22). This viewpoint, however, reflected the very thing which
David wanted to avoid, namely, assuming that victory came by
human effort alone. David reminded his men that their victory
had been given to them by the Lord (v. 23). David evidently
used a precedent established by Moses to solve the problem. He
reminded the men that the spoils belonged to all the people of
Israel, not only to those who fought in the battle (v. 24; cf.
Num. 31:25-54). David's decision evidently continued in force

and became a military policy for many years in Israel (cf. II Macc. 8:28-30).

When David returned to Ziklag, he took a large portion of the spoils which he had recovered and sent it to the elders of Judah and to friends in various cities. This was an important move on David's part because it re-established contacts with the leaders of Judah. His act was perhaps a way of expressing gratitude for the protection they had afforded him in the hills of Judah when he was pursued by Saul. Such an act would also be a means of demonstrating his loyalty to the people of Judah. This was made necessary because of his long association with the Philistines (a year and seven months). Among the towns to receive goods from David was the town of Hebron which was to become the capital of his first kingdom (v. 31).

III. THE DEATH OF SAUL AND JONATHAN (31:1-13)

A. *The Battle at Gilboa* (31:1-10)

Chapter 31 continues the history begun in 28:1. It was probably not very long after Saul's visit to En-dor that the battle took place. The Israelites had assumed that if they made Mt. Gilboa their final line of defense, they would be safe. They calculated that the Philistines would limit their battle to the valley of Jezreel and would not follow them into the mountains. This assumption, however, was a false one, for the Israelites were badly defeated in the field and the Philistines did pursue them into the mountains of Gilboa. There the sons of Saul were slain. It is with a sense of sorrow that one reads of the death of Jonathan (v. 2). Among those associated with King Saul, he appeared to be the only one with practical insight and a deep love for David. Saul's son, Ish-bosheth, was evidently not involved in the battle (or escaped), for he survived to become king over Israel for a brief period of time (cf. II Sam. 2:8-10).

As the battle continued in the area surrounding Gilboa, Saul was struck by the archers (v. 3). The phrase "he was sore wounded of the archers" is better translated from the Hebrew text as "he was greatly alarmed regarding the archers." In all likelihood the Philistines had sent out a specially trained detachment to find Saul. The welfare of the king in battle was very important for the morale of the troops on both sides. A similar procedure was practiced by the Syrians in their conflict with Ahab and Jehoshaphat (II Chron. 18:28-34). Saul's great fear was that the Philistines would take him captive while still alive and abuse him to the shame of Israel (v. 4; cf. the treatment of Samson, Judg. 16:23-31). In desperation Saul asked his armorbearer to slay him so he would not be taken alive by the Philistines; but the armorbearer refused to do this, for he was afraid he would be seen killing the king and his own life would be taken. In complete frustration and fear Saul attempted to commit suicide by falling on his own sword. According to this narrative, Saul's death was occasioned by this event (v. 6). However, some question has been raised about the details of the narrative in the light of the Amalekite's story recorded in II Samuel. Many feel that Saul's death was ultimately brought about by the Amalekite. The various views on this problem will be dealt with in the next chapter.

When the Philistines finally got to Saul, they cut off his head, stripped off his armor and sent it into their principal cities. The cutting off of the head was not an uncommon procedure in battles of this period. One should remember that David adopted the same practice in his defeat of Goliath, an act the Philistines had probably not forgotten (cf. I Sam. 17:51). The armor of Saul was placed in the house of their idols, a practice designed to encourage the faith of people with regard to the strength of their gods. Remember that the Ark of the Covenant was placed in the house of Dagon as a war trophy (cf. I Sam. 5:1-12). Notice also that David had taken the head of Goliath and placed it in Jerusalem (17:54). Later on the sword of Goliath was found in the sanctuary at Nob near the ephod (cf. I Sam. 21:9). It might well be that the Lord's refusal to permit David to build the temple was related to these practices. Perhaps the Lord, in this way, prevented David's turning the temple into a house of war trophies following Philistine customs. The armor of Saul ended up in the "house of Ashtaroth," one of the principal fertility deities in Philistia and Canaan.

The bodies of Saul and his sons were fastened to the walls of the city of Beth-shan, approximately two miles from the bat-

Mound of Beth-shan (in background) where the body of Saul was taken by the Philistines after his death (I Sam. 31:10). Levant Photo Service

tle area. Beth-shan was a very important fortress city in the Jordan Valley to the east of Megiddo. It guarded the vale of Jezreel which led up from the Jordan to the great plain of Esdraelon. The Egyptians had great interest in this city as evidenced by discoveries at this site. During the early part of the twelfth century B.C., Ramses III attempted to re-establish the empire of his forefathers and built a frontier military post at Beth-shan and stationed a garrison there. A number of objects have been recovered at the site which are attributable to the work of Ramses III. After about 1050 B.C., it was taken over by the Philistines as evidenced by both Biblical and archaeological data. In stratum V, excavators discovered a temple in the northern part of the mound. Many feel that this might be the "house of Ashtaroth" mentioned in I Samuel 31:10.

B. *The Burial of Saul* (31:11-13)

Word reached the inhabitants of Jabesh-gilead that the Israelites were defeated and that the mutilated bodies of Saul and his sons were hanging on the walls of Beth-shan. The men of Jabesh-gilead had not forgotten Saul's intervention on their behalf at an earlier period of time (I Sam. 11). In addition to that, it should be remembered that some of the inhabitants of Jabesh-gilead were Benjamites by marriage after the great Benjaminite War as described in the latter chapters of the Book of Judges. The valiant men of the city arose and travelled all night. They took the bodies of Saul and his sons, burned them and buried them in Jabesh (vv. 11-13). The parallel passage in I Chronicles 10:12 omits the fact that the bodies of these men were burned, perhaps because the burning of the body was at times a sign of shame (cf. Lev. 20:14; 21:9). A fast of seven days was proclaimed in mourning for this great champion of Israel.

While the life of Saul is a study in contrasts, and at times impossible to fully understand, there is a sense in which Saul wins our sympathy. He was a hero in Israel and a man who was necessary for the unification and strengthening of the nation. Unfortunately, while Saul resolved military conflicts, he was unable to care for the inner conflicts of his own soul and the spiritual problems which he encountered throughout his life. In the classical sense, Saul could not be called a great king, but that his achievements were many is clear from David's exquisite elegy recorded in II Samuel 1. Whatever military and judicial victories may have been attributed to Saul, they are overshadowed by his tragic spiritual failures.

22 (II Samuel 1–4)

DAVID: KING OF JUDAH

The journey which led to the throne was a long and arduous one for David. It was an experience in the agony of defeat and sorrow on one hand, but at other times the thrill of victory. David was a man of many talents. He was a musician, writer, leader and man of valor. Because of such capabilities he was eminently qualified for the highest position in Israel. The book of II Samuel continues the story of David's rise to the throne and covers his forty years of reign. The book opens with David's accession over Judah and closes just before his death.

Because of the exquisite presentation of the historical events in the book of II Samuel we know more of David than any other man in Israel's history. His deeds, innermost thoughts, and failures are there for all to examine. Complementing the narratives in Samuel are David's writings found in the book of Psalms and a parallel history recorded in the book of II Chronicles.

The book of II Samuel divides itself naturally in two sections: (1) David's rule over Judah (1:1–4:12) and (2) David's rule over all Israel (5:1–24:25). Some commentators have found it advantageous to divide the book by its spiritual content rather than historical. In this case the book would be divided as follows: (1) David's triumphs (1:1–12:31) and (2) David's troubles (13:1–24:25).

The book of II Samuel begins much as the book of I Samuel ends, on a note of sadness. The death of Saul was a tragic turn of events for the people of Israel. Their aspirations, hopes and futures appeared to have been crushed through the humiliating defeat of the Israelite armies at Gilboa. It was in such tragic circumstances that Israel's new champion made his appearance. The task of saving Israel from total destruction was one of great difficulty and complicated by many pressures. Spiritual sensitivity and imaginative leadership were the qualities that characterized David, Judah's first king. But perhaps there is another quality which should be observed in the life of David. Far too

269

often David's military valor, political genius and spiritual insights
are emphasized to the exclusion of a very basic attribute of David; namely, his keen emotion. David was a man of sensitive
character, and his love for his friends was not hidden. His sorrow
for those whom he respected was perfectly genuine and pure.
The book of II Samuel opens with one of the most eloquent expressions of sorrow, in the most genuine sense, recorded in ancient history.

I. THE LAMENTATION OF DAVID (1:1-27)

A. *The News of Saul's Death* (1:1-16)

David was still in the town of Ziklag when he received word
of Saul's death (v. 1; cf. I Sam. 30). This news did not reach
David until the third day of his return to Ziklag (v. 2). Upon
hearing the news he rent his clothes and put earth upon his head
in a public demonstration of mourning and sorrow (cf. Josh. 7:
6; I Sam. 4:12; Job 2:12). The news of Saul's death and the
defeat of Israel was brought to David by a man who identified
himself as an Amalekite (vv. 8, 13). The Amalekites are well
known to us because they were long-standing enemies of Israel.
They attacked Israel shortly after they had left the land of
Egypt (Exod. 17:8-13), and during the wilderness journey they
created problems for the tribes (Deut. 25:17). They evidently
were not strong enough during the period of the judges to attack Israel alone, but joined in a number of coalitions against Israel (cf. Judg. 3:13; 6:3). Saul was commanded to completely
destroy these peoples because of the destruction they wrought in
Israel. While Saul enjoyed a major victory, he did not fully
obey the command of God and thus brought upon himself God's
judgment (cf. I Sam. 15:4 ff.).

The messenger who appeared to David was probably one of
those who escaped the wrath of Saul. It should also be remembered that David had just recently fought the Amalekites because they had invaded the town of Ziklag and had taken David's wives captive. It is highly doubtful that this young man
was among the Amalekites whom David fought. In all probability he was a mercenary soldier who had joined Saul's forces. Notice that he described himself as one who had come "out of the

camp of Israel" (v. 3: cf. v. 2, "out of the camp of Saul"). Of course, it is entirely possible that the Amalekite had no official relationship to the armies of Saul at all and was merely wandering through the battlefield in an attempt to recover whatever booty he could. However, this appears unlikely in the light of the heat of the battle that took place.

According to the Amalekite's story, he "happened by chance" to come upon Mt. Gilboa, where he found Saul (v. 6). When he reached Saul, he was badly wounded and at the point of death.[68] Saul described his condition as one of great anguish or agony (v. 9, Heb. *šābāṣ*).[69] Realizing that Saul's condition was hopeless he followed the request of Saul and slew him, an act which Saul's armorbearer refused to do (cf. I Sam. 31:4). Presumably, Saul's wounds were so severe that there was no possible way of removing him from the battle field.

Scholars have generally questioned the veracity of the Amalekite's story. It is their view that "the Amalekite invented this, in hope of thereby obtaining the better recompence from David."[70] Those maintaining this view feel that the Amalekite saw an opportunity for political recognition.

Others, however, have attempted to harmonize the material found in I Samuel with the Amalekite's story. It is their viewpoint that the Amalekite did find Saul still alive, but mortally wounded, and brought his life to an end at Saul's request. It is clear from the punishment David assigned that he considered the Amalekite's story as the truth. David's revenge upon the Amalekite was not prompted by mere hatred of the Amalekites, although in the light of his recent conflict with them this may have been a factor. The death sentence was given primarily because

---

[68]Examples of attempted suicide are rare in Scripture. There are, however, three examples: Ahithophel (II Sam. 17:23), Zimri (I Kings 16:18) and Judas (Matt. 27:5).

[69]The Hebrew noun *šbṣ* occurs only here and is difficult to translate. Some suggestions are "cramp," "dizziness" or "giddiness." (See Goldman, *op. cit.*, p. 187; also Brown, Driver and Briggs, *op. cit.*, p. 990).

[70]C. F. Keil and F. Delitzsch, *op. cit.*, p. 286. See also H. D. M. Spence, *op. cit.*, p. 445; Francis Nichol, *op. cit.*, p. 602; and Fred Young, "I and II Samuel," *The Wycliffe Bible Commentary*, Charles Pfeiffer and Everett F. Harrison, eds. (Chicago: Moody Press, 1962), p. 293.

this Amalekite had slain the Lord's "anointed" (vv. 14-16). This
was a deed which David himself refused to do a number of times
(cf. I Sam. 24 and 26).

B. *David's Lament for Saul and Jonathan* (1:17-27)

The sorrow which David expressed over the death of Saul and
Jonathan was genuine. There was no pretense or superficiality
in the actions of David. His recorded elegy over the fallen and
the dead is one of the most eloquent in all Scripture.

> It is one of the finest odes of the Old Testament: full of lofty
> sentiment, and springing from deep and sanctified emotion, in
> which, without the slightest allusion to his own relation to the
> fallen king, David celebrates without envy the bravery and
> virtues of Saul and his son, Jonathan, and bitterly laments their
> loss.[71]

Another description of David's response is as follows:

> David's elegy is not supremely great poetry; it "stands out
> as the genuine outpouring of a noble heart, a heart too great to
> harbour one selfish thought in this dark hour of his country's
> humiliation" (Kennedy).[72]

David's elegy is divided into two parts. The first section describes David's sorrow over both Saul and Jonathan, and is introduced by the expression, "How are the mighty fallen" (vv.
19-24). The second section describes David's sorrow over Jonathan alone and is also introduced by the lament, "How are the
mighty fallen" (vv. 25-27). There are several expressions in this
portion of Scripture which deserve special treatment because of
their apparent ambiguity. Verse 18 speaks of teaching the children of Judah "the bow." The words, "the use of," do not appear
in the original. Quite evidently "the bow" was popular with
the people at that time, for it was recorded in the "Book of
Jasher." This book was referred to as early as Joshua 10:13. It
seems to have been composed of ballads accompanied by prose

---

[71]C. F. Keil and F. Delitzsch, *op. cit.*, p. 288.
[72]S. Goldman, *op. cit.*, p. 189.

introductions dealing with important events and great men in the early history of Israel. David also gave instruction that the news of Saul's death and the humiliation of the nation should not be told in Gath (v. 20). This expression uttered by David apparently became a proverb in later times (cf. Mic. 1:10). It should be remembered that David resided in Gath when he lived among the Philistines (cf. I Sam. 21:10, 12; 27:2-4).

Included in the poetic descriptions of this national tragedy is the following statement: ". . . for there the shield of the mighty is vilely cast away, the shield of Saul, as though he had not been anointed with oil" (v. 21, KJV). It is clear that the translators regarded this expression as referring to the anointing of Saul. In other words, he had been cast aside as though he had never been anointed king. A better interpretation, perhaps, is that Saul was likened to a shield, left in the field to rust after the battle. Shields made of metal were commonly oiled in order to be polished and protected (cf. Isa. 21:5).

That Saul had brought a degree of prosperity to the nation is clear from David's words in verse 24. The wars of Saul were many times successful and, in fact, enriched the nation of Israel (cf. I Sam. 14:47).

II. THE CROWNING OF DAVID (2:1-32)

A. *David's Rule at Hebron* (2:1-11)

1. *The Second Anointing of David* (2:1-4)

With the death of Saul, it would seem a perfectly natural thing for David to go immediately to Judah and Israel in an attempt to occupy the throne for which he had been anointed by Samuel. But such was not the spiritual character of David. He recognized that the throne of Israel came only by divine right and only in accordance with God's will. Thus the second chapter of this book begins with David's inquiry regarding his move to Judah. The inquiry was, doubtless, made through the high priest, Abiathar, who was with him (I Sam. 22:20–23:10). The answer of the Lord came immediately, and David was commanded to go to the city of Hebron in the southern hill country. Hebron is located approximately twenty miles south of Jerusalem and

Hebron, where David was first made king (II Sam. 2:1-4, 11).
Levant Photo Service

between fifteen and twenty miles away from the town of Ziklag where David was residing. It was an ideal place for the
capital in Judah since it was situated near the center of the tribe.
It was well protected, being located in the mountains, and it
had a long sacred history. David was no stranger to this area,
for on a number of occasions he was forced to hide in the caves
and valleys in the Hebron vicinity as Saul attempted to capture
him. David was also more recently remembered by the gifts
that he sent to the elders of Hebron after his defeat of the Amalekites (cf. I Sam. 30:31). In obedience to the Lord's command,
David and his two wives, Ahinoam the Jezreelitess and Abigail,
accompanied him to Hebron. His other wife, Michal, it will be
remembered, had been given to a man by the name of Phalti
and at this time was living in Benjamite territory (cf. I Sam. 25:
43-44). When David reached the territory of Judah, he was
warmly received and recognized as the king of that territory.
David's first anointing was only in the presence of his father and
his brothers (I Sam. 16:13); now, however, he stood before the
whole tribe of Judah and was publicly anointed (v. 4). Following the anointing, he received word of the heroic efforts of
the men of Jabesh-gilead who had rescued the mutilated bodies
of Saul and his sons and had buried them.

2. David's Message to Jabesh-gilead (2:5-7)

The town of Jabesh-gilead is generally identified with the site
known as Tell Abu-Kharaz which is located about two miles east
of the Jordan River and twenty miles south of the Sea of Galilee.
After hearing of the heroism of the men of Jabesh-gilead, David performed his first formal act as king, and it was indicative
of his wisdom and temperament. He commended the men of
Jabesh-gilead not only on their heroic deeds in rescuing the
bodies of Saul and his sons, but for the fact that they had shown
this kindness to the "Lord's anointed." David fully recognized
the love that the peoples of Jabesh-gilead had for the king because of the protection Saul had accorded the people on a previous occasion (cf. I Sam. 11:1-11). David was also fully aware
of the fact that if he could win the alliance of those faithful followers of Saul, he would have gone a long way in breaking down

any animosity that would build up between himself and the followers of Saul. It should be noted, however, that David's motives were characterized by more than mere political opportunism. His act was one of genuine kindness and sincerity. In addition to this, David may have offered some form of protection to the city, which at this stage was without royal leadership.

3. Ish-bosheth Made King (2:8-11)

Abner, a relation of Saul (I Sam. 14:50), attempted to maintain the dynasty of Saul by placing Saul's surviving son Ish-bosheth upon the throne. This man was brought to the city of Mahanaim and was there established as king over the territory of Transjordan. It is questionable whether Ish-bosheth had any significant political or military influence in the larger west bank area. The city of Mahanaim was apparently one of some importance and influence since it was chosen as the capital of that territory. Its importance is verified by the fact that it is mentioned in Shishak's victory inscription as *Mhnn*. Shishak (She-Shonk I) was the founder of the Twenty-second Dynasty in Egypt and is well known to us as the one who in Biblical history raided Judah in the fifth year of King Rehoboam. The fact that Abner made one of Saul's sons king indicates that the dynastic principle was not unknown among the Israelites at that time.

The original name of this king was most likely Esh-baal (Heb. *'ešbā 'al*) according to I Chronicles 8:33; 9:39. This name literally means "man of Baal" (or perhaps "man of the Lord"). On the basis of Ugaritic parallels some have suggested the meaning *it-ba al* ("Baal lives"). Because of the implication of the name Baal as it related to the Canaanite pantheon (and probably because of the actions of this man) the name was changed to Ish-bosheth (Heb. *'iš bōšet* which literally means "man of shame"). In Hosea 9:10 (cf. Jer. 3:24) the word Baal is placed in parallel with the term *bōšet*. There is no doubt that the change of the name had reference to his personal shame in addition to the stigma of the name Baal (cf. Ps. 35:26). That the changing of names was not uncommon among the Hebrew scribes is evidenced by the following examples: (a) Mephibosheth (II Sam.

4:4) was substituted for Merib-baal (I Chron. 8:34; 9:40) or
Meri-baal (I Chron. 9:40). (b) Jerubbesheth (II Sam. 11:21)
was substituted for Jerubbaal (Judg. 6:32; 8:35).

B. *The Battle of Gibeon* (2:12-32)

Once Ish-bosheth had been declared king of the northern
kingdom, it was only a matter of time before a military confrontation would occur between the two kingdoms. This took
place at a little town approximately eight miles northwest of
Jerusalem. The modern village located there today is known as
El-Jib, situated approximately twenty-five hundred feet above
sea level. The beautiful valley which surrounds this tell is very
fertile and probably was the means by which the inhabitants

The "pool" at Gibeon (El-Jib). The circular stairway leads to a tunnel
which is 45 feet long and led to the water room (II Sam. 2:13). Levant
Photo Service

were sustained through its long history. Excavations were carried on at El-Jib for four seasons beginning in 1956. These expeditions were conducted under the leadership of James B. Pritchard. The discoveries made there are most helpful to the Bible student. Identification of El-Jib as ancient Gibeon was made sure by the recovery of a number of jar handles dating from the seventh century B.C. On these jar handles were a number of inscriptions including the name of the town, Gibeon. Among the important industries at ancient Gibeon was the making of wine. This has been verified by the discovery of wine vats dating to the pre-exilic period.[73] Most spectacular of all the discoveries, however, was a large shaft leading to a pool, now identified with the pool mentioned in this chapter (cf. v. 13). This pool was cut down into a solid rock and was cylindrical in shape, measuring 37 feet in diameter and 35 feet deep. At the base of this cut the excavators discovered a circular stairway which continued by means of a tunnel down another 45 feet. This ultimately led to the water room which could be used by the people at all times, but especially during those periods when the enemy was outside the walls.[74]

When the men of Abner and the men of Joab arrived at Gibeon, they sat down on opposite sides of the pool, perhaps not intending an immediate conflict, but Abner presented Joab with a challenge which is recorded in the fourteenth verse. "Let the young men now arise, and play before us. And Joab said, Let them arise." This verse has been difficult for many to interpret in the light of the context. It is obvious that Abner and Joab were not talking about the playing of games in the modern sense of "games." The expression "play" (Heb. śāhaq) has a wide variety of uses in the Old Testament. It can refer to the playing of a game or to play in terms of celebration (cf. II Sam. 6:21). But the significance of the term here is clearly related to combat as the context shows. Twelve men who were selected from the

---

[73]See James B. Pritchard, "Industry and Trade at Biblical Gibeon," *The Biblical Archaeologist*, XXIII, 1 (Feb., 1960), p. 23 ff.

[74]For a further discussion of this site see James B. Pritchard, *Gibeon, Where the Sun Stood Still* (Princeton, N. J.: Princeton University Press, 1962).

tribe of Benjamin and twelve from among the servants of David gathered near the pool and combat between these two groups was initiated. The results were inconclusive and this led to a larger battle between the two armies. The concept of battle by representation was not new for this was the principle employed in the David-Goliath confrontation (I Sam. 17).

The fashion in which the twenty-four contestants fought has been a problem for commentators to handle. Up until recent years no parallels were known in the ancient Near East which could help to shed light on the nature and purpose of such an encounter. The most significant contribution to this problem was made in an article by Y. Yadin.[75] In this article he pointed out that a relief from Tell Halaf shows two men engaged in exactly this type of combat: each grasping the other's head with one hand and with the other plunging a blade into the other's side. While this discovery does not explain the particular purpose of this type of encounter, it at least provides a significant parallel. It might well be that in the near future new discoveries will shed further light on the nature and purpose of this particular type of combat.

The brief battle that followed was a demonstration of the superiority of David's men. That there were not great numbers involved in the battle is clear from the fact that only twenty men were slain in David's army and 360 in the army of Israel (vv. 30-31). During the pursuit of Abner's men, Asahel chased Abner. Asahel was the brother of Joab and Abner did not want any part of a direct encounter with this young man. He recognized that if he should slay Asahel a blood feud would develop. He gave warning to Asahel to forget his pursuit, but Asahel realized that if Abner could be slain he would have removed one of David's chief enemies and the principal power behind King Ish-bosheth in the north. The confrontation could not be avoided, however, and Abner was forced to slay the brother of Joab. The expression "the fifth rib" (v. 23) is merely a reference to the abdomen of the individual (cf. 3:27; 4:6; 20:10). There is

---

[75]Y. Yadin, "Let the Young Men, I Pray Thee, Arise and Play Before Us," *Journal of the Palestine Oriental Society*, XXI (1948), pp. 110-116.

no question that while this was not a major war, it was the beginning of long hostilities between the north and the south.

III. ABNER AND DAVID (3:1-39)

A. *The Family of David* (3:1-6)

That hostilities continued between the men of Abner and the men of Joab is evident by the opening phrase of verse 1. The "long war" described does not refer to continual fighting, but a continuing state of hostility between the two parties (cf. v. 6). The list of David's sons born during his seven-and-a-half year reign at Hebron is given in verses 2 through 5. Some of the sons are well known to us by virtue of their subsequent actions; the others we know only by name. Of particular interest is the fact, however, that Absalom was the son of a foreign princess (v. 3). This is not without interesting implications with regard to Absalom's later rebellion.

B. *Abner's Submission to David* (3:7-26)

It is rather clear that Ish-bosheth was hardly a skillful king. He had the throne only by virtue of his relationship to the former king. His suspicion with regard to Abner led to further conflict in the royal court. The charge laid against Abner is recorded in verse 7 and constituted a serious charge. The harem in the ancient Near East was considered the property of a king's successor and, therefore, taking a woman who was part of the harem of the previous king was interpreted as a type of claim to the throne. Abner's action (if really carried out) was clearly a violation of royal rights and was called into question (cf. II Sam. 12:8; 16:21; I Kings 2:22). The response of Abner to this charge was a very strong one. He asked if he should be considered a dog (v. 8). Dogs in the ancient Near East were something thoroughly contemptible. They were chiefly found prowling around the towns in a half-wild condition, living off offal and garbage. The King James Version obscures the original at this point, for it should not read "a dog's head which against Judah," which is a translation taken from the Vulgate, but should read "a dog's head which belongs to Judah." Ish-bosheth was clearly not in a position to challenge the power of Abner. This is made clear in verse 11 and indicates that Ish-bosheth was extremely weak. He had no real power apart from Abner and his men. Abner concluded that the future of the northern kingdom was rather dark under the leadership of such an incompetent monarch and decided to change his allegiance from Ish-bosheth to David. This was initiated by sending messengers to David with the proposition that a league be formed between his men and the men of David. To this David agreed, with one condition; namely, that his wife, Michal, should be returned to him (v. 13). This led to a personal meeting between Abner and David along with the elders of Israel (vv. 17-21). When Joab heard of the private meeting, he was less than enthusiastic, for he regarded Abner as the archenemy to David's throne and could see nothing in such a meeting except an attempt to deceive (vv. 22-26).

C. *The Murder of Abner* (3:27-39)

When Abner returned to Hebron to solidify the political agreements, he was met by Joab who took him aside and slew him (v. 27). Joab was quite clearly interested in revenge for the slaying of Asahel, his brother. He may also have been considering the protection of David (cf. v. 25). More likely, however, Joab was also thinking of the future. At that time he was general of the armies of Judah. If Abner were accepted by David as an ally, Joab's military position might be in danger. Therefore, his deed was, in fact, a protection of his own military prestige. The murder of Abner put David into a very embarrassing situation, for it would appear to the elders in the north that the whole plot had been conceived by David to eliminate his enemy. To prevent this type of rumor from developing, David immediately issued a public denouncement of the crime and denied any personal participation in the murder. The strong curse uttered by David in verse 29 indicates that he did not consider the act as justified. It should be remembered that Abner had slain Asahel in battle unwillingly and in self-defense. It should also be noted that Hebron was a city of refuge (Josh. 21:13) and in such a city not even the avenger of blood might slay the murderer without a trial (cf. Num. 35:22-25). Thus Joab violated basic laws established within Israel. The public mourning of

David and his genuine sorrow were quite impressive to the people (cf. vv. 32-36). The people in the north as well as the south recognized that David was genuinely sorry for the unnecessary death of Abner and they were pleased at the response of the king. It indicated that it was not David's desire to secure a kingdom by means of intrigue or murder.

IV. THE ASSASSINATION OF ISH-BOSHETH (4:1-12)

With the death of Abner the hands of Ish-bosheth were "feeble" (Heb. "were slackened"). Without Abner, Ish-bosheth had no real support for the throne. It is probable that Ish-bosheth was unpopular with many of his own countrymen. They must have been frustrated by the inability of Ish-bosheth to strengthen and expand their government. This led to his assassination at the hands of two men. They entered his house at noontime while he rested from the heat of the day and smote him. Following this, they took his head and brought it to David to prove the success of the assassination plot. They, perhaps like the Amalekite of Chapter 1, thought that such an act would secure political favor in the eyes of David. But these men, like the Amalekite, had miscalculated the character of David. He considered the throne a sacred office not to be secured by murder and bloodshed. David was thoroughly convinced that God had promised him the throne of Israel and that in due time that throne would be his. The two murderers were judged by David and found guilty of murder. As a result, they were condemned to death (vv. 10-12) and their bodies were hung over a pool in Hebron as a public denouncement of their deeds (v. 12; cf. Deut. 21:22). Ish-bosheth was buried with full military honors in the sepulchre of Abner.

One cannot help but be impressed with the ethical and political sophistication that David brought to Israel's politics. This was in contrast to the approach adopted by King Saul. David did not follow the philosophy that the end justifies any means. He was convinced of the providential and sovereign control of his God. He believed that in the proper time the way would be open for the unification of the land and the establishment of one throne.

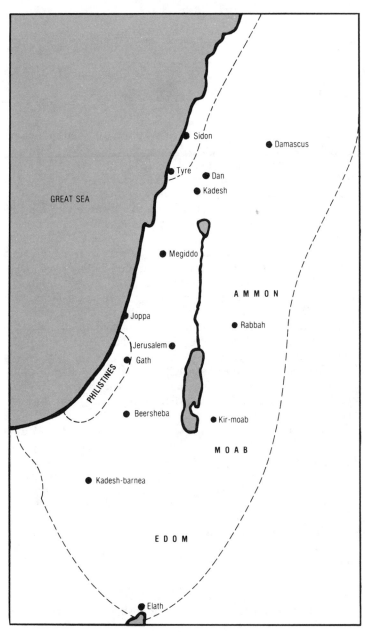

The Empire of David

23

ONE KING ... ONE KINGDOM

After seven-and-one-half years of division and failure, it became apparent that the nation of Israel could not afford the luxury of such division any more. David, who had long been recognized as a champion of Israelite causes, had already proven himself a worthy king in Judah. The inability of Ish-bosheth to strengthen the northern tribes, the continued success of the Philistines in warfare and the humiliating defeat suffered by Abner's men at Gibeon made it clear that the only practical solution to their problems was to recognize David as king over all the land. Thus, with the third anointing of David, the kingdom was united and on the way to firm establishment. The decision of the elders was fully vindicated, for in less than five years David was able to bring strength and unity to a nation that was badly divided. In addition to that, he created a strong capital at Jerusalem and quickly achieved international recognition for the sovereignty of Israel. David's efforts were so successful that a really serious foreign threat did not occur until after the reign of Solomon. The same skill and prudence which characterized the boyhood days of David (cf. I Sam. 16:18; 18:5, 14, 30) now brought success to him as king.

The story of David is one of the most intriguing found anywhere. This account of unparalleled success should not be attributed to mere human wisdom, prudence, and military genius. The real key to David's rise to power was the fact that God's hand was upon him. When he was first anointed by Samuel, he was only a shepherd boy, caring for a few sheep in the hills of Bethlehem. In the chapters before us we now see David on the royal throne in Jerusalem, caring for the whole flock of Israel.

I. THE LAND UNITED (5:1-25)

A. *David Anointed King over Israel* (5:1-5)

Following the disastrous reign of Ish-bosheth, the elders of the tribes to the north were left with no real alternative but to recognize the royal authority of David. The fact of the matter is that from a military point of view their very survival depended on such a decision. The appearance in Hebron of a large group of representatives from the north must have been impressive. Included in the great numbers were elders and many warriors (cf. v. 3 and I Chron. 12:23-40). The elders cited three reasons why the land should be unified. First, they recognized that David had been divinely appointed as king over Israel (v. 2). Second, they reminded David of their common heritage (v. 1; cf. Gen. 29:14; Judg. 9:2; II Sam. 19:12). Finally, they recognized the fact that David had played an important role in Israel's military history (v. 2). The nature of kingship as viewed by the elders is instructive. They were not concerned with military needs alone. Appropriately, David was considered a shepherd for they requested that he should "feed" the people, Israel (Heb. *tir 'eh* — "thou shalt pasture"; cf. 7:7). Like Saul (I Sam. 9:16; 10:1) and Solomon (I Chron. 29:22), David was to be a "captain" (Heb. *nāgîd*) over the nation of Israel. The former expression probably referred to the larger realm of civil responsibility, whereas the latter term had reference primarily to military affairs. The third anointing of David came when he was thirty years old, and, according to verse 4, he reigned for a period of forty years. It is clear that the number forty is a rounded figure of his total reign; however, the information supplied in verse 5 indicates that the reign of David extended for a short time over forty years (cf. 2:11; I Chron. 3:4 with I Chron. 29:27).

B. *The Capture of Jerusalem* (5:6-8)

Once David was recognized as king over all the tribes, it was inappropriate that his throne should remain in Hebron which was centrally located in the tribe of Judah, but certainly not easily accessible to the northern tribes. David had to look for a suitable location which would not give political advantage to either the north or the south. The two factions would be very sensitive to the location of the new capital with regard to this point. David selected the city of Jerusalem which was near the border of Judah and Benjamin. His selection was a wise one because Je-

rusalem had not been an Israelite city up to this time. It had
been able to maintain its independent status under the rule of
the Jebusites (cf. Josh. 15:63). Judah was successful in defeating the Jebusites on one occasion, but was not able to occupy
or control the site permanently (Judg. 1:8-9). The Benjamites
were also unsuccessful in an attempt to take the city on a permanent basis (cf. Judg. 1:21 with 19:11-12). In the fourteenth
century B.C. the city of Jerusalem was closely aligned with Egypt
and apparently depended on Egypt for help in its defense. Now
that Egypt was weak, the defense of the city rested on the Jebusites alone.

Jerusalem was also an attractive selection as a capital because
of its position in the highlands, which made it easy to defend.
Because it is approximately 2500 feet above sea level it is a very
comfortable place in which to live. The Jebusites who controlled
the city were the descendants of the third son of Canaan (cf.
Gen. 10:16; I Chron. 1:14). These Canaanite peoples evidently
had dwelt in the hills ever since the time of Moses (cf. Num.
13:29; Josh. 11:3) and, in particular, in the Jerusalem area (Josh.
15:8; 18:16).

The Jebusites were very confident about their ability to defend
the city. After all, they had successfully maintained control of
Jerusalem ever since the days of Joshua. Why, then, should they
fear the Israelite armies at this point? Their challenge to David indicates they were rather arrogant regarding their ability
to hold the site. In effect, they told David that the city could
be defended by the lame and the blind and he would still be
unable to occupy it (v. 6). The particular significance of the expression "blind and lame" has been subject to a number of viewpoints on the part of commentators. J. Sidlow Baxter, apparently
following some Rabbinic traditions, argues that the "lame and the
blind" were actually Jebusite gods.[76] This interpretation appears rather doubtful, however. It is not likely that the Jebusites would refer to their deities as "lame and blind." Furthermore, if they were referring to gods, why did they not specifically
say that? The preferred interpretation of this phrase is that:

[76]*Op. cit.,* p. 214.

The Jebusites relied upon the unusual natural advantages of their citadel, which stood upon Mt. Zion, the mountain shut in by deep valleys on three different sides; so in their haughty self-security they imagined that they did not even need to employ healthy and powerful warriors to resist the attack made by David, but that the blind and lame would suffice.[77]

The particular method employed by Joab in capturing the city is not made entirely clear from the terms used in verse 8. David suggested that men should enter the city by means of the "gutter" (Heb. ṣinnôr). The precise meaning of this word is a problem. The only other occurrence of the term in the Old Testament is in Psalm 42:7 where it is translated "water spout" (A.V.) and "water falls" (ASV.). Most commentators interpret this as a water conduit or a water course which went under the walls into the Jebusite city. On the basis of cognate parallels William F. Albright suggests that the word should be translated "hooks" or "scaling hook,"[78] but this view has not gained wide acceptance.

From the book of Chronicles it is clear that it was actually Joab who took the city and defeated the Jebusites (I Chron. 11:6). Evidently Joab and some of his men entered the city secretly by means of the water conduit, a tactic which the Jebusites had evidently not considered. In any event, the project was a success and in a very brief period of time David had complete control of the city.

C. *The Capital Established* (5:9-16)

After gaining control of the city, David immediately took steps to refortify it to guarantee its future protection. This was done by rebuilding "Millo" and sections inside the city (v. 9). The particular meaning of "Millo" is not completely known. It almost always occurs with the article. It was apparently an important part of the fortification of the stronghold of the city, perhaps that section which protected the most vulnerable part of the city

---

[77]Keil and Delitzsch, *op. cit.*, p. 315. Cf. also Francis Nichol, *op. cit.*, p. 620.

[78]"The Old Testament and Archaeology," *Old Testament Commentary*, H. C. Alleman and E. E. Flack, eds. (Philadelphia: 1954), p. 149.

in the north. Both Solomon (I Kings 11:27) and Hezekiah (II Chron. 32:5) recognized the importance of this fortress and took steps to strengthen it.

The selection of Jerusalem as the new capital was a political move of sheer genius on David's part. Its neutrality would make it attractive to the tribes in the north as well as the tribes in the south. Even more significant is the fact that David could defeat the Jebusites who had controlled the city for almost four hundred years. This certainly demonstrated his ability to achieve military goals. The result of this victory was a decided boost to David's popularity (v. 10). International recognition of David's throne came very quickly. To the northwest Hiram, king of Tyre, sent messengers to David and offered cedars, carpenters and masons to build a palace for the new king. The use of cedar in royal palaces was greatly desired by ancient Near Eastern monarchs. This is evidenced from the abundance of Egyptian literature which refers to certain ships going to Byblos to acquire that very kind of wood. The offer of Hiram not only had political implications, but economic as well. The Phoenicians had a lot to gain by establishing trade with Israel. They could supply lumber and goods from the western Mediterranean world. The tribes of Israel could provide most types of grain and food stuffs. Thus, a very significant friendship was established, one which was continued into the reign of Solomon (I Kings 5:1; 6:1, 38; 7:1; 9:10-14; II Chron. 2:3). David's prosperity in Jerusalem was not only evident in his ability to establish long-term political and economical contacts with the Phoenicians, but also in his multiplication of wives (vv. 13-16). A large harem was always a sign of wealth and prestige among ancient monarchs. However, he did so in violation of clear Biblical commands with regard to Israel's king (cf. Deut. 17:17). While polygamous practices are not condemned at this point, they are indirectly judged in the troubles that arise later in the royal court.

D. *The Capital Protected* (5:17-25)

1. *The Reason for the Philistine Attack* (5:17)

There is some doubt among scholars as to the precise chronology of events described in these verses. Many feel that the Phi-

listine battle herein described occurred before the capture of
Jerusalem. Others argue that the events were very closely related
and the Philistine war occurred immediately after David's enthronement in the city. In any event, it is significant that the
Philistines decided to move against David at this point. Quite
evidently David's previous enthronement at Hebron was not considered a serious threat to Philistine interest. The nation of Israel was badly divided and anarchy characterized political
trends in the north. But when David was recognized as king
over all the land, and unification was secure, the Philistines were
made aware of the fact that their success in the highlands was
perhaps coming to an end. They, therefore, decided to attack
immediately to prevent Israel from further uniting their military forces.

2. The Battle Described (5:18-25)

The attack of the Philistines occurred in two phases. The
first is described in verses 18 through 21. Their original plan
was to approach Jerusalem from the southwest through the
valley of Rephaim (cf. Isa. 17:5). Notice that David immediately asked divine help. The habits David had formed as a
young soldier now played an important role in his life as king.
The Lord's answer was affirmative with the guarantee of victory
(v. 19). David met the enemy at Baal-perazim and there defeated
them. The encounter was an overwhelming victory for David
and his men for the Philistines were so badly routed that they
even left their images behind to be burned (v. 21).[79] The
second attack started from the same location (v. 22). This time
David was instructed by the Lord to use a well-known tactic of
outflanking the enemy. He was commanded to send a group of
men behind the enemy, thus making them vulnerable to attacks
on all sides (vv. 23-25). Again, the effort was a complete success for David. The Philistines were routed from Geba to Gezer
(v. 25).[80]

---

[79]The Hebrew word for "images" is 'āṣāḇ ("idol," cf. I Sam. 31:9). In
the parallel passage the term used in 'eloh'm (I Chron. 14:12).

[80]The text of verse 25 reads Geba, but this is generally regarded as a
scribal error, for both the LXX and I Chron. 14:16 read Gibeon. The location of Gibeon (northwest of Jerusalem) also favors this latter reading.

Wilderness of Judah. Levant Photo Service

3. *The Importance of the Victory*

David's victory over the Philistines at this stage was significant for several reasons. It indicated that the capital had been fully established and Israel was now a force with which to be reckoned. The victory certainly must have produced a great deal of confidence in the people regarding David's ability. Finally, this was an encouragement to David and a stabilizing factor among his officials.

II. A NEW HOME FOR THE ARK (6:1-23)

A. *An Incomplete Journey* (6:1-11; cf. I Chron. 13—16)

David planned that Jerusalem should not only be the political center of the kingdom, but the religious as well. In order to establish Jerusalem as the spiritual center of Israelite life, the

presence of the Ark was needed. The Ark, at this time, was located in the town of Baale of Judah (v. 2), which is another
name for the city of Kirjath-jearim (Josh. 15:9; I Chron. 13:6).
Evidently the Ark had remained at Kirjath-jearim ever since the
day of its return from the Philistines after the death of Eli
(I Sam. 7.1). With the destruction of Shiloh by the Philistines and
the death of the priests located at Nob, Kirjath-jearim apparently was the best suited location for the Ark during these troubled
years. One writer has suggested that the Ark was, in effect, under Philistine suzerainty during this time. The following discussion is interesting although not conclusive:

> We know that Kirjath-jearim was a member of the Gibeonite
> league (Josh. 9:17) and therefore a predominantly Amorite or
> Canaanite city; and it is probable therefore that it remained
> under Philistine suzerainty, although not situated in Philistine
> territory, even when Saul had succeeded in a large measure
> in throwing off the Philistine yoke. . . . Its ultimate recovery
> stands in close connection with David's repeated victories over
> the Philistines.[81]

Before the Ark was brought to Jerusalem, David's plan was
discussed with the leaders of Israel (cf. I Chron. 13:1-4). He
evidently had their complete consent before initiating this important project. Unfortunately, while David sought general counsel on moving the Ark, he failed to take care in the method
employed in its removal. The Ark was placed on a "new cart"
(v. 3) and brought out of the house of Abinadab which was located on a hill.[82] According to the law, the Ark was to be carried by the sons of Kohath (Num. 4:4-15; 7:9), and not borne
on a cart or other vehicle (Exod. 25:14-15; Num. 4:5-8). It will
be remembered that the Philistines returned the Ark on a new
cart; but this, of course, was an entirely different situation (cf.
I Sam. 6:7-14). Everything went well for David until the cart
reached the rough, rocky threshing floor of Nachon. As the Ark

---

[81]S. Goldman, op. cit., p. 220.
[82]The Hebrew word gb'h should probably be translated here rather than
made a proper name. The word means "hill" and is so translated elsewhere
(Gen. 49:26; Exod. 17:9, etc.).

shook upon the cart, Uzzah put his hand on it to steady it. This
was a serious violation of the law (Num. 4:15). It was clear that
only the priest and the descendants of Aaron were permitted to
handle the Ark. The violation here was similar to that which was
recorded at Beth-shemesh (I Sam. 6:19). As a result of this,
Uzzah was slain by God and the failure of David's plan brought
anger to him (v. 8). Remembering the tragedy at Beth-shemesh,
David would not move the Ark any further, but placed it in the
house of Obed-edom, the Gittite, who was a Levite of the family
of Korah and later one of the doorkeepers of the Ark (cf.
I Chron. 15:18-24; 26:4 ff.).

B. *The Triumphal March* (6:12-23)

After a delay of three months David returned to the house of
Obed-edom to secure the Ark and attempt to take it to Jerusalem.
The Ark was moved only six paces in order to be sure that all
was in accordance with the Lord's will. Following this, a sacrifice was given to God in thanksgiving (v. 13). The removal of
the Ark to Jerusalem was no small affair in the eyes of David.
He was overwhelmed with emotion as he thought of the spiritual
and practical implications of its presence in Jerusalem. The evidence of his joy is witnessed in the fact that he "danced" before
the Lord with all his might. The Hebrew word for "danced" is
mekarkēr which literally means to "whirl" or to "whirl around."
While the occasion was a thrilling one for David, it was somewhat less than that for David's wife, Michal. When she saw
David leaping and dancing before the Lord, she viewed this as
a despicable act in the eyes of the public (v. 16). It is interesting to note that the historian identified her as "Saul's daughter"
rather than the wife of David. Perhaps her actions and attitude
in this situation were more characteristic of her father than of
her husband. She may have objected to David's actions because
it was more common for the women to act this way than for the
men (cf. Exod. 15:20-21; Judg. 11:34; I Sam. 18:6). Her displeasure, however, was more likely tied in with her insensitivity
to the religious significance of this occasion. Her speeches to
David were characterized by sarcasm and bitterness (cf. v. 20).
This brought a quick and decisive response from David in which

he pointed out that he had no intention of changing his behavior purely on her behalf. He planned to continue to "play"
before the Lord,[83] and "be more vile than this" (better translated, "I will be more lightly esteemed than this"). As a result of
this estrangement, Michal had no children until the day of her
death (v. 23; cf. 20:3; I Chron. 15:29).

III. THE KING'S DESIRE (7:1-29)

A. *David's Proposal and God's Response* (7:1-17)

Only one thing troubled David as he viewed the situation in
Jerusalem after the Ark had been placed there. The Phoenicians
had built him a beautiful palace of cedar, but the dwelling place
of the Ark was quite unimpressive (vv. 1-2). It was David's desire that the Ark should rest in a temple worthy of its importance. In order to ascertain God's will in this matter, he consulted with Nathan, the prophet (vv. 2-3). While this is the first
mention of Nathan, he, in all probability, had an important role
in the court of David prior to this time, most likely in the capacity of an advisor. Later he figured prominently in the story of
Bathsheba (II Sam. 12:1 ff.) and in the determination of succes-
sion to the throne (I Kings 1:11 ff.). According to I Chronicles
29:29 he, along with Gad, was one of the chroniclers of David's
reign (cf. II Chron. 9:29). The answer that Nathan gave was
affirmative, but quite clearly too hasty. Nathan judged the arguments of David and considered them to be valid. That evening
the Lord spoke to Nathan and instructed him to return to David
with a negative answer, thus, not permitting him to construct
the temple at that time.

By studying this context, along with other passages, one is able
to discover at least four reasons why David's request was rejected: (1) A historical argument (v. 6). A sophisticated temple
had not been required up to this point, so why now? (2) Had
God asked for this (v. 7)? In other words, the request did not
come from the Lord, but from David alone. (3) He was not
permitted to build this temple because he had ". . . shed much

---

[83]The Hebrew is *sihaqti* from *sahaq*. This is the same word used in 2:14.

blood upon the earth" (I Chron. 22:8; 28:3). His many years as
a warrior involved him in the bloodshed of hundreds and therefore made his candidacy inappropriate for such an important
task. It is also possible that under David the temple might become a treasure house of war trophies (cf. I Sam. 17:54 with 21:
9). This was a common practice among the Philistines in whose
land he had dwelt for over a year (I Sam. 5). (4) It was too
soon to build the temple. David's judgment as to the security of
the city was evidently inaccurate. It is clear from I Kings 5:3-4
that the destruction of the city was indeed possible at this time
in David's life.

Nathan's conversation with the king on the next day must have
been a very difficult one for him. God's response was not wholly
negative, however, for David was reminded of the fact that he
was the recipient of a sovereign call (v. 8) and had survived to
this day because of divine protection (v. 9). In this he found
encouragement (v. 10). While David would not be permitted
to build a house for the Ark, the Lord promised him that a
greater house would be built which would be established forever (v. 13). The Davidic covenant was a very important af-
firmation of God's intention to complete that which He had
promised to Abraham (Gen. 12). This covenant consisted of
three essential elements: (1) a posterity (vv. 12, 13, 16), (2)
a throne (vv. 13, 16; cf. Luke 1:32) and (3) a kingdom (vv. 13,
16; cf. Luke 1:33). The nature and scope of this covenant are
such that their fulfillment could not have been realized in the
days of Solomon, but will find their ultimate fulfillment in Christ
through the establishment of His kingdom on earth (cf. Isa. 9:
6).

B. *Worship and Praise* (7:18-29)

The response of David is an exquisite example of true submission to God's will. Rather than mourning the loss of his well-con-
ceived plans, David rejoiced in the promise of future blessing.
In this section of the chapter David recognized the sovereignty
of his Lord and the right of God to change his plans. David
was also thoroughly convinced of the perfection with which God
controls the affairs of men. The whole history of Israel up to

this point was an evidence of God's inerrant working among His people (cf. v. 23 ff.). The attitude expressed by David should be that which characterizes all believers as God's will is clearly revealed. In the light of such humiliation, it is not difficult to see why God called David "a man after His own heart."

IV. A SUMMARY OF DAVID'S WARS (8:1-18)

While the wars of Saul were characteristically defensive in nature, the wars of David took on the character of being offensive and led to expansion of the borders of Israel. The chapter before us describes the successful campaigns of David as they related to the surrounding nations. It is evident that David took geography and natural resources into consideration as he planned the expansion of Israel's borders.

A. *The Defeat of Philistia and Moab* (8:1-2)

It is not surprising that David waged campaigns against the Philistines who were at this time Israel's most bitter enemies. He was successful in subduing them and confining their military activity to a small area. In addition, he took the town of Metheg-ammah which translated means "bridle of the mother city." This was another name for the city of Gath, which was one of the principal towns of the Philistine pentapolis (I Chron. 18:1).

The fact that David conducted a campaign against Moab indicates a change of attitude on his part concerning these people. He had previously enjoyed rather good relations with Moab as indicated by their willingness to provide asylum for David's parents when he was a fugitive from Saul (cf. I Sam. 22:3-4). The reason for David's change of attitude has been attributed to a deception on the part of the Moabites resulting in the death of David's parents; however, this tradition cannot be verified. According to verse 2 only one-third of the captives were permitted to live after David's victory.[84]

B. *Victory over the Arameans* (8:3-12)

Having subjected the Philistines to the west and the Moabites

---

[84]Cf. J. Davis, *Biblical Numerology*, p. 82.

to the east, David turned his attention to the north and the kingdom of the Arameans. One of the key areas was the kingdom of
Zobah, a small territory west of the Euphrates and northeast of
the city of Damascus. David's victory over King Hadadezer
helped to secure the northern borders of Israel and to provide a
buffer zone from enemies further north. David's efforts in that
area were very successful, leading to the capture of many horses
and chariots (v. 4). David "houghed" the chariot horses; that is,
the horses were disabled by cutting the back sinews of their
hind legs. This rendered the animals unfit for use in war (cf.
Josh. 11:6-9). David did, however, keep a hundred chariots out
of this booty (v. 4). To guarantee protection for the northern
borders of his kingdom he established garrisons near Damascus.
Notice that after these victories David seized the shields of
gold that belonged to the servants of Hadadezer and brought
them to Jerusalem. Could it be that these were taken as war
trophies? It is not impossible to conceive that among the interests of David in building a temple was to provide a place to store
trophies such as these.

C. *The Defeat of Edom* (8:13-14)

The Hebrew text indicates that David fought "Arameans in
the valley of salt" (v. 13). It is highly doubtful, however, that
the term "Aramean" is the correct one. The text of verse 13 appears to have suffered from a copyist error. On this point almost
all commentators are agreed. According to I Chronicles 18:12,
the title of Psalm 40, and the immediate context of this chapter,
Edom, not Syria, was the enemy defeated in the valley of salt.
The geographic proximity of the valley of salt to Edom is clearly
seen in II Kings 14:7. In the light of the foregoing evidence,
most scholars feel that the text should read Edomites rather than
Arameans. A careful study of the Hebrew letters indicates a
confusion of *dalet* and *resh* by the scribes. David's victory over
the Edomites in the territory south of the Dead Sea was important because it gave David access to the very rich copper
mines of the Arabah. Furthermore, it placed control of important
trade routes from the gulf of Aqaba in David's hands.

D. *David's Court Officials* (8:15-18)

In addition to being a skillful warrior and a good leader, David was a successful organizer as evidenced by this portion of the text. The military organization was headed up by Joab, the son of Zeruiah (v. 16). The scribal organization within the royal court included a "recorder" (Heb. *mazkîr* — "rememberer") and a "scribe" (Heb. *sōpēr*). The particular functions of a recorder and the scribe apparently were different and most likely were parallel to similar Egyptian offices. Other texts indicate that the recorder was an important individual in the royal court (cf. II Kings 18:18-37; II Chron. 34:8; Esth. 6:1). According to verse 17 David had two priests over the land, Zadok and Ahimelech. The appointment of Ahimelech as one of the priests is interesting, for he was the son of Abiathar, the only one to escape Saul's senseless massacre of the priests of Nob (cf. I Sam. 22:11-20). Some scholars have felt that the appointment of Ahimelech to the high priesthood was to repay a debt to him or to salve a troubled conscience over the lie that caused the slaughter; however, this is not so indicated in the text. The personal bodyguard of the king was made up of two groups of men known as the Cherethites and Pelethites (v. 18; cf. 15:18; 20:7, 23; I Kings 1:38, 44; I Chron. 18:17). The Cherethites were many times associated with the Philistines and may have been part of that nation (I Sam. 30:14; cf. Ezek. 25:16; Zeph. 2:5).

V. DAVID AND MEPHIBOSHETH (9:1-13)

David's kindness to this surviving son of Jonathan is significant. This move on his part was prompted by two things: (1) The covenant which he had made with Jonathan, and (2) the attempt to end any conflict between his household and the household of Saul. The events described in this chapter probably took place about fourteen years after the death of Jonathan since Mephibosheth was then five years old (4:4) and now had a young son (v. 12). The kindness of David was genuine, however. It was a "kindness of God" (v. 3). Mephibosheth apparently was no threat to the throne of David, for he was lame in both feet (vv. 3, 13). Mephibosheth was brought to the royal court of David and there given food and shelter (v. 11).

VI. THE AMMONITE-SYRIAN WAR (10:1-19)

When David was a fugitive, he evidently was able to find asylum and protection among the Ammonites under Nahash (v. 2). When Nahash died, his son took the throne. David attempted to secure peaceful relations with him, but the advisors of the king interpreted this as an attempt to spy out the city and to ultimately overthrow it (v. 3). David's men were humiliated by having half their beards cut and half the garments cut away. The shame was so great that they were not able to return to Jerusalem until their beards had grown back (v. 5). The Ammonites were really in no position to encounter David in warfare by themselves, so they "hired" Arameans from the north from the kingdoms of Bethrehob and Zoba. According to I Chronicles 19:6 Hanun, king of the Ammonites, paid one thousand talents of silver to hire horsemen and chariots. This gives some indication of the crucial nature of the upcoming battle.

The first encounter with Joab and the troops of Israel ended in defeat for the Ammonite-Aramean coalition. Joab, by skillfully using his troops, was able to outflank them and defeat them. The Arameans no longer viewed the situation from the standpoint of mere professional obligation, for the security of their towns was now at stake. A second encounter followed which is described in verses 15 through the end of the chapter. Again Joab and his men were victorious over the Arameans as they marched down from the north. This victory completely humiliated the Ammonites and brought peace with the Arameans to the north (v. 19). Thus, David had secured all of the borders of Israel and expanded them so that the empire had now reached the greatest height of his career.

24 (II Samuel 11–14)

SHAME AND SORROW

The greatest victories are sometimes annulled by foolish mistakes. David's unparalleled success had made it possible for him to enjoy all the comforts of royal life. No longer did he need to be in the field of combat since capable leadership was provided by Joab and there were no more immediate serious threats to the kingdom. It was in these circumstances that David's greatest failure occurred (cf. I Kings 15:5). It was tragic indeed that such a brilliant career should be marred in this manner; however, it is well known that Satan is most effective in his approaches when the believer is comfortable and successful.

I. DAVID'S SIN WITH BATHSHEBA (11:1–12:31)

A. *The Occasion of the Sin* (11:1)

That David was free from military responsibility because of his previous successes is made clear in the first verse of this chapter. Under David's leadership the armies of Israel had soundly defeated the Ammonite-Syrian coalition (10:13-19). When David left the battlefield, the victory was clearly Israel's. The only operation that remained was the final conquest of the capital city of the Ammonites, Rabbah (11:1). The information provided in verse 1 indicates that the time when David committed this sin was the spring of the year. The Authorized Version implies that this event took place "after the year was expired," but this is a poor translation of the original. A better rendering would be "after the return of the year" (Heb. *litšûḇat haššānāh*). The precise meaning of this expression is made even clearer by the next clause, which states that this was the time of the year "when kings go forth to battle."[85] It was during the spring that armies normally conducted their campaigns because

---

[85]For another view on this problem, see S. Goldman, *op. cit.*, pp. 243-244.

of the favorable weather and the availability of food (cf. I Kings 20:22, 26). The winter season was cold and wet, thus making many roads impassable.

While the main armies of Israel surrounded the city of Rabbah, smaller army units were sent throughout the land and they "wasted the country of the children of Ammon" (I Chron. 20:1). "After the custom of ancient warfare, while the army was besieging Rabbah, foraging parties were sent out to lay waste the country and cut off any stragglers. Cf. I Sam. 13:17-18."[86]

B. *The Sequence of Sin* (11:2-5)

It was toward evening, following David's afternoon rest, that he saw Bathsheba washing herself and found her very attractive. David's palace was situated high on Mount Ophel which gave him a view over the many homes which were built along the slopes of that mountain. It was during these moments of idleness and inactivity that David was most severely tempted by Satan. One has well summarized the situation in this way:

> Satan chose this moment to bring upon the king of Israel a temptation that was to cause him deep humiliation and disgrace. David tragically forgot that there was an enemy greater than men. Feeling himself strong and secure against his earthly enemies, intoxicated by his prosperity and success, while receiving the plaudits of men, Israel's honored hero and saint was thrown off his guard. Imperceptibly the inner defenses of his soul had weakened, until he yielded to a temptation that transformed him into a shameless sinner.[87]

The sequence of David's sin is most instructive. There are three key verbs which describe the process by which David was led into adultery. According to verse 2 he *saw* a woman washing herself. The next step was *inquiry* (v. 3) by which he discovered not only the name of the woman, but also the fact that she was married to Uriah the Hittite. The third step, recorded

---

[86]F. Gardner, "II Samuel," *Ellicott's Commentary on the Whole Bible* (Grand Rapids: Zondervan Publishing House, n.d.), II, p. 471.
[87]Francis Nichol, *op. cit.*, p. 646.

in verse 4, was his *participation* in sin. The sequence of sin described in these verses is not new. Looking back to the garden of
Eden one can see a similar sequence described. In Genesis 3:6
we are told that Eve "*saw*" that the tree was good for food and
she "*desired*" to have a portion. Finally she "*took*" of the fruit.
This sin was not consummated in seclusion, for Adam later became involved (Gen. 3:6). The result was the loss of purity,
glory, and fellowship with God (Gen. 3:7). The same sequence
is also attested in the story of Achan recorded in Joshua 7.
Achan, we are told, "*saw*" the various objects in the destroyed city
of Jericho. He found these very attractive and "*coveted them*"
and then "*took*" them (Josh. 7:21). This, of course, led to disaster
and death for him and for the members of his family. In the light
of the above examples of temptation, failure and sin, one is reminded of the admonition of James that "when lust hath conceived it bringeth forth sin" (James 1:15). David's sin was not
one of ignorance, for having inquired as to the identity of the
young lady, he was informed that she was the wife of Uriah, one
of David's best soldiers (cf. II Sam. 23:39). The fact that David
knew that Bathsheba was married made this sin even greater.
Verse 4 indicates that David sent messengers to take Bathsheba.
Commentators are not sure that this was a seizure by force. Some
are inclined to believe that Bathsheba's bathing in view of the
royal palace was intentional and that her actions were characterized by easy submission to all of David's commands. Others
feel that Bathsheba bathed in privacy and David's view of her
was a mere accident. According to this view, she was taken by
force to be part of the royal harem of the king. While Bathsheba was obviously a woman of beauty there is some evidence
that she lacked discretion on various occasions (cf. I Kings 2:13-
22). In a short time it became clear that the sin could no longer
be completely concealed or forgotten (v. 5). The sin that David
committed was, according to law, punishable by death (cf. Lev.
20:10).

C. *The Results of Sin* (11:6-27)

Unwilling to face up to his sin and confess it, David attempted
to cover up that which he had done. Through the process of de-

ceit and evil maneuvers he attempted to make the conception
look perfectly natural. The first attempt of David is recorded in
verses 6 through 12. When Uriah returned from Ammonite territory he was taken to the king's palace and given gifts from the
king to take home, but Uriah refused the liberty offered to him
and remained at the king's house. Verse 11 gives the impression
that Uriah refused the king's offer on the grounds of inequity.
His fellow soldiers were out in the field suffering hardship, so
why should he enjoy such luxury and ease? The second attempt of David to get Uriah home is recorded in verse 13. This
time he permitted Uriah to eat with him and in the process
made him drunk, but this again failed for Uriah refused to return to his home. The persistent refusal of Uriah to return home
has raised suspicion in the minds of some as to whether or not
Uriah had been informed of the situation.

There is no question that Uriah was a capable soldier and one
of David's best. That he was a Hittite might indicate that he was
hired as a mercenary soldier, a professional with outstanding
skill. It is also possible, of course, that he was a proselyte to the
Israelite faith.

In any event, scholars are divided as to whether or not Uriah
had been informed with regard to David's relationship to Bathsheba. One writer says, "It is quite unnecessary to suppose that
Uriah had any suspicion of what had been done. His conduct
and language is simply that of a brave, frank, generous-hearted
soldier."[88] However, it appears more likely that Uriah may have
known of his wife's unfaithfulness. "Her visit to David was
known to the palace servants, and it is unlikely that David's
court was more discreet and less addicted to malicious gossip
than royal courts have been throughout all history."[89]

The third attempt of David to cover up his sin was the resort
to murder. The accomplishment of this task is described in verse
15 and following. By means of a royal letter Joab was commanded to place Uriah in the most difficult battle, so as to guarantee his death. Joab accomplished this goal by preparing an

---

[88]F. Gardner, op. cit., p. 471.
[89]S. Goldman, op. cit., p. 245. See also C. F. Keil and F. Delitzsch,
op. cit., p. 384.

attack against the city gate of Rabbah which was probably the most heavily defended part of the city (v. 23). This led to the death of Uriah. It appears that David, at this point, had lowered himself to the evil devices of his predecessor, King Saul. Saul earlier had attempted to take the life of David by similar maneuverings (I Sam. 18:25). When Bathsheba heard of her husband's death, "she mourned" (v. 26). As to the precise nature of this sorrow, Adam Clarke observes "the whole of her conduct indicates that she observed form without feeling the power of sorrow. She lost a captain and got a king for her spouse; this must have been deep infliction indeed, and therefore . . . 'she shed reluctant tears, and forced out groans from a joyful heart.' "[90] Following the period of mourning[91] she became the wife of David (v. 27). While it might appear that the devices of David had concealed his sin before the general public, God, who is omniscient, knew of the whole affair (v. 27).

D. *The Confession of Sin* (12:1-25)

1. *Nathan's Message* (12:1-14)

The very fact that David's sin and subsequent repentance are recorded in such detail is, in itself, quite unique as viewed from the vantage point of ancient Near Eastern literature generally. The record of David's failure is perhaps one of the strongest proofs of divine inspiration of Scripture. It was not normal for scribes to record the failure of ancient Near Eastern monarchs. Furthermore, the particular ethic conveyed in these chapters is likewise unique. To the eastern mind, for a king to take the wife of a subject was quite normal and considered as within the rights of an absolute sovereign. The fact of the matter is, few kings of the ancient Near East would have taken the trouble to attempt to conceal such sin. The fact that David went to great lengths indicates that Israel was dominated by moral principles far superior to those of her neighbors. It is generally agreed that

---

[90]*Clarke's Commentary* (New York: Carlton and Phillips, 1854), II, p. 336.

[91]The usual period of mourning was seven days (cf. Gen. 50:10; I Sam. 31:13).

the appearance of Nathan before David took place approximately one year after his marriage to Bathsheba (cf. 11:27 with 12: 14-15). For David, that year was one of the most bitter and frustrating in all his life. Psalm 32 appears to be a reference to these events, and verses 3 and 4 are very vivid descriptions of the effects that concealed sin has on one's life.

a. *The method of approach* (12:1-6). Nathan's approach to David on this very difficult occasion was both skillful and effective. With the use of a parable[92] he was able to both reveal David's sin and allow David to indict himself. The illustration was an appropriate one, for David knew how attached one could become to a lamb as a pet since he had been a shepherd for a good part of his life. It is also obvious that Nathan was employing David's knowledge of the law to make his sin clear. As Nathan described the arrogance of the rich man who seized that precious new lamb from the poor man, one can imagine the indignant response of David. In effect, Nathan was describing David's seizure of Bathsheba, who was precious to Uriah.

b. *The application* (12:7-12). Once David had recognized the injustice involved in the parable, Nathan was then prepared to make the application to David. In very clear, concise language he told David, "Thou art the man" (v. 7). This was no easy task for Nathan who had been with David for many years. He acted here as a true prophet in the exposure of sin (cf. Mic. 3:8). As a result of David's sin the Lord had promised a twofold punishment upon him and his household. First of all, during his lifetime his house would be characterized by rebellion and sin (vv. 11-13). The second phase of divine punishment involved the death of that child born through adultery (v. 14). While some might consider the punishment given by God to have been unjust, it should be remembered that David had committed two sins both of which required the death penalty (adultery, Lev. 20:10, and murder, Lev. 24:17). Therefore, the response of God was a just and merciful one.

c. *The confession* (12:13-14). David's confession must be regarded as genuine. He made no excuses for his sin and did not

---

[92]Note the use of parables elsewhere: 14:2-11; I Kings 20:35-41.

attempt to conceal his guilt any longer. The full expression of David's confession can be studied in Psalm 51, which is an important commentary on verse 13.

The whole story of David's temptation, fall, and punishment should not be a cause for despair, but instruction in the righteousness of God and His mercy toward the sinner. David's ". . . . fall, as St. Augustine has said, should put upon their guard those who have not fallen, and save from despair those who have."[93]

2. Death and Life (12:15-25)

After Nathan's departure, the child born to Bathsheba became very sick and ultimately died. David concluded the fasting period and then arose to look toward the future. There does not appear to be any bitterness in his heart; on the contrary, this tragedy led him to bend the knee in worship to his God (v. 20). By Bathsheba David was given another son, whose name is familiar to all students of the Old Testament, Solomon (vv. 24-25).

E. The Defeat of Rabbah (12:26-31)

This portion of the chapter resumes the narrative begun in Chapters 10 and 11 (verse 1). The material in the remaining part of Chapter 11 and the early part of Chapter 12 is therefore parenthetical. It is interesting to note that David's sin with Bathsheba does not appear in the parallel Chronicles account. Joab was able to complete the siege of the capital city and take it. He called David to the site of Rabbah so that David might enter the city and be declared the victor over that town lest Joab receive national recognition for the victory (v. 28). The victory over this city was significant, and involved the capture of many precious objects (v. 30). Verse 31, which describes the activities of David following this victory, presents a difficult problem. The Hebrew text is not entirely clear as to the nature of David's activity. Two views have emerged regarding the interpretation of the passage. The first view considers the implements mentioned as instruments of torture and death. The second clause of

---

[93]F. Gardner, op. cit., p. 471.

the verse would then be translated "he sawed them in pieces with the saw and with iron harrows." If this translation is adopted, it is necessary to make a change in the Hebrew text, for as it stands the text literally reads *wayyāśem bammegērāh* ("and he put them under saws"). To arrive at the above translation, the expression *wayyāśem* would need to be changed so as to read *wayyāśar* (from the root *śûr*).[94] The above translation seems to be the one adopted by the writer of Chronicles (cf. I Chron. 20:3). This, in effect, means that David punished the Ammonites with bodily mutilation. Many have objected to this conclusion. As one commentator observes, "such cruelties would be in accord with the common customs of the time, but not with David's character."[95]

The other view is that the Hebrew text should remain as it presently stands in the Samuel passage and read, "and he appointed to labor with saws"; that is, the Ammonites were put to various forms of slave labor.[96]

II. AMNON AND TAMAR (13:1-39)

The events recorded in this chapter most likely took place after David's marriage with Bathsheba and the war with the Ammonites. The events described in the following chapters relate to the history of David's court and the tragedies which followed his sin with Bathsheba. There is no question as to the cause and effect relationship between David's sin on the one hand, and these events as punishment on the other.

A. Amnon's Crime (13:1-22)

The story of Absalom, Tamar, and Amnon is tragic and disheartening. Unfortunately, we cannot claim that such events occurred only once in history. The tragedies of this chapter have been repeated many times since the days of David. Men have refused the counsel of Scripture and thus have paid the price of sin and its immediate consequences.

From II Samuel 3:3 we know Absalom and Tamar were the

---

[94]See C. F. Keil and F. Delitzsch, *op. cit.*, p. 395.
[95]Francis Nichol, *op. cit.*, p. 654.
[96]*Ibid.*

children of Maacah, daughter of Talmai, king of Geshur. Absalom, according to this verse, had been born to David in Hebron. Amnon was the oldest son of David, by Ahinoam, the Jezreelite (3:2).

The story that follows describes Amnon's love for Tamar, the beautiful sister of his step-brother, Absalom. His love for her, however, was not genuine. It involved no more than infatuation and sensuous desire. His desires for her became so strong that he became ill. Her upright behavior prevented an easy approach. It was through the advice of a "friend" that he was able to deceive her and commit his sin (v. 3 ff.). When word of his evil deed reached David, he was extremely angry, but found himself incapable of appropriate and stern discipline. This, of course, is understandable in the light of his own failures in the area of moral restraint (cf. v. 21). Absalom developed a bitter hatred for Amnon and for two years sought an occasion to take his life (vv. 22-23).

B. *Absalom's Revenge* (13:23-39)

The hatred that Absalom had for Amnon was precipitated mainly by Amnon's abuse of his sister; however, it is not impossible that Absalom's hatred for him also involved the fact that Amnon was the first-born and, therefore, probably the heir to the throne after David. When the occasion finally presented itself, Absalom took the necessary steps to bring the life of Amnon to an end. When David received word of this tragedy, he tore his garments and prostrated himself to the ground in sorrow (v. 31). The comfort offered by Jonadab was something short of genuine consolation (vv. 32-33). Absalom, recognizing the possibility of the king's wrath, fled from the royal court and went to Talmai, king of Geshur (v. 37). David's mourning lasted over a long period of time and his separation from Absalom continued for a period of approximately three years (v. 38).

III. THE RETURN OF ABSALOM (14:1-33)

A. *Joab's Plot* (14:1-20)

Joab had great concern for the disposition of David. David's broken heart and despondent countenance would have a disas-

Entrance to Tomb 302 at Tekoa. Used in the Iron II (900-600 B.C.) and Roman Periods. Courtesy Tekoa Archaeological Expedition

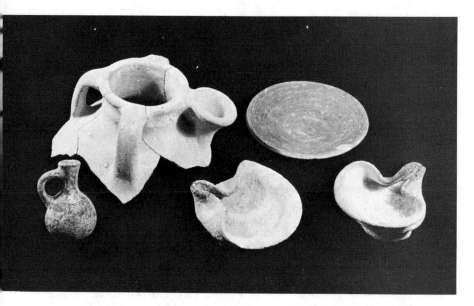

Iron Age II Pottery and Lamps from Tomb 302 at Tekoa. Excavated in 1968. Courtesy Tekoa Archaeological Expedition

1968 Tomb Excavations at Tekoa under the supervision of the author. Courtesy Tekoa Archaeological Expedition

trous effect on the morale of both the armies and the people of Israel. He therefore took immediate steps to reconcile the two. This was once again done by the use of a parable.

In order to approach David in a subtle manner so as not to reveal his own intentions, Joab sent to Tekoa and there sought out "a wise woman." It is interesting to observe the mention of Tekoa here and in 23:26. Tekoa was a rather important site during this period of time. The city had a long history in Scripture and, of course, is most well known to us as the home town of the prophet Amos. The mound of Tekoa lies approximately five miles south of Bethlehem and for centuries has remained in ruins. It was not until 1968 when the Tekoa Archaeological Expedition first began excavations at the site that some of the history of this significant town was illuminated. It was the author's privilege to be supervisor of Field III in that expedition, which involved the excavation of the ancient tombs. In addition to work done on the churches on the top of the mound, five tombs were excavated, some of which dated back to the ninth century B.C. A fine collection of pottery indicated rather extensive occupation of the site during the days of the prophet Amos.[97]

The parable given by the wise woman was immediately recognized by David as a device of Joab to reconcile David and Absalom (v. 19). David, however, did not appear to be greatly disturbed by the fact that Joab used this woman to convey his feelings to him.

B. *The Return and Restoration of Absalom* (14:21-33)

David recognized the effect that Absalom's separation was having on his own life. With reservation he agreed to bring Absalom back to Jerusalem again. This was done, but the restoration was somewhat incomplete. For two years Absalom did not enjoy the privilege of entering the royal court of David (cf. vv. 24, 28).

---

[97]For further information on the Tekoa excavations see Martin H. Heicksen, "Tekoa: Excavations in 1968," *Grace Journal*, X, 2 (Spring, 1969), pp. 3 ff. Also John J. Davis, "Tombs Tell Tales," *Brethren Missionary Herald*, XXXI, 10, p. 16 ff.

Mound of Tekoa, home of the "wise woman" who helped Joab (II Sam. 14:2) and of Ira, one of David's "mighty men" (II Sam. 23:26). Excavations were begun here in 1968 under the Tekoa Archaeological Expedition, Martin H. Heicksen, Director. Courtesy Tekoa Archaeological Expedition

Finally, Joab stepped in again and encouraged the king to completely restore Absalom. David finally agreed to forgive Absalom of the past deed and permit him full court privileges (v. 33). What appeared to be a step toward peace later turned out to be the first step in the development of another tragedy in the royal court of David.

25

TURMOIL IN JERUSALEM

The concluding chapters of II Samuel are filled with the misfortune that characterized the last days of David's reign. The full effects of Nathan's prophecy were now being realized (cf. II Sam. 12:1 ff.). The royal court experienced insurrection, disappointment, and sorrow. The rebellion of Absalom and the humiliation of David described in the chapters that follow were fully anticipated in Nathan's prophecy (cf. II Sam. 12:1 ff.). It is important to observe that the prophetic statements of Nathan were not vague generalities, but were explicit and to the point. David not only experienced rebellion within his own household, but public humiliation brought by several individuals. The greatest turmoil experienced by David was not from the armies that surrounded Israel, but from the tension and anarchy from within. Some of this was due to his own failure in disciplining his sons, and much of it was due to the effects of his sin which was quite clearly a turning point in his successful career. While David enjoyed the opportunity of gathering materials for the temple and securing the borders of Israel, it was not his lot to realize the blessing of peace and tranquillity in the royal court during the last years of his reign.

I. REVOLT AND HUMILIATION (15:1–19:8)

A. *The Insurrection Planned* (15:1-12)

Not long after the restoration of Absalom to the royal court, he sought every opportunity to capture the imagination and the hearts of the people. Verse 2 informs us that he rose up early and made a daily appearance at the gate where legal business was commonly conducted. When controversy arose he consistently took the side of the oppressed and used this occasion to raise questions about the judicial capabilities of his father (v. 3). Along with this was the constant suggestion that if he were made a judge in the land, justice would be more equitable (v. 4). Thus, after a period of time Absalom had gained a rather large following, especially among those who had opposed David from the beginning.

Verse 7 is problematic in that it indicates that a period of forty years transpired before Absalom brought about the full insurrection; however, it is clear that the number forty is not the best reading of the text at this point. The Lucian edition of the Septuagint and the Syriac read "four years" instead of forty. This is the number suggested by Josephus in *Antiquities*, VII. 9.1. The point at which these four years began was probably Absalom's return to Jerusalem. If this were the case, it would mean that two of these years were spent in turning the people's hearts from David (II Sam. 14:28).[98]

In order to have freedom and to make the insurrection successful, Absalom requested permission to return to Hebron to pay a vow made some years earlier (vv. 7-8). All of this, of course, was a subtle disguise to have freedom in planning the insurrection.[99] Rebellion against the throne was very carefully prepared and executed. While at Hebron, Absalom sent spies throughout the various tribes of Israel to encourage sympathy for his cause and to organize the insurrection. The right-hand man and advisor of Absalom was Ahithophel the Gilonite. This man had been David's counsellor for some years, but he evidently had never really supported the throne genuinely and this is understandable in the light of his relationship to Bathsheba. A comparison of II Samuel 11:3 and II Samuel 23:34 indicates that Ahithophel was the grandfather of Bathsheba. It is not impossible that ever since the violent death of Uriah, Ahithophel had been looking for an opportunity for revenge. With the rebellion of David's son, Absalom, his opportunity had arrived.

The insurrection of Absalom enjoyed a degree of success, at

---

[98]The Talmud reckoned the "forty years" from the time when the Israelites demanded a king. Ralbag (1288-1344) suggested the figure represented the time from David's anointing by Samuel. See S. Goldman, *op. cit.*, p. 275.

[99]One is reminded of the deceit employed by Amnon to accomplish evil goals (II Sam. 13:6-7).

least for a period of time. This success is not accounted for merely on the basis of the political skill or genius of Absalom. He was free to work this deceit because of the laxness of David toward his sons in matters of discipline (I Kings 1:6). It is also possible that in those years David lacked the resolute firmness that was needed for the implementation of consistent discipline. Furthermore, there most likely was a very strong anti-Davidic feeling in Hebron. Many people in Hebron had probably not forgiven David for changing the capital from Hebron to Jerusalem and took this occasion to express their dissatisfaction at that move. It was for this reason that Absalom returned to the place of his birth. There he could be assured of a sympathetic ear.

B. *The Flight of David* (15:13–17:29)

David's response to the news of Absalom's rebellion is somewhat surprising and puzzling. Could it be that such a brilliant king would be so easily deceived by the obvious actions and intentions of his son? Duff Cooper, an English author, acutely observes that David must have refused "to listen to what he did not want to hear. He could not bear to think that his lovely, charming son might be guilty of harboring thoughts of rebellion; and when evidence to that effect was brought to him he preferred to dismiss it."[100] When David was informed of the widespread discontent with his leadership and the organized insurrection of Absalom, he fled the city, perhaps recognizing that the strength of the opposition in Jerusalem would be more than he could overcome at that moment. Leaving quickly with his friends and faithful bodyguards, the Cherethites and Pelethites (15:18), the king began his long humiliating journey. This must have been one of the darkest moments in David's life, for his humiliation did not come at the hands of great Philistine kings or outstanding monarchs from Egypt, but from his own son whom he had restored to royal favor.

At first he considered the presence of the Ark of the Covenant very important and therefore took it with him (vv. 23-24); how-

---

[100]*David.* Quoted in S. Goldman, *op. cit.,* p. 277.

ever, it was later decided that the Ark could not guarantee success, and it was returned to Jerusalem. This act on the part of David indicated that he had now turned the whole situation over to God for final disposition. He was convinced that God would work out His will to perfection. When David heard that Ahithophel, one of his more capable advisors, had joined the rebellion, he employed the services of Hushai, an aged advisor and friend, to infiltrate Absalom's court organization. This was done in order that he might counteract the proposals of Ahithophel.

As David continued his journey from Jerusalem eastward, he was met by the servant of Mephibosheth whose name was Ziba. He brought a few gifts and two asses for David and the royal family, a small price to pay for advancement and recognition by the king. Ziba apparently convinced David that Mephibosheth had cast his lot with Absalom, a story that David should not have accepted immediately since he did not have the opportunity to confirm it, but the tension and pressure of the moment had dulled the keen judicial senses of David so that he believed the story without question and honored the request of the servant. Commentators have agreed that it is rather doubtful that Mephibosheth would have so easily joined the revolt of Absalom. As a cripple he had little to gain by being involved in a revolution of this type. Surely he did not suppose that friendship with Absalom would open up the way for his accession to the throne.

As David continued eastward to Bahurim he was met by Shimei, a member of Saul's household. He evidently stood on the hill that overlooked the road followed by David and his company and cast stones at the king and his servants (16:5-6). He cursed David, charging that he was "a bloody man and a man of Belial" (Heb. *'iš haddāmîm we'iš habbelîyā'al*). It could well be that Shimei was accusing David of the murders of Abner (3:27-39), Ish-bosheth (4:1-12), and Uriah (11:15-27). The patience and restraint that David showed on this occasion were most amazing indeed. One should recall the very opposite attitude in David's response to the slanderous words of Nabal (I Sam. 25:2 ff.). On that occasion he was prepared to take the life of that man without hesitation. It will be remembered that through the wisdom of Abigail he was spared the embarrassment of meaningless retaliation. That lesson had been well learned and the patience

exhibited on this occasion indicated that David had committed
the whole affair into the hands of his God. It is also possible that
David regarded the charges of Shimei as justified to the extent
that he had committed murder with regard to Uriah. Chapter
16 concludes with Absalom's entry into Jerusalem and the organization of his royal court (vv. 15-23).

That the rebellion of Absalom had been generally successful
and widespread is indicated by the response of the elders of
Israel to the suggestion of Ahithophel (17:4). They were prepared to accept the suggestion to slay King David and remove
any possibility of restoration to the throne. As one remembers
the Davidic covenant recorded in II Samuel 7, it becomes apparent that this situation must have been a tension-filled, drama-
packed one. Providentially the Lord took control of the situation
through the counsel of Hushai who advised Absalom in such a
way as to give David time to organize and to prepare for a military encounter with the forces of Absalom. The proposal of
Hushai seemed not only workable, but desirable in the eyes of
the elders. The two major points of Hushai's counterproposal
were (1) there was need of a larger army than Absalom had at
his command at this time. In other words, an encounter with
David with such a small army would result in a humiliating defeat for the young king. (2) Playing on the arrogance and pride
of the king, Hushai suggested that the king himself lead the
army into battle. This appeal to his vanity worked, and the result was that David had the additional time needed to organize
his own forces in defense of his throne (17:5-23). The humiliation of failure was too much for Ahithophel and he committed
suicide (v. 23).

C. The Death of Absalom (18:1–19:8)

Absalom was quite sure of a victory. He reorganized the armies under the leadership of Amasa (17:25) and had gathered a
considerable number of people together from the various tribes.
However, it is clear that Absalom had not calculated the continued popularity of David and the support which he had among
many of the tribes. David and his men gathered themselves together at the site known as Mahanaim, probably a fortified city

not far from the ford of Jabbok. In preparation for the encounter
David divided his men into three companies (18:2). The three-
pronged attack was a common military maneuver of this period
(cf. Judg. 7:16; I Sam. 11:11; 13:17). David gave specific instruction that Absalom, his son, should not be harmed if he participated in the battle (v. 5). As it turned out, the newly, and
probably poorly, organized armies of Absalom were no match for
the seasoned soldiers of David. A slaughter of over 20,000 men
was the result of this encounter (v. 7). More tragic for David,
however, was the death of Absalom. As Absalom rode upon a
mule, his head was caught in the branches of an oak tree and
while suspended in this tree he was slain by Joab's men (vv.
9-17). Joab, of course, was a ruthless, cold military leader. He
did not view Absalom as the son of David, but as an enemy of
David and a threat to his throne. With this in mind, he took the
life of Absalom in disobedience to David's specific command. It
might be pointed out that Absalom's death did not result from
excessively long hair which was caught in the tree as is usually
suggested. The text merely indicates that he was suspended
from the tree by his head (v. 9). David was quickly informed
of the victory and also of the tragic death of his son. The concluding words of Chapter 18 should be a sober reminder to all
believers that sin has far-reaching and tragic consequences. Surely David did not anticipate uttering the words recorded in verse
33 when he engaged in adulterous acts with Bathsheba. The
pitiful cries of David are a solemn warning that there is a price
attached to sin and disobedience.

The sorrow and mourning of David became a matter of concern of Joab. His sad disposition was apparently affecting the
morale of David's armies, and a stern rebuke from Joab helped
David to get control of himself and look toward the future (19:
1-8).

II. RETURN AND RESTORATION (19:9—21:14)

The return of David to Jerusalem and his restoration to the
throne were not a simple process. The bitter sentiments of some
of the people against David as encouraged by Absalom were
slow to die out. It took considerable diplomatic communication

to restore David in the eyes of many of his countrymen (19:9-40). In addition to this problem there was the developing political division between Israel in the north and the tribe of Judah to the south. This division had been developing over a long period of time. The viewpoints in this strife came out in the open as David prepared to return to Jerusalem and resume his authority. The two political parties were attempting to gain favor and recognition in the royal court. The return of David to Jerusalem was marked not only by victory and rejoicing, but also by tragedy and revolt. Joab, who did not appreciate competition for his position, took the life of Amasa, the military general under Absalom (20:4-12). Joab also pursued a man by the name of Sheba who evidently tried to organize another revolt against the throne. Sheba probably assumed that if Absalom could achieve success, he could use the same forces and the same sentiments to his own end. However, Sheba was captured and slain, thus was removed the final threat to the security of the throne (20:13-22).

Sometime in the latter days of David's reign the land was plagued by a famine which lasted for three years (21:1); however, it is evident from verse 7 that the events here narrated must have occurred after David had come to know Mephibosheth. The reason for the famine is given in the latter part of verse 1 of this chapter; namely, because Saul had slain the Gibeonites. This is the only reference to the fact that Saul had committed an offense against the Gibeonites. The details of Saul's action are not given, but his motives are (v. 2). Some feel that this is a reference to the slaying of the priests of Nob (I Sam. 22:18) to whom the Gibeonites were attached as laborers. In slaying the priests, Saul had destroyed their means of support and was, therefore, virtually guilty of slaying them. Others feel that Saul was merely trying to rid the land of the remnant of heathen in order that Israel and Judah might move and grow in more freedom. In any event, it should be observed that covenant-making was no small part of life in the ancient Near East. The covenant made by Joshua some four hundred years before Saul was still valid and had to be respected (cf. Josh. 9:15 ff.).

According to verse 2, the Gibeonites were descendants of the Amorites. This presents a problem because according to Joshua 9:7 and 11:19 the people of Gibeon were Hivites. In many listings of the native inhabitants of Palestine the Hivites are clearly distinguished from the Amorites (see Gen. 10:16-17; Josh. 9:1; 11:3; 12:8). The problem is probably resolved by recognizing that the term "Amorite" is often employed in a comprehensive sense somewhat equivalent to the word "Canaanite" as meaning any of the inhabitants of Canaan (cf. Gen. 15:16; Deut. 1:27). The term "Amorite" sometimes denotes more particularly the inhabitants of the hill country of Palestine as distinct from the Canaanites of the plain (Num. 13:29; Deut. 1:7, 20).

The Gibeonites came to David requiring restitution for the injustice done to them. They would not settle for a mere payment of silver or for the death of any Israelite except the sons of Saul (21:4-6). David probably recognized the legitimacy of their complaint and willingly turned over the sons of Saul to them. The question has been raised as to whether one can reconcile the death of Saul's sons with the command of Moses in Deuteronomy 24:16. Rabbi Jochanan's comment on this problem was, "It is better that a law of the Torah should be overridden than God's name should be publicly profaned (by the failure to expiate Saul's breach of the oath to the Gibeonites)."[101] However, it is more likely that Saul's sons had been directly implicated in the attack on the Gibeonites and therefore received just punishment for their own evil deeds.

III. CONFLICT WITH THE PHILISTINES (21:15-22)

The events described in these verses probably span a period from the revolt of Absalom to the last days of David. It is apparent that the Philistines took the occasion of Absalom's revolt and the subsequent confusion to attack the borders of Israel. The record of these battles is a summary of a number of encounters that took place during this period of time. The battle fought at Gob presents a problem with regard to information concerning the death of Goliath (v. 19). According to this verse, the man who killed Goliath, the Gittite, was Elhanan. It will be noted that the words "the brother of" are not part of the Hebrew text. This expression does occur in the parallel account of I Chronicles

---

[101]*Yebamoth.* Quoted in S. Goldman, *op. cit.,* p. 277.

20:5. To solve the problem of the reading of this verse in Samuel some have suggested that there were two Goliaths, having the same name and both descendants of the Gittites.[102] Most commentators, however, feel that the reading of the text in I Chronicles is the correct one and that the text of II Samuel suffers from a minor scribal omission.[103]

IV. APPENDIX (22:1–24:25)

A. A Psalm of Praise (22:1-51)

The psalm before us reflects the thinking of David in his later years. He was able to look back over the years of blessing and divine provision, giving him victories over his enemies and establishing his throne. This psalm appears as Psalm 18. Interestingly, verse 1 of this chapter provides the basis for the title of Psalm 18. This is a psalm of triumph and deliverance. There is recognition of David's problems and God's deliverance (vv. 2-21). The psalm also asserts the integrity of David and the just dealings of God with him throughout his career (vv. 22-46). While some have attempted to deny Davidic authorship to this psalm, the majority of commentators recognize the hand of David in its composition. The psalm clearly reflects the attitudes and the involvements of King David. There is no other individual who could have given such intimate expression to the frustrations and joys of kingship as expressed in this psalm.

B. David's Last Words (23:1-7)

The last words of David are not to be regarded as his final testament, which is recorded in I Kings 2:2 ff., but his last formal utterance and perhaps the last psalm which he composed. It is interesting that the Hebrew text of verse 1 uses the expression ne 'um dāwid. The Hebrew term ne 'um is generally employed to indicate a direct divine utterance or a message given through the prophets. The word is not usually employed to designate ordinary human speech, although false prophets many times em-

---

102See S. Goldman, op. cit., p. 324.
103C. F. Keil and F. Delitzsch, op. cit., p. 466.

ployed the word in order to give credibility to their message (cf. Jer. 23:31).

The identification of David as "the sweet psalmist of Israel" is interesting and informative. Some scholars have regarded this expression merely as an indication that David was the subject of many of the songs of Israel; however, in the light of the words that precede and follow this expression, it seems clear that authorship is involved. Furthermore, it is made clear in verse 2 that the songs of David were the result of divine inspiration.

C. A Gallery of Mighty Men (23:8-39)

The remainder of this chapter is occupied with a list of some of David's outstanding soldiers. This list also appears in I Chronicles 11:11-41 with slight variations. These were men who rendered to David outstanding service and were responsible for his numerous military successes. It is interesting to note that among the great men of David, Uriah the Hittite is listed (v. 39).

D. The Numbering of the People (24:1-25)

The first verse of this chapter presents a problem because of the parallel passage in I Chronicles 21:1-6. According to the Samuel passage it was the Lord who moved David to number the people of Israel. This assumes, of course, that the antecedent of the pronoun "he" is the Lord. In the parallel passage of Chronicles, however, it clearly states that Satan was the one who moved David to number the people (I Chron. 21:1). A number of suggested solutions have been given to this problem. One writer argues that it was the "anger of Jehovah" that prompted David to number the people of Israel and Judah.[104] This view takes the subject of the first independent clause and makes it the subject of the second independent clause. While this is remotely possible, it most certainly makes the grammar very awkward and strained. A second view translates the Hebrew word śāṭān found in I Chronicles 21:1 as "an adversary" rather than the personal name Satan. It was an adversary of David who prompted

---

[104]Abarbinel, quoted in John Gill, *An Exposition of the Old Testament* (London: Wm. H. Collingridge, 1853), II, p. 311.

him to muster the people together for warfare.[105] Those supporting this theory argue that there is no article prefix to the noun as in Job 1:6, 7, 8; 2:1, 2. The term, therefore, must have reference to someone other than Satan himself. They also point out that Hadad and Rezon were "satans" to both Solomon and Israel (I Kings 11:14-23, 25). It is the latter usage of the term that they feel the writer of Chronicles was employing. Other commentators have felt that it was Satan himself who initiated David's numbering of the people, perhaps in disobedience to a command of God.[106] Those holding this view point out that God could not be angry with David if He had moved David to commit this act. The final viewpoint proposed by scholars, and that which appears to be most popular, is that the Chronicles account and the Samuel account merely reflect two aspects of the same incident. Satan was the immediate cause of David's action, but, theologically speaking, God was the ultimate cause in that He did not prevent the incident from occurring. In other words, it was actually Satan who instigated the pride and ambition that led David to increase the size of his army, perhaps unnecessarily.[107] In the light of all factors involved, it appears that the last view is preferable.

Another problem associated with this passage is the nature of David's act. In what did David's sin consist? A number of suggestions have been given. Josephus felt that David forgot the commands of Moses in that he did not collect a half of a shekel for the Lord for every head counted.[108] Others have suggested that it was the attitude of David that brought God's anger and condemnation. David commanded the census out of an attitude of pride and vanity, and the purpose of the numbering was to serve selfish ends only. Others feel that David was over-expand-

[105]Arthur Hervey, "II Samuel," *The Holy Bible with Explanatory and Critical Commentary*, W. F. C. Cook, ed. (New York: Scribner, Armstrong & Co., n.d.), II, p. 458.

[106]Joseph Bensen, *Bensen's Commentary* (New York: Carlton and Porter, n.d.), I, pp. 948-949.

[107]See Francis Nichol, *op. cit.*, p. 710; F. Gardner, *op. cit.*, p. 507; and C. F. Keil and F. Delitzsch, *op. cit.*, p. 503.

[108]*Ant.* VII.13.1 (cf. Exod. 30:12).

ing his military potential and perhaps placing upon the people excessive burdens.

In any event, it is clear that God was dissatisfied with perhaps the motives, goals and the actions of David, and brought judgment. David, interestingly enough, was given a choice of punishment (v. 13). He selected the three days of pestilence and this resulted in the death of 70,000 men according to verse 15. The repentance of David and his sacrifice to the Lord caused the Lord to cease judgment upon the people and to have mercy upon David (vv. 16-25).

The book of II Samuel, therefore, concludes on a note of sorrow just as it began. David had enjoyed moments of great success and yet, in spite of his wisdom and political genius, as a father he failed within his own household. David's greatest heartaches came not from the enemies on the outside, but from his own family. It was not the weak hands of David that failed him, but a weak heart which allowed him to enter into an adulterous relationship with Bathsheba. The results of David's reign, however, were not all negative. It is very clear from a military and political point of view that David had fully established the kingdom of Israel. He had given its borders recognition and protection. He had achieved international respect and recognition for Israel in a very brief period of time. This great kingdom soon was to pass into the hands of Solomon, a young man with equal capabilities and gifts.

I KINGS 1-11

26

(I Kings 1–5)

SOLOMON: THE EARLY YEARS

The continuation and the conclusion of the story of the United Monarchy are found in the first eleven chapters of the Book of I Kings. The accounts of the death of David and the rise of Solomon are filled with intrigue and excitement. The early years of Solomon were golden years of prosperity and success. Solomon received a kingdom which was well established and internationally recognized; however, in the process of time, through the economic and physical exploitation of the land, Solomon's power and influence began to decline.

I. INTRODUCTION TO THE BOOKS OF KINGS

A. *The Title*

The Hebrew title to the books is *melākîm* ("kings") and, like I and II Samuel, they were originally one book. The books of Kings get their title from the type of leadership characteristic of that period. The Septuagint calls these books the Third and Fourth Books of the Kingdom. The First and Second Books of the Kingdom were the books of Samuel. Kings continued as an undivided book in the Hebrew text until the time of Daniel Bomberg (1516-1517). I Kings begins with the death of David and the accession of Solomon and concludes with the reign of Jehoram in Judah and Ahaziah in Israel. II Kings continues the account of Ahaziah's reign and concludes with the destruction of the kingdom of Judah.

B. *Author*

Ancient Jewish tradition found in the Talmud asserts that Jeremiah was the author of the books of Kings. This theory has some credibility, for there are striking similarities between parts of the Kings and material found in the book of Jeremiah (cf. II Kings 24:18–25:30 with Jer. 52). Also in favor of this theory is

327

the fact that there is no mention of Jeremiah himself in chapters which deal with Josiah and his successors. It is quite clear, however, that the major portion of material in the books of Kings represents a composite authorship. The final chapters of the books must have been written by someone other than Jeremiah, for Jeremiah was in Egypt at that time (cf. Jer. 43:1-8), and the description is that of one living in Babylon. The historian makes it plain that he had at least three sources for this history (I Kings 11:41; 14:19, 29). A number of individuals were associated with first-hand reports on specific material.[109]

Whoever the writer, it is quite clear that he wrote by divine inspiration and had uttered prophetic truth. No court historian normally would have included the failures and humiliations of King Solomon in the record. The balance, character and the theological content of the material indicate that the Holy Spirit guided in the ultimate production of the record.

C. The Purpose

The fundamental purpose of the books of Kings is to continue the history of the theocracy until its conclusion in the Babylonian exile. Even though the author's chief concern was with the Davidic line, he included considerable material which dealt with the fortunes and failures of the Northern Kingdom. The writer's approach to the subject matter was from the standpoint of the plans and purposes of God as they related to His chosen people. The writings are intensely theological and yet extremely practical. The books of Kings are very important to the Bible student because they give him the cultural and historical background of the ministry of Israel's great prophets.

D. Basic Outline of I Kings

1. *The Reign of Solomon* (1:1–11:43)
   a. Solomon's Accession to the Throne (1:1–2:11)
   b. Solomon's Establishment of the Kingdom (2:12–5:18)

---

[109]Nathan, Ahijah, and Iddo (II Chron. 9:29), Shemaiah and Iddo (II Chron. 12:15), Iddo (II Chron. 13:22), Isaiah (II Chron. 26:22; 32:32) and Jehu (I Kings 16:1).

II. SOLOMON'S ACCESSION TO THE THRONE (1:1–2:11)

A. *David's Illness* (1:1-4)

The chapter before us describes the last court intrigue of David's life. At this point he was extremely old and quite ill. According to II Samuel 5:4 he had reached the age of seventy years. As far as can be determined, he was the oldest of the Hebrew kings on record. King David was so weak at this time that he had to be put under the constant care of a young maid by the name of Abishag, a Shunammite (v. 3). It was probably clear to both David and his servants that his days were few in number.

B. *Adonijah's Attempt to Usurp the Throne* (1:5-53)

When Adonijah received word of the serious illness of his father, he immediately took steps to achieve recognition as Israel's next king. Verse 6 gives three reasons why he made his move toward the throne. First, his father had not "displeased him at any time in saying, Why hast thou done so?" Apparently David had never disciplined Adonijah and had never questioned his activities. Thus, he had a free hand in gathering about him court officials and court personnel in Jerusalem. Secondly, he was an attractive man, and such attractiveness would make him a desirable candidate for the throne. Thirdly, he was the oldest living son now that Absalom was dead. David's first-born son, Amnon, was killed by Absalom (II Sam. 13:28 ff.). Chileab (or Daniel, I Chron. 3:1) probably died at a rather young age since nothing is recorded of him. David's third son, Absalom, was slain by Joab's men in battle (II Sam. 18:15).

Adonijah must have commanded the interest of many important individuals. For example, he was able to gain the support of Joab, the captain of the host (v. 7). In addition to that, Abiathar the priest also supported him. Abiathar, it will be remembered, was the great-grandson of Eli (I Sam. 14:3; 22:20), who was descended from Ithamar, the son of Aaron (I Chron. 24:3). A number of court officials, however, refused to join in the proposed move of Adonijah. Those who remained faithful included Zadok the priest, Benaiah, Nathan the prophet, Shimei, and Rei (v. 8). This did not discourage Adonijah, and he proceeded to conduct a public sacrifice in En-rogel (v. 9).

When Nathan the prophet received word of the intentions of Adonijah, he immediately made an appeal to Bathsheba to intercede on the behalf of Solomon. Apparently David had, at an earlier time, solemnly promised to Bathsheba and perhaps to Nathan that Solomon would be the next king. This promise on the part of David might have been made at the time of Solomon's birth, or perhaps on the occasion of Absalom's rebellion and death. In any event, Bathsheba proceeded to inform David of the intentions of Adonijah and pleaded on Solomon's behalf. David recognized the danger at hand and called for Zadok the priest in order that Solomon might be properly anointed and declared Israel's next king (vv. 32-39). Zadok took the oil from the tabernacle and anointed Solomon (v. 39). This was then followed with the public proclamation of the Solomonic anointing and his accession to the throne (v. 40).

While this was going on, Adonijah had organized a banquet which included prominent people from Jerusalem, including Joab and those who supported his claims to the throne. His "ten shekel a plate fund raising dinner" was going along quite smoothly until the shouts of recognition for Solomon were heard outside the building. It was not long before the guests realized that they had committed themselves to a losing cause, and little by little they left the banquet (v. 49). It did not take Adonijah very long to realize that his attempts to take the throne were abortive and his life was now in danger. In order to secure mercy he fled to

the tabernacle and there caught hold on the horns of the altar
(v. 50). Solomon, evidently, did not consider Adonijah a serious
threat any longer and granted him mercy as long as he relin-
quished any further claims to the throne.

C. David's Charge to Solomon (2:1-11)

David's final admonitions to his son Solomon were, first of all,
spiritually and theologically oriented (vv. 1-4). David made it
clear that obedience to the Word of God was the key to prosperity (v. 3; cf. Josh. 1:8; Ps. 1:2). Following this admonition, he
cited certain individuals who should be removed from the royal
court in order that further trouble should not develop. Among
those to be removed was Joab who had murdered Absalom (II
Sam. 18:14 ff.) and Amasa (II Sam. 19:13; 20:8-10). Joab had
also supported Adonijah in his attempt to seize the throne
(I Kings 1:7). The second individual cited by David for punishment was Shimei (v. 8). David recalled the curses and the stones
thrown by Shimei when he had to flee during the rebellion of Absalom (II Sam. 16:5-13). Even though Shimei sought pardon
after the rebellion, it was possible that he might turn against the
throne again. David's instructions in this area were not all negative, however. He remembered the kindness of Barzillai, the man
who helped sustain him in those days of confusion and humiliation when he had to flee Jerusalem as a result of Absalom's revolt (II Sam. 19:31 ff.). Barzillai was to be given preferential
treatment as a reward for his faithfulness to the throne.

After a very eventful reign of approximately forty years (v.
11), David died and was buried in Jerusalem (v. 10; cf. Neh. 3:
15-16).

III. THE KINGDOM ESTABLISHED AND ENRICHED (2:12–5:18)

A. The Removal of David's Adversaries (2:12-46)

The first individual to fall under the punitive wrath of Solomon
was Adonijah, who had not ceased in his attempt to secure royal
recognition. This time Adonijah came to Bathsheba, Solomon's
mother, and requested that Abishag, one of David's concubines,

be given to him as a wife (vv. 13-17). Bathsheba, not fully understanding all the intentions of Adonijah, went to Solomon and
presented Adonijah's request. Solomon immediately recognized
the intentions of Adonijah. The harem of a king was the sole
property of his successor and a sign of royalty. Having already
failed in his first attempt to take the throne, Adonijah was attempting by a more subtle means to gain his objectives. Solomon
immediately recognized the plan and condemned him to death
(vv. 22-25).

Following this, Abiathar the priest was removed from office and
Zadok became the sole priest at this time (vv. 26, 27, 35). Joab heard of the executions and the moves of Solomon and decided to plead for mercy. He did this in the same manner as
Adonijah had done at an earlier time (cf. v. 28 with 1:50). To
take hold on the horns of the altar was to claim the right of sanctuary, but it should be noted that this right was denied to a wil-
ful murderer (cf. Exod. 21:14). Because of Joab's murders and
his participation in the revolt led by Adonijah, he, like Adonijah,
was slain (vv. 31-35). The last individual to fall under the wrath
of Solomon was Shimei. His death did not come merely as a result of his cursing David, but because of his refusal to follow special restrictions placed upon him by King Solomon (vv. 36-45).
The removal of these individuals cleared the way for a complete
rebuilding of the royal court and a guarantee of its firm establishment.

B. *Political Alliance with Egypt* (3:1-3)

It is interesting to compare the political and military strategies
of Israel's first kings. King Saul, on the one hand, was occupied
with defensive military measures for the most part. His reign
was characterized by reactions to Philistine raids and military
pressure put on Israel from other areas. David, on the other
hand, not only defended the territory which Israel held, but also
expanded her borders and secured those borders with the use of
a series of fortresses. David also initiated and expanded Israel's
commercial resources. Agreements with the Phoenicians regarding trade had been reached. David also used the process of
royal marriage for the purpose of securing royal alliances and

concluding treaties. Such a practice was common in the ancient Near East. It will be remembered that in the very early days of David's reign he employed this approach by marrying the daughter of Talmai, king of Geshur (II Sam. 3:3; I Chron. 3:2).

Solomon, however, brought to Israel its most complete and intricate organization. He initiated major changes in Israel's military system by introducing chariotry as an essential fighting force. As will be noted later, he organized the Northern Kingdom into twelve administrative districts to provide food for the royal court. Solomon expanded previous commercial contacts and created new commercial monopolies. He also embarked upon a very energetic building program which was carried out in various parts of the land.

The marriage of Solomon to Pharaoh's daughter is something of great significance (3:1). "As far as we know, there is no real example of Pharaoh's daughter given in marriage to a foreign royal house, although the pharaohs quite frequently married daughters of foreign rulers."[110] We know for example that Kadash-manharbe, king of Babylon, did ask for the hand of Akhenaton's daughter and was flatly refused in rather strong language. In Amarna Letter IV, the following words appear as an answer from King Akhenaton: ". . . from of old, a daughter of the king of Egypt has not been given to anyone."[111] The marriage of Solomon to Pharaoh's daughter, therefore, has important political and military implications. It indicates, on the one hand, that Egypt, under the leadership of the Twenty-first Dynasty, was extremely weak. On the other hand, it indicates the military and political superiority of the Solomonic empire over Egypt. The precise identity of Solomon's father-in-law in Egypt is not completely clear at this point. The most widely accepted candidate is Psusennes II who was the last king of the Twenty-first Dynasty. Malamat, however, suggests the possibility of Simanon, the pred-

---

[110]A. Malamat, "The Kingdom of David and Solomon in Its Contact with Egypt and Aram Naharaim," *The Biblical Archaeologist*, XXI (Dec., 1958), p. 97.

[111]Amarna Tablet EA, 4, II, 6-7, quoted in A. Malamat, *Ibid.*, p. 98. Cf. also A. Malamat, "Aspects of the Foreign Policies of David and Solomon," *Journal of Near Eastern Studies*, XXII, 1 (Jan., 1963), p. 10.

ecessor of Psusennes.[112] Further proof of Solomonic prestige is
seen in the dowry given to Solomon on the occasion of his marriage. The city of Gezer, which had been taken by the Egyptians, was used as a wedding gift (I Kings 9:16).

C. A Prayer for Wisdom (3:4-28)

While at Gibeon worshipping (v. 4), Solomon received a
dream in which the Lord asked him what he would desire (v.
5). In all probability this dream represented God's answer to a
previous request on the part of Solomon. The use of dreams as a
means of divine revelation was not uncommon either in this period or in later periods. Solomon's response included a recognition of God's faithfulness to the throne (v. 6), and perhaps most
significant, a recognition of his inexperience (v. 7). The expression "I am but a little child" does not mean that Solomon
was a young boy when he took the throne. Josephus, for example, asserted that Solomon was only fourteen years old at this
time.[113] This idea is not correct, for "little child" is merely an
assertion of humility and a recognition that from the standpoint
of experience, he was like a child. His principal request, as he
viewed the greatness of his task (v. 8), was that he might be
given "an understanding heart to judge thy people" (v. 9). It is
instructive, indeed, that Solomon brought to the throne a very
high view of the people of God. He looked up to his task, not
down to it. The attitude and request of Solomon pleased the
Lord and his prayer was answered (vv. 10-15). The proof of
God's blessing in Solomon's life and the fact that he had been
given the gift of practical wisdom is seen in the concluding
verses of this chapter which describe one of his first judicial
cases (vv. 16-28).

D. Organization of the Kingdom (4:1—5:18)

1. The King's Officials (4:1-20)

The court organization adopted by Solomon was principally
that established by David. The significant difference between

---

[112]"The Kingdom of David and Solomon in Its Contact with Egypt and
Aram Naharaim," p. 99.
[113]*Ant.*, VIII.7.8.

David's list of officers (II Sam. 8:16-18; 20:23-26) and Solomon's
is that the first officer in David's was the captain of the host,
whereas the first officer listed in Solomon's court was the priest
(v. 2). Basically, Solomon's organization of the royal court represented an expansion of the system established by David. One
of the offices was the "recorder" (v. 3) which Jehoshaphat held
during David's reign (I Chron. 18:15) and apparently continued
to hold into the reign of Solomon. This office was, in effect, that
of a court annalist whose duty it was to record events as they
occurred and who probably was responsible for the official archives of the realm (cf. II Kings 18:18-37; II Chron. 34:8). The
"captain of the hosts" was Benaiah (v. 4), with Zadok and Abiathar as the chief priests. Adoniram was set over the "tribute"
(v. 6), which is better translated "forced labor" or "levy." This
office was evidently established in the latter part of David's reign
(II Sam. 20:24), for his earlier list of offices does not include the
one here mentioned (cf. II Sam. 8:16-18).

Solomon organized the Northern Kingdom and Transjordan
into twelve districts headed up by one governor in each district.
The twelve districts had no consistent relationship to the original
division of land among the twelve tribes, but were related primarily to the twelve months of the year.[114] Each governor was
responsible for supplying the needs of the royal court for one
month (v. 7). In order to guarantee the fidelity of several of the
governors, his daughters were given to them as wives (cf. vv.
11, 15).

2. The Wealth of the Kingdom (4:21-28)

Solomon's prestige and power reached all the way from the
river Euphrates in the north to the border of Egypt (v. 21). The
amount of food required for one day in the royal court was so
significant that it was included in the official record found in this
chapter (vv. 22-23). Solomon's success was also witnessed in his
ability to guarantee property rights and secure peace for the
land (v. 25). His military strength and the expansion of the char-

---

[114]See Yohanan Aharoni and Michael Avi-Yonah, *The Macmillan Bible
Atlas* (New York: The Macmillan Co., 1968), p. 72.

iot forces were a particular characteristic of Solomonic organization. Verse 26 indicates that Solomon possessed "forty thousand
stalls of horses for his chariots." The parallel passage in II Chronicles 9:25 reads "four thousand." Quite evidently the Kings passage reflects a copyist's error and the better reading is "four thousand."

3. The Fame of the King (4:29-34)

While only a few proverbs of Solomon have actually been preserved, it seems clear from verse 32 that he was known for many
proverbs and songs. The fact that he had a keen interest and
understanding of natural phenomena, as noted in verse 33, might
be a clue to the authorship of both Ecclesiastes and the Song of
Solomon.

4. Building Preparations (5:1-18)

As Solomon began to make preparations for the building of
the temple, he was contacted by Hiram, king of Tyre, who had
had earlier trade agreements with David (v. 1; cf. II Sam. 5:11).
Since the land was now enjoying relative peace (vv. 3-4), it was
possible for Solomon to initiate and complete the building of
the temple. A formal written agreement was drawn up between
Solomon and Hiram including not only the exchange of materials,
but also laborers (cf. vv. 6-12 and II Chron. 2:11 ff.). Josephus
stated that copies of the letters between Hiram and Solomon
were still in existence in the days of Menandar (ca. 300 B.C.)
and could be seen in the archives of Tyre.[115] In order to guarantee success for the project, Solomon "raised a levy out of all Israel" (v. 13) and as far as can be determined this was the first
major levy ever raised from the tribes. During the reign of David, strangers were used in this manner (I Chron. 22:2), and apparently Israelites were used only in a limited way. It will be
remembered that Samuel warned Israel that such a policy would
result from monarchial leadership as Israel desired it (I Sam. 8:
16). The requirement for those taken in levy was that they were
to work one month out of three (v. 14). This was done in order

---

[115]*Ant.*, VIII.5.3.

that there would not be widespread discontent. Much of the skilled work, however, was done by Hiram's men who were known for their outstanding ability (vv. 6, 18). The use of the word "stonesquarers" (v. 18) is probably not the best translation of the Hebrew. The correct reading of the Hebrew text is "Giblites." These were the inhabitants of Gebal or Byblos (cf. Ezek. 27:9), an important coastal city of Phoenicia.

While Solomon achieved a high degree of organization and effective production, it led to rapid and widespread bureaucratization in his kingdom. This, in turn, led to the rapid decline of tribal rights and reduction of the force of covenant law. That Solomon's policies ultimately led to widespread discontent was made clear when Rehoboam took the throne after Solomon's death (cf. I Kings 12:3-4). While the days of Solomon were indeed the golden days of monarchial success, they were also days of personal and tribal humiliation. Solomon's success came at the high price of individual freedom and tribal sovereignty.

27 (I Kings 6–11)

SOLOMON: THE GREAT YEARS

The wealth and splendor of the Solomonic kingdom were unparalleled in Hebrew history. Solomon was successful not only in territorial expansion and the establishment of foreign alliances, but brought to Israel sophistication in government operations. The chapters before us give significant insight into the wealth and power of the kingdom of Israel during Solomon's reign. His great achievements included construction of the temple and a magnificent palace in Jerusalem, as well as other structures of note throughout the land. His commercial and domestic policies produced tremendous wealth and prestige within the kingdom. Solomon achieved a degree of international recognition which was never matched in the remaining years of Israel's history.

I. THE TEMPLE (6:1–9:25)

A. *The Date of Construction* (6:1)

The chronological information supplied in this verse is of great importance to Bible students. If it is numerically correct, the date of the exodus must be placed in the middle of the fifteenth century B.C. According to the information supplied, the fourth year of Solomon represented a point in time which was 480 years after the exodus from Egypt. The fourth year of Solomon is generally regarded as being 967/966 B.C. This being the case, the exodus would have taken place approximately 1445 B.C. This date, however, conflicts with what some scholars feel to be stronger evidence in favor of a thirteenth century B.C. date for the exodus. In the light of what they feel to be more compelling evidence, this verse is considered symbolic and the "four hundred eighty" merely represents twelve generations of forty years each and, according to this view, is not intended to be taken literally. However, this interpretation has serious weaknesses. In the first place, the text is in no way poetic or symbolical. It appears in a serious narrative portion and is a very important state-

Air View of Jerusalem showing the Temple area and Old City. Matson Photo Service

ment in the light of the subject matter discussed. Second, it is in agreement with other Biblical data regarding the time lapse between the exodus and the rise of the monarchy.[116] Third, while the Septuagint gives the figure 440 years instead of 480, the Hebrew text does not have any significant variants.[117] In the light of these considerations, therefore, it seems advisable to accept the numerical data as being accurate and dependable.

B. *Its Size and Appearance* (6:2–9:25)

The temple proper was 60 cubits long and 20 cubits wide (v. 2), exactly double the dimensions of the Tabernacle (cf. Exod. 26:16, 18). If the cubit is regarded as eighteen inches, then the floor plan of the temple would have been 90 x 30 feet. The temple proper was divided into two sections. The inner room or the most Holy Place was a cube measuring 20 x 20 x 20 cubits (6:16, 20). The other room or the outer chamber called the Holy Place measured 40 x 20 cubits.

The finishing work and decoration of the temple proper were nothing short of spectacular. The floor and walls were made of stone covered with cedar and then overlaid with gold (I Kings 6:16, 21, 22). Around the temple proper, on the two sides and back, special chambers were added (6:5-6). In front of the temple there was a porch which measured 20 cubits long and 10 cubits wide (6:3). Two large pillars stood in front of the temple which were given the names Jachin and Boaz (7:21).

Even though nothing remains of Solomon's temple in Jerusalem, one is able to reconstruct major portions of the temple on the basis of archaeological data. Excavations of the Oriental Institute of the University of Chicago at Tell Tainat (ancient Hattina) in Syria have recovered a small chapel dating to the eighth century B.C. This temple has some very similar features to those of the temple of Solomon.[118] Of even greater interest, however, is the

---

[116]See pp. 17-18.

[117]Josephus gives the figure variously as 592 or 612 (*Ant.*, VIII.3.1 and XX.10.1).

[118]See G. E. Wright, *Biblical Archaeology* (Philadelphia: The Westminster Press, 1957), p. 136 ff.

An isometric plan drawn by H. D. Hill depicting the residence (foreground) and chapel (background) of the eighth century B.C. rulers at
Tell Tainat. Courtesy of the Oriental Institute, University of Chicago

discovery of an Israelite (Kenite?) temple dating to the tenth
century B.C. at Tell Arad.

Together with its side rooms, it was a building over sixty-five
foot long, and forty-nine foot broad, occupying a vital part of
the relatively small citadel. The entrance was on the eastern

side, with the holy of holies toward the west. Its original plan
was simple and symmetric . . .[119]

The temple of Solomon was constructed with Phoenician skilled
labor and included a number of Phoenician influences; however,
the temple should not be regarded as solely Phoenician in its design. Its plan was probably based on the general layout of the
Tabernacle and its layout follows traditions associated with that
structure rather than contemporary cult centers.

In the Holy of Holies was placed the old Mosaic Ark of the
Covenant, with its two golden cherubims above the mercy seat.
The Ark had an added feature in Solomon's temple in that it was
placed between two additional figures of cherubim made of olive
wood and overlaid with gold (cf. 6:23, 28; II Chron. 3:10-13).
Inside the Holy Place was the altar of incense covered with cedar and overlaid with gold (6:20, 22; 7:48). Instead of the single
golden candlestick as in the Tabernacle, there were now ten. Five
were placed on one side and five on the other side of the Holy
Place. Instead of only one table of shewbread, there were now
ten, five on each side of the room with all utensils made of gold.
The inner court had the familiar brazen altar of burnt offering
and the "bronze sea" which, in effect, took the place of the "la-
ver" of the Tabernacle. It was given the name "moulten sea" because of its great size.[120]

In addition to the seven years used to complete the temple
(6:37-38), Solomon spent thirteen years constructing his own palace (7:1). The "house of the forest of Lebanon" mentioned in
verse 2 has been regarded by some as to have been a structure
built in the mountains of Lebanon. Others suppose that Solomon's house (v. 1), the house of the forest of Lebanon (v. 2),
and the house of Pharaoh's daughter (v. 8) were three distinct
and separate buildings in Jerusalem. Yet another view on these

[119]Yohanan Aharoni, "Arad: Its Inscriptions and Temple," *The Biblical
Archaeologist*, XXXI, 1 (Feb., 1968), p. 19.
[120]For further details on the temple and its furnishings see "Temple."
The International Standard Bible Encyclopedia, V, pp. 2930-2936, and
G. Ernest Wright, "The Steven's Reconstruction of the Solomonic Temple,"
The Biblical Archaeologist, XVIII, 2 (May, 1955). Also, Merrill F. Unger,
Archaeology and the Old Testament, pp. 228-234.

expressions is that they merely reflect three sections of the one
main palace known as the "king's house" (9:10). One thing is
clear, however, and that is that Solomon embarked upon a massive building program not only in Jerusalem, but in other parts
of the country as well. In I Kings 9:15 we are informed that
his building projects included Millo, the wall of Jerusalem, Hazor, Megiddo and Gezer. A great deal of archaeological light has
been shed on the work at Megiddo and particularly at Hazor.[121]

II. SOLOMON'S COMMERCIAL ENTERPRISES
(9:26–10:29)

According to I Kings 9:26-28 and 10:22 (II Chron. 8:17-18),
Solomon had an extensive fleet of ships located at Ezion-geber
which is located on the Gulf of Aqaba. In all probability the
port was under the supervision of Phoenicians who were known
for their shipbuilding capabilities (cf. 10:22). Archaeological
work conducted at Tell el-Kheleifeh or Biblical Ezion-geber indicates that it was not only extensively occupied in the days of
Solomon, but was used as a smelting operation. Among other
structures found at this site was a well-built structure with high
floors designed and used either as a storehouse or granary.[122]
Regarding the smelting activities carried on at Ezion-geber, Nelson Glueck says the following:

> . . . We should like to underscore the fact that industrial and
> metallurgical activities did indeed take place in the various
> periods of occupation of Tell el-Kheleifeh. Copper slag was
> definitely found in the excavations as well as remnants of copper
> implements and vessels. There was, however, little slag compared
> to the great masses of slag marking numerous Iron I and early
> Iron II copper mining and smelting sites in the Wadi Arabah
> where mining and smelting activities also were carried on in
> Middle Bronze I and late Chalcolithic times.

---

[121]See articles in the *Biblical Archaeologist* by Yigael Yadin: XIX, 1
(Feb., 1956); XX, 2 (May, 1957); XXXII, 3 (Sept., 1969). D. Ussishkin,
"King Solomon's Palace and Building 1723 in Megiddo," *Israel Exploration
Journal*, XVI, 3 (1966), pp. 174-186.

[122]Nelson Glueck, "Ezion-geber," *The Biblical Archaeologist*, XXVIII. 3
(Sept., 1965), p. 75.

A reconstruction drawing of the NE gate at Megiddo (Stratum IV).
Courtesy of the Oriental Institute, University of Chicago

A Pink-buff Clay Liver Model discovered at Megiddo (Stratum VII).
Courtesy of the Oriental Institute, University of Chicago

A Reconstruction of Building 338 at Megiddo as seen from the NE according to a drawing by L. C. Woolman. Courtesy of the Oriental Institute, University of Chicago

Limestone Altars, Offering Stands and Other Objects found at Megiddo dating to the eleventh century B.C. Courtesy of the Oriental Institute, University of Chicago

The small amount of slag at Tell el-Kheleifeh may be explained by the difference in metallurgical operations as carried out in Wadi Arabah and at Tell el-Kheleifeh. At the latter place, they were devoted, we believe, to remelting the globules of copper ore obtained through several metallurgical processes in the Wadi Arabah smelting sites, in order to shape them in more easily salable ingots or to pour the molten metal into molds for manufacturing purposes. This process would have produced no slag.[123]

New light has also been shed on the nature of Solomon's "navy" or "fleet of Tarshish." Recent studies have indicated that the navy of Solomon was, in effect, a specialized "smeltery" or "refinery fleet" which was responsible for bringing smelted metal home from the colonial mines. The Phoenicians were also probably very much engaged in this activity.[124] In addition to carrying slag and metal materials, Solomon's ships also went to Ophir. This was carried out in collaboration with Hiram, king of Tyre (10:22). The term "Ophir" probably includes most of the region of South Arabia and was commonly associated with the production of fine gold in the Old Testament (cf. I Kings 10:11; Job 22: 24; Ps. 45:9; Isa. 13:12). Solomon was able to strengthen his ties with the Arabian merchants by virtue of the visit of the queen of Sheba (10:1-13). Many of the objects brought to Israel by Solomon's merchant fleet came from such distant places as Africa, Arabia and parts of the Mediterranean world.

One of Solomon's very important enterprises was the trading of horses and chariots (10:28-29). Many of the purchases made were probably for his own armies, but it is also possible that he provided horses and chariots for other countries as well, perhaps acting as a middleman in the commercial negotiations (cf. 10:26 with 4:26).

In spite of the commercial success of Solomon in these various areas, it is rather clear that near the end of his reign he ran into financial difficulty. After the construction of the elaborate temple and palaces in Jerusalem, he was required to pay Hiram, king

---

[123]*Ibid.*

[124]See W. F. Albright, *Old Testament Commentary*, p. 51, and his "New Light on the Early History of Phoenician Colonization," *Bulletin of the American Schools of Oriental Research*, LXXXIII, 83 (Oct., 1941), p. 21.

of Tyre, for the wood and labor used. Unlike earlier agreements, he was not able to give Hiram food products from Israel. Instead he gave him twenty cities located in the land of Galilee (9:10-13). This exchange was not satisfactory with Hiram. In all probability the cities were unimportant and nonproductive.

III. APOSTASY AND ITS CONSEQUENCES (11:1-43)

The latter years of Solomon's reign were marked by gradual apostasy and departure from the law. The many marriages which he concluded for purposes of alliance began to influence his spiritual life. In addition to the daughter of Pharaoh, verse 3 indicates that he had 700 wives and princesses as well as 300 concubines. In order to make royal marriages effective it was evidently necessary to build temples for the more important wives living with him in Jerusalem (vv. 5-8). International marriages commonly required the recognition of foreign deities and the intermarriages of Solomon with important princesses of other lands were no exception. The result, Scripture says, was that his wives "turned away his heart after other gods" (v. 4). This practice on the part of Solomon diminished the effectiveness of the true temple and made it difficult for the people to distinguish between the true and the false. Foreign deities were given official recognition and this certainly made it difficult to maintain true worship in Israel. As a result of Solomon's disobedience and deep involvement in apostasy, God raised up a number of adversaries to frustrate and humiliate the very proud king. Among these were Hadad the Edomite (v. 14) and, to the north, Rezon, a renegade from the Aramaean kings. Within Israel itself a revolt was led by Jeroboam because of the heavy levies placed upon the people of Israel (v. 27). The result of all of this was the clear prophecy that following Solomon's death the kingdom would be divided. Jeroboam was to receive ten tribes to the north (v. 31) and was to uphold God's promise to David, while the house of David would maintain control in the south (v. 32). The turmoil of the final years of Solomon's reign and the division of the kingdom was the direct result of his involvement in idolatry (vv. 33-40). Following the death of Solomon, his son Rehoboam took the throne (v. 43).

This brief look at Solomon has been sufficient to demonstrate his greatness as a king and leader. He was uniquely blessed by God with wisdom above all his contemporaries. The mere possession of wisdom, however, did not guarantee spiritual success. The materialistic interests of Solomon ultimately led him to open idolatry in violation of the law. His life, therefore, is a solemn reminder that wisdom and intellectual genius are really worthwhile only when they are made subject to God's Word.

Part Three

SOLOMON TO THE EXILE

Studies in Kings and Chronicles

John C. Whitcomb

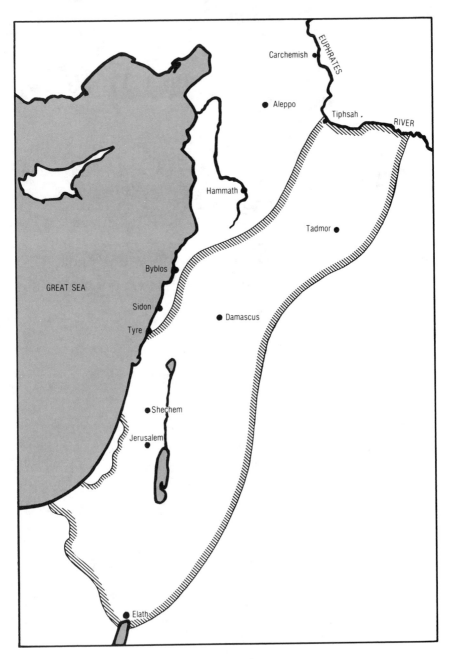

The Empire of Solomon

28
SOLOMON'S APOSTASY AND JEROBOAM'S REBELLION

I. THE GLORY AND WISDOM OF SOLOMON
(I Kings 3–10)

Solomon's was surely the most glorious kingdom the world has yet seen. It was certainly not the largest, nor even the most prosperous, but the wisdom of its king and the perfection of its government and the quality of its religion made it glorious beyond comparison. The Lord Jesus Christ paid indirect tribute to this fact when He compared Solomon's glory to the perfection of a God-created flower (Luke 12:27) and Solomon's wisdom to His own (Matt. 12:42).

It seems entirely possible, in fact, that discerning men such as Nathan the prophet, Ahijah the Shilonite, and Iddo the seer (II Chron. 9:29) could have considered Solomon to be the long-awaited Seed of the Woman (Gen. 3:15), the Shiloh from Judah in the prophecy of dying Jacob (Gen. 49:10), the Star and Sceptre of Balaam's vision (Num. 24:17), and the final House Builder of II Samuel 7:13. Judah and Israel were now as "many as the sand which is by the sea in multitude, eating and drinking and making merry" (I Kings 4:20), an apparent fulfillment of God's promise to Jacob (Gen. 32:12 — "I will surely do thee good, and make thy seed as the sand of the sea, which cannot be numbered for multitude"). Furthermore, Solomon practically claimed to be the Messiah in Psalm 72, as he pondered the significance of the Queen of Sheba's visit (72:10, 15).

In one of those very rare occasions in Bible history when God spoke to a man in his dreams, Solomon was asked a very searching question: "Ask what I shall give thee" (I Kings 3:5). We may be sure that God would not have asked such a question of just anyone, for only those who are already in God's grace and God's will have the incomparable privilege of guaranteed answers to universal requests (cf. John 15:7). And Solomon's answer confirms this, for he asked for "an understanding heart to judge thy people, that I may discern between good and evil" (I Kings 3:9; cf. James 1:5). God not only granted that specific request, but added riches and honor as well (I Kings 3:13), providing the perfect historical example for Jesus' promise that if we seek the kingdom of God and His righteousness first, "all these things shall be added unto you" (Matt. 6:33). Solomon's wisdom apparently did not include any details of God's prophetic plan for Israel and the nations, but it was unparalleled in the realms of jurisprudence (I Kings 3:28), administration (I Kings 4:20, 29; 5:12), poetry (I Kings 4:32), natural science (I Kings 4:33), architecture and engineering (I Kings 5:1–7:51; 9:15-22), and commercial enterprise (I Kings 9:26–10:29).[1]

In the midst of all this glory and wisdom, however, one fatal weakness remained – a sinful human nature. Solomon had wisdom, wealth, and power. But he was a sinner! At the end of his life he sadly confessed: "Surely there is not a righteous man upon earth, that doeth good, and sinneth not" (Eccles. 7:20). This is exactly why he could never have crushed the serpent's head (Gen. 3:15) and thus fulfilled mankind's basic need of a Redeemer (Job 19:25). As Solomon's glory faded, and his royal successors brought great disillusionment to the godly remnant, prophets began to point more and more to the coming of an Ideal King who would neither sin nor fail (cf. Isa. 9:6-7). Not Solomon, but the Christ, would fulfill God's ultimate purpose for His people.

II. MULTIPLYING WIVES (I Kings 11:1-8)

During the first twenty-four years of Solomon's reign it might appear that Pharaoh's daughter was his only wife (cf. I Kings 3:1; 6:37–7:1). This might be concluded from the statement in 11:1 that "Solomon loved many foreign women, together with the daughter of Pharaoh." And this would be a highly desirable interpretation, for God does not approve of polygamy (Matt. 19:5) and He blessed Solomon marvellously during those years. On the other hand, it must be recognized that God had also

---

[1]For an analysis of these aspects of Solomon's reign, see the previous study in this series: John J. Davis, *The Birth of a Kingdom* (Grand Rapids: Baker Book House, 1970), pp. 327-337.

richly blessed David during the early years of his reign, and that in spite of a polygamous household (II Sam. 3:1-5; 5:12-16). Furthermore, the Song of Solomon implies a God-honoring relationship between Solomon and the Shulamite maiden at a time when he already had sixty queens and eighty concubines (Song of Sol. 6:9, 13). Finally, Solomon must have married Naamah the Ammonitess a couple of years *before* he became king, and thus before he married Pharaoh's daughter, for Rehoboam was forty-one when Solomon died at the end of a forty-year reign (I Kings 14:21; II Chron. 12:13).[2]

Why did God permit David and Solomon to multiply wives? God had said to David through Nathan the prophet: "I gave thee thy master's house, and thy master's wives into thy bosom" (II Sam. 12:8). But this must be understood as God's *permissive* will, even as our Lord explained with regard to divorce: "Moses for the hardness of your heart *suffered* you to put away your wives: *but from the beginning it hath not been so*" (Matt. 19: 8). Not only did Moses specifically warn kings against multiplying wives to themselves (Deut. 17:17), but he also gave the tragic examples of multiple wives in the homes of Abraham (Gen. 16:1-6) and Jacob (Gen. 34:30; 35:21 ff.). Jealous wives (Gen. 30:16) and spoiled children (I Kings 1:6) were the inevitable fruit of polygamy, and Solomon had to lament over his son Rehoboam: "who knoweth whether he will be a wise man or a fool? yet will he have rule over all my labor wherein I have labored, and wherein I have showed myself wise under the sun" (Eccles. 2:19). Thus, God, in His providence, saw to it that both David and Solomon suffered severely for establishing polygamous households.

But the one consideration that must have overridden all others in the thinking of Solomon was the desire to establish diplomatic ties with the hundreds of city-states and kingdoms of the eastern Mediterranean and the Fertile Crescent. The most effective way to confirm a commercial or political treaty with a

---

[2]In the light of Abijah's statement that "Rehoboam was young and tender-hearted" (II Chron. 13:7) when he became king, some have suggested that instead of being forty-one, he was only twenty-one (compare II Chron. 36:9 with II Kings 24:8 for the age of Jehoiachin).

foreign king was to marry one of his daughters and give her a prominent position in the court. Theoretically a king would think twice before offending a father-in-law. This was a common and accepted practice among ancient rulers, and Solomon (contrary to the known will of God) conformed to this standard.[3]

However, multiplying wives was only the beginning of contradictions and disasters. Each wife, as a true representative of her father's kingdom, brought with her the religious paraphernalia and the priests of her god. As we shall see in Chapter 30, Jezebel brought with her from Phoenicia 850 prophets of Baal and Asherah when she came to Israel to be Ahab's queen (by arrangement of their fathers Omri and Ethbaal who planned thus to cement a political treaty).

Let us attempt to picture the situation that began to develop around Jerusalem during the last fifteen or twenty years of Solomon's reign. It must have been like Massachusetts Avenue in Washington, D.C., lined with the embassies and legations of many nations — little islands of foreign culture within the borders of the United States. A few years ago I visited this section of our capital city and walked into a fabulously beautiful Moslem mosque crowned with a white limestone minaret piercing the sky above. The costly structure was built with contributions from fifteen predominantly Moslem countries of Africa and Asia, so that there, on that 30,000 square-foot portion of American soil, the god Allah is officially honored!

So it was during Solomon's declining years. Shrines to pagan gods with attending priests and guardian queens dotted the hills surrounding Jerusalem. And there they remained for *three hundred years* — inviolable and untouched even during the reigns of such reforming kings as Asa, Jehoshaphat, Uzziah, and Hezekiah. At last, during Josiah's great reform movement toward the end of the seventh century B.C., these "high places" around

---

[3]The decipherment of the Nuzi tablets reveals that it was an accepted practice of Abram's day for a barren wife to give her handmaid to her husband to beget children that would be legally hers (Gen. 16:2; cf. K. A. Kitchen, *Ancient Orient and Old Testament* [Chicago: Inter-Varsity Press, 1966], p. 154).

the city were destroyed (II Kings 23:13). And two centuries after that, Nehemiah pronounced God's sad epitaph on Solomon's folly: "Did not Solomon king of Israel sin by these things? yet among many nations was there no king like him, and he was beloved of his God and God made him king over all Israel: nevertheless even him did foreign women cause to sin" (Neh. 13:26).

III. THE REBELLION OF JEROBOAM (I Kings 11:9-40)

In view of the enormity of Solomon's sin, it is remarkable that God showed grace toward him in two distinct ways. First, he was allowed to live out his days as the ruler of a united kingdom. Second, his son would be permitted to rule over part of the kingdom instead of losing it all (I Kings 11:12-13). This promise of grace both in time and extent of the judgment was really God's way of honoring the Davidic Covenant of II Samuel 7.

It is also fascinating to observe how God was preparing for the fateful day of kingdom division long in advance of Solomon's spiritual defection, and even before his reign began! For example, Hadad the Edomite fled to Egypt (I Kings 11:14-19) and Rezon of Syria rose to power even before David died (I Kings 11:23-25). God is never taken by surprise when humans fail, but His resources of grace are more than sufficient for those who trust Him (cf. Rom. 5:20).

It can be demonstrated that Jeroboam's rebellion (I Kings 11: 26, 40) was the climax to a very extensive background of events in Israel's history. Jeroboam's tribe — Ephraim — was a very proud tribe. Joshua, the conqueror of Canaan, was an Ephraimite. The tabernacle was first located at Shiloh within their tribal boundaries; and, for that matter, one of the very first places where Abram built an altar in the Promised Land was within their territory, too (Bethel — Gen. 12:6-8). It was apparently for such reasons as these that the Ephraimites chided with Joshua about the small size of their territorial allotment: "Why hast thou given me but one lot and one part for an inheritance, seeing I am a great people, forasmuch as hitherto Jehovah hath blessed me?" (Josh. 17:14).

Later, when Gideon (of the tribe of Manasseh) defeated the Midianites by a spectacular and supernatural victory, the jealous Ephraimites chided him with these bitter words: "Why hast thou served us thus that thou calledst us not when thou wentest to fight with Midian?" (Judges 8:1). It was only by a soft answer that Gideon avoided a civil war then and there. But the Ephraimites did not fare so well when they denounced Jephthah of Gilead for not calling them to lead the battle against Ammon (Judges 12:1). A rugged frontiersman of illegitimate origin (Judges 11:1-3), Jephthah challenged their insufferable pride and cut off their retreat across Jordan by demanding the Shibboleth password, slaughtering 42,000 of them in the bloodiest civil strife in centuries. Thus subdued, the Ephraimites submitted to Philistine conquest and also to the reign of Saul of Benjamin and David of Judah.

But in the process of time the pride of Ephraim raised its head again. The colossal burdens of taxation and forced labor that Solomon imposed on all the tribes for building programs that centered largely in Jerusalem (I Kings 9:15) proved too much for Ephraim and other northern tribes. Although they were overawed by the wisdom and glory of Solomon, smoldering resentment was nevertheless present according to their later complaint to King Rehoboam: "Thy father made our yoke grievous" (I Kings 12:4).

IV. JEROBOAM'S PLOT

It was against a background such as this that a young Ephraimite named Jeroboam came to the forefront. Ambitious and highly competent, he was soon placed by Solomon over the Ephraimite work crews that labored in Jerusalem. In consultation with his fellow workers an assassination plot was hatched, and Jeroboam went back to Ephraim to rally support. Ahijah the Shilonite met him on the way and confronted him with God's proposal. If he would desist from this murderous plot and honor the Davidic kings and Zadokian priests in Jerusalem, God would give him ten tribes and a perpetual dynasty in the north. This was a magnificent and gracious offer, but Jeroboam, like Ahaz two centuries later (cf. Isa. 7:11-12), was not content

with God's plan and provision. And this brought about his ultimate ruin. As it turned out, his plot was a failure (compare
I Kings 11:26b with 11:40a); and barely escaping with his life,
he fled to Egypt to bide his time.

V. THE DIVISION OF THE KINGDOM

After the defeat of Absalom, David had unwisely contributed
to the inferiority complex of the northern tribes by favoring Judah at his triumphal recrossing of the Jordan (II Sam. 19:9-15).
Their pride thus wounded, the men of Israel denounced the
men of Judah (II Sam. 19:40-43), and then joined in the rebellion of Sheba. The battlecry of Sheba is interesting — "We have
no portion in David, neither have we inheritance in the son of
Jesse: every man to his tents, O Israel" (II Sam. 20:1). The expression as used here was idiomatic for "return to your homes."
Israel no longer lived in tents, but the memory of nomadic days
had not yet faded away. A half century later, the northern
tribes used the very same battlecry when Jeroboam led the
revolt against the dynasty of David and the kingdom was split
(I Kings 12:16).

Jeroboam was a very clever and industrious man. Utilizing
the building skills he had developed under Solomon (I Kings
11:28), he established two northern capitals: *Shechem*, near the
border of Ephraim and Manasseh at the location of Mount Ebal
and Mount Gerizim where Joshua had first dedicated the Promised Land to Jehovah (Josh. 8:30-35), and *Penuel* across the Jordan (I Kings 12:25). This trans-Jordan capital may have been
necessitated by the anticipated invasion of Pharaoh Shishak
(his former protector — I Kings 11:40), which occurred in the
fifth year following the division of the kingdom (I Kings 14:
25). Later on, for an unknown reason, he established another
west-Jordan capital at Tirzah (I Kings 14:17; 15:33).

VI. JEROBOAM'S NEW RELIGION

The greatest challenge that confronted Jeroboam, however,
was not Egypt but Jerusalem. Three times a year, in accordance
with God's revealed plan, the nation went up to Jerusalem to
worship Jehovah (Lev. 23; cf. Exod. 23:17). As the Levites

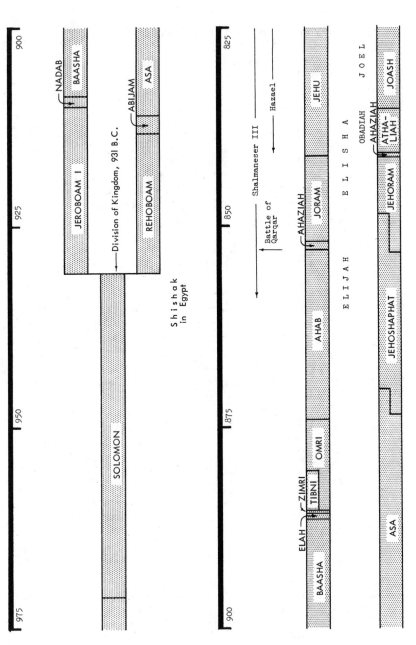

2. Time Chart: 975 to 825 B.C.

would instruct the people concerning the significance of the sacrifices, they would probably also take occasion to refer to Rehoboam as the legitimate Davidic king who reigned in Jerusalem. Before long, the people from northern tribes might begin to draw certain conclusions concerning Jeroboam, namely, that he was both illegal and unnecessary.[4]

Filled with such fears, Jeroboam adopted drastic measures to bring these influences to an end. He revolutionized the religion of Israel by changing (1) the symbols of religion, (2) the centers of worship, (3) the priesthood, and (4) the religious calendar. First of all, he changed the symbols of Israel's religion. Instead of golden cherubim above the ark, Jeroboam substituted two golden calves. Calves or bulls were sacred to the Egyptians, and during his stay in Egypt Jeroboam had doubtless become fascinated by the popularity of this cult. Unfortunately for Israel, Jeroboam was able to find in the first high priest Aaron a precedent for using a golden calf as a worship symbol. Aaron, pressured by the demands of idolatrous Israelites in the wilderness, not only fashioned a calf from the golden earrings of the people, but even exclaimed: "These are thy gods, O Israel, which brought thee up out of the land of Egypt" (Exod. 32:4). Not that Aaron was denying Jehovah completely; for on the following day he proclaimed a feast to Jehovah (Exod. 32:5). In other words, Aaron presented the calf as a visible symbol of Jehovah's strength and power.

In like manner, Jeroboam, determined to satisfy the desire of the average Israelite for a spectacular symbol of his God, probably assured the people that these calves were intended only to *point to* Jehovah. And, after all, this was nothing really new, but was merely an amplification of that form of Israel's wilderness religion which Aaron himself had established! Thus Jeroboam assumed the position of high priest himself, and by a clever mixture of popular pagan idolatry with the name of Jehovah, brought forth a compromise religion far more dangerous for the nation than out-and-out paganism could ever be. Like Satan, his supreme master, he attempted to pose as an angel of

---

[4]See pp.365-366, for an analysis of Abijam's taunt of the northern king as recorded in II Chronicles 13:4-11.

light and a minister of righteousness (II Cor. 11:14-15), and thus succeeded in "slaying" his tens of thousands. Twenty-one times after this, Old Testament writers refer to Jeroboam as the one who "made Israel to sin" (I Kings 14:16, etc.).

In the second place, Jeroboam established two new worship centers at Bethel and Dan. These were clever choices, for *Bethel* ("house of God") had been Jacob's worship center where Jehovah had spoken to him twice (Gen. 28; 35). *Dan* was also significant because Jonathan, a grandson of Moses, had established there on the very northern extremity of the land a worship center and a dynasty of priests for the tribe of Dan during the many years that the tabernacle was at Shiloh (Judges 18:30-31). Why bother to go all the way to Jerusalem to worship Jehovah when these God-honored places, newly equipped with Aaron-style calves, were ready at hand?

Thirdly, a new religion demanded a new priesthood. It would be utterly futile to attempt to persuade Levites to function in such a context, so Jeroboam opened priestly privileges to the highest bidders. Even in the days of the judges, when "every man did that which was right in his own eyes" (Judges 21:25), it was considered a special blessing to have a Levite for a priest (Judges 17:13). But now that the iniquity of the Israelites was becoming full, even this downward shift became possible (I Kings 12:31). Utterly disgusted at this drastic departure from divinely revealed tradition, the vast majority of priests and Levites fled southward to Judah, taking with them the remnant of true believers from the northern tribes and leaving behind them a situation of near-total apostasy (II Chron. 11:13-17).

In the fourth place, Jeroboam changed the religious calendar. To have no religious calendar at all would have been as foolish as to have no symbols, worship centers, or priests. A substitute religion, rather than no religion, has always been Satan's supreme goal (cf. Rev. 13). The seventh month, with its Feast of Trumpets (first day), Day of Atonement (fifteenth day), and Feast of Tabernacles (fifteenth to twenty-second days), was the climax of the religious year. So Jeroboam simply shifted the calendar one month ahead to the eighth month, "the month which he had devised of his own heart" (I Kings 12:33), doubtless making its ceremonies even more spectacular (if possible!) than its counterpart in Judah. In our own day, religious movements which possess the least Biblical truth often have the most elaborate ceremonies and the most impressive worship centers.

VII. THE PROPHET FROM JUDAH (I Kings 13)

No matter how deep the spiritual darkness of Israel became, God always had a human channel available through whom His Word could be proclaimed. King Jeroboam was proudly burning incense on his new altar in Bethel, when an unnamed prophet from Judah burst upon the scene, announced that a future Davidic king named Josiah[5] would desecrate the altar (cf. II Kings 23:15-20 for the fulfillment 300 years later), and confirmed the spectacular prophecy with an equally spectacular sign. Jeroboam's effort to stop him was met with divine judgment, and his plea for mercy was met with divine grace; but in neither case did the king truly repent of his sins.

God had commissioned the unnamed prophet to utter his curse and return immediately to Judah without eating or drinking in the spiritually contaminated land of Israel (compare the somewhat similar experience of Amos at Bethel during the reign of Jeroboam II 200 years later — Amos 7:10-13). So when Jeroboam, deeply impressed with the prophet's supernatural powers and thinking that he could bribe him into using his magic to the advantage of the kingdom, offered him food and a reward, the prophet utterly refused. But the next test was too hard for him. An old prophet in Bethel, who probably had once served the Lord but had compromised away his spiritual usefulness, invented a message from God to deceive the prophet. Said he, "I also am a prophet as thou art; and an angel spake unto me by the word of Jehovah, saying, Bring him back with thee into thy house, that he may eat bread and drink water" (I Kings 13: 18).

The prophet believed the trumped-up message, accepted the invitation, and died under God's judgment as a result. Why was the penalty so severe? Was it really his fault? Our approach

---

[5]Another remarkable example of this type of prophecy was the naming of Cyrus 150 years in advance (Isa. 44:28; 45:1).

to this problem is exceedingly important. God's Word, from Genesis to Revelation, indicates clearly that it *is* possible to recognize God's voice through the convicting and illuminating work of the Holy Spirit. No other supporting evidence is really needed, or that would outweigh God's own voice in importance to the human heart. The unnamed prophet knew God's command. He also knew that God does not contradict His own Word. Therefore, as the apostle Paul stated, "Though we, or an angel from heaven, should preach unto you any other gospel than that which we preached unto you let him be anathema" (Gal. 1:8). So when the old prophet claimed the unnamed prophet *could* eat and drink in Israel, his heart should have detected the hiss of the Serpent and his lips should have cried out, NO!!

The fact that the old prophet was deeply touched by the unnamed prophet's testimony and punishment in no way modifies the tragedy of the episode. What Satan could not do by outward persecution, he accomplished through inward enticement. Not only the old prophet of Bethel, but all subsequent "sons of the prophets" in Bethel, Gilgal, Jericho, and elsewhere must have pondered this vivid lesson whenever they ministered the message of the Holy One of Israel.[6]

VIII. THE END OF JEROBOAM'S DYNASTY

We are surprised to learn that Jeroboam had a godly son, Abijah, even as Saul had his Jonathan. We are also surprised to learn that God's way of honoring this lad was to permit him to die of sickness and be buried in a grave! "For he only of Jeroboam shall come to the grave, because in him is found some good thing toward Jehovah, the God of Israel, in the house of Jeroboam" (I Kings 14:13). So horrible was the judgment awaiting the royal family (I Kings 14:10-11) that to avoid it by dying in bed would be a great blessing!

Therefore, Jeroboam's purely pagan plot to deceive the blind old prophet Ahijah by a disguise (like Saul with the witch of

---

[6]It is only in the light of such severe lessons that we can properly explain the episode described in I Kings 20:35-36 (see comments, p. 380).

Endor) not only failed, but became God's means of pronouncing doom upon his dynasty (which ended only two years after his own death) and of unveiling the first frightening suggestion of national deportation to Assyria (I Kings 14:15; cf. Deut. 29:28). Thus ended the reign of the great Kingdom-divider, the great calf-worshipper, the man "who made Israel to sin."[7]

---

[7]For a study of Jeroboam's disastrous confrontation with Abijam of Judah (II Chron. 13), see pp. 365-366.

29

THE FIRST SOUTHERN KINGS

I. REHOBOAM (I Kings 12, 14; II Chron. 10–12)

It is probable that Rehoboam's mother was a worshipper of the heathen deity, Molech, since she was an Ammonitess (I Kings 14:21; cf. 11:7). And not only this, but she had to compete with seven hundred other "wives" for the affections of an apostate king (I Kings 11:3). Such was the "home life" and the "spiritual environment" in which Rehoboam grew to manhood. Is it any wonder, then, that "he did that which was evil, because he set not his heart to seek Jehovah" (II Chron. 12:14)?

Immediately upon assuming his responsibilities as king, Rehoboam revealed his utter incompetence for this high office (cf. Eccles. 2:18-19). He rejected wise counsel concerning the demands of the northern tribes and followed the proud and immature ideas of "the young men that were grown up with him" (I Kings 12:8).[1] The result, of course, was open rebellion and a permanent split in the kingdom, exactly as God had prophesied through Ahijah (I Kings 12:15; cf. 11:30-35). Barely escaping from Shechem with his life, Rehoboam rallied Judah and Benjamin for a great civil war which was averted only because God intervened. Speaking to the king through Shemaiah the prophet, the Lord explained that the split in the kingdom was neither a chance occurrence, nor a mere human scheme, nor was it accomplished by Satan's power — "this thing is of me" (I Kings 12:24). Not until the nation experiences its great regeneration during the Tribulation will God reunite the two kingdoms into one (cf. Ezek. 37:15-23).

Somewhat chastened by this sad turn of affairs, Rehoboam followed Jehovah for about three years (II Chron. 11:17). It was at this time that the remnant of true believers in each of the northern tribes began to follow the priests and Levites in the

---

[1] On the question of Rehoboam's age at the death of Solomon, see p. 353.

permanent abandonment of their homes because of Jeroboam's religious revolution (II Chron. 11:13-15; cf. 13:9). Just as the forced exile of hundreds of thousands of godly French Huguenots brought incalculable blessing to surrounding nations in the seventeenth century A.D., so this influx of spiritually-minded Israelites "strengthened the kingdom of Judah and made Rehoboam the son of Solomon strong, three years" (II Chron. 11:17) and modified God's otherwise negative evaluation of his entire reign: "in Judah there were good things found" (II Chron. 12:12).

In a vain and ridiculous attempt to match the glory of Solomon, Rehoboam took eighteen wives (including granddaughters of Jesse, David, and Absalom) and sixty concubines, and begat eighty-eight children (II Chron. 11:18-23). Proud of his harem, building projects, and great prosperity, Rehoboam forsook the Lord. This time, God's instrument of chastening and humiliation was Shishak, king of Egypt, equipped with 1200 chariots, 60,000 horsemen, and countless soldiers (II Chron. 12:1-4).[2] Because of a timely repentance at the preaching of Shemaiah the prophet (I Chron. 12:5; cf. I Kings 12:22), Rehoboam and the kingdom were spared the tragedy of total defeat and subjugation at the hands of the Egyptians. (How the situation had changed since the early days of Solomon when the pharaoh was happy to give his daughter to the king of Israel!) Stripping the temple of all its golden vessels and ornaments symbolized the fact that the glory had already begun to depart. The continuance of the southern kingdom for another three hundred years is a marvellous tribute to the longsuffering of God!

II. ABIJAM (I Kings 15:1-8; II Chron. 13)

The author of Kings dismisses Abijam with very few words, none of them encouraging (I Kings 15:1-8). But in II Chroni-

---

[2]Shishak has left to us some references to this campaign on the outside wall of the great temple at Karnak in southern Egypt, though he doesn't mention Jerusalem (cf. ANET, pp. 242 f. and 263 f.; the map in The Macmillan Bible Atlas, p. 77).

cles 13 we learn of a great victory that God gave to him against Jeroboam of Israel. The victory was unique, not only because of the vast number of Israelites slain (500,000), but also because of the special appeal which Abijam made to the northern enemy and their apostate king (II Chron. 13:4-12). With amazing skill and bitter sarcasm, Abijam exposed the rottenness of Jeroboam's administration which was built upon "worthless men, base fellows" (II Chron. 13:7), and the folly of his man-made religion, propped up by "the golden calves which Jeroboam made you for gods" (II Chron. 13:8) with the sacred offices being staffed by any non-Levite who could pay the price — "a young bullock and seven rams" (II Chron. 13:9)!

In contrast to this hollow sham, said Abijam, we Judeans have the true God (Jehovah), legitimate Aaronic priests, atoning sacrifices, the original table of showbread and the golden candlestick. (How these pointed reminders of happier days and God's ways must have stung the conscience of many a northerner!) Furthermore, declared the bold young king, we have *the ultimate weapon* — "behold, God is with us at our head, and his priests with the trumpets of alarm to sound an alarm against you" (II Chron. 13:12). The magnificent speech ended with a plaintive appeal: "O children of Israel, fight ye not against Jehovah, the God of your fathers; for ye shall not prosper."

But even while he pretended to listen to this "summit meeting" oration, Jeroboam was plotting the destruction of his enemies by means of an ambushment. Jehovah, however, had the final word; for through the fervent prayers of godly Judeans and their Jericho-like trumpet blasts and expectant shouts, He brought an unparalleled destruction to Jeroboam's army from which he never recovered (II Chron. 13:20).

We might conclude from all this that Abijam (or Abijah, as the Chronicler calls him) was one of the greatest southern kings. However, the last two verses of this chapter tend to modify our praise and to help us to recognize (especially in the light of I Kings 15:1-8) that Abijam was capable, like his father (cf. II Chron. 11:4, 17; 12:6, 12), of occasional acts of faith in a life of general disobedience to the revealed will of God.

III. ASA VERSUS ZERAH (I Kings 15:9-15; II Chron. 14–15)

Rehoboam and Abijam, two unrighteous but occasionally obedient kings, were followed by Asa and Jehoshaphat, two righteous but occasionally disobedient kings. One great disaster, shared in common by the first three southern kings, was Maacah, a granddaughter of the spoiled and ambitious Absalom. As a sort of Jezebel of Judah, she was Rehoboam's wife, Abijam's mother, and the "Queen Dowager" who held the reins of power in the early days of Asa's administration (the word "mother" in I Kings 15:10 should be translated "grandmother," his own mother presumably having died when he was a child). We are amazed at the boldness of young Asa in deposing Maacah "because she had made an abominable image for an Asherah" (I Kings 15:13). He not only cut down her Asherah, but he also burned it in the Kidron valley!

The conflict with Baasha described in I Kings 15:16-22 cannot be properly understood apart from some immediately preceding events outlined for us in II Chronicles 14 and 15. Early in Asa's fifteenth year (897 B.C.), God permitted an Ethiopian army (or an Ethiopian-backed Arabian army, judging from the kind of spoils mentioned in II Chron. 14:15) of enormous size to invade Judah. Presumably the peace and prosperity of Asa's early years lulled the people into complacency and pride (note the emphasis on "quiet" and "rest" in II Chron. 14:1, 5, 6, 7), and the nation took its blessings for granted.

Zerah's invasion cured the nation of this problem! On behalf of his people, Asa uttered one of the great prayers of Bible times: "Jehovah, there is none besides thee to help, between the mighty and him that hath no strength: help us, O Jehovah our God; for we rely on thee, and in thy name are we come against this multitude. O Jehovah, thou art our God; let not man prevail against thee" (II Chron. 14:11). With this, "a terror from Jehovah" (II Chron. 14:14, ASV margin) fell upon the enemy and they fled for their very lives. Once again, faith and prayer proved to be the secret and irresistible weapon of God's people, "for the weapons of our warfare are not of the flesh, but mighty before God to the casting down of strongholds" (II Cor. 10:4).

At the moment of victory, the Spirit of God spoke powerfully to Asa through a prophet who appears only once in the Old Testament — Azariah the son of Oded. The message was simple and clear: obedience brings blessing, and disobedience brings defeat (in II Chron. 15:3-6 either Azariah or the Chronicler provided a vivid reminder of the tragedies that stemmed from national disobedience during the days of the judges). The final words had an electrifying effect upon king and people through the Spirit of God: "But be ye strong, and let not your hands be slack; for your work shall be rewarded" (II Chron. 15:7). Hearing this, Asa's enthusiasm for reform and revival was fanned into a white heat. Even northern tribes were affected, and, surprisingly, the tribe of Simeon too, concerning which so little is heard after the time of Joshua (II Chron. 15:9). The resulting influx of believers from the northern tribes into Judah not only alarmed Baasha of Israel (as we shall see), but also provided the necessary dynamic for a spontaneous and widespread revival.

The Great Revival of the third month (the Feast of Weeks?) of Asa's fifteenth year was noteworthy for its intensity and zeal. Not only did the people renew their covenant promises "with a loud voice and with shouting and with trumpets and with cornets," but they determined to kill any man or woman who refused to be revived!

Two important points must be made here. In the first place, Israel was the only nation in history which God ruled through royal and priestly mediators. Therefore, "church and state" were almost a unity, and a religious offense was at the same time a crime against the state! The worship of any other god brought public execution (cf. Exod. 22:20); and even close relatives were responsible for exposing the offender and taking the leading part in his execution (Deut. 13:6-11).

Secondly, the very fact that people who did *not* seek Jehovah were executed proves that regeneration could not have been the prerequisite for "revival" in ancient Israel. Those who *conformed* to the religious regulations of the nation and *avoided* the worship of other deities were accepted as legitimate citizens of the theocracy and were exempt from the penalties of the law. In the Christian dispensation, however, false worship is *never* to be dealt with by physical punishment (I Cor. 5:12-13), and "revival" can occur *only* in the hearts of *regenerated* people (cf. II Cor. 13:5). Having made this distinction, we must also recognize that God's desire for Israel was always individual regeneration first of all (Ezek. 36:27), and then revival of *heart-religion* (Deut. 10:16; Jer. 4:4). Thus, Isaiah (1:10-20), Micah (6:6-8), and Hosea (6:6) all denounced mere outward conformity to ceremonial requirements without a corresponding revival of the heart.

IV. ASA VERSUS BAASHA (I Kings 15:16-22; II Chron. 16)

Second Chronicles 15 ends with a summary statement about the peacefulness of the early years of Asa's reign (cf. 14:6). The correct translation of II Chronicles 15:19 is: "there was no war unto the five and thirtieth year of the reign of Asa" (instead of "no more war" as in ASV). But we know that Zerah's invasion occurred in his fifteenth year (II Chron. 15:10). Therefore, the Chronicler must be measuring these years from the division of the kingdom in 931 B.C., for the 15th year of Asa's own reign was also the 35th year of the Divided Kingdom. Such an interpretation, strange though it may seem at first glance, actually solves two chronological problems of considerable importance. First, it eliminates the anomaly of Baasha waiting twenty-one years to block the southward flow of his citizens (II Chron. 15:9; 16:1). Second, and more important, it eliminates the absurdity of Baasha invading Judah nine years after he had died (cf. I Kings 15:33)![3]

Thus, Baasha's invasion of Judah and his fortification of Ramah (five miles north of Jerusalem) were his Berlin wall response to the powerful magnet of revival in Jerusalem to the south (cf. II Chron. 15:9). The king of Israel realized full well that it was his most stalwart citizens, the very life blood of the nation, who were leaving him, and he took drastic means to stop the flow.

Asa panicked when he saw this happening. Instead of trusting the Lord, as he had done only a few months earlier when

---

[3]For a full discussion of this and other chronological problems during the period of the Divided Kingdom, see Edwin R. Thiele, *The Mysterious Numbers of the Hebrew Kings* (Grand Rapids: Wm. B. Eerdmans Publishing Co., 1965), pp. 59 f.

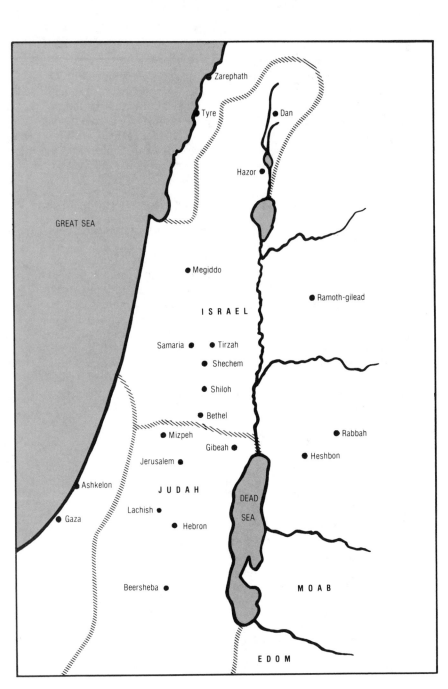

The Kingdoms of Israel and Judah

Zerah the Ethiopian invaded the land (II Chron. 14:9), he leaned heavily upon the arm of the flesh. Taking out of the temple the gold and the silver he had recently dedicated to God (cf. II Chron. 15:18), he sent it to Damascus, to Ben-hadad king of Syria, bribing him to break his commercial treaty with Baasha and to attack his northern borders. If Asa's conscience disturbed him, he must have suppressed it with the rationalization that the end justifies the means. After all, did not the plan succeed? Was this not sufficient evidence that God honored the plan? Baasha withdrew from Ramah to cope with the threat from the north, and Asa commanded his people to dismantle the fortifications at Ramah and to use the materials to build two fortresses, Geba and Mizpah, three and four miles to the east and northwest, as his own defense system against Baasha.

One day soon after this, while congratulating himself for his cleverness, Asa heard a knock on his palace door. It was the last person in the world he wanted to see — Hanani the seer, God's prophet! Without being invited to speak, Hanani delivered God's message to Asa: (1) you could have conquered Syria as well as Israel if you had trusted Me; (2) you have already seen how God answered your prayers and destroyed the Ethiopians; (3) God's eyes have "legs" that carry them throughout the whole world to bring special blessings to those who truly trust Him; and (4) because of your deliberate sin, you will have wars to the very end of your reign.

These words from the God of Heaven came upon the king like a clap of thunder. Completely losing control of himself, he lashed back at God by putting His prophet into "the house of the stocks" (ASV margin) and oppressing others who dared to question his royal policies or who came to the support of Hanani. In the light of all this, it is indeed a remarkable testimony to God's grace that He could direct the Chronicler to write: "the heart of Asa was perfect all his days" (II Chron. 15:17; cf. I Kings 15:14). When applied to men, the term "perfect" never carried the idea of sinless perfection (cf. I John 1:8, 10). Instead, it characterized a person who trusted God and used His appointed means (through Levitical sacrifices) to confess and receive atonement for sins committed. Thus, Job was "perfect" before he was even tested (Job 1:1), and Jehovah was able to

say of David that he "kept my commandments, and followed me
with all his heart, to do that only which was right in my eyes"
(I Kings 14:8), even though he was guilty of some horrible
crimes. The only *absolutely* perfect man who ever lived was our
Lord Jesus Christ.

Asa not only outlived Baasha, but also Omri, the founder of
a dynasty of fanatical Baal-worshippers (see Chap. 30). Toward
the end of his reign, which came twenty-seven years after the
revival and the defeat of Baasha, Asa must have turned away
from God again. As a result, he was smitten with a great and
loathsome disease in his feet. Instead of turning to God and His
prophets, he turned to pagan (foreign?) physicians who were
probably little more than witch-doctors. Two years later he died
and was buried in a bed filled with sweet spices and surrounded
with incense burners (cf. Jer. 34:5). Thus ended the long reign
of the godliest king to sit on the throne of Judah until Hezekiah
and Josiah.

V. JEHOSHAPHAT (II Chron. 17–20)

The character and reign of Jehoshaphat constitute a fascinating study in contrasts. On the one hand, some of his spiritual
attainments were almost without parallel in the history of the
kingdom. But on the other hand, he repeatedly and flagrantly
involved himself and his people in alliances with the husband
and two sons of wicked Queen Jezebel. Thus, by his refusal to
exercise spiritual discernment with regard to the utter apostasy
of Israel, he practically cancelled the spiritual benefits that came
from his reforms in Judah. The application of this lesson to the
ecumenical pressures which pastors of fundamental churches
must face in our own day is quite obvious.

Jehoshaphat's reign began impressively. He was *against* Israel
(II Chron. 17:1), and "he walked in the first ways of his father
David" (II Chron. 17:3 — an intentional contrast to the post-
Bathsheba phase of David's career). Even more impressive is
the record of Bible-teaching teams, consisting of princes as well
as priests and Levites, "who taught in Judah, having the book of
the law of Jehovah with them; and they went about throughout
all the cities of Judah, and taught among the people" (II Chron.
17:9). As a result, God gave him such honor and prestige that

even the Philistines and Arabians brought tribute (II Chron. 17:11).

Approximately halfway through his twenty-five year reign, however, Jehoshaphat made a decision that in later years almost brought his kingdom and the Davidic dynasty to destruction: "he joined affinity with Ahab" (II Chron. 18:1) by accepting the pagan Athaliah, daughter of Ahab and Jezebel, as his son's wife. The alliance became so strong through this marriage that Jehoshaphat really had no choice when Ahab urged him to join in a battle against Ramoth-gilead.[4] Barely escaping with his life, Jehoshaphat returned to Jerusalem only to receive a scathing denunciation from God through the prophet Jehu (II Chron. 19:2). It was at this time that his son Jehoram became the co-regent.[5]

Now Jehoshaphat launched a new series of reforms in Judah "and brought them back unto Jehovah, the God of their fathers" (II Chron. 19:4). Judges were appointed in all fortified cities, and were admonished to do their work as unto the Lord, avoiding all bribes (vv. 4-11). This was just what was needed to face the next crisis — an invasion of Moabites and Ammonites from the east. Gathering the nation before the temple court, the king prayed a prayer of faith and of child-like trust in Jehovah. The remarkable response from heaven came through a Levite named Jehaziel: "Fear ye not, neither be dismayed by reason of this great multitude: for the battle is not yours, but God's. . . . ye shall not need to fight this battle: set yourselves, stand ye still, and see the salvation of Jehovah with you . . ." (II Chron. 20:14-17; cf. Exod. 14:13-14). The victory was total, the spoils were enormous, and "the fear of God was on all . . . countries, when they heard that Jehovah fought against the enemies of Israel" (II Chron. 20:29).

In spite of all these blessings, and in spite of his tragic experience with Ahab, Jehoshaphat joined with wicked Ahaziah of Israel in a shipbuilding project at Ezion-geber. The Lord denounced this alliance through the prophet Eliezer and destroyed the ships (II Chron. 20:35-37). Even worse, his son Jehoram,

[4]For a discussion of this battle and Jehoshaphat's part in it, see pp. 381-384.

[5]Edwin R. Thiele discusses the chronology of this period in *The Mysterious Numbers of the Hebrew Kings*, pp. 64-71.

upon becoming co-regent, murdered his six younger brothers
and some of the princes (II Chron. 21:4). As a result, Jehoram
received a letter from Elijah the prophet denouncing him and
predicting a horrible death (21:12-15). Still refusing to learn
the lesson of separation from apostasy, Jehoshaphat joined himself and his army to Joram of Israel in an expedition against
Moab (II Kings 3:4-7). It was only by the grace of God, through
Elisha's special intercession on behalf of Jehoshaphat (in spite
of the presence of Joram), that both armies were spared a
total catastrophe (II Kings 3:8-27).[6]

Thus, Jehoshaphat made his mark in Judah's history as a king
who did "that which was right in the eyes of Jehovah" (I Kings
22:43); but appended to this official evaluation of his reign were
these tragic words in red ink: "And Jehoshaphat made peace
with the king of Israel" (I Kings 22:44). May God help us to
keep our record of Christian life and service pure and clean by
"cleansing ourselves from all defilement of flesh and spirit, per-
fecting holiness in the fear of God" (II Cor. 7:1).

------

[6]See pp. 405, 407 for a study of this battle.

4. View of the hill of Samaria where Omri established his capital
after abandoning Tirzah. Courtesy, Matson Photo Service.

30

OMRI AND AHAB — DYNASTY OF BAAL

I. THE DYNASTY ESTABLISHED (I Kings 16:15-34)

Omri was founder of the fourth dynasty in the Kingdom of Israel. Jeroboam and Baasha were founders of the first two dynasties, but they were each followed by sons who reigned only two years. The third dynasty hardly deserves such a title, for it lasted only a week! Zimri, who had murdered Baasha's son, himself died in a siege seven days later when Omri, captain of the army, attacked him in the capital city of Tirzah. Within five years, Omri crushed a rival to the throne (Tibni) and greatly strengthened the kingdom by purchasing a strategic hill called Samaria (see illustration on following page) and building a new, well-fortified capital there. So important was this move from an international standpoint that for over a hundred years the Assyrians called Israel "the land of Omri."[1]

Omri's other claim to fame (or rather, infamy) was the sealing of an alliance with Phoenicia through the marriage of his son Ahab to Jezebel, daughter of Ethbaal, king of the Sidonians. To make Jezebel feel perfectly at home, Ahab erected a temple for Baal in Samaria, thus officially abandoning the compromise calf-cult of Jeroboam. Possibly he appealed to the example of Solomon, who had encouraged his foreign wives by erecting pagan shrines for them around Jerusalem (I Kings 11:7).

As a measure of the wickedness of the new dynasty, a prominent citizen of Bethel publicly defied the curse of Joshua upon Jericho. Joshua had not prohibited all future settlement in this city, but only its *fortification* (Josh. 6:26 — "gates"), for it was inhabited again not long after his day (Judges 3:13). It is true that God's warnings of coming judgment may lie dormant for many centuries, but they must not be lightly defied or challenged. So Hiel's presumption cost him two of his sons, and the entire nation must have been stunned by this spectacular dem-

---

[1]Pritchard, *ANET*, pp. 284, 285.

onstration that God will fulfill His promise: "I watch over my word to perform it" (Jer. 1:12).

II. AHAB AND BEN-HADAD (I Kings 20)

But this was only a mild warning from Jehovah. The next blow was a three-year drought followed by the slaughter of 450 prophets of Baal at the hand of Elijah.[2] But still the message did not get through to the sinful heart of Ahab. Therefore another disaster loomed over the horizon in the person of Ben-

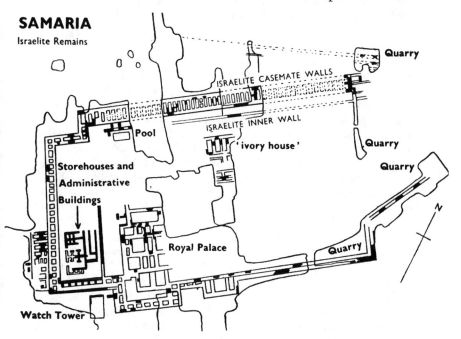

Plans of Samaria, capital of Israel, with its stout casemate defense walls, royal palace and House of Ivory. Courtesy, Inter-Varsity Fellowship.

---

[2]See discussion in Chapter 31.

hadad, king of Syria (I Kings 20:1), who laid siege to Samaria. Realizing that he had overextended his supply lines, Ben-hadad tried to strike a bargain with Ahab: "Thy silver and thy gold are mine; thy wives also and thy children, even the goodliest, are mine" (I Kings 20:3). When Ahab quickly accepted these terms (including the loss of Jezebel!), the greedy king demanded even more and thus lost everything, being foiled by his own clumsy frankness. Wicked though he was, Ahab was not totally devoid of the courage of a king. To Ben-hadad's ridiculous boasting, Ahab replied with calm dignity, "Let not him that girdeth on his armor boast himself as he that putteth it off" (I Kings 20:11).

Ahab was still king of Israel, in spite of his spiritual blindness, and God honored him to the extent of speaking encouraging words to him through a prophet on three different occasions (I Kings 20:13, 22, 28). Ben-hadad was overconfident. He and his thirty-two kings were drunk in their tents and therefore hardly knew what hit them. Blaming the slaughter of their soldiers on a theological miscalculation (I Kings 20:23), the Syrians attacked again and failed even more disastrously (I Kings 20:29-30), the reason being theological rather than military (I Kings 20:28).

It is important to recognize that *all* of Israel's military victories were won by obeying the Lord. Of no other nation can such a statement be made. Joshua prevailed against Amalek only when Moses' arms were held high in prayer (Exod. 17: 8-13). His attack on Ai failed because of Achan's sin (Josh. 7). God cut down Gideon's army to a mere 300 in order that he would not trust in the arm of the flesh (Judges 7:2). In fact, if Israel really trusted in the Lord only one soldier would be sufficient to chase 1,000 and two could put 10,000 to flight (Deut. 32:30). Zechariah tells us that at the close of Israel's tribulation period "he that is feeble among them at that day shall be as David; and the house of David shall be as God, as the angel of Jehovah before them" (12:8). For us, too, "though we walk in the flesh, we do not war according to the flesh" (II Cor. 10:3). In fact, said the great apostle, "I glory in my weaknesses, that the power of Christ may rest upon me. Wherefore I take pleasure in weaknesses . . . for Christ's sake: for when I am weak, then am I strong" (II Cor. 12:9-10).

Ahab made the fatal mistake of assuming, in the hour of Ben-hadad's humiliation, that *he*, not Jehovah could dictate the terms. Instead of executing God's enemy, Ahab, like Saul before him (I Sam. 15:9), decided to spare the captive king and accomplish his own purposes through him. Apparently he wanted a strong kingdom in Damascus to serve as a buffer between Israel and Assyria, instead of trusting Jehovah to be his wall of defense (cf. Isa. 26:1). Also, there would be the privilege of having Israelite bazaars in the very important commercial center of Damascus (I Kings 20:34). Outwardly impressive, the plan was actually nearsighted and cruel, for Ahab not only had to take his army to fight the Assyrian king, Shalmaneser III, at Qarqar along with other western kings (853 B.C.), but shortly thereafter had to lead his weary army against Ben-hadad, the very king he had just pardoned. This not only cost him his life but the lives of many of his men.

Assyrian battle scene. The royal chariot with three occupants is protected by soldiers armed with bows and daggers. From relief of Ashurnasirpal II at Nimrud. Courtesy, Inter-Varsity Fellowship.

God's method of exposing Ahab's blunder is fascinating. An unnamed "son of the prophets" was instructed by God to get wounded at the hand of a fellow prophet and then deliver a message of doom to the king through his head bandages. The first prophet refused (not surprisingly!), and was therefore killed by a lion on the highway. What severe discipline for the preparation for God's representatives! We *must* assume that this young prophet, like all true believers, had the God-given capacity to discern the voice of God (John 10:27; I John 4:1), and, therefore, like the unnamed prophet from Judah who suffered an identical fate (I Kings 13:24), was guilty of elevating his personal desires above the known will of God (cf. the experience of Jonah). A second prophet cooperated with this strange command, sorely wounding his friend, and the king received the message of God in such a forceful way that "he went to his house heavy and displeased" (I Kings 20:43).

III. NABOTH'S VINEYARD (I Kings 21)

This, of course, is the background to the tragedy of Naboth's vineyard. Morose and disconsolate, the childish king wanted a new toy with which to play. When his whim was thwarted, he sulked homeward "heavy and displeased" (cf. I Kings 20:43), and pouted on his dining room couch. When Jezebel asked for an explanation, he gave only a partial answer. Naboth had said, "Jehovah forbid it me, that I should give the inheritance of my fathers unto thee" (I Kings 21:3). The Lord had prohibited the outright and perpetual sale of any inherited property to someone who was not in the immediate family (Lev. 25:23; cf. Micah 2:1-2) because the land belonged to *Jehovah* and had been given to the families of Israel as a foretaste of blessings and privileges (Micah 4:4).

Ahab knew, of course, that Jezebel would laugh at such a law. Amazed that a *king* would accept "no" for an answer, she proceeded to do what any Phoenician ruler would do under such circumstances: simply destroy the uncooperative citizen.[3] Jeze-

---

[3]Years before, Samuel had warned Israel that land-grabbing would be the typical policy of kings (I Sam. 8:14).

bel was careful, however, to honor Jewish law to the extent of
obtaining *two* witnesses (Deut. 17:6) and making a legitimate
accusation (cf. Lev. 24:16). The mock trial is a painful reminder of what our Lord experienced at the hands of men
even more guilty than Jezebel (Matt. 26:59-67; 23:32-36; I Thess.
2:14-16). Naboth's sons were stoned too (II Kings 9:26), and
thus the property had no heir. As Ahab went to possess it, his
chariot was followed by two officers, Jehu and Bidkar, who later
recalled this vivid scene and helped to fulfill Elijah's terrible
judgment (II Kings 9:25). So Naboth's blood (like that of Abel
— Heb. 12:24) cried out to God, even while being licked up by
scavenger dogs, and God heard that cry (I Kings 21:19).[4]

IV. AHAB'S LAST BATTLE (I Kings 22)

Jehoshaphat, the king of Judah, was partly responsible for the
disastrous campaign against Ramoth-gilead, for he had "joined
affinity with Ahab" (II Chron. 18:1) by marrying his son Jehoram
to Athaliah, daughter of Ahab and Jezebel (II Chron. 21:6; 22:
2-3), at least ten years earlier (cf. II Kings 8:17 with 26). So
when Ahab celebrated this reunion with his southern relatives by
providing a huge banquet (II Chron. 18:2), Jehoshaphat was
really in no position to deny Ahab's urgent request to help him
recapture the border town of Ramoth-gilead from the hands of
the Syrians. Ahab was especially anxious for the battle, because
Ben-hadad had betrayed his covenant of three years earlier
(I Kings 20:34) in taking this trans-Jordan territory from
Israel. What Jehoshaphat expected to gain from such a campaign is not at all clear.

Having already decided to go to battle with Ahab, Jehoshaphat
now decided to inquire of Jehovah. It was somewhat late for
this, but his insistence on hearing from a genuine prophet of
Jehovah (I Kings 22:7-8) was doubtless the very factor that
saved his life in the battle. Ahab, having anticipated such a
request, had trained four hundred men to imitate the prophets
of Jehovah (were these formerly Jezebel's 400 prophets of the
Asherah?), being careful to use Jehovah's name (I Kings 22:

---

[4]See pp. 398-399 for an analysis of Elijah's confrontation with Ahab at
Naboth's vineyard (I Kings 21:17-29).

11, 12, 24). One of them, a certain Zedekiah, even made horns of iron to match the vivid imagery of Moses' final blessing upon the Joseph tribes: "his horns are as the horns of the wild ox: with them he shall push the peoples, all of them, even to the ends of the earth" (Deut. 33:17). This was apparently sufficient to convince Jehoshaphat in spite of all that Micaiah, the 401st prophet, could say.

Micaiah, the son of Imlah, was truly one of God's great ones. His testimony stood out if for no other reason than that Ahab hated him (I Kings 22:8). The king, with itching ears, was anxious to hear his own desires echoed by the mouths of his well-trained prophets (II Tim. 4:3), but here was one who remained utterly aloof from the superimposed ecumenism of the new state religion. He was urged to conform his words to theirs and thus to rubber-stamp the king's plan. At first glance, it would seem that Micaiah succumbed to the pressure (I Kings 22:15), but Ahab's angry response shows clearly that Micaiah's tone of voice intentionally betrayed the insincerity of his words. Then came the straight message, at the king's own request: Israel would be defeated and Ahab would die (cf. Samuel's message to Saul at Endor — I Sam. 28:19).

God confirmed the judgment with a parabolic vision, which explained in story form the complete sovereignty of God in manipulating the evil devices of men. If the king and his false prophets thought they could control the outcome of battles and even their own destiny by purely magical means, the truth of the matter was that they, like Satan their master, were under *God's* control (cf. Gen. 50:20; Ps. 76:10; Dan. 4:17), having willfully sold themselves to sin's dominion (cf. I Kings 21:20). In the vision, the spirit who volunteered to entice Ahab's prophets may have been a personification of the spirit of false prophecy, as in Zechariah 13:2 (cf. I John 4:6). God had given up these wicked men to judicial hardening, and their doom was sealed (cf. Rom. 1:24-32), as exemplified by the blasphemous response of Zedekiah and God's personal judgment upon him (I Kings 22:24-25).

The last recorded appeal of Micaiah as he was dragged off to prison ("Hear, ye peoples, all of you" — I Kings 22:28b) may not have turned the two kings from their course of action but in the marvellous providence of God it found lodgment in the hearts of two parents a hundred years later who named their son in his honor: Micah. It is significant that Micah's first recorded words were the final ones of his namesake: "Hear, ye peoples, all of you" (Micah 1:2). No one can fully measure the impact of one godly life upon the hearts of other men, but God assures us that it is great (Dan. 12:3).

Ahab's determination to disguise himself during the battle reveals two facts: (1) he was essentially pagan in his concept of God's knowledge; and (2) his death was even more obviously the work of God. The enemy did not recognize him, but "a certain man drew his bow at a venture, and smote the king of Israel between the joints of his armor" (I Kings 22:34). The Achilles' heel of Ahab was not the crack in his armor but his willful rebellion against God. And once a man has made God his enemy there can be no escape: "though they hide themselves in the top of Carmel, I will search and take them out thence; and though they be hid from my sight in the bottom of the sea, thence will I command the serpent, and it shall bite them . . . and I will set mine eyes upon them for evil, and not for good" (Amos 9:3-4).

Fatally wounded, Ahab bravely held himself up in his chariot to encourage his men, and died as the sun set. It was not his magnificent ivory-inlaid palace of Samaria (I Kings 22:39) that welcomed him home this time, but the same dogs that licked the blood of Naboth. And so God clearly vindicated His faithful prophet Micaiah, who had staked his claim to the true prophetic office on the certainty of this event: "If thou return at all in peace, Jehovah hath not spoken by me" (I Kings 22:28).

It is hard not to be astounded at the stupidity of Jehoshaphat. Rushing into the battle with his royal robes flowing in the wind, he was a perfect target for the enemy. King Ben-hadad commanded his men to concentrate on Ahab, for whom he had no love in spite of great mercy previously received (I Kings 20:34). Thinking he was the king of Israel, the Syrian captains pursued after the defenseless and desperate Jehoshaphat. Whatever armor he may have had was useless, but he "cried out" to Jehovah in one of the most famous "foxhole prayers" of Bible history. "And Jehovah helped him; and God moved them to depart from him" (II Chron. 18:31), because in spite of his inconsistencies

384 SOLOMON TO THE EXILE

and compromises he basically had done "that which is right in the eyes of Jehovah" (I Kings 22:43; II Chron. 19:3).

It is true that God spared his life, but upon his return to Jerusalem Jehoshaphat was severely rebuked by Jehu the seer in words which are rich in warning to Christians today who feel that the Lord's work can best be promoted by cooperation with unregenerate religious leaders: "Shouldest thou help the wicked and love them that hate Jehovah? for this thing wrath is upon thee from before Jehovah" (II Chron. 19:2). To this, we may add the words of the apostle Paul: "Be not unequally yoked with unbelievers: for what fellowship have righteousness and iniquity? or what communion hath light with darkness . . . or what portion hath a believer with an unbeliever?" (II Cor. 6:14-15).

V. THE DESTRUCTION OF AHAB'S DYNASTY

When King Ahab permitted his wife Jezebel to kill Naboth for the sake of obtaining his vineyard, God sent Elijah to denounce him for his sin. Among other things, Elijah said: "Behold, I will bring evil upon thee, and will utterly sweep thee away, and will cut off from Ahab every man child" (I Kings 21:21). In startling fulfillment of this grim prophecy, the following judgments fell upon Ahab's family:

(1) Ahab himself was slain by an enemy arrow, in spite of every effort to disguise himself (I Kings 22:34).

(2) Ahab's son Ahaziah died childless after a fall in his palace (II Kings 1:1-17).

(3) Joram, Ahab's second son, and Ahaziah of Judah, his grandson, were killed by Jehu (II Kings 9:24, 27).

(4) Ahab's wife, Jezebel, was likewise killed by Jehu (II Kings 9:33).

(5) Ahab's seventy sons (by various concubines) were beheaded by the elders of Israel at the command of Jehu (II Kings 10:1-10).

(6) Jehoram of Judah, son-in-law of Ahab, lost all of his wives and sons except Athaliah, their son Ahaziah, and a daughter, Jehosheba (II Chron. 21:17).

(7) Jehoram himself died of a horrible disease (II Chron. 21:19).

(8) Some of Jehoram's male relatives and descendants were killed by Jehu (II Kings 10:13; II Chron. 22:8).

(9) All the rest of his male relatives and descendants were killed by Athaliah herself, with the exception of Joash (II Chron. 22:10).

(10) While she reigned in Judah (841-835 B.C.), Athaliah was the *only* living representative of Ahab's family besides her daughter Jehosheba and her little son, Joash, who was also the *only* male representative of David's line.[5] Thus, when Athaliah was finally slain (II Kings 11:16; II Chron. 23:15), the amazing prophecy of Elijah was fulfilled; for both Jehosheba and Joash were led into Jehovah's spiritual family by the high priest Jehoiada, the husband of Jehosheba and the foster-father of Joash (II Chron. 22:10-12).

"He that being often reproved hardeneth his neck shall suddenly be destroyed, and that without remedy" (Prov. 29:1). "It is a fearful thing to fall into the hands of the living God" (Heb. 10:31).

[5]Athaliah was probably not Ahab's actual daughter, but rather a daughter of Omri whom Ahab and Jezebel adopted and indoctrinated into the deeper mysteries of Baalism after Omri died in 874 B.C. Her youngest son Ahaziah was born no later than 863 B.C. (II Chron. 22:1-2), so she must have been born no later than 880 B.C., several years before Ahab and Jezebel were married. See H. J. Katzenstein, "Who Were the Parents of Athaliah?" *Israel Exploration Journal* 5 (1955), p. 194.

31

ELIJAH: FROM THE BROOK CHERITH
TO THE JUNIPER TREE

I. THE APPEARING OF ELIJAH (I Kings 17:1)

Like a meteor suddenly flashing across the darkened sky, Elijah appears on the scene without genealogy, without historical background, and without warning. One thunderous judgment from heaven through his lips and he disappeared without a trace — "As Jehovah, the God of Israel, liveth, before whom I stand, there shall not be dew nor rain these years, but according to my word" (I Kings 17:1).

God permitted neither debate nor dialogue between His prophet and Ahab, the apostate king of Israel (compare Elisha's attitude toward Ahab's son, Joram — II Kings 3:14). The king was left to stagger for three more years under the colossal judgment of an unrelieved drought, six months of it having been experienced already (compare I Kings 18:1 with Luke 4:25 and James 5:17). Not that the nation had no warning at all. Centuries before, Moses had said that national apostasy would cause the rains to cease (Deut. 11:17; 28:24). And now that Jehovah had been officially repudiated, His providential blessings upon this land came to an end.

II. ELIJAH AND THE RAVENS (I Kings 17:2-7)

To prevent His prophet from being besieged by the desperate entreaties of the dying and the dire threats of Ahab and Jezebel (who doubtless concluded that it was the magical power of Elijah rather than Jehovah that had cast this evil spell upon their land), the Lord whisked him away to a secluded spot just east of the Jordan in the rugged hill country of Gilead. We may also assume that Elijah himself needed this time of retreat and this spectacular reminder that God alone was his source of supply and strength. As the ravens fed him each morning and evening, Elijah was made aware of the basically supernatural character of his ministry in a day of desperate spiritual darkness when Israel stood at the crossroads of her destiny. So titanic was this struggle that Elijah on at least one later occasion needed to be fed by God again under a juniper tree through angelic agency (I Kings 19:5).

III. ELIJAH AND THE WIDOW OF ZAREPHATH
(I Kings 17:8-24)

And yet, even this miraculous supply had its God-appointed limitations. When the brook dried up, no supernatural fountain appeared. Elijah was now commanded to proceed to Zarephath, a Phoenician coastal town (the modern Sarafand) between Tyre and Sidon. It was not that there were no widows in Israel who could help him. The Lord Jesus explained (Luke 4:25) that in His sovereign grace God chose a woman who, though a believer in Jehovah, was not even an Israelite, in order to rebuke the utter apostasy of His people (see a similar rebuke in Matt. 8:10 — "I have not found so great faith, no, not in Israel"). Furthermore, it was a special rebuke to Queen Jezebel, for she never dreamed that Elijah would be hiding in her own homeland (I Kings 18:10)!

The widow of Zarephath was subjected to a very severe test of faith and she passed it. When Elijah challenged her to give him the last morsel of food, "she went and did according to the saying of Elijah" and was richly blessed for her obedience. Our Lord later enunciated this principle: "Seek ye first his kingdom and his righteousness, and all these things shall be added unto you" (Matt. 6:33).

Her final test was to trust Elijah's God concerning her dead son. It was not "to bring her sin to remembrance" (I Kings 17:18) that God permitted this to happen (she still clung to the popular superstition that the proximity of a prophet enabled God to see one's sins more clearly — a superstition that has not completely died even in our day!). Rather, God allowed this tragedy to occur in order that He might be glorified through it (cf. John 9:3). Great is the mystery of God's providential purposes! As God's instrument for bringing this boy back to mortal life, Elijah became a true forerunner of the Lord Jesus Christ (see p. 411 for comparison between the work of Elijah and Christ).

The widow not only received back her son, but also regained her confidence that her remarkable guest was indeed God's man.

IV. THE PROPHETS OF JEHOVAH (I Kings 18:4, 13)

By the third year after the miracle of the widow's son, the drought had taken its devastating toll in the land. Whatever the fate of the people might have been, Ahab was desperately concerned about his horses, for they were his first line of military defense (I Kings 18:5).[1] A few years after this drought in the year 853 B.C., Assyria's king, Shalmaneser III, informs us that Ahab appeared at Qarqar in Syria with 2,000 chariots; so his efforts to save his horses must not have been totally unsuccessful.[2]

Ruins of horse stables with hitching posts and mangers, probably from the period of Ahab, at Megiddo. Courtesy, Oriental Institute.

[1] These ruins of horse stables at Megiddo very likely date to the reign of Ahab.
[2] Cf. Pritchard, *ANET*, p. 279.

The rainless skies were not caused by Elijah's magical powers as Ahab and Jezebel thought ("Is it thou, thou troubler of Israel?" I Kings 18:17; cf. Josh. 7:25 concerning Achan), but by their own persecution of the prophets of Jehovah (I Kings 18:4) and replacement with 850 Baal and Asherah prophets imported from Phoenicia and supported from the royal treasury (I Kings 18:19). The one hundred surviving "prophets of Jehovah" were probably the same as the "sons of the prophets" who knew of Elijah's forthcoming translation to heaven (II Kings 2:3, 5). They may even have traced their heritage back to the prophetic guilds of Samuel's day (I Sam. 19:20). But Elijah must not have considered their testimony to be very outstanding; for in spite of the fact that Obadiah had saved a hundred of them alive in caves (there are about 2,000 caves in Mt. Carmel alone), Elijah still insisted that "I, even I only, am left a prophet of Jehovah" (I Kings 18:22). The Lord corrected this statement by assuring him that seven thousand had not bowed the knee to Baal (I Kings 19:18). Nevertheless, it must be admitted that if these one hundred prophets were the nucleus of the prophetic schools at Bethel and Jericho (II Kings 2:3, 5), they were in great need of systematic instruction in the things of God (cf. II Kings 2:15-18).

V. ELIJAH ON MOUNT CARMEL (I Kings 18:19-39)

The contest on Mt. Carmel was a spectacular vindication of the uniqueness and sovereignty of Jehovah in a day of satanic darkness. Never in all history was the point more clearly made that "no idol is anything in the world and there is no God but one" (I Cor. 8:4). The three-and-one-half-year famine had doubtless shaken the confidence of many in the ability of Baal, the god of fertility, to answer their prayers. But if any yet hesitated, Elijah's demonstration would remove every excuse for following this vile system of worship.

The issue was crystal clear: "If Jehovah be God, follow him; but if Baal, then follow him" (I Kings 18:21). God has never tolerated middle-of-the-road, lukewarm compromises in spiritual matters. The Lord Jesus warned the church of Laodicea with these words: "I know thy works, that thou art neither cold nor hot: I would that thou wert cold or hot. So because thou art lukewarm, and neither hot nor cold, I will spew thee out of my mouth" (Rev. 3:15-16). These words certainly do not mean God does not care whether people believe Him or not, but they do mean that nothing can be quite so dangerous to the spiritual vitality of a church or nation as the presence and prominence of those who profess to know God but by their works deny Him (Titus 1:16). The church of Jesus Christ today would be enormously strengthened if all those who profess to be its friends, but who secretly deny the authority of its Lord, would depart from it. A mixed multitude can only bring compromise and spiritual defeat to God's people.

Elijah gave every possible advantage to the 450 prophets of Baal (did Jezebel's 400 prophets of the Asherah stay home as a "back-up team"?). He not only permitted himself to be outnumbered four hundred and fifty to one, but also chose a prominent hill near the Baal centers of Phoenicia where the power of this deity would presumably be greater. He gave them the privilege of choosing the best bullock, and of having most of the day to exercise their skills in evoking a response from their great god. All the people (including representatives from all twelve tribes — I Kings 18:19-20) agreed that the contest was a fair one (I Kings 18:24), though Jezebel's absence may suggest her deep misgivings about such a contest.

Elijah's analysis of the plight of the Baal prophets is instructive. That there was a humorous aspect to the whole episode is undeniable, and Elijah was God's spokesman in pointing this out (for a similar exposure of the utter folly of idolatry, see Isa. 44: 9-20). The evils of idolatry are twofold: (1) it involves a forsaking of nature's testimony to the conscience that only one true God can exist; and (2) it pictures God (or the gods) in terms of human sin and frailty (compare the double denunciation in Jer. 2:13). In the light of such religious irrationality on the part of God-created minds and hearts, it is understandable that "He that sitteth in the heavens shall laugh . . ." (Ps. 2:4). So Elijah taunted these desperate men in their well-deserved hour of public humiliation: "Cry aloud; for he is a god: either he is musing, or he is gone aside [a euphemistic expression], or he is on a journey, or peradventure he sleepeth and must be awaked!"

We, too, must laugh at such a concept of deity. For we have a God whose presence permeates and penetrates the highest heaven, the lowest Sheol, and the uttermost part of the sea (Ps. 139:8-9). Not only can He be contacted, but He is inescapable, for He fills both heaven and earth (Jer. 23:24). And as for alertness to the cries of His people, "he that keepeth Israel will neither slumber nor sleep" (Ps. 121:4). So accustomed are we to hearing such truths that we tend to take them for granted. But the otherwise clever and clear-thinking Greeks, unenlightened by the Word of God, populated Mt. Olympus with deities which reflected their sinful human imaginations about the God who created them (cf. Acts 17:16, 29). Only if God condescends to reveal Himself to men in a special way can they grasp anything of His true character.

But, there was also a tragic side to this great summit meeting. Hundreds of men who had devoted their lives to promoting the cult of Baal now sank to the desperate expedient of slashing their own bodies with knives in order to provoke their god to respond, if for no other reason, then at least out of sympathy for their physical agonies. Jehovah had long since warned His people against doing such things (Lev. 19:28; Deut. 14:1), not only because the body is sacred (I Cor. 6:19, ASV), but because human efforts and sacrifices apart from faith in God's revealed will are utterly worthless (cf. Micah 6:6-8). And so it is today — millions are destroying their lives and even their eternal destinies out of loyalty to such gods as materialism and blind evolutionism (to say nothing of the gods of false cults and religions), which can neither save men's souls nor even answer their prayers.

The calm assurance and dignity of Elijah provide a startling contrast to the heated frenzy of the pagan prophets. Gathering the people, he quickly rebuilt the local Jehovah altar (apparently tolerated by the Lord because Jerusalem was now inaccessible to His northern worshippers — I Kings 19:10; Romans 11: 3; cf. II Chron. 16:1) that had been thrown down by Baal's worshippers. Drenched with twelve jars of sea water, and having only one man of like passions with us (James 5:17) to offer a short prayer on its behalf, this second-choice bullock (I Kings 18:23) seemed a poor candidate for heavenly acceptance. But the great difference lay in the fact that Elijah's God *actually existed* and that Elijah was *His servant!*

That Jehovah could *answer by fire* had already been demonstrated in spectacular ways to Abraham (Gen. 15:17), Lot (Gen. 19:24), Aaron's sons (Lev. 10:2), and Solomon (II Chron. 7:1). No mere lightning bolt was this; for stones, dust, and even the sea water all vanished, along with the bullock and the wood. Truly "our God is a consuming fire" (Deut. 4:24; Heb. 12:29) — and may all mankind take heed!

Ridiculous beyond expression is the modern liberal suggestion that "Elijah poured naphtha, which he obtained from a nearby source, on the altar and that he used a magnifying lens to focus the sun's rays and ignite the fire."[3] It is "Christian rationalists" such as this who would explain Jesus' walk upon the sea in terms of a shallow sand bar, or the feeding of the five thousand as an emotional response of the crowd to a boy's willingness to share his lunch, so that they all spontaneously took out the lunches they had selfishly hidden in their garments! Church members of some denominations would be surprised to learn how many such men occupy positions of great influence in their church-supported institutions of higher learning today.

VI. THE EXECUTION OF FALSE PROPHETS
   (I Kings 18:40)

What shall we say of Elijah's treatment of the humiliated prophets of Baal? Should he not have reckoned their public disgrace sufficient punishment? Or should he not, perhaps, have enrolled them in the prophetic schools for indoctrination courses in the hope that they might gradually repent of their false religious concepts and turn to Jehovah? God, who knows the utter depths of human depravity (Jer. 13:23; 17:9), had already settled the question. False prophets were to die without mercy (Deut. 13:5; 18:20; cf. 7:2), for their words, like a deadly cancer, would spread confusion, unbelief, and ultimate disaster to all who heeded them (II Tim. 2:17).

---

[3]Refuted in *The New Bible Commentary: Revised* (Grand Rapids: Wm. B. Eerdmans Publishing Co., 1970), p. 344. For an excellent discussion of the entire Mt. Carmel episode, see Leon J. Wood, *Elijah, Prophet of God* (Des Plaines, Ill.: Regular Baptist Press, 1968), pp. 80-94.

Far more dangerous to the well-being of any people than thieves or even murderers are the disseminators of doctrinal error (Isa. 9:14-17; Matt. 23:15). If pollution of our natural resources and human bodies is becoming a national concern in America, what about the pollution of our minds and souls? Churches that emphasize social and political reform more than the Word of God are contributing to the ruin of the very nation they profess to love. The only churches that can expect Christ's commendation are those which examine and expose those who falsely claim to be Christ's representatives (Rev. 2:2). And so Elijah, rather than following his personal inclinations, obeyed God's Word (even as Samuel did when he "hewed Agag in pieces before Jehovah in Gilgal" — I Sam. 15:33), and led the nation in exterminating these promoters of theological error (see Zech. 13:3).

VII. ELIJAH'S DEFEAT (I Kings 18:41—19:6)

Baal, the supposed god of weather and fertility, had been totally discredited before the nation. Now Jehovah, the true Ruler of all nature, opened the windows of heaven "and there was a great rain." Perhaps in order to touch the king's heart and to convince him that he had no personal enmity against him, Elijah ran before Ahab's chariot along rain-soaked and muddy roads to the winter palace of Jezreel about fifteen miles to the east of Mt. Carmel.

But here the great prophet, physically and emotionally exhausted, made his greatest mistake. Instead of personally confronting Jezebel with what *Jehovah* had done, he allowed Ahab to tell Jezebel "all that *Elijah* had done." With astounding boldness, in her hardened depravity, Jezebel decided to intimidate Elijah with a threat on his life. (It is possible, however, that Jezebel feared his great power as a magician, for otherwise it seems that she would have killed him on the spot.) Unfortunately, the mere threat proved sufficient, for Elijah temporarily took his eyes from the Lord and, filled with fear, fled for his life.

Surprising though it may seem, this is one of the clearest evidences of the divine inspiration of this history. For if mere men had composed the account, they could hardly have resisted the temptation to omit or at least modify the record of their hero's spiritual failure. But this is the thing we need most to understand: apart from our blessed Saviour, no one, not even an apostle (cf. I Cor. 9:27; Gal. 2:11), is free from the disastrous potential of a sinful nature. Noah, Abraham, Moses, David, Solomon, and even John the Baptist, experienced failure and defeat because of sin. "Now these things happened unto them by way of example; and they were written for our admonition. . . . Wherefore let him that thinketh he standeth take heed lest he fall" (I Cor. 10:11-12). Sinless perfection is a mere dream this side of heaven (I John 1:8-10), and God has been gracious to us in revealing that even Elijah "was a man of like passions with us" (James 5:17).

But the story of Elijah also proves this: "there hath no temptation taken you, but such as man can bear: but God is faithful, who will not suffer you to be tempted above that ye are able; but will with the temptation make also a way to escape, that ye may be able to endure it" (I Cor. 10:13). Elijah's failure is a deafening warning to the spiritually proud and complacent. But God's tender intervention on his behalf is a soothing reminder that "God is faithful" and that there is no need to despair. Like Jeremiah, who more than once wrote out his official resignation from the ministry (cf. Jer. 9:2; 20:7-18), Elijah prepared a formal speech for the Lord's record book: "It is enough; now, Jehovah, take away my life; for I am not better than my fathers" (I Kings 19:4).

This, of course, was no time for formal speeches and great decisions. The poor man was totally exhausted (having travelled 150 miles from Jezreel to Beersheba, plus another day's journey, leaving his servant behind because he apparently had no intention of returning to his native land). Therefore the tender Shepherd of Israel (Isa. 40:11) simply ignored the speech, put His weary prophet to sleep, and commanded an angel to feed him when he woke up.

And so we too need to learn that things are never quite so bad for us as they may seem, for "we know that to them that love God all things work together for good" (Rom. 8:28). Elijah was not finished, because God was not finished. His greatest work was still in the future, even beyond the time of his departure from this world.[4] And that is true of each of us, too, if we love the Lord. For it is written, "Eye hath not seen, nor ear heard, neither have entered into the heart of man, the things which God hath prepared for them that love him. But God hath revealed them unto us by his Spirit (I Cor. 2:9-10).

[4]See p. 403.

32

ELIJAH: FROM MOUNT HOREB TO HEAVEN

I. INSTRUCTION AT HOREB (I Kings 19:1-18)

Sometimes our service for God is hindered by neglect of the normal needs of the body for proper rest and nourishment: "It is vain for you to rise up early, to take rest late, to eat the bread of toil; for so he giveth unto his beloved sleep" (Ps. 127: 2). And so Elijah, after the terrific strain of his ministry on Mt. Carmel and his 150-mile marathon race from Jezreel to Beersheba and beyond, needed physical therapy at the hands of a tender angel. Rested, fed, and strengthened by the Lord, he journeyed 200 miles south from the vicinity of Beersheba across the trackless wilderness to the rugged mountain range of Horeb, to Mount Sinai, "the Mount of God" (cf. Exod. 3:1, 12; 4:27; 24:13). In fact, it may be that God led him to "*the* cave" (19:9, definite in Hebrew) where Moses was covered by God's "hand" lest he should see God's "face" (Exod. 33:22). Just as Moses desperately needed God's encouragement to lead the nation in a time of deep apostasy (Exod. 33:3-6, 15), so Elijah needed the same vision of God in his time of near despair.

God's instruction of the defeated prophet came in four phases. First, the deep probing of his heart: "What doest thou here, Elijah?" (compare God's question to Adam in Gen. 3:9). Elijah's answer revealed his keen disappointment and impatience with God's ways and an exaggerated pessimism concerning the condition of the nation. Why did not God strike Jezebel dead in his presence and then cause a great host of men to follow his spiritual leadership?

With the prophet's true attitude fully exposed, Jehovah now graciously showed him by a series of visual aids the drastic limitations of this method of dealing with men and nations. Great winds, earthquakes, and fires can quickly destroy men's lives (as God will demonstrate during the Great Tribulation — Rev. 6–18), but only by the "still small voice" of the Holy Spirit

396

can men be regenerated through the patient teaching of His Word (John 3:3-8; II Tim. 2:23-26).

Elijah's problem was shared by two of Jesus' own disciples, James and John, the sons of Zebedee. When a Samaritan village refused them hospitality because they were heading toward Jerusalem, James and John desired to consume them with fire from heaven — Elijah-style! But for this they were rebuked by the Saviour: "Ye know not what manner of spirit ye are of . . ." (Luke 9:55). And this in essense was God's rebuke to Elijah at Horeb.

This did not mean that judgment and destruction of sinful men had no part in God's program for Israel. God is not only gracious (I Kings 19:12; Exod. 34:6), but righteous (I Kings 19: 17; Exod. 34:7). Thus the third phase of his Horeb indoctrination course was that God *will* judge the wicked — in His own time and way! Hazael, Jehu, and Elisha were each to wield swords, though in very different ways, and Elijah would *directly* (in the case of Elisha) or *indirectly* (in the case of Hazael, II Kings 8:8-15; and Jehu, II Kings 9:1-10) launch them into their ministries of judgment.

The fourth point in God's instruction was this: in spite of outward appearances, God *is* doing a work in the hearts of men — "Yet will I leave me seven thousand in Israel . . . which have not bowed unto Baal" (19:18). So has it ever been from Adam to the present: "A remnant according to the election of grace" (Rom. 11:5). It may come as a shock to those with little understanding of the height of God's holiness and the depth of man's depravity that the remnant of true believers is so small. This was Abraham's problem too, when he assumed that there were probably fifty righteous men in Sodom — or at the *very least*, ten (Gen. 18:22-33). Our Lord warned us that "few there be that find" eternal life (Matt. 7:14). But in the light of the frightening fact that apart from God's special grace *none* would be saved (Rom. 3:9-30), it should be a constant source of amazement that the Holy Spirit has transformed so many people (Rev. 7:9), and such unlikely people (I Cor. 1:27-28), and under such unusual circumstances (cf. Phil. 4:22). Zealous to do our part in fulfilling God's great commission to the church, we must also be content with His gracious sovereignty in dealing with the nations.

II. ELISHA ANOINTED (I Kings 19:15-21)

Perhaps Elijah never fully realized the significance for Israel of the anointing of Elisha. This great yet humble successor to the prophet of fire would have a ministry several times as long as Elijah's and one that would be filled with both miracle and blessing for many. We may assume that the two men had met before, even as Jesus had met Andrew, Peter, James and John several months before He called them to a life of ministry as fishers of men (cf. Matt. 4:19 with John 1:35-42).

Elisha was apparently a wealthy farmer, for he plowed with twelve yoke of oxen (he probably had eleven servants, each with one yoke); but when he heard God's call through Elijah, he forsook all and followed him. His desire to bid farewell to his parents was not a sign of hesitation on his part (contrast Jesus' rebuke of another potential disciple — Luke 9:61-62). Instead, it was a desire to present a clear testimony to family and friends that God had called him to a great life work (compare Matthew's farewell testimony banquet — Luke 5:27-29).

III. AHAB HUMILIATED (I Kings 21:17-29)

It would be interesting to know what Ahab had been thinking about Elijah since he fled from the face of Jezebel. Had his magic powers left him, or had Jezebel and her four hundred prophets of the Asherah proven too much for him? But Ahab had not seen the last of God's prophet! As well might Ahab have sought to escape the presence of God in the uttermost part of the sea as to hide from the one whom God had specially prepared to activate the feeble conscience of Israel's monarch.

Having been goaded by Jezebel into the cold-blooded murder of Naboth and his sons (see pp. 380-381), Ahab stood at last in the beautiful vineyard he had so long coveted (cf. Isa. 5:8). Suddenly, like a nightmare become incarnate, Elijah appeared at the vineyard and pronounced judgment upon the guilty king. Even as Saul feared and even pursued Samuel because of his own guilty conscience (I Sam. 16:2; 19:22; 28:11), so now Ahab lashed out at his supposed tormentor: "Hast thou found me, O mine enemy?" (cf. I Kings 18:17). It has always been true, from the blood of righteous Abel to the death of the most recent Christian martyr, that the unsaved world seeks to alleviate the pressure of offended conscience by attacking those who speak God's Word (compare the fate of *Micaiah* in I Kings 22:27; *Hanani* in II Chron. 16:10; *Zechariah* in II Chron. 24:20-22; and *Jeremiah* in Jer. 26:8). It was a compliment to Elijah to be counted as an enemy of this royal murderer, for "friendship of the world is enmity with God" (James 4:4).

Elijah quickly explained that the king was really his *own* worst enemy! It was true that Jezebel had "stirred up" her husband to do things that had alienated the Lord and His prophet, and we may even go a step further and recognize that it was Satan who had stirred up Jezebel. But the *ultimate* fact, the fact that sealed his eternal doom, was that Ahab "did *sell himself* to do that which was evil in the sight of Jehovah" (I Kings 21:25). Two important points need to be made here. First, sin is a *personal* responsibility. Adam set the pattern for us all when he blamed Eve for his sin (Gen. 3:12; and Eve blamed Satan! — Gen. 3:13). But the partaking of the forbidden fruit was Adam's *own* fault, for the Scriptures make it perfectly clear that "by one man" sin entered into the world (Rom. 5:12) and that "*Adam was not beguiled*" (I Tim. 2:14). Secondly, sin is not freedom at all, but is the worst possible kind of *slavery* (Rom. 6:16; 7:14).

The blistering judgment had its appropriate effect upon Ahab. Recalling, perhaps, the fate of the 450 at Mt. Carmel, he humbled himself before Jehovah and "went softly." Weak rather than vicious in character (like Zedekiah the last king of Judah), Ahab's conscience was still functioning slightly. And because of this single response to his conscience, God extended his dynasty a dozen years! How vastly important in God's sight is our feeblest response to His Word! Only eternity will tell. How many months Ahab continued to go "softly" we cannot guess; but the following chapter (see comments, pp. 381-384) makes it clear that, like Pharaoh, he hardened his heart again.

IV. AHAZIAH DESTROYED (I Kings 22:51-53; II Kings 1)

Though Ahaziah's name honored Jehovah ("Jehovah has grasped" — thus named by Ahab and Jezebel to please Jehoshaphat?), he made no concessions whatsoever to Israel's God. During his brief reign a joint ship-building enterprise with Jehoshaphat was destroyed by the Lord (II Chron. 20:37), and the Moabites ceased their vast tribute of wool to Israel (II Kings 1:1; 3:4). But his greatest claim to infamy was a futile military campaign against a one-man army named Elijah.

Seriously injured by a fall from the upper chamber of his palace, Ahaziah sent messengers to Philistia (about forty miles west) to inquire at a shrine of the god Baal-zebub at Ekron, thus showing himself to be a true son of Jezebel. The real name of this Syrian deity was Baal-zebul ("Lord of life"), but the Jews called him Baal-zebub ("Lord of the flies") in derision. By the time of Christ, this deity had become a symbol of Satan (Matt. 12:24).

However, the king's messengers were stopped en route by God's war machine, equipped with nothing but a garment of hair and a leather girdle. This dress was a forceful rebuke of the sinful luxury of the aristocracy of Israel, and became such a symbol of prophetic power that false prophets would "wear a hairy mantle to deceive" (Zech. 13:4)! Speaking of Elijah's later counterpart, John the Baptist, our Lord asked: "What went ye out to see? a man clothed in soft raiment?" (Matt. 11:8; cf. 3:4). But it was more than his rough garments and rugged visage that gave Elijah power against Baal's henchmen — it was special authority from God Himself.

In the full fury of his wrath at this blatant challenge to his royal will, King Ahaziah flung one entire company of soldiers, and then another, against the impudent prophet, only to discover, to his horror, that the fire that fell at Mt. Carmel could consume people as well as bullocks! The third captain saw the light, surrendered to Elijah, and accompanied him to Samaria while the prophet personally (contrast I Kings 19:1) confronted the king with his appointed doom. Ahaziah's younger brother, Jehoram (Joram), far more diplomatic in his willingness to make outward concessions to Jehovah (II Kings 3:2, 10), but equally wicked in the sight of God (II Kings 3:13a), took the throne as the last of the Omri kings (cf. I Kings 21:29).

V. HEAVEN WITHOUT DYING (II Kings 2:1-18)

Of Enoch's departure from this world it is simply recorded that he "walked with God: and was not; for God took him" (Gen. 5:24). Thus, "by faith Enoch was translated that he should not see death" (Heb. 11:5). Elijah was the only other man in history to share such an experience. In his hour of despair he had prayed: "O, Jehovah, take away my life" (I Kings 19:4). Not only was he not permitted to die then, but he never did die! This was God's way of honoring one who had sought so zealously to honor Him in a time of utter apostasy.

The prophet's march to heaven began at upper Gilgal (not the famous Gilgal of Joshua 4:20 near the bank of the Jordan) and moved steadily eastward and downward through Bethel and Jericho to the Jordan River. It was a testing time for young Elisha, for his master asked him three times to tarry behind (II Kings 2:2, 4, 6). Like Ruth the Moabitess, when encouraged by Naomi to avoid the uncertainties of a new adventure with the God of Israel, Elisha too may have replied: "Entreat me not to leave thee, and to return from following after thee; for whither thou goest I will go. . . . Jehovah do so to me, and more also, if ought but death part thee and me" (Ruth 1:16-17). For such courage and faithfulness, Elisha was promised a "double portion" of Elijah's spirit if he saw his master go up to heaven. The double portion was the portion of the firstborn son; namely, twice as much as any other son (cf. Deut. 21:17). In other words, he would be Elijah's true successor in the prophetic ministry.

Refusing to be distracted by the unspiritual curiosity of the "sons of the prophets" (see discussion, p. 389) who had been told by the Lord a little of what might happen to him, and wielding his mantle like the rod of Moses, Elijah walked across the Jordan on dry ground. But this was nothing compared to what happened next. As the two men talked, they were suddenly parted from each other by a fiery chariot and horses from heaven (the chariot was the mightiest military instrument known to the ancient world and was therefore symbolic of God's incomparable power — Ps. 104:3-4; Isa. 31:1; 66:15; Hab. 3:8-9). While his faithful companion watched in wonder, Elijah was swept into the third heaven by a supernatural whirlwind leaving only his mantle for Elisha to cling to as the token of his new position and power.

Elijah left this earth in the year 852 B.C., and nearly nine hundred years later appeared again! Moses also appeared with him near the top of a high mountain in the presence of Jesus and three disciples. They talked with Jesus about His forthcoming death — a topic of never-ending fascination to dwellers in heaven (Luke 9:27-36; cf. I Peter 1:12; Rev. 5:9, 12). But the purpose of this appearance was to glorify Jesus, not Moses and Elijah. For when Peter foolishly ("knowing not what he said") suggested the erection of *three* tabernacles, thus putting Moses and Elijah on a par with Jesus, a cloud immediately overshadowed the two prophets, "and lifting up their eyes, they saw no one, save Jesus only" (Matt. 17:8). Great though they were in the history of Israel, Moses and Elijah were mere men, and sinful ones at that.[1]

---

[1] See Alva J. McClain, *The Greatness of the Kingdom* (Chicago: Moody Press, 1968), pp. 181, 337, 457, for helpful discussions of Elijah's future ministry to Israel.

33

ELISHA: FROM THE JORDAN TO SHUNEM

I. A NEW BEGINNING (II Kings 2:13-18)

Like Joshua, the tried and proven successor to Moses, who crossed the Jordan by the miraculous power of God, Elisha exercised his new prophetic authority by wielding the mantle of his master, and "the Jordan was driven back" (Ps. 114:3b). Even if the nation rejected him, at least the forces of nature seemed fully aware of the "double portion" of Elijah's spirit that was now his, and this must have been most encouraging to the young prophet. If the enemies of God thought that His power was crippled by the disappearance of Elijah, they would soon discover otherwise!

On the west bank of the Jordan, Elisha was greeted by fifty sons of the prophets (II Kings 2:15). They had known that Elijah would be taken by the Lord (II Kings 2:5), but they refused to believe Elisha's story about his master's bodily ascension. Refusing to argue with such immature minds concerning an experience so spiritually precious (just as our Lord never publicly proclaimed His virgin birth, and Paul waited fourteen years before sharing his experience in the third heaven — II Cor. 12: 1-4), he sent the stubborn students on a futile three-day expedition to recover the broken body of Elijah from the trans-Jordan mountains.

II. BETHEL AND THE BEARS (II Kings 2:23-25)

Leaving the region of Jericho (see p. 408 for a discussion of the miracle of healed waters), Elisha climbed fifteen miles to the city of Bethel, retracing his steps with Elijah. But before he could visit the school of the prophets there (II Kings 2:3), he was challenged by a large mob of irresponsible young delinquents. The expression "young lads" (II Kings 2:23) certainly

403

does not mean little children.[1] The same term is used of David when Samuel anointed him (I Sam. 16:11), and by then David had already established a reputation as "a mighty man of valor" (I Sam. 16:18), having killed a lion and a bear (I Sam. 17:34-37). So these were young unmarried men, perhaps from twelve to thirty years of age, idle and "vile fellows of the rabble" (Acts 17:5) who were available for hire to perpetrate almost any act of violence. And in the light of their words to Elisha, and his response, it seems highly probable that the calf-worshipping priests of Bethel had masterminded this plot, in order to discredit and humiliate Elijah's successor.

The taunt, "Go up . . . go up," may have been intended as a mockery of the supposed ascension of Elijah. If even the sons of the prophets at Jericho refused to believe Elisha's story of this stupendous miracle, what could be expected from the unbelievers in Israel? And the expression "thou baldhead" was one of extreme contempt. They were pronouncing a divine curse upon him, for which baldness was often the outward sign (cf. Isa. 3: 17a, 24).

Since this was an *official* challenge to his God-appointed ministry, Elisha "cursed them in the name of Jehovah," and in remarkable fulfillment of Moses' warning against national apostasy, two wild animals leaped upon the mob and forty-two were wounded ("if ye walk contrary unto me . . . I will send the beast of the field among you, which shall rob you of your children . . ." — Lev. 26:21-22). This was a shocking, but comparatively mild warning to the nation of what would soon follow if the general apostasy continued. However, instead of repenting of their sins and turning to God, "they mocked the messengers of God, and despised his words, and *scoffed at his prophets,* until the wrath of Jehovah arose against his people, till there was no remedy" (II Chron. 36:16). No wild animals could match the savage cruelty that would be heaped upon this hard-

---

[1]Critics of the O.T. concept of Jehovah love to emphasize the youth and innocence of these lads. Thus, H. W. F. Saggs states that the O.T. "records, with obvious satisfaction, the fate of forty-two cheeky urchins, cursed by Elisha and in consequence eaten by bears" (*The Greatness That Was Babylon,* New York, Mentor Books, 1968), p. 240.

ened people by that specially-prepared rod of God's anger, the
Assyrian army; and that rod would strike within four generations.[2]

III. THE MOABITE CAMPAIGN (II Kings 3)

When King Ahab died, the Moabites rebelled against Israel.
Ahaziah was unable to cope with this crisis, so it was left to his
brother, Joram. In the providence of God, a most remarkable
inscription was discovered in 1868 (see illustration, p. 406)
which contains the actual words of Mesha, king of Moab: "As
for Omri, king of Israel, he humbled Moab many years, for
Chemosh was angry at his land. And his son [Ahab] followed
him and he also said, 'I will humble Moab.' In my time he
spoke thus, but I have triumphed over him and over his house,
while Israel hath perished for ever!"[3]

Determined to recover his lost source of tribute, Joram recruited the services of the ever-willing Jehoshaphat (cf. I Kings
22:4; II Chron. 20:35-37), the father-in-law of his sister Athaliah.
In addition, he enlisted the king of Edom, who had reasons of
his own to seek revenge upon Moab (cf. II Chron. 20:23, where
"Mt. Seir" refers to Edom).

As the combined armies moved across the barren wilderness
south of the Dead Sea, no fresh water could be found, and their
plight became desperate. King Joram blamed Jehovah for this;
but Jehoshaphat, remembering that God had spared his life
because of his desire to hear a true prophet (I Kings 22), once
again asked for a prophet of Jehovah. When a servant suggested
Elisha, he recognized his name; but it is surprising that his
presence in the expedition was not known before this. Possibly
he intended to serve in the capacity of a modern chaplain,
providing systematic instruction for the few officers and men
who would be willing to hear God's Word.

God greatly honored the young prophet by bringing these
three kings to his feet! Later, the king of Syria would do the
same (II Kings 8:9) — a true foretaste of the day when "all

---

[2]See Richard Messner, "Elisha and the Bears," *Grace Journal* (Spring,
1962).

[3]Pritchard, *ANET*, p. 320.

The Moabite Stone. This inscription records Israel's conquest of Moab and the successful revolt of Mesha, king of Moab. Courtesy, Oriental Institute.

kings shall fall down before him [the Messiah], and all nations shall serve him" (Ps. 72:11; cf. Isa. 49:23). But Elisha, unimpressed by the array of royalty, denounced Joram to his face: "What have I to do with thee? get thee to the prophets of thy father, and to the prophets of thy mother" (II Kings 3:13). In other words, Baal's worshippers should consult Baal's prophets. The privilege of answered prayer is granted by God only to those who ask "according to his will" (I John 5:14). But for the sake of Jehoshaphat, whose outward compromises disguised a heart that loved the Lord, Elisha agreed to consult Jehovah.

At first glance, it would seem strange that Elisha would ask for a minstrel to play for him. This was not to awaken any latent magical powers of the prophet, as Joram probably assumed, but was rather for the purpose of calming his distraught soul in order that he might concentrate upon God Himself. Similarly (though the situation was quite different) when David played on his harp, "Saul was refreshed, and was well, and the evil spirit departed from him" (I Sam. 16:23; cf. I Chron. 25:1). Music is one of God's greatest means for thrilling man's heart with His glory and grace (Ps. 150:3-6; Eph. 5:19; Rev. 5:8-9), and Elisha was fully aware of this fact. God heard the fervent prayer of His prophet and not only filled the region with water but also delivered the enemy into their hands.

Seeing his hopes for victory deteriorating, the desperate king of Moab offered his eldest son as a sacrifice to the god Chemosh on the top of the city wall. This was the supreme act of devotion to a pagan deity, and Jehovah had long since warned Israel against such abominations (Deut. 12:31; Micah 6:7).[4] The superstitious (and increasingly polytheistic) Israelites were so terrified at the prospect of what Chemosh, the god of Moab, would do in response to this supreme sacrifice, that they gave up the siege and returned to their own land![5] And so it was, as in the days of Elisha's predecessor, that the nation continued to halt between two opinions as to who their God really was.

---

[4]For an explanation of God's command to Abraham to sacrifice Isaac, see David Dilling, "The Atonement and Human Sacrifice," *Grace Journal* (Winter, 1964).

[5]See George Harton, "The Meaning of II Kings 3:27," *Grace Journal* (Fall, 1970).

IV. WATER, OIL, POTTAGE, LOAVES AND AXE-HEADS
   (II Kings 2:19-22; 4:1-7, 38-44; 6:1-7)

One of the truly outstanding truths about our God is that He concerns Himself with apparently insignificant people and their little problems. He is so great that He must humble Himself just to look into the universe He created (Ps. 113:6)! But the same transcendent God "raiseth up the poor out of the dust and . . . maketh the barren woman to keep house, and to be a joyful mother of children" (Ps. 113:7-9)! While maintaining the orbits of stars and planets, He also numbers the very hairs of our heads (Matt. 10:30). This must be so, if He is truly God, for even human minds realize that *total control* of a system must include the control of all the minute parts and events that make up that system. That seems to be the message of these portions of Scripture.

The miracles of Elijah's brief ministry were mainly spectacular in character, involving the entire nation. But even then, it was not beneath the dignity of Elijah (and Elijah's God) to care for the needs of a widow in Zarephath by miraculous intervention (I Kings 17:13-24). Elisha's ministry, on the other hand, involved numerous "small" miracles by which the temporal needs of God's servants were graciously met.

First was the healing of Jericho's waters (II Kings 2:19-22), a miracle of blessing that stands in sharp contrast to the miracle of cursing which followed (see pp. 403-405). Even as God commanded Moses to use a tree as a symbol of His power to purify the brackish waters at Marah (Exod. 15:25), so Elisha used salt. Obviously, neither the tree nor the salt had any intrinsic powers. To this very day, tourists are shown "Elisha's pool" near the town of Jericho — if nothing else, at least a token of the deep impression this miracle has made upon the minds of men.

Second was the miracle of the widow's oil (II Kings 4:1-7). A poor seminary student died, leaving nothing but unpaid debts for his widow. To make matters worse, her two sons were about to be taken by the creditor to work for him until the debt was paid. This may seem cruel to us, but it is important to note that the creditor is not depicted as a villain in this episode. Bond-service for debt payment was part of God's plan for Israel, but

He also safeguarded this system from abuses (Lev. 25:39-55; Matt. 18:25). Instead of denouncing the creditor, Elisha commanded the widow to pay her full debt (II Kings 4:7). God commands His people to honor their rightful obligations (cf. Rom. 13:8), even under inconvenient circumstances.

The increasing of the widow's oil supply was proportionate to her faith and obedience in borrowing the empty vessels. It must have been somewhat embarrassing to explain to her neighbors why she needed all of these; but even though the miracle took place behind closed doors, the whole neighborhood must have rejoiced in the results when they saw their oil-filled pots being sold and payment made to the creditor instead of the widow surrendering her two sons to the creditor. When the veil has been removed, we will find that God has not only supplied all our needs, but has done so in the most glorious possible way (Phil. 4:19).

The third and fourth "minor miracles" in Elisha's ministry (II Kings 4:38-44) involved food supplies for hungry seminary students at upper Gilgal (cf. II Kings 2:1). One student, possibly meditating on Elisha's fascinating theology lectures, carelessly gathered some poisonous wild cucumbers to add to the luncheon stew. God graciously overruled this potential tragedy for good and demonstrated once again that He "will add all these things unto us" if we seek His interests first.

Soon afterwards a believer from a nearby town brought the first recorded "seminary offering" — an inadequate supply in the form of barley loaves and grain. Gehazi revealed his typical lack of faith (cf. II Kings 4:27; 6:15), but God chose to multiply the offering and thus to anticipate the far greater miracle of our Lord beside the Sea of Galilee. Little things become great when they are dedicated to God.

Last, and perhaps most fascinating of all, was the miracle of the floating axe-head (II Kings 6:1-7). Could anything have been less important in the history of Israel than the loss of an iron axe-head in the Jordan by a careless student? Perhaps not, in man's estimation; but the event must be seen in proper context to be appreciated. The theological students at Jericho suffered in their studies from inadequate housing facilities. The great prophet of God was asked to join with them in their little venture of faith, the construction of a dormitory. Inexperienced and poorly equipped (their tools were borrowed), they nevertheless worked with zeal and for the glory of God. Is the great God of the universe interested in such projects? We might laugh at their feeble effort, but God's question is this: "Who hath despised the day of small things?" (Zech. 4:10). When the horrified student saw the borrowed tool sink deep into the river, both he and his companions gained a never-to-be-forgotten insight into God's loving concern for His own when He put forth His hand and "made the iron to swim." Later, the Lord Jesus taught a frustrated disciple a similar lesson when He commanded a fish to pick up a coin from the depth of the sea and bring it to the shore (Matt. 17:27). God, not man, determines which events are the most important.

V. THE SHUNAMMITE'S SON (II Kings 4:8-37)

On the northern edge of the Plain of Esdraelon, north of Jezreel and east of Mt. Carmel, was a little town named Shunem. Like Bethany near Jerusalem, it will always be remembered as the place where one returned from the realm of death to mortal life.

The background to the miracle may not be spectacular, but it is full of interest. A wealthy lady of Shunem provided a "prophet's chamber" in her home for Elisha's convenience during his frequent travels in that region. Desiring to show her a special favor in response to her gracious hospitality, Elisha offered to speak for her to the king or to the captain of the host if she had any complaint against a neighbor or government official. The prophet apparently had access to the royal court at this time because of the victory over Moab which he was instrumental in achieving (II Kings 3). But she lived in peace with her neighbors and needed no special intercession (II Kings 4:13).

This was the setting for two of the greatest miracles of the Old Testament. First, God granted to her a son when her husband was old (like the fathers of Isaac and John the Baptist). Second, when this miracle boy (whose name is not even recorded!) died, he was brought back to life again. The Scriptures make it very plain that the Shunammite's son did not merely fall into a coma (cf. II Kings 4:20, 32; 8:5). It is also quite clear that no mere sacred object (Elisha's staff) or ceremony (laying it on the child's face) could bring life.

Somehow, the Shunammite woman knew that Gehazi lacked the depth of faith that Elisha possessed. And so, hurrying to Mt. Carmel (ten miles to the west) where she and others had received from Elisha systematic instruction in God's Word in times past, she insisted on seeing the prophet himself in her hour of deepest need (II Kings 4:24, 27, 30). Gehazi, whose spiritual shallowness was later fully exposed (II Kings 5), was completely helpless in the presence of death, even with Elisha's equipment and methods at his disposal. This is an exceedingly important point. God is a glorious Person, and cannot be manipulated by sinful man under any circumstances.

Doubtless remembering Elijah's explanation to him of how God had raised the widow's son at Zarephath (I Kings 17), Elisha demanded privacy and time for fervent prayer. Elijah had stretched himself three times upon the dead child before God granted life. But Elisha did this only twice, and after the first time he could detect warmth returning to the boy's flesh. Why God directed Elijah and Elisha to employ such methods we cannot know; but it is emphatically clear that God, not the methods, brought life. But great as these miracles were, we cannot help but contrast them with the simplicity and majesty of our Lord's work of raising the dead: a mere word (Lazarus and the widow of Nain's son) or touch of the hand (Jairus' daughter).

Elisha then warned the Shunammite to take her family to Philistia to escape a seven-year judgment-drought upon the land, which probably coincided with the final years of King Joram (II Kings 8:1). When she returned, she found that her property had been confiscated, but she also found that the Omri-Ahab dynasty had been destroyed (in the persons of Queen Jezebel and her son Joram), and that Jehu was now on the throne. Gehazi was telling Jehu about Elisha's miracles, especially the raising of the Shunammite's son. Just then, they were brought into the king's presence and received his assistance in regaining her property. Thus did Jehovah honor His prophet, even in high places.

34

ELISHA: MIRACLES IN LIFE AND IN DEATH

I. NAAMAN THE SYRIAN (II Kings 5)

The miraculous healing of Naaman the Syrian actually occurred *later* than the events of Chapters 6 and 7, and the first part of Chapter 8; for in these chapters Gehazi, Elisha's servant, is seen in positions of honor (cf. II Kings 6:17; 8:4). This would be unthinkable if he had already experienced the permanent curse of leprosy (II Kings 5:27). Thus, the cursing of Gehazi must have occurred soon after his visit with the king (II Kings 8:1-6).

Apparently lepers were not ostracized from society in Syria, or else Naaman had proved himself so indispensable to the king (probably Hazael at this time) that his leprosy was tolerated. In the marvellous providence of God, a servant girl from Israel attended his wife and boasted of Elisha's great power to help people, even to raising the dead (II Kings 4:35). If only Christians today would speak this enthusiastically about the powers of their great Saviour!

When the king of Syria heard about the Israelite prophet, he immediately prepared an enormous gift for the king of Israel (more than $80,000 in value), assuming that the king would then bribe his court prophet to perform his magical powers on behalf of this foreign dignitary. But the king of Israel (possibly Jehoahaz by this time, because Jehu would have known about the powers of Elisha — II Kings 8:4) not only ignored Elisha but took the request as a subtle means of exposing his human frailty as a royal representative of Jehovah.

Elisha was deeply offended by this willful ignoring of his position as God's prophet, even as Elijah had challenged King Ahaziah for sending to a foreign god for help (II Kings 1:3). It is encouraging at least that the king must have acknowledged his error, and sent Naaman, in all his military splendor, to the door of Elisha's humble abode (cf. II Kings 3:12; 8:8). A greater contrast can hardly be imagined!

To put this mighty one into the right position before Jehovah, Elisha refused to see him personally, and instructed him to wash seven times in the muddy Jordan. No magic incantation or mysterious handwaving (nor all the clean waters of the rivers of Damascus) could solve this man's problem — only the direct intervention of the living God. Would he be willing to do a very simple and apparently foolish thing, believing that God could meet his need according to His promise? That is the essence of the gospel as it goes forth to men today. The vast majority of men consider the crucified Jesus to be an utterly foolish way to deal with the leprosy of sin (I Cor. 1:23); but to those who have taken God at His word, such a message has become the very power and wisdom of God (I Cor. 1:24; Rom. 1:16).

Naaman must have felt rather silly coming up the sixth time with nothing to show for it; but the seventh time, like the final encirclement of Jericho (Josh. 6:16, 20), was the moment of miracle. With skin as fresh and clean as a little child's (cf. Matt. 18:3), the deeply grateful foreigner returned to offer thanks (like the Samaritan leper of Luke 17:15) and give Elisha a gift. Much in the way of testimony and principle was at stake here. If Elisha accepted the money, Naaman would have been confirmed in his view that even Jehovah's miracles are for hire, just as Simon Magus thought he could buy the power to bestow the gifts of the Spirit (Acts 8:18-20).

Another superstitious view Naaman had was that no god could be properly worshipped except in his own land. Therefore, he would take some of Jehovah's land back to Damascus with him! Also, while accompanying his master in public worship in the heathen temple, he would pray to Jehovah while bowing to Rimmon (or Hadad), the god of Damascus. It will be remembered that the apostle Paul was willing to make large concessions to weak believers on non-essential matters (Acts 18:18; 21:26; I Cor. 8:13; 9:22; 10:28); and in spite of the problems inherent in this passage, we must assume that Elisha considered Naaman to be ill-prepared for advanced instruction in the worship of Jehovah at this moment. Thus the concession: "Go in peace" (II Kings 5:19).

Now comes a shattering blow to this otherwise refreshing scene: "But Gehazi . . ."! Our hearts are deeply wounded, as was Elisha's (II Kings 5:26) at the shocking betrayal by Gehazi, and even more by the spoiled vision of God's free grace that Naaman doubtless carried with him to the grave. The plot was well executed. The money and the raiment were not to be for himself, but for two poor students preparing for the ministry. Naaman doubled the amount of money requested, glad at last for the opportunity to pay for his healing (cf. II Kings 5:15-16), and even sent two servants to carry the garments and the 150 pounds of precious metal all the way to Gehazi's house.

Should not Elisha's servant have guessed that God would see him? How blinding sin can be! Elisha clarified Gehazi's vision (compare the earlier experience recorded in II Kings 6:17): with multitudes of people in desperate spiritual need and false prophets abounding, was this a time for God's servants to seek wealth (to say nothing of seeking it by dishonest means)? In proportion to his privileges, so also was his judgment — perpetual, inheritable leprosy! And thus, for one more of God's privileged servants came the judgment that Paul feared so much: "lest by any means, after that I have preached to others, I myself should be rejected" (I Cor. 9:27).

II. ELISHA AND THE SYRIAN ARMY (II Kings 6:8-23)

Long before the healing of Naaman, while Ben-hadad I was still king of Syria (II Kings 6:24), a most remarkable thing happened: an entire Syrian army was captured alive by Elisha the prophet! It all began with a series of raiding expeditions against the eastern borders of Israel. When these were all systematically and mysteriously blocked, a servant of Ben-hadad suggested that Elisha was responsible (II Kings 6:12). Whereupon, the king sent an entire army, complete with chariots, to capture him! Possibly he hoped to bribe the prophet into becoming *his* court magician!

By night the army surrounded the city of Dothan, and early the next morning Gehazi looked in utter terror at the scene around him: "Alas, my master! how shall we do?" Elisha's calm reply provides one of the greatest assurances the believer can have: "They that are with us are greater than they that are with them" (cf. II Chron. 32:7; I John 4:4). Then Gehazi's eyes were opened, and things took on a new perspective: it is not God's people, but God's enemies who are surrounded and helpless (cf. II Kings 19:28)! When overwhelmed by the forces of evil, we too need to look up and see, with the eye of faith, the heavenly hosts that serve God night and day; for it is always true that "the angel of Jehovah encampeth round about them that fear him, and delivereth them" (Ps. 34:7).

The blindness which God inflicted upon the Syrians did not permanently damage their eyes, but was an intensive form of mental blindness. The only other occurrence of this Hebrew word (*sanwērîm*) describes the judgment of the Sodomites who attacked Lot's home (Gen. 19:11). Mocking the frustrated Syrians (as Elijah had mocked the Baal prophets on Mt. Carmel), Elisha led them to the capital (cf. II Kings 5:3) ten miles away, in what must have been one of the strangest looking processions in history!

The king of Israel (probably the wicked Joram) viewed this as an opportunity for an easy and cruel triumph over his hated enemy; but God could not honor a faithless ruler with such a victory. Furthermore, this would be one more opportunity to confirm in the thinking of the Syrians that "the kings of the house of Israel are merciful kings" (I Kings 20:31), because their God is a merciful God. The Syrians must have been greatly impressed, not only with Jehovah's mercy, but also with Elisha's superhuman insight, "for the bands of Syria came no more into the land of Israel" (II Kings 6:23).

III. THE SIEGE OF SAMARIA (II Kings 6:24–7:20)

After the lessons of the previous futile invasion had worn off, Ben-hadad determined to destroy Samaria once and for all (II Kings 6:24). As the siege continued, the plight of the surrounded Israelites became desperate. Even an ass's head (not ordinarily a choice item!) brought 80 shekels of silver; and four pints of dove's dung was worth five shekels of silver (for fuel). Just as God had warned through Moses long before, willful national rebellion against His Word would reduce His proud and privileged people to savage cannibalism (Lev. 26:29; Deut. 28:

53; cf. Lam. 4:10), as He gave them up to the outworking of
their own carnal desires.

Just like his mother Jezebel, King Joram placed all the blame
for this crisis upon God's prophet (II Kings 6:31; cf. I Kings
19:2). Undoubtedly Elisha had warned the king before the
siege began that such a judgment would come if the nation did
not repent. Joram now felt that a quick way to end the siege
would be to kill Elisha and thus break his evil spell upon the city
(II Kings 6:33). By such thoughts he demonstrated that he was
indeed a "son of a murderer" (a Hebrew idiom for murderer, or
possibly a reference to his father Ahab who had murdered Naboth). An executioner was immediately sent to behead the
prophet, but he was transfixed by the words he heard even as
the temple guards returned empty-handed from their commission to capture Jesus with the strangest of excuses: "Never man so
spake" (John 7:32, 46).

Within twenty-four hours, said Elisha, the famine would not
only be ended, but a whole measure of fine flour would sell for
a shekel! (Recall that during the siege *eighty* shekels would buy
only an ass's head.) And this fantastic deflation of prices would
be accomplished by courtesy of the Syrian army, which would
leave their rich supplies behind while fleeing from an army that
did not exist. Four humble and desperate men, ostracized from
the community because of their leprosy, were honored by God
with the great discovery (cf. Ps. 113:7-8); and fearing divine
punishment if they failed to share the good news with their
starving countrymen, they hurried back to Samaria to inform
the porter at the city gate. The analogy to our own situation is
obvious. God has utterly routed our great enemy through the
work of His Son. But if we, who have made the great discovery, fail to share it with those who are dying in their sins, we
will be held accountable to God (II Cor. 5:11-20). The responsibility we bear is far greater than that of the four lepers of
Samaria.

When the report of the lepers was confirmed, the half-starved
survivors poured out of the city gates and gorged themselves on
the fine flour and barley they found strewn all over the fields
(causing the black market in asses' heads and dove's dung to
collapse immediately!). The captain of the guard who had been

appointed by the king to supervise an orderly exodus through the city gate not only became a victim of the stampede but a literal fulfillment of Elisha's enigmatic and somber prophecy: "Behold, thou shalt see it with thine eyes, but shalt not eat thereof" (II Kings 7:17-20). We may be sure, however, that in the midst of all the rush and confusion few, if any, took the trouble to thank Elisha or Elisha's God for this miraculous intervention on their behalf (cf. Ps. 78:29-32; 106:15).

IV. ELISHA IN DAMASCUS (II Kings 8:7-15)

About ten years had passed since Elijah's ascension, and his successor now carried out a special commission God had entrusted to him — the anointing of Hazael to be king of Syria (cf. I Kings 19:15). The aged and sick king, Ben-hadad I, granted to Elisha a royal reception in Damascus. Sending his captain, Hazael, to meet him with a caravan of forty camels' burden of Damascene delicacies for a gift (somewhat inappropriate for the rugged prophet!), he hoped to purchase the prophet's magical healing powers for his own physical needs. Elisha's reputation was very high in Syria at this time, probably because of his single-handed conquest of the Syrian army at Dothan, and his merciful treatment of the captives (II Kings 6:23).

What did Elisha mean by his statement to Hazael: "Go, say unto him, Thou shalt surely recover; howbeit Jehovah hath showed me that he shall surely die"? At first sight, the statement seems to be completely contradictory. Why tell the king he would recover if God had revealed to the prophet that he would die? There are two ways to interpret these words. The first is that Elisha, knowing that wicked Hazael would not tell his master the truth concerning his imminent death, commanded him to carry out his lying scheme; just as God told Balaam to go with the messengers of Balak (Num. 22:20-22), and as Jesus told Judas to begin his diabolical work of betrayal (John 13:27). The second possibility is that it would not be the illness, but the murderous Hazael who would end the king's life. In either case, it is perfectly clear from the context (in spite of II Kings 8:13b) that Elisha did not put any wicked thoughts into Hazael's mind — they were already there!

As the Lord began to show the prophet what would happen
to thousands of Israelites at the hands of this cruel man, he
stared at him in fascination, and then broke down and wept.
And as we look back upon the fulfillment (II Kings 10:32; 13:
3-7, 22 — in the light of Amos 1:3-5), we may weep too.

Telling Ben-hadad only half of the prophet's words (II Kings
8:14), which in this situation was equivalent to uttering a complete lie, Hazael dipped a bedspread into water and smothered
him to death. We are not told whether Elisha actually anointed
Hazael or not (cf. I Kings 19:15), but his cold-blooded murder
of Ben-hadad demonstrated that a new scourge in the hand of
God was now ready (in spite of Hazael's mock humility — II
Kings 8:13) for the chastening of His stubborn people.[1]

V. THE DEATH OF ELISHA (II Kings 13:14-21)

Elijah's prophetic ministry lasted less than a decade; but his
great successor continued a ministry of miracle and teaching
throughout the reigns of Joram, Jehu, Jehoahaz, and Joash (or
Jehoash) — a total of at least fifty-five years! At last, the aged
prophet found himself upon his death-bed (II Kings 13:14). The
year was now about 795 B.C., and the king of Israel, Joash,
came down to visit him.

The natural sadness of the scene was magnified by the king's
reminder that Elijah had not died, but was raptured to heaven.
Would not God do the same for Elisha — one who had served
Him so long and so faithfully? But our Lord is not obliged to do
for one of His servants what He does for another, and we may
be sure that Elisha was well aware of this fact. If he had ever
asked the Lord for a repetition of Elijah's whirlwind rapture, we
can almost hear His reply: "If I willed that he should thus depart from the earth, what is that to thee? follow thou me" (cf.
John 21:21-23).

It is just possible, however, that Joash's quotation of Elisha's
cry, "My father, my father, the chariots of Israel and the horsemen thereof," was his way of saying: "I want to be *your* successor
and to inherit the portion of the firstborn that you received from

[1]See p. 420 for Elisha's part in the anointing of Jehu.

Elijah." If so, then the symbolic military campaign which Elisha told him to wage against Syria with bow and arrows was the test to determine his fitness for such a privileged position.

In any case, the king's half-hearted response to Elisha's command brought deep disappointment to the prophet. For forty years Hazael had attacked the Holy Land with unique cruelty and persistence; and now his son Ben-hadad II was on the throne to perpetuate his dreadful work (II Kings 13:3). Would King Joash be willing to trust Jehovah for full victory against the enemy? Apparently not, and for the same reason that Ahab had spared the life of Ben-hadad I many years before (I Kings 20: 34), namely, the worldly desire for military security through maintaining Syria as a buffer state against the even more frightful threat of Assyria.

We must assume that Joash understood perfectly the symbolism of the acts Elisha commanded him to perform (compare the iron horns in I Kings 22:11). Five or six strikes upon the ground with a handful of arrows meant total victory over Syria. Four or less would mean partial victory. Joash deliberately rejected God's way and chose his own. Therefore, so far from being a successor to Elisha's prophetic office, Joash was not even qualified to fulfill his own kingly office, and God gave him only limited victory against the enemy (II Kings 13:25).

VI. ELISHA'S POSTHUMOUS MINISTRY (II Kings 13:20-21)

Elisha was not taken to heaven in a whirlwind, but God granted him an experience recorded of no other in history. After he died and was buried, the body of an Israelite soldier killed while defending the land from Moabite invaders was hastily dropped into Elisha's sepulchre. As his body touched the bones of Elisha, his life was restored to him and he stood on his feet! If it could be said of Abel that "he being dead yet speaketh" (Heb. 11:4), we might say of Elisha that he, being dead, yet ministered! And if the other one whom Elisha raised from the dead (the Shunammite's son, now nearing sixty years of age) could have met this soldier, they would have agreed that even without a whirlwind ascension, Elisha was surely one of the greatest servants God ever had.

35

FROM JEHU TO THE ASSYRIAN CAPTIVITY

I. JEHU ANOINTED KING OF ISRAEL (II Kings 9:1-13)

Elisha had personally fulfilled the commission God had given to Elijah to anoint Hazael king of Syria (I Kings 19:15; II Kings 8:8-15); but he delegated to one of the "sons of the prophets" the task of finding and anointing Jehu to be king of Israel. Perhaps Elisha wanted to avoid giving the impression that he was personally responsible for or in favor of the policies of Jehu.

The rush and confusion of Jehu's anointing seemed to be prophetic of the entire career of this mad militarist. As Jehu and his captains were seated in a council of war in Ramoth-gilead near the battlefront, a wild-eyed young prophet burst upon the scene, invited Jehu into a nearby house, anointed him as king of Israel with the primary commission of annihilating the dynasty of Omri and Ahab, and then fled away. When the captains found out what had happened, they immediately improvised a throne, placed their garments beneath him as an act of homage (as many did for the Lord Jesus at His triumphal entry into Jerusalem), blew the trumpet and shouted, "Jehu is king" (compare Absalom, II Sam. 15:10; and Solomon, I Kings 1:39).

II. JORAM AND JEZEBEL SLAIN (II Kings 9:14-37)

Determined to get back to Jezreel before Joram could hear of the coronation and organize his forces, Jehu drove "furiously" (same root as the word used for the "mad" prophet, II Kings 9:11) in his chariot with a company of soldiers. The wounded Joram, anxious to hear news of the battle, sent messengers to enquire, "Is all well?" (II Kings 9:17, ASV margin). Increasingly suspicious of foul play, Joram took Ahaziah (his sister's son, now king of Judah), and dashed forth, in spite of his infirmities, to confront Jehu face to face. Like a mighty magnet, Naboth's blood drew the kings to the fateful spot where Elijah had pronounced doom upon Ahab and his dynasty (I Kings 21:21-22). Unrepentant to the last, and with the judgment of God ringing

in his ears, Joram king of Israel died like his father, and his
nephew suffered a like fate soon afterward.

Jezebel knew what was coming. If she had to die, she would
do so like a Phoenician queen, with painted eyes, set hair, and
with defiance spewing from her mouth: "Is it peace, thou Zimri,
thy master's murderer?" (II Kings 9:31). Zimri had boldly destroyed Baasha's dynasty, but paid the penalty by dying in
flames a week later (I Kings 16:9-20) while under attack from
Omri, Ahab's father. The palace eunuchs were doubtless glad
to demonstrate their loyalty to the new king by throwing Jezebel
to her death. Once again God's word was fulfilled to the letter
as her body was devoured by scavenger dogs because of Jehu's
unintentional (?) delay in granting her the burial of "a king's
daughter."

III. JEHU, THE SCOURGE OF GOD (II Kings 10:1-36)

Intoxicated by his spectacular victory over Ahab's widow, son,
and grandson, Jehu now challenged the rulers and elders of Samaria to a formal combat to determine the destiny of the kingdom. By his various wives and concubines (cf. I Kings 20:3-5
and II Kings 10:1 for hints of the size of Ahab's harem) Ahab
had left seventy sons in Samaria who were cared for by foster-
fathers (compare the seventy sons of Gideon — Judges 8:30).
But it was perfectly obvious that not one of them had the character or experience to lead the nation in a struggle against Jehu.
So the nobles accepted the drastic terms of surrender and brought
to Jezreel seventy baskets containing the heads of Ahab's sons.
Mimicking the terror-tactics of the king of Assyria (to whom he
would bow in abject submission before the year was over),[1] Jehu
demanded that the heads be placed in two heaps at the entrance
of the city gate so that all who passed through would have second thoughts about any possible revolt. Shalmaneser III thus describes his method of handling conquered cities: "I slew with
the sword 300 of their warriors. Pillars of skulls I erected in front

---

[1]The Black Obelisk of Shalmaneser III, dated 841 B.C. (Jehu's first
year), shows Jehu bowing to the king (see Fig. 9). The caption begins:
"The tribute of Jehu, son of Omri; I received from him silver, gold. . ."
(ANET, p. 281).

The Black Obelisk of Shalmaneser III. In the second panel may be seen "Jehu, son of Omri" kneeling before the Assyrian king. The cuneiform text describes the tribute received by Shalmaneser. Courtesy, Oriental Institute.

of the town. . . . In the moat of the town I piled them up, I
covered the wide plain with the corpses of their fighting men, I
dyed the mountains with their blood like red wool. I erected
pillars of skulls in front of his town."[2]

Jehu then sought to gain the favor of the populace by pointing out that he had not personally executed Ahab's sons. Nevertheless, their death was clear evidence that God meant exactly
what He had said through Elijah the prophet (which Jehu had
heard with his own ears — II Kings 9:25). This does not necessarily mean that Jehu was a disciple of Elijah or of Elijah's God,
for he could favor a Jehovah-religion as opposed to a Baal-re-
ligion for purely political reasons (cf. II Kings 10:31). As a
right-wing patriot, he had probably headed up an increasingly
powerful opposition party within Israel against Ahab's foreign
religion, and was very anxious to gain favor with the "silent
majority."

Israelites bearing tribute from Jehu, king of Israel, to Shalmaneser
III, king of Assyria. It consists of silver, gold, vessels, buckets, a block
of antimony, staves, and fruit. From the Black Obelisk. Courtesy,
Inter-Varsity Fellowship.

This helps to explain Jehonadab's support of Jehu's drastic and
ruthless policies. Jehonadab was the founder of a strict sect of
Israelites (partly of Kenite extraction — I Chron. 2:55) who protested the corrupting influences of Canaanite culture by refusing
wine and returning to the nomadic life of Israel's earlier days
(cf. Jer. 35:1-11). He apparently was held in high respect by

---

[2]*ANET*, p. 277.

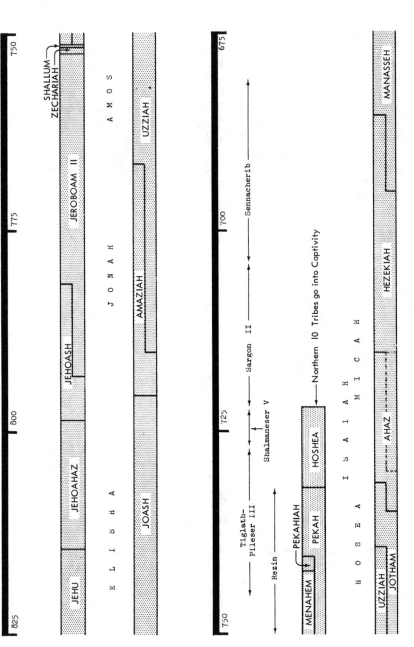

11. Time Chart: 825 to 675 B.C.

many, and Jehu was most happy to have his public endorsement of the great bloodbath that was now under way.

The slaughter of Ahab's henchmen in Jezreel (II Kings 10:11) and Samaria (II Kings 10:17), and the execution of Ahaziah's relatives (II Kings 10:12-14) would be expected under the circumstances. But the methods of deceit which Jehu employed in order to destroy Baal's followers in the name of Jehovah reveal his true attitude and could never be condoned (II Kings 10: 18-28). God does not need human lies to promote His truth (cf. Rom. 3:7-8), nor can He honor those who feel that such methods are necessary for the accomplishment of His purposes (compare the tragic consequences of David's lie to the high priest — I Sam. 22:22).

With a diabolical efficiency that may be compared to Hitler's scheme of duping Jews into thinking that gas chambers were only shower rooms,[3] Jehu and Jehonadab jammed the house of Baal with his most zealous worshippers and then had them slaughtered. "Thus Jehu destroyed Baal out of Israel" (II Kings 10:28), carrying to completion the negative aspects of the lifelong struggles of Elijah and Elisha. Ahab's family had refused the ministries and warnings of Jehovah's great prophets, so He sent to them a messenger they *would* understand.

For his zeal against this false deity, Jehu was honored with a dynasty that continued through four more generations and nearly a century (II Kings 10:30). But Jehu (like Nebuchadnezzar) was more of an instrument than a servant of Jehovah, and was spiritually incapable of promoting the true worship of Israel's God. Having destroyed Baal, he contented himself with Jeroboam's calf-cult at Bethel and Dan and "took no heed to walk in the law of Jehovah, the God of Israel, with all his heart: he departed not from the sins of Jeroboam, wherewith he made Israel to sin" (II Kings 10:31). Therefore, what he gained through zeal he lost through spiritual blindness, and Jehovah had to tell the prophet Hosea eighty years later to name his son Jezreel, "for yet a little while, and I will avenge the blood of Jezreel upon the house of Jehu, and will cause the kingdom of the house of Israel

---

[3]Cf. William L. Shirer, *The Rise and Fall of the Third Reich* (New York: Simon and Schuster, 1960), p. 970.

to cease" (Hos. 1:4). So the very deeds he supposedly performed
for Jehovah (II Kings 10:16 — "Come with me and see my zeal
for Jehovah") were an abomination to God because they were
not done out of a Spirit-filled heart and for the glory of God.

IV. JEHOAHAZ AND JEHOASH (II Kings 13:1–14:16)

In the very first year of his reign, Jehu, like other western
kings, was forced to pay homage to Shalmaneser III of Assyria.
Within a few years, however, Assyrian pressures were concen-
trated farther east, thus permitting Hazael of Damascus to begin his devastating campaigns against the entire trans-Jordan region (II Kings 10:32-33). Jehu had never fainted at the sight of
blood; but he met his match in this scourge from Damascus,
whose cruel treatment of Israelite captives brought tears to the
prophet who anointed him and who foresaw his evil works (cf.
II Kings 8:11-13).

Jehoahaz, the son of Jehu, was a religious carbon-copy of his
father, bowing before the calf at Bethel which Jeroboam had set
up. For this, Jehovah permitted Hazael to slash deep into his
kingdom and decimate his army, leaving him only ten chariots
(compared to Ahab's two thousand!). Perhaps the author of
Kings was speaking ironically when he suggested further reading
on Jehoahaz "and his might" (II Kings 13:8)!

When, in desperation, he temporarily abandoned his golden
calf and turned directly to the Lord in prayer, God graciously
"gave Israel a saviour, so that they went out from under the
hand of the Syrians" (II Kings 13:5). But who was this "saviour"? It was either an unnamed general, or the son of Jehoahaz
who "recovered the cities of Israel" (II Kings 13:25), or possibly
even his grandson Jeroboam II ("he saved them by the hand of
Jeroboam" — II Kings 14:27).

Jehoahaz was followed by another calf-worshipper named Joash (or Jehoash). He was notable for his bedside visit with the
dying Elisha; for his three victories against Syria (II Kings 13:
25); and for his complete victory over Amaziah, the "Thistle
King" of Judah.[4] By now, it was becoming quite obvious that

---

[4]See pp. 441-442.

Jehu's "reforms" were almost totally worthless from a spiritual standpoint and that Satan was the unseen victor in the affairs of the northern kingdom.

V. JEROBOAM II TO PEKAHIAH (II Kings 14:23–15:26)

Jeroboam II may be considered as the greatest of the northern kings, even though he followed the spiritual pattern of his apostate fathers. During his long reign of forty-one years he succeeded in extending the borders of Israel far beyond Damascus, almost to the Euphrates, as God had promised Abraham (Gen. 15:18). Jeroboam's military successes were predicted by the prophet Jonah, who had doubtless returned by now from Nineveh (14:25). In fact, it may have been the repentance of the Ninevites that brought about a lull in Assyrian campaigns to the west during the reign of Jeroboam II, thus permitting him to move unchallenged deep into Syrian territory. Israel's prosperity during this era is clearly reflected in the writings of Hosea (12:8; 13:6), Amos (6:4-6), and Isaiah (28:1). But it was only a calm before the storm, for prosperity brought complacency, pride, and insensitivity to the voice of the Lord (Amos 7:10-13; cf. James 5:1-6).

The death of Jeroboam II in 753 B.C. was the beginning of the end for the northern kingdom. Within two years Zechariah his son died at the hand of an assassin (thus bringing a hasty fulfillment of God's promise of four generations of royal descendants to Jehu – II Kings 15:12); and the assassin himself (Shallum) was slain by an utterly calloused soldier named Menahem (II Kings 15:14; cf. v. 16). Note the remarkable similarity of these events to those 130 years earlier, when Elah, after a two-year reign, was assassinated by Zimri, who in turn was brought to death a few days later by Omri. As in the final phase of the Roman Empire, one general after another seized the throne and the populace paid less and less heed to the bewildering game of intrigue, military takeover, and sham rule.

It was in the days of King Menahem that the dreadful spectre of Assyrian conquest loomed over the eastern horizon. For more than a generation Assyria had been relatively quiescent (a result of the ministry of Jonah in Nineveh?) with weak emperors such

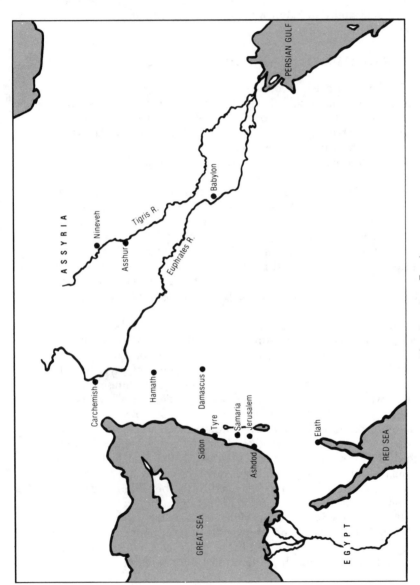

The Assyrian Empire.

as Shalmaneser IV, Ashurdan III, and Ashur-ninari V upon the throne. But in 745 B.C. an exceedingly vigorous general took the reins of government under the title Tiglath-pileser III (and the name Pulu following his conquest of Babylon — II Kings 15:19; cf. I Chron. 5:26, where "and" should be translated "even"), and whipped the Assyrian army into a state of incomparable efficiency and zeal. Moving westward in 743 B.C., he conquered

Relief showing Tiglath-pileser III, king of Assyria.
Courtesy, Inter-Varsity Fellowship.

several small kingdoms. "As for Menahem, I overwhelmed him like a snowstorm and he . . . fled like a bird, alone, and bowed to my feet."[5] Sixty thousand Israelite "men of wealth" had to pay fifty shekels of silver each (a thousand talents was three million shekels), at the command of Menahem, to buy off the Assyrians (II Kings 15:20).

VI. PEKAH AND HOSHEA (II Kings 15:25–17:23)

Menahem's "dynasty" lasted only two years beyond his own death, for his son Pekahiah was slain by one of his generals, Pe-

---

[5]Pritchard, *ANET*, pp. 283-284.

kah the son of Remaliah. Furthermore, it appears that Pekah had
already long since established himself as a pretender to the
throne and a leader of the anti-Assyrian party especially in the
trans-Jordan region of Gilead (II Kings 15:25), for he dated the
beginning of his reign retroactively to the beginning of Menahem's.[6]

It was only a year after Pekah took the throne that King Uzziah of Judah died as a leper, and Isaiah saw the vision of Je-
hovah-Christ upon the throne of heaven (Isa. 6:1). With the
powerful Uzziah now dead, Pekah began to exert great pressure
upon Judah to join his western confederacy of anti-Assyrian
states. But when Ahaz became co-regent with his politically
weak father, Jotham, in Judah and refused to join, Pekah of Israel and Rezin of Syria invaded the southern kingdom, killed
120,000 soldiers and took 200,000 captives, who were soon released under threat of divine judgment (II Chron. 28:5-15). A
few months later Pekah and Rezin plotted to replace Ahaz with
a Phoenician puppet (son of Taleel — Isa. 7:6), invaded Judah
again[7] and "went up to Jerusalem to war against it, but could
not prevail against it" (Isa. 7:1; cf. II Kings 16:5) because Ahaz
had in the meantime succeeded in bribing Tiglath-pileser III to
attack Damascus and northern Israel (II Kings 15:29; 16:7-9;
II Chron. 28:20). Pekah and Rezin were now mere "tails of
smoking firebrands" (Isa. 7:4) because Jehovah was not their
Head (Isa. 7:7-9).

Thus, the great darkness of Assyrian deportation fell first upon
the land of Galilee (cf. Isa. 9:1). Utterly terrified by the prospect of total collapse under the iron fist of Tiglath-pileser III,
the majority of Israelites now backed Hoshea's plot to remove
Pekah and to come to terms with Assyria. As the great conqueror explained it: "They overthrew their king Pekah and I
placed Hoshea as king over them. I received from them ten talents of gold, 1,000 talents of silver as their tribute, and brought
them to Assyria."[8]

[6]Thiele, *Mysterious Numbers,* pp. 123-124.
[7]Cf. Edward J. Young. *Studies in Isaiah* (Wm. B. Eerdmans Publishing
Co., 1954), pp. 145-151.
[8]Pritchard, *ANET,* p. 284.

In spite of the fact that Hoshea was the least wicked of the northern kings (II Kings 17:2), the kingdom collapsed anyway, thus demonstrating that it was rotten beyond recovery. Five years after Hoshea became king, Tiglath-pileser III died, and the new Assyrian emperor, Shalmaneser V, demanded a continuation of the heavy tribute. However, the burden became unbearable and Hoshea apparently was forced by his leaders to seek out an alliance with the Egyptians. Such treachery was, of course, intolerable to the Assyrians, who promptly imprisoned Hoshea and began a long siege of the well-fortified capital city of Samaria (724-722 B.C.). Just after the siege ended, Shalmaneser V died, and Sargon II (cf. Isa. 20:1) claimed the honor of having conquered the city.[9] "At the beginning of my royal rule I conquered the town of the Samarians.... I led away as prisoners 27,290 inhabitants of it and equipped from among them soldiers to man 50 chariots for my royal corps.... The town I rebuilt better than it was before and settled therein people from countries which I myself had conquered. I placed an officer of mine as governor over them and imposed upon them tribute as is customary for Assyrian citizens."[10] Before the days of Tiglath-pileser III, Assyrian monarchs had been content to raid and exact tribute from western countries. But now a drastic new method of shattering national morale and resistance was instituted — mass deportations of peoples from one end of the empire to the other. God had indeed prepared a "rod of his anger" to send against "a profane nation" (Isa. 10:5-6).

So tragic and shocking was this catastrophe that the author of Kings paused in the midst of his narrative to list about twenty reasons why God's judgment was so richly deserved (II Kings 17:7-18). God was not helpless to rescue Israel from her enemies. In fact, He was the One who raised them up and brought them to destroy His people. Nor had He broken His covenant

---

[9]Cf. Hayim Tadmor, "The Campaigns of Sargon II of Assur," *Journal of Cuneiform Studies*, vol. 12, no. 1 (1958), pp. 33-40. A. T. Olmstead and E. R. Thiele agree that the cuneiform evidence does not support Sargon's claim to be the conqueror of Samaria.

[10]Pritchard, *ANET, p.* 284.

Limestone relief of Sargon II, king of Assyria, from the palace at Khorsabad.

One of the colossal human-headed winged bulls that guarded the entrance to the palace of Sargon II at Khorsabad. Courtesy, Oriental Institute.

promises to the nation, for a remnant of each of the northern tribes had long since fled to the tribe of Judah to perpetuate their identity there (cf. II Chron. 11:16; Acts 26:7; James 1:1; and the reference to Anna "of the tribe of Asher" in Luke 2:36). We may imagine his tears falling upon the parchment as the author of Kings penned Israel's epitaph: "So Israel was carried away out of their own land to Assyria unto this day" (II Kings 17:23). And the tragedy was compounded because Judah refused to learn spiritual lessons from the experience of her sister kingdom to the north (II Kings 17:19; cf. Ezek. 16:46-59), thus explaining why the author of Kings was himself in far off Babylon when he completed his book (cf. II Kings 25:27-30).

VII. THE DESTRUCTION OF ISRAEL (II Kings 17:24-41)

Isaiah had predicted that the process of deporting Israelites and importing foreigners with the consequent destruction of the ethnic identity of the northern kingdom (and the formation of a new mongrel race called Samaritans) would take sixty-five years beginning in 734 B.C. (Isa. 7:8). Thus, "the king of Assyria" in II Kings 17:24 who completed this monumental task must have been Esarhaddon, the grandson of Sargon, whose reign ended in 669 B.C., exactly sixty-five years after Isaiah's prophecy. This is confirmed by the fact that the Samaritan half-breeds who hindered the work of Zerubbabel and Joshua in rebuilding the Jerusalem temple insisted that "we sacrifice unto him since the days of Esar-haddon king of Assyria, who brought us up hither" (Ezra 4:2).

It is noteworthy that so many Israelites vanished from the scene during those years that lions began to multiply beyond control. God had long since warned the nation: "If ye walk contrary to me . . . I will send the beast of the field among you, which shall rob you of your children, and destroy your cattle, and make you few in number; and your ways shall become desolate" (Lev. 26:21-22; cf. Exod. 23:29). Having utterly rejected the mild warnings of two she-bears in the days of Elisha (cf. II Kings 2:24), the land was now literally overrun with thousands of lions.

To meet this crisis, the new inhabitants called for a Jehovah calf-priest to be returned to Bethel to "teach them the law of the god of the land" (II Kings 17:27). The priest, however, must have felt somewhat hindered in his teaching ministry, for the golden calf had been carried away from Bethel to Assyria: "The inhabitants of Samaria shall be in terror for the calves of Beth-aven; for the people thereof shall mourn over it . . . because it is departed from it. It also shall be carried unto Assyria . . ." (Hos. 10:5-6).

If this priest set as his goal the mere perpetuation of the name of Jehovah in the northern regions he succeeded marvelously well. But the *worship* of Jehovah, even in the style of Jeroboam I, vanished permanently in the north (II Kings 17:34). Each group of importees from Babylon, Cuth, Hamath, Avva, and Sepharvaim (from various extremities of the Fertile Crescent — II Kings 17:24, 30, 31) maintained their basic loyalty to their own gods, and either added Jehovah to the already crowded pantheon or perhaps called their favorite god by the name of the local deity, Jehovah, whom they sought to placate by this means. "They feared Jehovah, and served their own gods, after the manner of the nations from among whom they had been carried away" (II Kings 17:33).

This was the final fruit of Jeroboam's break with Jerusalem and Judah: a stench in the nostrils of God and man. From this time onward, the southern Jews had "no dealings with the Samaritans" (John 4:9); and though the Samaritan people continue to the present hour, their numbers have dwindled to a mere handful and their national glory has departed forever.

36

FROM JEHOSHAPHAT TO HEZEKIAH

I. JEHORAM AND AHAZIAH OF JUDAH (II Chron. 21–22)

The fruits of Jehoshaphat's alliance with wicked Ahab and Jezebel of Israel (through the marriage of his son Jehoram to their daughter Athaliah) now became clearly evident. As is often the case with children, young Jehoram copied the weaknesses of his father but not his strengths, and not only entered willingly into a marriage relationship with the northern princess, but accepted wholeheartedly the pagan ways of her parents as well. Thus Queen Jezebel controlled both her husband and her daughter's husband, and through them permeated both Israel and Judah with the poisonous leaven of Baalism.

As soon as his father was dead, Jehoram eliminated his six younger and more righteous brothers (II Chron. 21:2-4; cf. v. 13) to whom their father had given many gifts and fortified cities in Judah (II Chron. 21:3). This was doubtless at the instigation of his wife Athaliah (21:6; 22:3), even as Jezebel had engineered the murder of Naboth and his sons at Jezreel. Jehoram's brothers, along with some of the nobility, apparently had sought to hinder his plan to introduce the outright worship of Baal in Judah (cf. II Chron. 23:17), and lost their lives as a result. Were these men true believers? Did they bear a consistent witness to Jehovah in those evil days? One of the great blessings of heaven will be a personalized study of the unabridged edition of God's Hall of Fame.

God's response to Jehoram's depraved and outrageous acts was drastic. First, He permitted Edom and Libnah to slip out of Judah's hand (II Chron. 21:8-10), even as Moab had earlier revolted from Israel (II Kings 3:5). Second, He permitted Philistines and Arabians to invade Judah, sack Jerusalem, and carry away the king's wives and sons, with the exception of Athaliah

435

and Jehoahaz (or Ahaziah).[1] Third, He directed Elijah, His special witness against Baal-worshippers, to write a letter to Jehoram, warning him of a horrible form of dysentery that would
come upon him (II Chron. 21:12-15), which brought him to an
untimely grave two years later. Fourth, Jehoram was deprived
of an honorable burial. "His people made no burning for him
like the burnings of his father [cf. II Chron. 16:14 for Asa] . . .
and he departed without being desired; and they buried him in
the city of David, but not in the sepulchres of the kings" (II
Chron. 21:19-20). Thus did Jehovah permit Satan's man to have
his little day in the sun, and then cast him forth "like an abominable branch. . . . thou shalt not be joined with them in burial,
because thou hast destroyed thy land, thou hast slain thy people; the seed of evildoers shall not be named forever" (Isa. 14:
19-20, concerning Satan's future tool, the Antichrist).

Ahaziah, Jehoram's son and successor, was, if possible, even
more wicked than his father; but he was cut off before the end
of his first year and therefore had less opportunity to display
his depravity. His mother, Athaliah, not only named him after
her evil brother in the north, but "was his counsellor to do
wickedly" (II Chron. 22:3). Furthermore, "the house of Ahab
. . . were his counsellors after the death of his father, to his destruction. He walked also after their counsel" (II Chron. 22:
3-5). A more discouraging background for a Davidic king can
hardly be imagined!

But Satan overreached himself when he bound Ahaziah so
closely to Ahab's family, for God's appointed hour for the destruction of that dynasty had come. While Ahaziah was in Jezreel visiting his wounded uncle Joram, Jehu, the scourge of
God, swept in from the eastern battlefront and killed the Israelite king. Horrified by what he saw Ahaziah fled by way of the
garden house (II Kings 9:27) southward to Samaria. There he

---

[1]It was at this time, apparently, that Obadiah denounced Edom for standing "on the other side, in the day that strangers carried away his [Jeru-
salem's] substance, and foreigners entered into his gates, and cast lots
upon Jerusalem" (Obad. 11). Such an early date for Obadiah is suggested
by the fact that Jeremiah (49:14-16) seems to quote from him, and not
the reverse. For supporting arguments, see Gleason Archer, *A Survey of
Old Testament Introduction* (Moody Press, 1964), pp. 287-91.

was captured, and brought in his chariot to Ibleam, halfway back to Jezreel, where Jehu ordered him to be killed (II Chron. 22: 9). However, the blow was not immediately fatal, and Ahaziah managed to escape westward up the ascent of Gur toward Megiddo where he finally died (II Kings 9:27).[2] While his body was being returned to Jerusalem for burial, forty-two of his cousins, who had somehow succeeded in escaping the slaughter inflicted upon their family by Philistines and Arabians (II Chron. 21:16-17), were intercepted and killed by Jehu on their way to visit the royal family in Jezreel (II Kings 10:12-14).

II. QUEEN ATHALIAH (II Chron. 22:10–23:15)

Satan, knowing that his time was short, stirred up Athaliah, his feminine Antichrist in Jerusalem, and "she arose and destroyed all the seed royal of the house of Judah" (II Chron. 22:10). The real surprise here is that there was anyone left for her to kill! In the marvellous providence of God, a baby son of Ahaziah was rescued by his aunt, Jehosheba, whose husband Jehoiada "just happened to be" the high priest at that time. Hiding him first in a bedchamber and then in the temple, they managed to prevent the queen (or anyone else) from knowing of his existence for six long years!

What must God's people have thought about God's promise to David: "Thy house and thy kingdom shall be made sure for ever before thee: thy throne shall be established for ever" (II Sam. 7:16)? Did some attempt to spiritualize the promise in the light of its apparent failure of fulfillment? Those who did were guilty of underestimating the Word of their God, for the literal interpretation of the prophecy had its vindication in a temple playroom. Even more complex for God's people was the problem of Jeremiah's curse upon the line of Jehoiachin (Jer. 22: 28-30) two centuries later. After Jehoiachin's death, where was the legitimate Davidic king? The answer was hidden in the genetic code of a woman who came from one of David's noncursed lines (Nathan — II Sam. 5:14; Luke 3:31), whose virgin-

---

[2]See the map depicting these movements in Aharoni, *The Macmillan Bible Atlas* (New York: The Macmillan Co., 1968), p. 85.

born Son could be adopted by a descendant of Jehoiachin (Joseph of Nazareth), thereby transmitting to this child the legal right to the throne without at the same time transmitting the curse! Truly, God's ways and thoughts are higher than ours, even as the heavens are higher than the earth (Isa. 55:9).

In the seventh year of Judah's tribulation period under Athaliah, the fulness of God's time finally came. The high priest Jehoiada secretly summoned to the temple five faithful captains together with the Carites,[3] representative Levites, and other godly leaders, and after making them swear their loyalty, showed them the crown prince. The experience must have been electrifying. There *was* a king in Judah! God's promises had *not* been frustrated by Satan! Thus, Jehoiada reminded them: "Behold, the king's son shall reign, as Jehovah hath spoken concerning the sons of David" (II Chron. 23:3).

Waiting until a Sabbath day, when more temple workers would be present, Jehoiada divided the incoming shift of priests and Levites into three groups to guard strategic points, while the outgoing group, instead of going to their homes, stayed in the temple to protect the king (II Chron. 23:8). The fact that all of this could be planned without the queen's knowledge shows how feeble her popular support really was by now.

Armed with David's weapons, the defenders of David's dynasty brought forth David's descendant, placed the crown upon him, presented to him a copy of God's Law (cf. Deut. 17:18-20), anointed him, and shouted, "Long live the king!!" Even as Adonijah heard too late the shouting at his brother Solomon's coronation (I Kings 1:41-53), so Athaliah found herself an unwilling spectator at her own abdication. Instead of panicking like Adonijah, however, she followed the example of her mother Jezebel and faced her enemies with fierce boldness, screaming "Treason! treason!" These were her last recorded words; for in just retribution for her blasphemies and murders, she was maneuvered away from God's house which her sons had ransacked (II Chron. 24:7) and was slain near the palace.

---

[3]The Carites were probably the "Cherethites" of II Sam. 8:18, who, along with the Pelethites and Gittites, were Philistine mercenary troops who were fiercely loyal to David and the Davidic dynasty (II Sam. 15:18; cf. I Sam. 30:14; Ezek. 25:16; Zeph. 2:5).

Thus ended the dynasty of Omri in its Judean extension, just seven years after its northern extension had been destroyed by Jehu. The mopping-up operations were quickly accomplished; for the people covenanted to serve Jehovah, and then destroyed Baal's temple, altars, images, and priest[4] without having to employ Jehu's deceptive methods at all (cf. II Kings 10:18-28).

III. JOASH, THE BOY KING (II Kings 12; II Chron. 24)

The forty-year reign of Joash may be divided into two parts — before and after the death of his spiritual guardian, Jehoiada. The statement that "Joash did that which was right in the eyes of Jehovah *all the days of Jehoiada the priest*" is ominous. Without the moral and spiritual courage of this high priest, Joash was as unstable as Lot without Abram. Therefore, God showed His mercy to the people of Judah by extending Jehoiada's life to an amazing 130 years![5]

One worthy project that Joash accomplished during the first phase of his reign was the repair of the temple. At first glance, II Kings 12:4-6 seems to imply that it took the priests twenty-three years to collect money for repairing the temple! However, the text does not state how long before his twenty-third year the project was started. There may be some hint of dishonesty among the priests or their "acquaintance" (II Kings 12:5, 7 — possibly money changers or assessors) in handling the offerings. At any rate, a voluntary offering system with a "Joash chest" proved more effective, and the precious metals (coinage had not yet been invented) were turned over to faithful workers who completed all the necessary repairs.

Then came Phase Two of the reign of Joash, and with it great tragedies. With Jehoiada dead, a group of left-wing no-

---

[4]The name of this priest, Mattan, may be an abbreviation for Mattan-baal ("gift of Baal"), just as Mattaniah meant "gift of Jehovah" (cf. II Kings 24:17).

[5]II Chron. 24:15. Thus, Jehoiada lived longer than anyone on record during the previous thousand years, since Amram, an ancestor of Moses, died at 137 (Exod. 6:20). We are disappointed, however, to see Jehoiada's concession to human frailty in giving two wives to young Joash (II Chron. 24:3).

bles caught the ear of the king and turned him from the Lord so completely that he actually commanded his men to stone Zechariah, the son of Jehoiada, for speaking out against the new apostasy. As the faithful prophet lay dying in the temple court, he cried out: "Jehovah look upon it and require it" (II Chron. 24:22).[6] And Jehovah *did* require it of Joash, for before the year was over, Hazael's army approached Jerusalem from the west, defeated the Judean army (II Chron. 24:23-24), and was finally bought off with temple treasures (II Kings 12:18). Joash himself was sorely wounded, and was later slain by two conspirators. The supreme indignity came when he was denied burial among the sepulchres of the kings, though Jehoiada was given this special honor (II Chron. 24:15-16, 25).

IV. AMAZIAH, THE "THISTLE KING"
(II Kings 14; II Chron. 25)

Amaziah's reign began well, with a wise handling of an emotionally-charged situation. Most ancient kings would have wiped out the entire family of an assassin to prevent further retaliation. But Amaziah entrusted this matter to the Lord and obeyed the Scriptures (II Chron. 25:4; cf. Deut. 24:16). Furthermore, he obeyed God's prophet by sending home 100,000 Ephraimite mercenaries, even though the hundred talents of silver had already been given to them and their humiliation would doubtless cause them to retaliate (II Chron. 25:5-10, 13). It is obvious that Judah's army had not yet recovered from the disastrous defeat in the days of Joash (cf. II Chron. 24:24), and therefore additional troops were needed for the campaign against Edom. But it is also true that spiritual principles had to take precedence over military ones; and not only was God able to give Amaziah a great victory over Edom without the Ephraimite soldiers (II Chron. 25:10-12), but He was also able to more than make up for the great financial loss (II Chron. 25:9).

That Amaziah should bow down and burn incense to the Edomite idols which were obviously not able to deliver even

---

[6]Many believe that Jesus referred to this event in Matthew 23:35. However, he spoke of "Zachariah son of Barachiah" who was a postexilic prophet (Zech. 1:1). The situation may have been quite similar. See J. Barton Payne, "Zachariah Who Perished," *Grace Journal* (Fall, 1967).

their own people (II Chron. 25:14-15) is so ridiculous as to be almost unbelievable. But how believable or rational is *any* sin? Not until the mind of man has surrendered to the Lord can it even begin to function properly (cf. Luke 8:35 – "in his right mind at the feet of Jesus"). So Amaziah had to be rebuked by God and suffer terribly in order that he (and we) might learn the folly of spiritual disobedience.

Idolatry clouded his mind so completely that instead of obeying God's prophet as he had done before the battle (II Chron. 25:10), he denounced him with bitter words: "Have we made thee of the king's counsel? forbear: why shouldest thou be smitten?" (II Chron. 25:16). God prevented him from actually smiting the prophet (as Asa and Joash had done in their moments of rebellion against God); but the thought was as bad as the deed, and even more alarming words came back upon his head: "I know that God hath determined to destroy thee, because thou hast done this, and hast not hearkened unto my counsel" (II Chron. 25:16).

All of this necessary background information to the disastrous battle with Jehoash of Israel is omitted by the author of Kings, who assumed that his readers were aware of the existence of at least this portion of the book of Chronicles.[7]

Doubtless Amaziah was able to convince his people that the war was necessary for the sake of national honor, but this time Jehovah was not with him (II Chron. 25:20). Supremely confident of his invincible power after (1) defeating the Edomites completely, (2) capturing and then enlisting the help of their gods, and (3) silencing Jehovah's meddlesome prophet, Amaziah challenged the king of Israel to a military contest in revenge for the damaging border raids by the malcontent mercenaries whom he had previously rejected at Jehovah's insistence (II Chron. 25:13). But the king of Israel, astounded at Amaziah's ambitious pride, cut him down to size with a well-phrased fable: A worthless and despicable thistle once tried to

---

[7]Similarly, the author of Kings omitted the reason for Baasha's fortification of Ramah (I Kings 15:17) because the full story was available in II Chron. 15:9 ff. More frequently, however, the Chronicler assumes the reader's knowledge of the book of Kings.

put himself on a par with stately cedar trees until a passing beast accidentally stepped on him, and his ambitious plans came to a sudden end![8] In other words, O Amaziah, pitiful "thistle king" of Judah, stay in your own league and be content with the little trophies you have already won, lest you and your kingdom should come to disaster!

But Amaziah did not discern God's voice through the fable; thus he suffered a staggering defeat at Beth-shemesh (just west of Jerusalem), saw six hundred feet of the northern wall of his capital city broken down, and lost hostages as well as temple treasures (II Chron. 25:21-24). Furthermore, Amaziah henceforth lost the confidence of his people; Uzziah his son was made co-regent while still a teen-ager; and conspirators finally succeeded in killing Amaziah at Lachish.

V. KING UZZIAH, THE LEPER (II Chron. 26)

The story of King Uzziah, or 'Azariah" as his name is spelled in the book of Kings, is remarkably similar to that of Asa, Joash, and Amaziah. Running well in the beginning, all of these kings became preoccupied with their own success and prosperity (which God gave them in the first place) and were sorely chastened with disease, military defeat, and (in the case of Uzziah) leprosy. "He that thinketh he standeth, let him take heed lest he fall" (I Cor. 10:12).

The tremendous influence which God's prophets had upon their contemporaries may be judged by this statement concerning King Uzziah: "he set himself to seek God in the days of Zechariah, who had understanding in the vision of God: and as long as he sought Jehovah, God made him to prosper" (II Chron. 26:5). We know nothing of this prophet Zechariah (possibly named after the one whom Uzziah's grandfather had commanded to be stoned), but his influence upon both king and kingdom may be compared to that of Jehoiada the high priest in the early years of Joash. In a real sense, therefore, all of Uzziah's great achievements during these early years of his long reign (defeating enemy nations; building cities, towers, and

---

[8]The only other fable in the Bible was uttered by Jotham, a son of Gideon, concerning trees that sought for a king (Judges 9:8-15).

cisterns; raising cattle and fruit trees; equipping his army with
the "latest" weapons) can be attributed to Zechariah who encouraged the king to "seek God." Thus, Uzziah "waxed exceed-
ing strong" (II Chron. 26:8) and "was marvellously helped" (II
Chron. 26:15).

All of this is the background for one of the greatest falls in
Old Testament history. The similarity to Satan's fall from heaven
is striking: "when he was strong, his heart was lifted up" (II
Chron. 26:16).[9] But why did Uzziah desire to "burn incense
upon the altar of incense"? Because he was no longer satisfied
with being a mere king, and desired to be a "divine king" like
some of his contemporaries, especially in Egypt.[10] But the
depth of this sin can be measured only by the sacredness of the
position he was usurping, namely, the position of the great
Priest-King, our Lord Jesus Christ who alone is qualified to sit at
God's right hand as "a priest for ever after the order of Melchizedek" (Ps. 110:1, 4), indeed, as "a priest upon his throne"
(Zech. 6:13). It was God's revealed plan that no Aaronic priest
should ever sit upon David's throne (cf. Gen. 49:10; Heb. 7:14),
and no descendant of David should ever be an Aaronic priest.
Uzziah clearly understood this clear distinction between kings
and priests in Israel and thus was guilty of deliberately defy-
ing God.

With great moral courage, Azariah the high priest and eighty
priests with him confronted Uzziah and denounced him in the
name of the Lord. The moment he responded with anger instead of repentance, leprosy broke out on his forehead,[11] and

---

[9]Cf. Isa. 14:13 — "thou saidst in thy heart, I will ascend into heaven";
and Ezek. 28:17 — "Thy heart was lifted up because of thy beauty." Thus,
the New Testament pastor was not to be a novice, "lest being puffed up
he fall into the condemnation of the devil" (I Tim. 3:6).

[10]It is possible that Uzziah wanted to be another Melchizedek (Gen.
14:18). Jeroboam I similarly attempted to combine royal and priestly
functions in himself (cf. I Kings 12:27-33).

[11]Miriam was similarly punished for intruding into the God-given au-
thority of Moses. The verb "spake" in Numbers 12:1 is feminine! For
excellent discussions of leprosy, see McClintock and Strong, *Cyclopedia of
Biblical, Theological, and Ecclesiastical Literature*, Vol. V (Grand Rapids:
Baker Book House, reprinted 1969); and Patrick Feeny, *The Fight Against
Leprosy* (New York: American Leprosy Missions, Inc., 1964).

in great terror the king rushed out of the temple, followed by
eighty-one priests thrusting him out. The final decade of his
life was spent in a separate place, crying out, "Unclean, unclean,"
to all who passed by (cf. Lev. 13:45-46). A more tragic end to
an otherwise glorious reign can hardly be imagined. But from
a broader aspect, Uzziah symbolized the condition of the entire
nation before God. As Isaiah the prophet confessed when he
saw the Holy One of Israel in the year that King Uzziah died,
"Woe is me! for I am undone; because I am a man of unclean
lips, and I dwell in the midst of a people of unclean lips" (Isa.
6:5).

VI. JOTHAM AND AHAZ (II Chron. 27–28)

Very little is written about King Jotham in Scripture, possibly
because his reign was overlapped largely by co-regencies with
his father, Uzziah, and son, Ahaz. Though he was a godly man,
his reign was somewhat colorless. He built some cities and towers, and won a foreign war (which is not mentioned in Kings).
The only significant adverse comment is that "he entered not
into the temple of Jehovah" (II Chron. 27:2). Was he trying to
honor his father who was smitten with leprosy in the temple,
or was he superstitiously fearful of suffering the same fate?
Nevertheless, "Jotham was mighty because he ordered his ways
before Jehovah his God" (II Chron. 27:6).

Ahaz was a shocking contrast to his godly father. In fact, he
ranks among the most wicked rulers of the southern kingdom,
in a class with such blots on the Biblical record as Jehoram,
Athaliah, Manasseh, Jehoiakim, and Zedekiah. His personal
contribution to the record of royal depravity was to burn alive
some of his own children as sacrifices to the god Molech, setting
an example which Manasseh later followed (II Chron. 28:3; 33:
6; cf. Lev. 18:21). God's response to this was to permit an
Ephraimite to kill another of his sons (II Chron. 28:7), so that
when Hezekiah finally became king he had no brothers to challenge him.

This was a time of great turmoil in Palestine, as Assyrian armies under the brilliant leadership of Tiglath-pileser III repeatedly crushed these small western kingdoms with burdens of
tribute and threats of mass deportation. Pekah of Israel was

launched to the throne on a wave of anti-Assyrian feeling, and he determined to bring Judah into his western confederacy.[12] When Judah, now ruled by Ahaz, refused to cooperate, Pekah of Israel and Rezin of Damascus invaded their southern neighbor and carried off many captives to Samaria and Damascus (II Chron. 28:5-15). While in Damascus as a captive, Ahaz sacrificed to the gods that smote him. "But they were the ruin of him and of all Israel" (II Chron. 28:23).

After his release, and the release of 200,000 of his citizens from Samaria, Ahaz was attacked by Edomites from the southeast and Philistines from the west. Furthermore, Israel and Syria prepared to invade Judah again (II Kings 16:5; Isa. 7:1). Jehovah offered to encourage his faith with a spectacular sign (Isa. 7:11), but with mock piety Ahaz brushed this gracious offer to one side: "I will not ask, neither will I tempt Jehovah" (Isa. 7:12).

Thus, rejecting all of God's warnings through Isaiah, Ahaz followed through with his desperate plan of bribing Tiglath-pileser III to attack Damascus and Israel. He may have justified this move by appealing to Asa's example (who hired Ben-hadad of Syria to attack Baasha of Israel), but Isaiah warned him that he was playing with fire and that the Assyrian would ultimately destroy Judah also (Isa. 7:17–8:8). Ahaz received a foretaste of this in his own lifetime, for "Tiglath-pileser king of Assyria came unto him, and distressed him, but strengthened him not" (II Chron. 28:20). The more he gave to Tiglath-pileser the more was demanded of him, until he had to strip the temple and his own palace to make payments, "but it helped him not" (II Chron. 28:21).

It was not that Ahaz neglected Tiglath-pileser. In fact, as soon as the Assyrians conquered Syria (732 B.C.), the Judean king hurried to Damascus to pay his personal respects to the great king (II Kings 16:10). While there, he saw the great altar that Tiglath-pileser erected for the glory of Asshur, sent for Urijah the priest to copy and duplicate it, and hastened to demonstrate his loyalty to his Assyrian overlords by worshipping exclusively at

---

[12]For a discussion of Pekah's policies, see p. 430.

this replica within the temple court in Jerusalem. He even set Jehovah's altar to one side (II Kings 16:10-16), made other drastic changes in temple arrangements "because of the king of Assyria" (II Kings 16:18), and finally "cut in pieces the vessels of the house of God and shut up the doors of the house of Jehovah" (II Chron. 28:24).

But if Ahaz thought he could gain a solid and lasting friendship with Assyria by such means, he was utterly mistaken. He was now in the "big leagues" of international intrigue and political depravity, where truth, honesty, faithfulness, and love were unknown entities. Having deliberately abandoned Jehovah, he and his little kingdom (the remaining refuge for God's people in the world) were now hopelessly enmeshed in Satan's web. "Forasmuch as this people have refused the waters of Shiloah that go softly . . . the Lord bringeth upon them the waters of the River, strong and many, even the king of Assyria, and all his glory . . . and it shall sweep onward into Judah . . . and the stretching out of its wings shall fill the breadth of thy land, O Immanuel" (Isa. 8:6-8).

Ahaz died and was buried in dishonor. And such would have been the fate of his kingdom too were it not for Hezekiah his son, whose faith in Jehovah in an hour of ultimate crisis was God's reason for extending the nation's existence yet another hundred years.

37

HEZEKIAH AND THE ASSYRIANS

I. THE GREAT REVIVAL (II Kings 18:1-8)

With the probable exception of Josiah, who lived a hundred years later, Hezekiah was the most godly descendant of David ever to sit upon the throne (II Kings 18:5; cf. 23:25). His reign began with a great revival of true religion in Judah, the effects of which reached even to the northern tribal territories (II Chron. 30:5-27).

From a negative standpoint, there were much destruction and removal of the symbols of pagan idolatry that had accumulated during his father's reign (II Kings 18:4; cf. II Chron. 31:1). Among the things destroyed was the *brazen serpent* which Moses had made in the wilderness seven hundred years earlier (Num. 21:8-9)! Instead of serving as a reminder of the blessed truth that salvation comes by obedient faith in God's promises (cf. John 3:14-15), the famous relic had become an idol before which men bowed and offered incense! Therefore the young king did to it what we should be prepared to do to *anything* that positions itself between us and God — see it for what it really is (Nehushtan — a mere "piece of brass," ASV margin), and *destroy* it! So it was that Paul's converts at Ephesus saw their books on magical arts in a new light, gathered them into a huge pile, and "burned them in the sight of all . . . so mightily grew the word of the Lord and prevailed" (Acts 19:19-20). "My little children," wrote an aged apostle, "guard yourselves from idols" (I John 5:21).

From a positive standpoint, Hezekiah opened the temple doors which Ahaz his father had closed (II Chron. 29:3; cf. 28:24), commissioned the priests and Levites to cleanse the temple (II Chron. 29:4-19), offered appropriate sacrifices (II Chron. 29:20-36), planned a special passover which had to be delayed one month because so few were ceremonially qualified (II Chron. 30:1-4), and invited people from every tribe, not only from the south, but also from the northern areas that had suffered the loss

of their king and capital city a few years earlier (II Chron. 30:
5-12).

II. TRIBUTE TO SENNACHERIB (II Kings 18:13-16)

It is apparent that Hezekiah did not fully count the cost in
one decision he made during the early years of revival and reformation: "he rebelled against the king of Assyria, and served
him not" (II Kings 18:7). This was not a particularly courageous
act at the time, for the Assyrian army was preoccupied in the
eastern part of the empire for several years, and Sargon II died
in 705 B.C. But now the picture had changed drastically. In
701 B.C., Sennacherib, having consolidated the empire and reorganized the army following the death of his father, moved
westward to punish various kings, including Hezekiah, and to
force them once again to pay heavy annual tributes to Nineveh.[1]

Hezekiah was utterly terrified at this sudden and unexpected
confrontation with the mighty Assyrian army, and therefore allowed himself to be caught in a trap of his own making. "The
fear of man bringeth a snare, but whoso putteth his trust in
Jehovah shall be safe" (Prov. 29:25). Instead of trusting God,
he asked for terms of peace, which is exactly what any worldly
ruler would have done under the circumstances (cf. I Kings
20:4). In the words of our Lord, "what king, as he goeth to encounter another king in war, will not sit down first and take
counsel whether he is able with ten thousand to meet him that
cometh against him with twenty thousand? Or else, while the
other is yet a great way off, he sendeth an ambassage, and asketh
conditions of peace" (Luke 14:31-32). The tribute imposed
upon Judah was enormous (nearly $2,000,000), and Hezekiah
had to empty both the temple and palace treasuries, and even to
strip the gold from the doors and pillars of the temple (II Kings
18:16).[2]

---

[1] In a clay prism, Sennacherib lists the following familiar cities and
countries which were conquered and forced to pay tribute during the
701 B.C. campaign: Sidon, Arvad, Byblos, Ammon, Moab, Edom, Ashdod,
Ashkelon, Ekron, and Joppa (*ANET*, pp. 287, 288).

[2] In anticipation of Sennacherib's next move, Hezekiah had a tunnel
cut under Mt. Zion to bring the water of Gihon spring into the city (cf.
II Kings 20:20; II Chron. 32:3, 4, 30; and for the inscription cut into
the wall of the tunnel, *ANET*, p. 321.)

The Siloam Tunnel cut by Hezekiah (II Kings 20:20). This 1,750-foot conduit brought the waters of the Spring Gihon inside the city of Jerusalem. Courtesy, Matson Photo Service.

III. SENNACHERIB'S FIRST THREAT (II Kings 18:17-37)

His appetite whetted by Hezekiah's easy surrender to his demands, Sennacherib determined to take everything (compare the effort of France and England to appease Hitler by giving him the outer borders of Czechoslovakia in 1938). It was very important to the Assyrian commander to eliminate Jerusalem as a potential threat on his left flank as he faced the Egyptian army to the south. Therefore he sent three highly trained military ambassadors to terrify the Jews of Jerusalem into immediate surrender: *Tartan* ("Field Marshal"; cf. Isa. 20:1), *Rab-saris* ("Chief Eunuch"; cf. Jer. 39:3), and *Rabshakeh* ("Chief Officer").

The location of the confrontation was significant: "the conduit of the upper pool, which is in the highway of the fuller's field" (II Kings 18:17). It was here, on the high ground overlooking the city from the northwest, where laundrymen (fullers) found sufficient water for their trade, that Isaiah had challenged wicked Ahaz thirty-three years earlier with a divine alternative: either trust Jehovah or face the Assyrians (Isa. 7:3-17). Ahaz, on behalf of his people, made his decision, and God's warning was now being fulfilled.

Hezekiah sent Eliakim, Shebnah, and Joah to meet the three Assyrian ambassadors. But instead of discussing the matter privately, Rabshakeh insisted on using the occasion as a means of terrifying the curious Jews who were crowded along the walls of the city (II Kings 18:26; cf. II Chron. 32:18). Not only did he shout at them with a loud voice, but he also spoke in Hebrew so he could be clearly understood. Does this mean that he went to the trouble of learning Hebrew, or did he speak through an interpreter? The Jewish delegation begged him to speak to them in Aramaic, the commercial and diplomatic language of the Fertile Crescent (which by this time was replacing the more cumbersome Akkadian language). He not only refused to do so, but insulted the people of the city (II Kings 18:27). In our own day, the utter frustration and futility of engaging in "peace talks" with Communist leaders comes vividly to mind by way of comparison.

Rabshakeh used six arguments to pressure the Jews into the immediate surrender of their city. The first, third, and fifth were mundane and practical reasons; but the second, fourth, and sixth were religious and theological in character. The *first argument* was actually quite valid: Egypt was an undependable and weak reed to lean upon as far as military alliance was concerned. Isaiah the prophet had repeatedly warned the Jews against heeding the pro-Egyptian party in Judah, which tended to grow in influence whenever pressure from Assyria increased (Isa. 30:2, 5, 7; 31:1). The people of Judah had already seen what happened to the northern kingdom when Hoshea "sent messengers to So king of Egypt" (II Kings 17:4), and not only received no help from him but thereby provoked the ultimate wrath of his Assyrian overlord (a century later King Zedekiah tried the same tactic and failed, too — Jer. 37:5-10). Rabshakeh didn't realize, however, that the real reason why Egypt was no help to Israel was that God blocked any alternative to trusting in Him.

The *second argument,* a theological one, must have seemed laughable to most of the listening Jews. Hezekiah had removed all the "Jehovah altars" throughout the land (II Kings 18:4; cf. II Chron. 31:1), and destroyed Moses' brazen serpent (II Kings 18:4). Surely, then, the Assyrians insisted, the Jews could no longer count on any help from Jehovah, whose honor and glory had thus been reduced by Hezekiah's fanatical iconoclasm! Such reasoning might have seemed impressive to idolaters who thought that the size and number of idols erected in honor of a particular deity would be a valid measuring-stick of the amount of blessing that could be expected from him; but even the average Jew could see through such religious logic (cf. Isa. 10:10-11).

Rabshakeh's *third argument* was simply that the Assyrian army was overwhelmingly large and powerful (II Kings 18:23-24; cf. I Kings 20:10). The point was undeniable, except that a gigantic army would presumably require just as much time to conquer a well-fortified city like Jerusalem as a moderate-sized army, and a lengthy siege was probably the last thing the Assyrians wanted to engage in at this time.

The most astonishing argument of all was probably the *fourth* one: "Am I now come up without Jehovah against this place to destroy it? Jehovah said unto me, Go up against this land, and destroy it" (II Kings 18:25). Nearly two centuries later, Cyrus of Persia claimed that Marduk, the god of Babylon, had "ordered him to march against his city Babylon."[3] But was this a mere propaganda technique? Isaiah had been warning Jerusalem for over thirty years that Jehovah would bring "the king of Assyria" to cause desolation in the land (Isa. 7:7-25; 8:7-8). Jehovah's words through His prophet must have electrified the complacent Jews: "Ho Assyrian, the rod of mine anger, the staff in whose hand is mine indignation! I will send him against a profane nation, and against the people of my wrath will I give him a charge, to take the spoil, and to take the prey, and to tread them down like the mire of the streets" (Isa. 10:5-6).

In view of the obvious cleverness of Rabshakeh, is it not possible that he had heard of Isaiah's sermons and determined to use them to his own political advantage? It seems clear that the Babylonian king was aware of Jeremiah's ministry and rewarded him accordingly after the fall of Jerusalem (Jer. 39:11-12); and the Medo-Persians presumably knew of Daniel's denunciation of Belshazzar before the fall of Babylon (Dan. 5:28; 6:3). There is one remarkable case of a foreign king who was told by Jehovah to kill a godly king of Judah if he blocked his way through Palestine (II Chron. 35:20-22). But we may be sure that this was not true of Sennacherib, "for he hath said, By the strength of my hand I have done it, and by my wisdom" (Isa. 10:13; cf. 10:7). Furthermore, God revealed to Hezekiah that these words from the lips of the Assyrian were *blasphemies* (II Kings 19:6, 22). Even if Rabshakeh did quote from Isaiah's sermons, he failed to consider the possibility that Jehovah's wrath upon Judah would be averted if the people repented of their sins and prayed to their God.

Rabshakeh's *fifth* argument (II Kings 18:31-32) must go down in history as one of the clumsiest and most transparent propaganda appeals on record. If you will just surrender unconditionally to us, said the Assyrian, we will provide for you free transportation to a beautiful land far away, where each of you will have a private cistern surrounded with vines, grain, and both olive and fig trees — like the Garden of Eden! The only problem with this impressive travel and settlement plan was that the sponsors had a very bad reputation! The Assyrians were

---

[3]*ANET*, p. 315.

experts in handling mass deportations from one end of the Fertile Crescent to the other, and heartless cruelty was their trademark (cf. Nah. 3:1-4, 19). Was Rabshakeh incapable of recognizing that the Judeans had a clear memory of what had happened to their northern neighbors just two decades earlier — at the hands of gentle and gracious Assyrians (cf. II Kings 17:23-24)?

Sixth, and finally, another religious argument (II Kings 18:33-35). (In our day of near-total secularism, it is difficult to appreciate how great a role religion played in the ancient Near East, even in military and political affairs.) Other gods, that had protected greater cities than Jerusalem (the gods of Hamath, Arpad, Sepharvaim, Hena, Ivvah, and even — how pitiful! — Samaria), had proven to be utterly ineffective against the might of Ashur, god of the Assyrians. So what could Jehovah do except to surrender His city to prevent its destruction? This argument, like the second one (II Kings 18:22), must have seemed quite unimpressive to those Jews who had any concept whatsoever of the absolute uniqueness of Jehovah.

The arguments were now ended. Could they be answered and refuted on a human level? No. What, then, could the Jews say to Rabshakeh? Nothing. "Foolish and ignorant questionings refuse, knowing that they gender strifes. And the Lord's servant must not strive . . ." (II Tim. 2:23-24). Hezekiah did the right thing in commanding his delegation: "Answer him not" (II Kings 18:36); for the only answer the Assyrians could possibly understand would be the language of action in the form of supernatural judgment.

IV. HEZEKIAH'S FIRST PRAYER AND GOD'S ANSWER (II Kings 19:1-7)

Having been thoroughly chastened by his experience with the Assyrians, Hezekiah now set the pattern for his people in following God's way of dealing with a great crisis: (1) self-humiliation — 19:1a; (2) going to the appointed place of worship — 19:1b; (3) consulting the Word of God through His prophets — 19:2; and (4) putting God's honor and glory above everything else — 19:4. If the thrice-holy God of Israel had honored the sincere repentance of a wicked king like Ahab (I Kings 21:29), and later honored the repentant prayer of another wicked king

named Manasseh (II Chron. 33:12-13), He would surely respond
to this kind of a prayer from this kind of a king. And Hezekiah
was not disappointed. The Lord promised through Isaiah that
the blasphemies of Rabshakeh would be dealt with. With regard to Sennacherib, God would maneuver him back to Nineveh
(possibly by a report of potential rebellion there) and cause him
to be killed at the hand of assassins (see comments on II Kings
19:37).

V. THE SECOND ASSYRIAN THREAT (II Kings 19:8-13)

The words "returned" and "heard" in verses 8 and 9 are not
the fulfillments of Isaiah's prophecy (II Kings 19:7) that the king
of Assyria would "hear" and "return." Instead, verses 8 and 9
refer to a temporary shift of strategy in southern Palestine in the
light of a new threat from Tirhakah king of Ethiopia (who had
apparently usurped control of Egypt). Realizing that his position
was now more dangerous than ever, Sennacherib sent his messengers back to Jerusalem to pressure the inhabitants to surrender without a siege. Nothing new was added to previous arguments except the gruesome example of several other great cities
that had refused to surrender to the mighty Assyrian army —
Gozan, Haran, Reseph, and Telassar (II Kings 19:12; cf. 18:34).
Even as Rahab admitted to the spies that the recent reports of
Jehovah's destruction of Sihon and Og caused all of their hearts
to melt in fear (Josh. 2:10-11), so now the example of recent
history must surely strike its mark in timid hearts.

VI. HEZEKIAH'S SECOND PRAYER AND GOD'S ANSWER
(II Kings 19:14-34)

The king's response to this fresh challenge is one of the most
encouraging examples of child-like trust in the entire Bible: "And
Hezekiah received the letter . . . and read it . . . and spread it
before Jehovah" (II Kings 19:14). How many of the discouraging
things of life do we "spread before Jehovah"? Not that He
doesn't already know all about them; but He commands us to cast
all our cares upon Him, for He cares for us (I Peter 5:7).

Hezekiah's prayer was effectual, because he knew his God and
he knew the issues in the light of God's Word: (1) Jehovah is
absolutely unique as the sovereign Creator — II Kings 19:15;

(2) a mere sinful man named Sennacherib had defied Him —
II Kings 19:16; (3) Sennacherib's boast that other gods had been
destroyed only confirmed the fact that they were not real gods
in the first place! — II Kings 19:17-18; (4) Jehovah would be glorified among all nations by the deliverance of Jerusalem — II Kings
19:19.

God's answer to this humble and discerning prayer involved
three distinct ideas: (1) Sennacherib is a mere instrument in the
hands of a sovereign God — II Kings 19:21-28; (2) the remnant
of Israel will prosper again — II Kings 19:29-31; and (3) the Assyrians will not touch Jerusalem — II Kings 19:32-34.

First of all, Sennacherib made a fatal miscalculation when he
thought that Jerusalem was just another city (II Kings 19:21-
22)! Other great cities may have their kings (cf. Isa. 7:8-9), but
Jerusalem also has a heavenly King who happens to be the Sovereign God of the entire earth! With insufferable pride, Sennacherib's army had destroyed one kingdom after another, like an irresponsible lumber company slashing down a beautiful forest (II
Kings 19:23). But the truth of the matter was that Jehovah had
long since planned and prepared the Assyrians for this very task
of destroying many cities (II Kings 19:25). The fact that they
couldn't resist him did not so much reflect Sennacherib's skill as
it did the irresistible purpose of Jehovah (II Kings 19:25), for
the Assyrian king was nothing but an axe, a saw, a rod, or a staff
in the hand of God (Isa. 10:15). To prove this, He would take
the raging, arrogant Assyrian by his nose and lips[4] and lead him
back to Nineveh (II Kings 19:28). What a comfort to God's
people today to know that He has "a hook in the nose" of their
arch-enemy, Satan, who can do *nothing* outside of the will of their
heavenly Father (Job 1:12; 2:6; Rev. 20:2).

Secondly, there was hope for the remnant of Judah (II Kings
19:29-31). The fruitful fields and vineyards which the Assyrians
had devastated (cf. Isa. 7:18-25) would be resown and replanted,
and by the third year the normal agricultural cycle would func-

---

[4]This was a cruelty which the Assyrians frequently inflicted upon their
captives. "Esarhaddon's relief at Zenjirli shows Tirhakah of Egypt and
Baalu of Tyre each with a ring in his nose and the cords in the hand of
the conqueror. Cf. II Chron. 33:11" (*The New Bible Commentary: Revised*), p. 363.

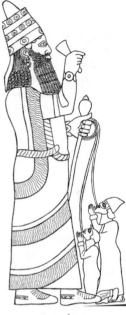

Relief of Esarhaddon, king of Assyria, from Zenjirli. Two royal captives are secured by ropes and rings through their lower lips.

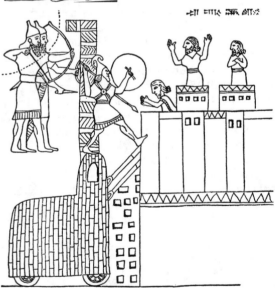

Assyrian mobile battering ram. It was to accommodate such a machine that Sennacherib would have built a ramp, or "cast a bank against" the wall of Jerusalem (II Kings 19:32). Note the falling bricks loosened by the ram and the distressed defenders of the city. Courtesy, Inter-Varsity Fellowship.

tion again. To encourage his people, it is quite possible that Hezekiah wrote Psalm 126. The first three verses of this psalm reflect the national and international astonishment that Jerusalem could be delivered so suddenly from such a peril (cf. II Chron. 32:22-23). Verse 4 is a prayer for the return of prosperity. And verses 5 and 6 are an encouragement to the remnant of Judah to sow their precious seed (instead of eating it), for even though it might involve weeping and tears, yet great joy would come with the harvesting of sheaves.

Finally, the threatened siege of Jerusalem would not material-ize at all, for Jehovah would defend it to vindicate His glory which had been blasphemed (cf. I Kings 20:28), and to honor the covenant promise He had made to David (II Sam. 7). The completeness of God's protection (no arrows, shields, or mounds) reminds us of the three friends of Daniel who emerged from the fiery furnace with no clothing burned, nor hair singed, nor even the smell of fire (Dan. 3:27)! There would be no question as to who had saved Jerusalem!

VII. THE ASSYRIANS DESTROYED (II Kings 19:35-37)

That very night (compare the death of the firstborn of Egypt — Exod. 12:29) the angel of the Lord (the pre-incarnate Christ) killed 185,000 Assyrian soldiers! Is this difficult for us to believe? In order to make the narrative more palatable to the "modern mind," some have pointed to a tradition recorded by the ancient Greek historian Herodotus (ii, 141) that mice once infested a camp of the Assyrian army and ate the bow-strings and leather shield handles. The actual truth of the tradition, we are told, is the presence of mice, which would have spread bubonic plague and thus destroyed the army. But would this many men die from such a cause in one night? It is also suggested that 185,000 is an exaggerated figure which somehow got into the text of II Kings. Note, for example, this unfortunate and irresponsible comment by an evangelical scholar: "there is no evidence outside of the Bible of such tremendous loss; in Chronicles it is much more moderate . . . a pestilence such as bubonic plague may have been behind both stories [i.e., Herodotus and II Kings]" (*New Bible Com-mentary: Revised*, Eerdmans, 1970, p. 363). Does every miracle

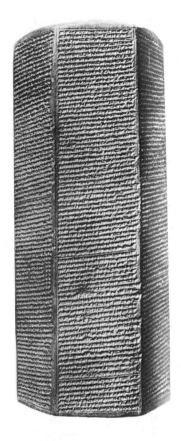

Hexagonal clay prism inscribed with the annals of Sennacherib, king of Assyria. Sennacherib boasts of conquering 46 strong cities of Judah and besieging Jerusalem. Courtesy, Oriental Institute.

ḫa - za - qi - a - ú	mat ia - ú - da - a - a
Hezekiah	the Judaean

kima	iṣṣuri	qu - up - pi	ki - rib	al	ur - sa - li - im - mu
like	a	caged bird	within	the city of	Jerusalem

al	sami - ti - šú	e - sir - šú
his	capital city	I shut up

Part of inscription appearing on Sennacherib's Prism. Courtesy, Inter-Varsity Fellowship.

recorded in the Bible have to be confirmed by outside sources before we can really believe it? Does the fact that II Chronicles 32:31 omits the number of soldiers killed contradict the number given in II Kings, *which is found also in Isaiah 37:36?* "Ye do err, not knowing the scriptures, nor the power of God" (Matt. 22:29).

However, those who are skilled at "reading between the lines" of Assyrian historical records find convincing evidence of a great Assyrian military debacle in Palestine at this time. In his famous Prism Inscription (see illustration, p. 458), Sennacherib states: "Hezekiah himself, whom the terror-inspiring splendor of my lordship had overwhelmed and whose irregular and elite troops which he had brought into Jerusalem, his royal residence, in order to strengthen it, had deserted him, did send me, later, to Nineveh, my lordly city, together with 30 talents of gold, 800 talents of silver...."[5] Now the fact that Sennacherib said nothing about conquering Jerusalem is tantamount to admitting a total defeat, for otherwise he would have gloated over the conquest in great detail. Furthermore, it was thirteen years before the Assyrians appeared in Palestine again.

Apparently it was shortly before the destruction of his army that Sennacherib returned to his capital city of Nineveh (cf. II Kings 19:7). Twenty years later (681 B.C.), as he was worshipping in his palace chapel, two of his sons (cf. Isa. 37:38) assassinated him and fled northward to the region of Ararat between the Black Sea and the Caspian Sea. Another son, Esarhaddon (681-669 B.C.), took the throne and completed the task of transplanting Israelites to the eastern parts of the empire and replacing them with other peoples (II Kings 17:24-41; cf. Isa. 7:8; Ezra 4:2).

In a fascinating inscription, Esarhaddon tells how his father Sennacherib preferred him above his older brothers, who thereupon "abandoned godliness, put their trust in bold actions, planning an evil plot."[6] Furthermore, Ashurbanipal, the son of Esarhaddon, gives us a hint as to how Sennacherib died: ". . . others, I smashed alive with the very same statues of protective deities

---

[5]*ANET*, p. 288.
[6]*Ibid.*, p. 289.

with which they had smashed my own grandfather Sennacherib
— now finally as a belated burial sacrifice for his soul."[7]

Fitting these scraps of information together, we may assume
that it was in revenge for being passed over as heirs to the
throne that Esarhaddon's older brothers crept into their father's
private prayer chapel and pushed over on him a gigantic statue
of Nisroch, his god. And thus the great and proud king of Assyria, who boasted that Hezekiah's God was utterly helpless, not
only lost his army at one flick of Jehovah's finger but was himself
crushed to death by the idol of a non-existent deity to whom
he had devoted his life.

_____

[7]*Ibid.,* p. 288.

38

HEZEKIAH AND THE BABYLONIANS

I. HEZEKIAH'S SICKNESS (II Kings 20:1-3)

There are several reasons for believing that Hezekiah's sickness and recovery, and the visit of the ambassadors from Babylon, took place *before* the attack by Sennacherib as recorded in the previous two chapters. In the *first* place, when God responded to Hezekiah's prayer and promised to heal him, He also promised: "I will deliver thee and this city out of the hand of the king of Assyria; and I will defend this city for mine own sake, and for my servant David's sake" (II Kings 20:6). Such a promise would seem unnecessary if the Assyrian army had just been destroyed and Sennacherib had returned to Nineveh.

Secondly, it would seem highly unlikely that Hezekiah could show the Babylonian ambassadors "all the house of his precious things, the silver, and the gold . . ." (II Kings 20:13), if he had just stripped both the temple and the palace of all their gold and silver (including the plating on the doors and pillars) to buy off the Assyrians (II Kings 18:15, 16). *Thirdly,* II Chronicles 32: 25-26 informs us that after God healed him, "Hezekiah rendered not again according to the benefit done unto him; for his heart was lifted up: therefore there was wrath upon him, and upon Judah and Jerusalem. Notwithstanding Hezekiah humbled himself for the pride of his heart, both he and the inhabitants of Jerusalem, so that the wrath of Jehovah came not upon them in the days of Hezekiah." It seems quite clear from this statement that the payment of heavy tribute and the threat of siege by Rabshakeh came *after* Hezekiah was healed of a deadly disease.

Why did the Lord tell Hezekiah to prepare to die? It is true, of course, that "it is appointed unto men once to die" (Heb. 9:27), but this is the only recorded instance of God telling a righteous man to prepare to die while he was still in the prime of life ("in the noontide of my days" — Isa. 38:10). The answer seems to be that God chose to use this means to chasten Hezekiah because of a growing pride of heart. The record in II Chronicles 29–31 of unparalleled blessings that were his during the early

461

years of revival and reformation is followed immediately by this ominous statement: "After these things, and this faithfulness, Sennacherib king of Assyria came, and entered into Judah . . ." (II Chron. 32:1). It is important to note that even *after* God healed him, "Hezekiah rendered not again according to the benefit done unto him; for his heart was lifted up . . ." (II Chron. 32:25).

The God who understands our thoughts afar off (Ps. 139:2) is jealous of our love and devotion to Him, and "whom the Lord loveth he chasteneth" (Heb. 12:6). "But I have this against thee, that thou didst leave thy first love. Remember therefore whence thou art fallen, and repent . . . or else I come to thee, and will remove thy candlestick . . ." (Rev. 2:4-5). Only in the light of such warnings can we understand the apparent severity of God's dealings with the sins of Moses (Num. 20:12), David (II Sam. 12:10-14), and Uzziah (II Chron. 26:16-21). We may assume, then, that if II Kings 20:1 were expanded, it would read: "In those days was Hezekiah sick unto death because Jehovah chastened him for the pride that was rising within his heart after so many years of prosperity and blessing."

Just as King David "fasted and wept" when the Lord brought a great sickness upon his and Bathsheba's child (II Sam. 12:16, 22), so now "Hezekiah wept sore" under the chastening hand of a gracious God who desires nothing but the best for His children (cf. Rom. 8:28, 32). It was not that Hezekiah's years of God-honoring service had been forgotten (cf. Heb. 6:10). It was not that he had borne no spiritual fruit at all. The fact of the matter is, that *only* those who bear fruit are chastened! "Every branch that beareth fruit, he cleanseth it, that it may bear more fruit" (John 15:2). May it never be forgotten that it was Hezekiah's repentant tears, rather than his great works, that brought the *miracle* of physical healing (II Kings 20:7), the *miracle* of Jerusalem's defense (II Kings 20:6), and the *miracle* of the retreating shadow (II Kings 20:8-11).

II. THE PROMISE OF RECOVERY (II Kings 20:4-7)

One of the more unpleasant tasks God imposed upon His prophets in those days was that of pronouncing judgment upon kings that had stepped outside of the will of God. Isaiah had already had very unpleasant experiences with Ahaz (Isa. 7:13), and it must have brought him great joy to see and to participate in Hezekiah's national reforms. Nothing could have been farther from his heart than to see now the untimely death of this great king. We can imagine his joy, therefore, when the Lord stopped him soon after he had given to Hezekiah the divine death sentence and told him to return to the king with the assurance that he would recover within three days and that fifteen years would be added to his life!

What would I do with the remainder of my life if God told me that I had just fifteen years to live? What did Hezekiah do with those years? The Bible does not say, for the last event recorded of his reign was the destruction of Sennacherib's army in 701 B.C. (which probably occurred less than a year after his sickness). It has been suggested that one reason why God prolonged his life was that he had no male heir to the throne (II Kings 21:1 states that Manasseh was only twelve when he began to reign). However, it is probable that Manasseh was a co-regent with his father for nearly ten years; because otherwise it would be impossible to fit the fifty-five years of his reign into this period of Judah's history, working back from the fixed dates of the Babylonian Captivity (see chronology chart, p. 480). In view of Manasseh's character (II Kings 21:1-18), Hezekiah's remaining years were not fruitful in passing on to his son the great truths God had taught him, though his godly influence must have been one factor in Manasseh's later deep repentance (II Chron. 33:12-13).

III. THE SHADOW THAT RETURNED (II Kings 20:8-11)

The statement that Hezekiah recovered (II Kings 20:7) obviously follows the giving of the sign that he would recover (II Kings 20:8-11). For the sake of clarity, therefore, verse 8 should be translated: "And Hezekiah *had* said unto Isaiah, What shall be the sign that Jehovah will heal me . . . ?"

It is instructive to contrast this request for a sign with the attitude of Ahaz, his father, who *refused* to ask for a faith-strengthening sign when the Lord promised to perform a spectacular miracle for him "either in the depth, or in the height above" (Isa. 7:11). Ahaz had already determined his course of action against Pekah and Rezin, namely, to call the Assyrians to his assistance; and he was not interested in committing himself to *God's* way as presented by Isaiah the prophet. Therefore his response ("I will not ask, neither will I tempt Jehovah" — Isa. 7:12) was pure unbelief cloaked in a garment of piety. As in the case of Moses, Gideon, Nathanael, and others, a sign could be of great help *only* if there was genuine faith already present.

The sign that God gave to Hezekiah was certainly one of the most spectacular miracles in Old Testament history. In the courtyard of the palace there was apparently a series of steps (not necessarily a sundial as we would think of it) so arranged that the shadow cast by the sun would give an approximation of the time. At the request of the king, and doubtless in the presence of a large group of officials (including foreign ambassadors?), the shadow moved *backward* ten steps (or "degrees")!

How did God actually accomplish this miracle? Did He cause the earth to stop its rotation and turn backwards a little? All true Christians would agree that He *could* have done such a thing, for by Him *all things* consist, or hold together (Col. 1:17). But the Bible makes it rather clear that this was *not* God's method; for in referring to this miracle, II Chronicles 32:24 states that Hezekiah "prayed unto Jehovah; and he spake unto him, and gave him a sign [Hebrew: *mopheth*]." But in verse 31 we are told that the Babylonians sent ambassadors to Hezekiah "to inquire of the wonder [*mopheth*] that was done *in the land*." Obviously, then, it was a *geographically localized miracle,* which did not involve a reversal of the earth's rotation, with shadows retreating ten degrees all over the Near East. Instead, the miracle occurred only "in the land" (of Judea); and, to be even more specific, it was only in the king's courtyard that "the sun returned ten steps on the dial whereon it was gone down" (Isa. 38:8).

It is the writer's conviction that a proper understanding of the nature of this great miracle helps us to understand what happened in the miracle of Joshua's long day (Josh. 10:12-14).[1]

---

[1]See J. C. Whitcomb, "Joshua's Long Day," *Brethren Missionary Herald* (July 27, 1963).

Since Joshua's need was a *prolongation of light* (not a slowing down of the earth's rotation), his need could be met by a supernatural continuation of sunlight and moonlight *in central Palestine* for "about a whole day" until Joshua's army could follow up its great victory and completely destroy the enemy.

The Bible teaches us that God does not unnecessarily multiply miracles. For example, Jesus did raise Lazarus, but He didn't remove the stone or the graveclothes. Furthermore, when the Flood ended, God promised to Noah that "while the earth remaineth . . . day and night shall not cease" (Gen. 8:22). This was confirmed to Jeremiah less than a century after the miracle in Hezekiah's courtyard: "If my covenant of day and night stand not . . . then will I also cast away the seed of Jacob . . ." (Jer. 33:25-26; cf. 31:36; 33:20-21). In other words, God has promised the earth would *not* cease rotating on its axis at the present rate until the very end of human history. Vague reports of a so-called "missing day in astronomy" must therefore be investigated with extreme caution.

IV. HEZEKIAH'S HEALING AND SONG OF THANKSGIVING (Isa. 38:9-20)

With his faith confirmed by the sign of the retreating shadow, Hezekiah gladly submitted to a fig poultice treatment on his deadly boil. The "cake of figs" did not heal him, but was a physical token of the work that God was doing, even as Jesus on one occasion put wet clay on the eyes of a blind man while healing him (John 9:6).

Isaiah's account of this miracle of healing (from which the authors of Kings and Chronicles apparently selected their materials — II Chron. 32:32) includes the song of thanksgiving Hezekiah wrote "when he had been sick and was recovered of his sickness" (Isa. 38:9). The beauty, depth, and pathos of this song demonstrate that Hezekiah was fully capable, under the direction of the Holy Spirit, of contributing significant portions to the poetical books of the Old Testament. That this song was to be used in public worship in the temple is clearly stated in verse 20: "We will sing my songs with stringed instruments all the days of our life in the house of Jehovah."

What happened to the other songs mentioned in verse 20?

Some scholars (Lightfoot, Thirtle, Scroggie) believe that they are the ten anonymous "Songs of Degrees" in the group of fifteen (Pss. 120-134). These psalms do have a certain similarity of style, and we have already seen that Hezekiah probably composed Psalm 126 (see p. 457). It has even been suggested that Hezekiah wrote the ten anonymous psalms of this group in memory of the ten steps the shadow returned, and then added five appropriate hitherto unpublished psalms from the pens of David and Solomon (compare Prov. 25:1) to bring the total to fifteen, in honor of the fifteen years God added to his life!

V. THE AMBASSADORS FROM BABYLON
(II Kings 20:12-15)

Merodach-baladan (Isa. 39:1; misspelled "Berodach" in II Kings) was twice king in Babylon, first from 722 to 710 B.C., when he was dethroned by Sargon II, and then again after Sargon died, from about 703 to 702 B.C., when Sennacherib defeated him again. The Jewish historian Josephus[2] suggests that Merodach sent his representatives to Jerusalem to gain an ally and to stir up additional trouble for the hated Assyrians. This seems highly probable as one of his motives, though the Bible indicates only two (less sinister) purposes: (1) to congratulate Hezekiah for his recovery — Isaiah and II Kings; and (2) "to inquire of the wonder [sign] that was done in the land" — II Chronicles.

The Babylonians were indeed fascinated by astronomic signs, for their national life revolved around the movement of planets and comets against the background of fixed stars and the predicted time intervals of solar and lunar eclipses. Expert "stargazers" (called "soothsayers" in Dan. 2:27) spent their lives taking amazingly accurate astronomic measurements in order to control the superstitious population through astrology. Isaiah challenged these men to save Babylon from divine judgment if they could: "let now the astrologers, the star-gazers, the monthly prognosticators, stand up, and save thee from the things that shall come upon thee" (Isa. 47:13). Because of these Babylonian astrologers, millions of heathen were "dismayed at the signs of

---

[2]*Ant.*, X.2.2.

heaven" (Jer. 10:2), and we must admit with sorrow that similar influence is gaining momentum even in so-called Christian America today.[3]

Thus, the Babylonians were particularly amazed and alarmed to hear about the return of the sun's shadow at the word of King Hezekiah of Judah, and they were convinced that he had some secret powers for manipulating the heavenly bodies. Perhaps a man such as this could be persuaded or bribed into accomplishing the destruction of Assyria by controlling the celestial signs!

Hezekiah was "glad" to see these ambassadors (Isa. 39:2), and thus failed an important spiritual test; for God allowed this to happen "to try him, that he might know all that was in his heart" (II Chron. 32:31). What did the test reveal — a deep suspicion of the motives of these pagans? An abiding concern for the glory of the God who had healed him and spared his life? No, his heart's desire was to convince these men that he was not a second-rate king according to the world's standards. And so, instead of learning about the uniqueness and holiness of Jehovah, and the necessity of acknowledging Him alone, they carried back to Babylon nothing more than a knowledge of silver, gold, spices, precious oil, and material treasures (II Kings 20:13). Thus, "Hezekiah rendered not again according to the benefit done unto him; for his heart was lifted up" (II Chron. 32:25).

VI. COMING JUDGMENT (II Kings 20:16-19)

The judgment that came upon Hezekiah and his people (who obviously shared his attitude of sinful pride and complacency) was twofold. *First,* within a matter of months the Assyrians would threaten Jerusalem with destruction, and it would be only by a timely repentance on the part of both king and people that the city would be spared ("therefore there was wrath upon him and upon Judah and Jerusalem. Notwithstanding Hezekiah humbled himself for the pride of his heart, both he and the inhabitants of Jerusalem, so that the wrath of Jehovah came not upon them in the days of Hezekiah" — II Chron. 32:25-26).

Second, the very Babylonians in whom he had delighted would

---

[3]*Time,* March 21, 1969.

some day strip his palace of everything (in fact, the Assyrians did this within a few months), carry his descendants into captivity, and make some of them serve as eunuchs in the palace of Babylon (II Kings 20:17-18; this probably does not refer to Daniel and his three friends "in whom was no blemish" — Dan. 1:4). Instead of collapsing before the Lord in deep repentance, Hezekiah's response (in the spirit of Neville Chamberlain after Munich in 1939) was incredibly and criminally shallow: "Good is the word of Jehovah which thou hast spoken. . . . Is it not so, if peace and truth shall be in my days?" (II Kings 20:19). Harold Stigers comments: "This was not a confession of sin. It was an expression of the 'peace in our time' policy, that short-sighted attitude that shows little concern for those on whom coming catastrophe shall fall. Therefore Isaiah could only turn to Jehovah and cry out, 'Comfort ye, comfort ye my people' (Isa. 40:1). Only after the predicted destruction would there come an end to Israel's sin of apostasy, and only then would true peace endure."[4]

---

[4]*Wycliffe Bible Commentary* (Moody Press, 1962), p. 362.

39

JOSIAH'S REFORMATION

I. MANASSEH AND AMON (II Kings 21:1-26)

In spite of the probability that Manasseh became king (or co-regent) about ten years before Hezekiah died, the godly influence of his father created only a negative reaction in the heart of this delinquent teen-ager. Shocking as this record of royal depravity may be, especially following the great revival of true religion in Hezekiah's day, we have ample illustrations from our own times of just such reversals. Cultured, and even godly, homes are no *guarantee* of high quality among children, because each child begins at zero, spiritually speaking (Ps. 51:5; 58:3). Children do not necessarily follow in the ways of their parents. Compare Ezekiel's analysis of the righteous father, the wicked son, and the righteous grandson (18:5-18) with Hezekiah, Manasseh (and Amon), and Josiah.

For half a century, Manasseh deliberately duplicated the depravity of the Canaanites whom Joshua was commissioned to destroy (II Kings 21:9; cf. II Chron. 33:9). In fact, he murdered so many righteous men in Jerusalem that the remnant became too small to spare the nation from total destruction, in spite of the noble reforming efforts of Josiah (II Kings 21:10-15; cf. 23:26). The fact that the majority of the people tolerated the utter paganism of Manasseh was God's reason for sealing the doom of the city and the temple, and there could be no escape. God even told Jeremiah: "Pray not thou for this people . . . for I will not hear thee" (Jer. 7:16; cf. 11:14; 14:11). Their hearts had been judicially hardened (cf. Isa. 6:9-12).

Included in the "innocent blood" that Manasseh shed (II Kings 21:16) may have been that of the prophet Isaiah himself; for Jewish tradition relates that he was "sawn asunder" (cf. Heb. 11:37).[1] Is it possible for a man as wicked as Manasseh to turn

---

[1]Whatever Manasseh may have done to Isaiah in the seventh century B.C., negative critics of the nineteenth century A.D. busied themselves in cutting Isaiah's book asunder, with "Deutero-" and other "Isaiahs" to explain away the magnificent predictive prophecies God gave to Israel through his pen (e.g., Isa. 44:28; 45:1).

to God in genuine repentance? Ezekiel said it was possible (18: 21-24, 27, 28), and II Chronicles 33:13 tells us that he did! For some offense against Ashurbanipal, the king of Assyria, Manasseh was dragged to Babylon "with hooks" (ASV margin; cf. II Kings 19:28). While in prison, "he besought Jehovah his God, and humbled himself greatly before the God of his fathers. And he prayed unto him; and he was entreated of him, and heard his supplication, and brought him again to Jerusalem into his king-

King Ashurbanipal shooting from saddle with bow and arrow. Relief from Nineveh, ca. 650 B.C. Courtesy, Inter-Varsity Fellowship.

dom. Then Manasseh knew that Jehovah, he was God" (II Chron. 33:12-13). Just as Joseph's brethren, while in prison, re-membered his desperate entreaties, their consciences being acti-vated by extreme adversity (Gen. 42:21), so now Manasseh must have recalled the teachings of his godly father and the warnings of the prophets whom he had slain (II Chron. 33:10).

How much of his 55-year reign was left after this we have no way of knowing, but it was now too late to reverse the trends he had initiated. His wicked son Amon cancelled these belated reforms and soon died at the hands of assassins.

II. JOSIAH'S INITIAL REFORMS (II Kings 22:1-7; II Chron. 34:1-13)

The author of II Chronicles lists for us in loving detail the chronological progress of Josiah's great reformation movement. Who it was in such a corrupt society that instructed and challenged him (apart from the Spirit of God) we are not told. At the tender age of *eight* he began to reign (II Chron. 34:1). At the age of *sixteen* "he began to seek after the God of David his father" (II Chron. 34:3). At about the same time, Ashurbanipal, king of Assyria, died and the once-mighty empire began to fall apart. At the age of *twenty* Josiah began to cleanse the land of all the tokens and instruments of idolatry (II Chron. 34:3-7). A year later the prophet Jeremiah began his ministry (Jer. 25:3). At the age of *twenty-six* Josiah began to repair the temple with money collected from the remnant of *all* the tribes, delivering it to Hilkiah the high priest (34:8-9).

III. FINDING THE BOOK OF THE LAW (II Kings 22:8-13)

In the process of cleansing the temple of the heaps of rubbish that had accumulated during the reigns of Manasseh and of Amon, the high priest Hilkiah discovered a copy of "the book of the law" (II Kings 22:8). Hilkiah gave it to Shaphan the scribe to read, who in turn came to the king. Mentioning first that the temple repairs were proceeding according to schedule, Shaphan then dropped a delayed-fuse bomb with enormous disruptive power — Jehovah's despised and neglected warnings of national judgment! King Josiah was utterly overwhelmed when he heard God's description of apostasy and its consequences echoing through the centuries from the time of Moses, and he feared that it might already be too late to bring the nation to repentance.

What was "the book of the law" that Hilkiah discovered? Some Bible students believe that it was the entire Pentateuch, while others claim that it was either the Book of Deuteronomy or just certain sections like Leviticus 26 and Deuteronomy 28 which enumerate the judgments God would bring upon His people if they continued to defy His Word. It is frankly quite difficult to imagine that a Davidic king could be unaware of such a significant portion of Scripture, especially when God had so clearly commanded that each king must "write him a copy of this law in a book, out of that which is before the priests and Levites: and it shall be with him, and he shall read therein all the days of his life" (Deut. 17:18-19). Did not even the priests and Levites have copies of the Law, which it was their special responsibility to teach to the people (cf. Lev. 10:11; II Chron. 17:9; 35:3; Neh. 8:7; Mal. 2:6-7)?

In seeking to answer this important question, we must remember that Manasseh had wiped out almost every trace of the true religion of Israel during a period of fifty years. As in the later persecutions of the Jews by Antiochus Epiphanes (168 B.C.) and of the Christians by the Roman emperor Diocletian (ca. A.D. 290), so also in Manasseh's persecution of Israel's godly remnant, it was probably a capital offense to possess a copy of the Scriptures. Thus, whatever copies of the sacred scrolls actually survived this period were probably hidden in caves like those near the Dead Sea where so many priceless manuscripts have been discovered.

In passing, we must comment on one of the most fantastic fables ever foisted upon the Church by "the father of lies." Nineteenth century A.D. negative critics of the Old Testament, especially a German scholar named Julius Wellhausen, insisted that the Book of Deuteronomy was invented by an unknown contemporary of King Josiah. Making the scroll to read like an original production of Moses himself, he planted it in the rubbish heaps of the temple in order that it might be discovered during the time of cleansing and repair! The true tragedy of this fantastic theory is that the vast majority of Old Testament scholars in Europe and America adopted it, and its influence continues to the present hour, even though the theory has experienced many modifications (see *The New Bible Commentary: Revised,* 1970, pp. 34-40).

IV. HULDAH'S PROPHECY (II Kings 22:14-20)

The king immediately requested that Jehovah be consulted through His appointed prophets concerning these fearsome words of divine warning. Was there yet hope for the nation? Five years before this, Jeremiah had begun his prophetic ministry in Judah; and Zephaniah was also proclaiming the word of the Lord. But apparently neither of these men was in Jerusalem at this time. So Josiah's official representatives went to a prophetess in Jerusalem named Huldah, who was probably an aunt of Jeremiah (II Kings 22:14; cf. Jer. 32:7).

This was not the first time that Jehovah had spoken to the nation through a woman. *Miriam,* the sister of Moses, was a prophetess (Exod. 15:20); *Deborah* led the nation in a time of crisis and composed an inspired song of victory (Judges 5); and Isaiah's wife was also called a prophetess (Isa. 8:3). In New Testament times we recall that Anna (Luke 2:36) and the four daughters of Philip the evangelist (Acts 21:9) received this special gift from God for speaking forth His infallible words of truth.

It is interesting that Huldah did not refer to Josiah as "the king" in her first reference to him, but simply as "the man" (II Kings 22:15). This was not disrespectful, but apparently was God's way of emphasizing the frailty of one who, though king, needed His help desperately. In spite of Josiah's well-meaning efforts, the reformation was essentially superficial; for almost everyone involved in this great "revival" was insincere except the king and a tiny remnant of true believers. Jeremiah seems to suggest this very problem when he says in one of his earlier sermons: "Judah hath not returned unto me with her whole heart, but feignedly, saith Jehovah" (Jer. 3:10). As has been true in all too many "revival meetings" since then, God was "near in their mouth, and far from their heart" (Jer. 12:2).

For these reasons, the judgment of God, though postponed, would be certain. Apostasy and paganism were too deeply entrenched in the hearts of the people to be rooted out by mere decrees emanating from the royal palace. But God would spare Josiah from seeing the coming national catastrophe, even as He had spared Hezekiah three generations earlier, "because thy heart was tender, and thou didst humble thyself before Jehovah, when thou heardest what I spake against this place" (II Kings 22:19).

It may seem strange indeed that God would have promised Josiah: "thou shalt be gathered to thy grave in peace" (II Kings 22:20), when, as a matter of fact, he was killed by an Egyptian pharaoh on the field of battle (cf. II Chron. 35:23)! The problem is solved, however, when we realize that for the Israelite, to die "in peace" meant to die in a state of fellowship with God as a true believer, whether in the front line of battle or at home in bed. In contrast to this, "there is no peace, saith my God, to the wicked" (Isa. 57:21).

V. THE COVENANT RENEWED AND REFORMS INTENSIFIED (II Kings 23:1-20)

Deeply shocked by the word of God through Huldah the prophetess, King Josiah gathered the leaders of the nation to the temple for a public reading of the newly-discovered portions of Scripture. Then he encouraged all the people to stand with him in a renewal of covenant vows to Jehovah.

As we read in the following verses some of the details of Josiah's great reform movement, we are astounded at the mass of idolatrous influences that had been allowed to accumulate in the kingdom, the capital city, and the temple courts:

(1) The paraphernalia of paganism were carted out of the temple and burned in the Kidron Valley, the ashes being used to defile the rival center of Israelite worship at Bethel (II Kings 23:4).

(2) The idolatrous priests (Hebrew, *Chemarim*; cf. Hos. 10: 5; Zeph. 1:4) were "put down."

(3) The Asherah (the idol of Baal's consort) was removed from the temple and burned.

(4) The tents that male Baal-cult prostitutes ("Sodomites") had set up in the temple courts were removed.

(5) Priests throughout Judah were recruited to defile idolatrous high places.

(6) The place of human sacrifice to Molech (god of Ammon) in the Valley of Hinnom, just south of the city, was defiled.

(7) Chariots dedicated to the use of the sun god were burned.
(8) Special heathen altars erected by Ahaz and Manasseh in the temple courts were destroyed.
(9) Sacred shrines which Solomon had erected for his foreign wives on the surrounding hills were destroyed (cf. I Kings 11:5-8).
(10) Jeroboam's rival altar at Bethel, and all other Samaritan altars, were destroyed and desecrated with the exhumed bones of their priests (cf. I Kings 13:2).
(11) All surviving calf-worshipping priests were slain.
(12) All mediums and wizards were removed from the land (cf. II Kings 21:6).

As we ponder this amazing list, we cannot help but ask what had been accomplished during the previous six years of reforms. It will be recalled that a great national purge of idols had begun in Josiah's *twelfth* official year (II Chron. 34:3), and the present purge took place in his *eighteenth* year. We can only conclude that the task was so gigantic that it took many years to complete. Furthermore, the reform movement may have started slowly because of fear of offending the Assyrian overlords. But as the collapse of Assyrian power following the death of Ashurbanipal became evident to all, and as Jeremiah's powerful messages struck deep into the consciences of the people, the reformation began to increase in momentum.

Some other important questions arise: Was anything accomplished by this great reformation? Were any of the fundamental spiritual problems of the people solved? Was there a widespread turning of hearts to the Lord? Was the nation now in a position to serve and glorify their God? The answer to these questions, unfortunately, is *no*. This might come as a great surprise to many in our own day who feel that their best energies should be spent on reform movements, purging the nation of this or that physical or moral evil. That such evils are ruining the nation and should be uprooted no sensible person would deny. But the problem is how to deal with the *source*, not the final product; with the *root*, not the ultimate fruit. Every true Christian is (or should be) concerned with the problems of environmental pollution, drugs, crime, pornography, governmental inefficiency, communism, war, etc., etc., which threaten the health, morals, and very existence of our society. But if the source and root of these problems is not recognized and dealt with in the light of God's Word, nothing of permanent value can be accomplished for anyone.

Our Lord told of a man (or, in our case, a nation) from whom an evil sipirt was expelled (Matt. 12:43). Returning "home," the spirit found there had been a great reformation — it was "empty, swept, and garnished." "Then goeth he, and taketh with himself seven other spirits more evil than himself, and they enter in and dwell there: and the last state of that man [or nation] became worse than the first. Even so shall it be also unto this evil generation." Here is the abiding lesson of Josiah's reforms. "Out of *the heart* come forth evil thoughts, murders. . ." (Matt. 15:19; cf. 12:33-35), and unless *the heart* is dealt with by the Holy Spirit speaking through His Word, there can be neither salvation nor permanent reformation (cf. Ezek. 36:26-27; Rom. 8:1-4; Eph. 2:1-10; Heb. 4:12).

VI. THE GREAT PASSOVER (II Kings 23:21-23; cf. II Chron. 35:1-19)

Full details of Josiah's great passover celebration in 622 B.C. are provided for us in II Chronicles 35. Three points of special interest should be noted in this account. *First,* it appears that conditions had deteriorated so badly in the temple since the days of Hezekiah that faithful Levites had removed and hidden the Ark of God (II Chron. 35:3)! Josiah ordered it to be returned, for there could be no proper observance of the passover without it. *Second,* the Levites showed extraordinary zeal in preparing passover lambs, not only for themselves, but also for the priests, the singers, and the porters (II Chron. 35:11-15; cf. Ezra 6:20). *Third,* this was the greatest passover since the days of Samuel the prophet 500 years earlier (II Chron 35:18), because of the obstacles that had to be overcome and because it was done with such great zeal and according to the Law (Hezekiah's passover had to be held in the second month because so many were ceremonially defiled — II Chron. 30:2, 3, 17-20).

VII. THE DEATH OF JOSIAH (II Kings 23:28-30; II Chron. 35:20-27)

The final years of Josiah's reign saw tremendous changes taking place on the international scene. Nineveh had finally fallen under the combined attacks of Medes and Babylonians in 612 B.C., and a remnant of the Assyrian army under Ashuruballit II fled westward to a stronghold on the Euphrates River named Carchemish. By 609 B.C., the Babylonian army was preparing to cross the Euphrates to conquer Syria, having by now consolidated their newly conquered territories to the east. Desiring to block a Babylonian move into Palestine, and to gain control of Syria for themselves, the Egyptians (whose power had increased in ratio to the decline of Assyria) determined to move north to Carchemish and back the Assyrians in their desperate last-ditch stand against the Babylonians.

The statement that "Pharaoh-necho king of Egypt went up against the king of Assyria to the river Euphrates" (II Kings 23:29) should better be translated: "*on behalf of* the king of Assyria, to the river Euphrates."[2] It was at this point that Josiah made his fatal mistake. Thinking, perhaps, that any friend of the hated Assyrians was an enemy of his, and boldly disregarding all prophetic warnings against meddling in international affairs, he quickly moved his army to Megiddo to block the Egyptian army.

Now came one of the strangest episodes in Old Testament history. The heathen king, Necho II of Egypt, informed Josiah that "God hath commanded me to make haste" and that if Josiah interfered with God's plan, God would destroy him (II Chron. 35:21). We would immediately dismiss such a statement as propaganda, of course, were it not for the explanation by the Chronicler that Josiah "hearkened not unto the words of Necho *from the mouth of God*" (II Chron. 35:22)! Furthermore, Necho must be believed, for Josiah *was* killed. What does this mean? Did Josiah lose his salvation because of disobedience? No, for Huldah had said he would die "in peace" (II Chron. 34:28). Was Pharaoh-necho a prophet of Jehovah? No, for God had

---

[2]J. Barton Payne in *The Wycliffe Bible Commentary*, p. 419.

spoken to pagan kings directly at various times without necessarily transforming their hearts (see Gen. 12:17-20; 20:3-7). We
may conclude that God wanted to maneuver the Egyptian army
to the Euphrates so that Nebuchadnezzar could destroy it as well
as the Assyrian army, and thus fulfill His warning that the
Babylonians would conquer and chasten Judah (see Jer. 25:
8-11).

Even more tragic than the fact of Josiah's death was the manner of his death. Disguising himself, as did Ahab (I Kings 22:
30), thus hoping to avoid the deadly wound that he must have
suspected God was planning for him, he challenged the Egyptian
army in the Valley of Megiddo, only to be pierced by an arrow
that was God's key to the grave where he would be "gathered
to his fathers in peace."

Great was the national mourning for Josiah. The great reformation was obviously over, for his sons offered no prospect of
walking in their father's footsteps. Someday, wrote the prophet
Zechariah a century later, Israel will mourn for the Messiah they
crucified, even "as the mourning of Hadadrimmon in the valley
of Megiddon" (12:11), a remarkable evidence of the intensity
and universality of Judah's mourning for Josiah. Jeremiah lamented for Josiah too (II Chron. 35:25; these lamentations are
not found in the Book of Lamentations which is concerned with
the fall of Jerusalem); and to protect the uniqueness of Josiah's
reputation, Jeremiah commanded the nation *not* to mourn over
the death of Jehoiakim (Jer. 22:18). Truly, Josiah was a great and
godly king; but it would take more than a Josiah to reverse the
nation's downward trend: "Though Moses and Samuel stood before me, yet my mind would not be toward this people: cast
them out of my sight, and let them go forth" (Jer. 15:1). In the
final chapter it will be our unpleasant responsibility to see how
God did this very thing.

40

THE BABYLONIAN CAPTIVITY

I. JEHOAHAZ/SHALLUM; THE EXILE TO EGYPT
(II Kings 23:30-34; II Chron. 36:1-4)

The tragic death of Josiah at Megiddo marked the end of true quality in the royal line of Judah until the return of Christ to sit "upon the throne of David . . . to establish it, and to uphold it with justice and with righteousness from henceforth even for ever" (Isa. 9:7).

As Pharaoh Necho marched his army to the Euphrates in June, 609 B.C., to help the Assyrian army block any further Babylonian advances towards the west, the people of Judah put Josiah's son Jehoahaz upon the throne in Jerusalem.[1] But his evil reign was a short one, for Pharaoh Necho deposed him at the end of the summer on his return from the Euphrates, and carried him off to Egypt, and elevated Eliakim to the throne. The prophet Jeremiah, who called Jehoahaz "Shallum," proclaimed an oracle against him: "He shall not return thither any more; but in the place whither they have led him captive, there shall he die, and he shall see this land no more" (Jer. 22:11-12). Little did Jeremiah realize that he himself would ultimately be dragged to Egypt in a miniature reversal of the Exodus, never to return to the land he loved (cf. Jer. 43, 44).

II. JEHOIAKIM, THE PROPHET HATER
(II Kings 23:34—24:7; II Chron. 36:4-8)

For some reason, Pharaoh Necho felt that Eliakim, a brother of Jehoahaz, would be a more dependable vassal. To improve Eliakim's image with the traditionalists in Judah, Necho changed his name to Jehoiakim. But this was hardly sufficient to offset

---

[1] In 609 B.C., Jehoiakim at 25 was the oldest son of Josiah; Jehoahaz was 23, and Zedekiah was only 10. In I Chron. 3:15, however, Jehoahaz/Shallum is listed as the last of four sons of Josiah.

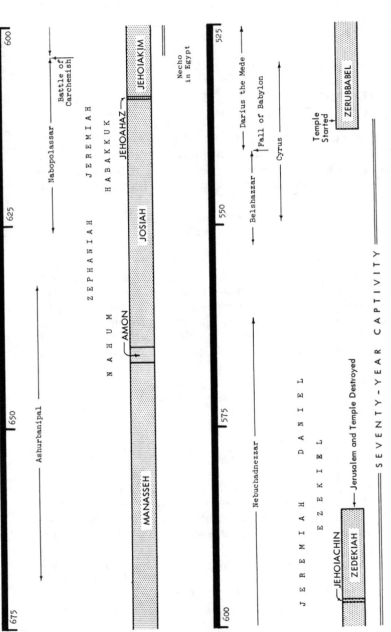

22. Time Chart: 675 to 525 B.C.

the vast unpopularity the new king must have incurred when he taxed the people heavily to pay tribute to the Egyptians (II Kings 23:35).[2] To make matters worse, while the people groaned under these burdens Jehoiakim built for himself a luxurious palace "ceiled with cedar and painted with vermillion" (Jer. 22:14) and then refused to pay the workers (Jer. 22:13).

Jehoiakim was probably the most consistently wicked king of Judah since Ahaz (cf. Jer. 22:15-17). He took a scroll of Jeremiah's sermons, calmly cut it into pieces, and threw it into the fire after hearing only three or four columns read (Jer. 36:20-26). He twice attempted to capture Jeremiah, but was thwarted through the intervention of God and friends (Jer. 26:24; 36:19, 26; cf. 1:19). However, he did kill the prophet Uriah who preached "according to all the words of Jeremiah" (Jer. 26:20-23).

In Jehoiakim's fourth year (the summer of 605 B.C.), Pharaoh Necho once again led his army to the Euphrates for a confrontation with the Babylonians. Nabopolassar, king of Babylon, was sick at home while his son Nebuchadnezzar led the army. Jeremiah had already prophesied that Nebuchadnezzar would not only win this battle but would also control Judah for seventy years (Jer. 25:1-11; cf. Hab. 1:1-17). And so the Egyptian army, led like sacrificial animals to the slaughter (Jer. 46:10), received wounds from Nebuchadnezzar that all the balm of Gilead could never heal (Jer. 46:2, 11). In a recently translated tablet, the official scribe of Babylon tells the story: "In the 21st year [605/04 B.C.] the king of Akkad stayed in his own land, Nebuchadnezzar his eldest son, the crown-prince, mustered [the Babylonian army] and took command of the troops; he marched to Carchemish which is on the bank of the Euphrates, and crossed the river [to go] against the Egyptian army which lay in Carchemish . . . [they] fought with each other and the Egyptian army withdrew before him. He accomplished their defeat and to non-existence [beat] them. As for the rest of the Egyptian army

---

[2]The progressive poverty of the nation may be detected in the amount of tribute that could be exacted. Hezekiah paid 300 talents of silver and 30 talents of gold (II Kings 18:14). But Jehoaikim could pay only 100 talents of silver and one talent of gold.

which escaped from the defeat [so quickly that] no weapon
had reached them, in the district of Hamath the Babylonian
troops overtook and defeated them so that not a single man
[escaped] to his own country. At that time Nebuchadnezzar
conquered the whole area of the Hatti-country [Syria, Phoenicia, and Palestine]."[3]

Sweeping into Palestine in pursuit of the Egyptians, Nebuchadnezzar's troops besieged Jerusalem until Jehoiakim surrendered.[4] The Chronicler says that Nebuchadnezzar "bound him
in fetters to carry him to Babylon" (II Chron. 36:6), but before
the plan was fulfilled something of urgent importance happened
that caused Nebuchadnezzar to change his mind. He received
word that his father Nabopolassar had died in Babylon on August 15. Realizing that the throne was now in jeopardy, he
forced Jehoiakim to promise loyalty as his vassal,[5] took the short
route across the Arabian desert to Babylon,[6] and sent some prisoners (including Daniel and his friends) the long way around.
The Babylonian Chronicle informs us that Nebuchadnezzar "sat
on the royal throne in Babylon" by September 6, 605 B.C., which
was only twenty-three days after his father died!

Like Hoshea, the last king of Israel, Jehoiakim must have felt
the increasing pressure of the pro-Egyptian party in his kingdom. After three years of paying tribute to Nebuchadnezzar, he
finally decided, against the vigorous warnings of Jeremiah (cf.
Jer. 36:29), to rebel against the Babylonian monarch (II Kings
24:1). But God raised up various marauding bands from the
north and east to harass Jehoiakim until he was finally killed in
early December, 598 B.C. Jeremiah had predicted that "they
shall not lament for him, saying, Ah lord! or, Ah his glory! He

---

[3]Donald J. Wiseman, *Chronicles of Chaldean Kings* (London: The
Trustees of the British Museum, 1956), pp. 67, 69.

[4]Daniel 1:1. The "third year of the reign of Jehoiakim" in this verse
is not a contradiction to "the fourth year of Jehoiakim" in Jer. 25:1, for
according to Daniel's Tishri reckoning Jehoiakim's fourth official year
would not begin until the fall of 605 B.C.

[5]This is implied in II Kings 24:1. Wiseman (*op. cit.*, p. 28) suggests
that the three-year servitude did not begin until 604 B.C.

[6]According to the Babylonian historian Berossus, as quoted by Josephus,
Contra Apionem, I, 19.

shall be buried with the burial of an ass, drawn and cast forth beyond the gates of Jerusalem" (Jer. 22:18-19; cf. 36:30). Furthermore, "he shall have none to sit upon the throne of David" (Jer. 36:30), which must have been an anticipation of the curse which would fall upon his son, Jehoiachin.

III. JEHOIACHIN, THE BROKEN VESSEL
(II Kings 24:8-16; II Chron. 36:9-10)

Jehoiachin's wicked reign began and ended when he was only eighteen years old, for he ruled for only three months and ten days (II Chron. 36:9).[7] Because of his father's treasonous acts, the Babylonian army besieged Jerusalem and finally captured it on March 15, 597 B.C. This date has finally come to light through the remarkably detailed Babylonian Chronicle: "the king of Akkad mustered his troops, marched to the Hatti-land, and encamped against the city of Judah and on the second day of the month Adar he seized the city and captured the king. He appointed there a king of his own choice, received its heavy tribute and sent [captives] to Babylon."[8]

The Judean prisoners going into captivity to Babylon. Babylonians followed the policy initiated by the Assyrians of deporting populations. Courtesy, Inter-Varsity Fellowship.

[7]He could hardly have been eight years old at this time, for he had wives (II Kings 24:15). Therefore the number "eight" in II Chron. 36:9 should read "eighteen" as in II Kings 24:8.
[8]Wiseman, op. cit., p. 73.

Jehoiachin, together with his mother Nehushta, his wives, and ten thousand of his leading citizens came out of the city to receive their judgment from the lips of Nebuchadnezzar himself: permanent deportation to Babylon. More treasures were taken from the temple (cf. Dan. 1:2 for the sacred vessels taken in 605 B.C.), leaving just enough sacred furniture for religious ceremonies to be carried on under the high priest Seraiah and the puppet king Zedekiah (II Kings 25:13-18).

Among the captives taken to Babylon at this time was a young priest named Ezekiel. Five years later, at the age of thirty, he began to prophesy to the exiles in Babylon, explaining why Jerusalem was doomed to destruction and why the Shekinah Glory had departed from the temple (Ezek. 1-33). Ezekiel continued to date his own ministry in terms of Jehoiachin's reign (Ezek. 1: 2), because as long as Jehoiachin lived he (*not* his uncle Zedekiah) was Judah's legitimate king. Moreover, Jeremiah made it clear that Jehoiachin was the *last* legitimate king of Judah, "for no more shall a man of his seed prosper, sitting upon the throne of David, and ruling in Judah" (Jer. 22:30).[9]

A remarkable series of Babylonian tablets have been discovered which list foreign prisoners who received rations from the royal storehouses from 595 to 570 B.C.

> Among them Jehoiachin (Yaukin), his five sons and eight other Judeans are named together with other royalty and craftsmen from places in Egypt, Philistia (Ashkelon), Phoenicia, Syria, Cilicia, Lydia, Elam, Media and Persia, some of which are mentioned in the prophecies of Jeremiah. Jehoiachin, held as a hostage, was still called "king of Judah." His royal estates in Judah continued to be managed, at least between 597 and 587, by "Eliakim, steward of Jehoiachin," impressions of whose seal were found at Debir and Bethshemesh.[10]

---

[9]Ezekiel explained that the kingship would be removed from Judah "until he come whose right it is" (21:27); namely, Christ. See pp. 437-438. for a discussion of how God solved this apparent contradiction of perpetual kingship through David (II Sam. 7) and a perpetual curse upon David's descendant, Jehoiachin.

[10]Donald J. Wiseman, *Illustrations from Biblical Archaeology* (Grand Rapids: Wm. B. Eerdmans Publishing Co., 1958), p. 73.

It seems probable that toward the close of Nebuchadnezzar's reign Jehoiachin was involved in some treasonous plot; for when Nebuchadnezzar died in 562 B.C., his son Evil-merodach "did lift up the head of Jehoiachin king of Judah out of prison; and he spoke kindly to him, and set his throne above the throne of the kings that were with him in Babylon, and changed his prison garments. And Jehoiachin did eat bread before him continually all the days of his life: and for his allowance, there was a continual allowance given him of the king, every day a portion, all the days of his life" (II Kings 25:27-30). We can understand this as Evil-merodach's effort to gain favor with subject peoples, especially the Jews, who might be tempted to revolt after the death of his powerful father.

Zerubbabel, who led nearly 50,000 Jews back to Judah in 537 B.C., was a grandson of Jehoiachin (Matt. 1:12). He knew that he could never be Judah's king because of Jeremiah's curse, but God compensated with the assurance that "I will make thee as a signet, for I have chosen thee" (Hag. 2:23; contrast Jer. 22:24).

IV. ZEDEKIAH, THE FICKLE PUPPET
(II Kings 24:17—25:7; II Chron. 36:10-21)

Having sent Jehoiachin to Babylon, Nebuchadnezzar placed his uncle Mattaniah on the throne, changing his name to Zedekiah ("Jehovah is righteous"!) and making him swear by Jehovah that he would remain loyal (II Chron. 36:13; Ezek. 17:11-21). It is just possible that Nebuchadnezzar refrained from destroying Jerusalem at this time because of the intervention of Daniel, who five years earlier had been established in the court of Babylon as the supreme interpreter of dreams (Dan. 2:1, 46-49). If so, he blundered seriously in not leaving Zedekiah in the hands of more qualified advisors, for the puppet king was apparently helpless to bring Judah into submission to Babylon even if he wanted to.[11] Zedekiah and the nobles who were permitted to remain in Judah convinced themselves that they were God's

---

[11] F. F. Bruce, *Israel and the Nations* (Grand Rapids: Wm. B. Eerdmans Publishing Co., 1963), p. 89.

chosen ones, while the exiles were being punished for their special sins. Both Jeremiah and Ezekiel denounced this attitude, explaining that Jehovah would henceforth treat the exiles as "good figs" (Jer. 24) and would "be to them a sanctuary for a little while in the countries where they are come" (Ezek. 11: 16). In fact, Jeremiah wrote a letter to the exiles stating that Jehovah had "thoughts of peace, and not of evil, to give you hope in your latter end" (Jer. 29:11).

In his fourth year (593 B.C.), Zedekiah had to appear before Nebuchadnezzar in Babylon, presumably to promise again that he would not betray his oath or look toward Egypt for help (Jer. 51:59-64). In the same year, the Lord instructed Jeremiah to prepare some "bonds and bars" as symbols of submission to Nebuchadnezzar, and to present them to the ambassadors of five western kingdoms in Jerusalem to take back to their kings. But all to no avail. Zedekiah's vacillation between submission to Babylon and flirtation with Egypt finally brought upon him the wrath of Nebuchadnezzar, as well as the wrath of Jehovah whose name Zedekiah had utttered in his oath of loyalty (Ezek. 17:11-21).[12] Because of this, Ezekiel referred to him as the "deadly wounded wicked one, the prince of Israel, whose day is come..." (Ezek. 21:25; cf. v. 14).

Nebuchadnezzar had long been distracted by military commitments elsewhere in his vast empire and even a revolt within his own army in 594 B.C.[13] But now he was free to bring his iron fist down upon rebellious Judah, whose day, like that of Zedekiah, had fully come. Using divination to decide whether to attack Rabbah of Ammon first, Nebuchadnezzar was led by God to move directly to Jerusalem, "to open the mouth in the slaughter, to lift up the voice with shouting, to set battering rams..., to cast up mounds, to build forts" (Ezek. 21:18-22). The final agony of Judah had begun.

Because the siege began in Zedekiah's ninth year, the tenth month, and ended in his eleventh year, the fourth month, it

[12]The solemnity and permanence of oaths uttered in the name of Jehovah are greatly emphasized in the Old Testament (cf. Num. 30:2; Ps. 50:14; 66:13-14; Eccles. 5:4).

[13] Donald J. Wiseman, Chronicles of Chaldaean Kings, pp. 36, 37, 73.

has generally been assumed that the siege lasted for eighteen months (January 588 to July 587 B.C.). However, the siege must have lasted *thirty months*, because Ezekiel states that it began in the tenth month of Jehoiachin's *ninth* year (Ezek. 24: 1) and the word of Jerusalem's destruction reached Babylonia in the tenth month of his *twelfth* year, exactly three years later (Ezek. 33:21). Thus, Jerusalem fell on July 18, 586 B.C., and six months later the tragic news came to Ezekiel in Babylon. In the light of Ezekiel's clear chronology, it becomes obvious that the author of Kings was using a Tishri dating system (with the first day of the seventh month being the beginning of the king's official year) in II Kings 25, so that the tenth month would be *early* in his ninth year, and the fourth month would be *late* in his eleventh year. This allows sufficient time for the many events to transpire during the siege as described in Jeremiah 32, 33, 34, 37, and 38.

While Ezekiel was faithfully and graphically portraying to the exiles in Babylon the inevitability of Jerusalem's fall, Nebuchadnezzar's forces drew near to the city. The very day the siege began, Ezekiel's wife died (Ezek. 24:1, 15-24) — a drastic sign to the exiles that Jehovah's sanctuary, "the desire of your eyes," was doomed. In the meantime, Jeremiah was suffering intensely at the hands of his countrymen in Judah, who considered him to be a traitor for counselling surrender to Babylon.[14] As a reward for his faithfulness in delivering God's Word without compromise, Jeremiah was plotted against by the citizens of his own home town (Jer. 11:18-23), beaten and put into the stocks (Jer. 20:1-3), publicly challenged by false prophets (Jer. 28:1-11), thrown into various prisons (Jer. 37:15, 21), and even lowered into a deep cistern full of mire (Jer. 38:6).

Several months after the siege began, Pharaoh Hophra came up into Judah with a large army; and the Babylonians, perhaps recalling the serious losses they suffered at the hands of Pharaoh Necho in a clash at the border of Egypt in 601 B.C.,[15] decided to withdraw from Jerusalem temporarily. In the meantime,

---

[14]Compare Jer. 18:18; 20:7-10; 21:1-14; 25:8-11; 27:1—28:17; 29:24-32; 32:1-5, 28-36; 34:1-5, 17-22; 37:7-10, 17-19; 38:1-6, 17-23.

[15]Cf. Donald J. Wiseman, *Chronicles of Chaldean Kings*, p. 29.

Painting of Nebuchadnezzar's Babylon showing the bridge over the Euphrates, the great ziggurat and the temple of Marduk. Courtesy, Oriental Institute.

Painting of Nebuchadnezzar's Babylon showing the Procession
Way passing through the Ishtar Gate. Courtesy, Oriental Institute.

Zedekiah and the people of Judah had agreed under pressure to release their Hebrew bondservants in obedience to God's law (cf. Exod. 21:2-11); but when the Babylonian army withdrew, they immediately broke their covenant (Jer. 34:8-21)! Therefore, God assured them that the Egyptians would depart permanently and the Babylonians would destroy the city even if their army consisted of nothing but wounded men (Jer. 37:6-10; 34: 22; Ezek. 17:17).

The final months of the siege of Jerusalem brought Zedekiah to the edge of despair. Secretly and frequently calling for Jeremiah to hear some encouraging word from Jehovah, he was given the clear alternative: surrender to Nebuchadnezzar and not only live in peace but save Jerusalem as well; or keep on resisting and be totally shattered by the Babylonians (Jer. 37:16-17; 38: 14-23). The Chronicler tells us that one of the reasons why God judged Zedekiah is that "he humbled not himself before Jeremiah the prophet speaking from the mouth of Jehovah" (II Chron. 36:12). The story of this confrontation between God's weeping prophet and the fickle and godless king of Judah is almost without comparison in Scripture for its tragic overtones. Vacillating between the demands of his nobles on the one hand, and a superstitious fear of Jehovah on the other hand, Zedekiah permitted Jeremiah to be alternately humiliated and protected (Jer. 32:1-5; 37:21; 38:10). The pitifully irresponsible puppet ruler of Judah was therefore directly responsible for the destruction of Jerusalem and the temple (Jer. 38:23).

The end came swiftly and the picture is sickening to contemplate. On July 18, 586 B.C., the city walls were breached and the enemy moved in.[16] Zedekiah and some of his leaders fled

---

[16]Donald J. Wiseman writes: "The severe nature of the final siege of Jerusalem in 589-587 B.C. is shown by the utter devastation of Judah which took place at this time. In the debris of the guardroom by the city gate of Lachish eighteen inscribed potsherds were found. Some, invoking the name of Yahweh, mention restriction of movement and the 'princes who weaken the hands,' perhaps the very opponents of Jeremiah. The majority were messages passing between Hosha'yahu, the commander of an outpost, and Ya'ush, military governor of Lachish. Letter No. IV ends: 'and let my lord know that we are waiting for the fire-signals of Lachish according to the indications which my lord has given, because we

toward Jericho, but were easily overtaken by the Babylonians who promptly dragged them to the main military headquarters at Riblah in Syria. Standing before the mighty monarch to whom he had sworn loyalty in the name of Jehovah, Zedekiah was forced to watch his sons and the chief priests and the nobility of Judah being slain before his eyes. Then he was blinded so that the memory of this horrible scene would never depart from him (Jer. 39:6-7; II Kings 25:6-7, 18-21). Jeremiah had warned Zedekiah that he would look into the very eyes of Nebuchadnezzar (Jer. 32:4; 34:3); but Ezekiel prophesied that he would not see Babylon with his eyes (Ezek. 12:6, 12, 13). These

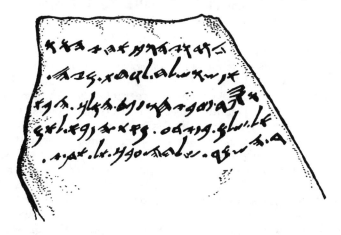

Drawing of an inscribed ostracon from Lachish. This letter, written in cursive Hebrew of the time of Jeremiah, was found in a small guard-room under the gate-tower of Lachish, ca. 589-87 B.C. Courtesy, Inter-Varsity Fellowship.

cannot see (the fire-signals of) Azekah.' Jeremiah (6:1; 34:7) mentions 'fire-signals' and tells how Lachish and Azekah were focal points in the Babylonian campaign. Lachish, Bethshemesh and Debir, which showed signs of increasing poverty after the war of 597 B.C., now fell, their gates and fortifications were pulled down, the buildings set on fire and the sites, as in many other places in Judah, were abandoned or only sparsely inhabited thereafter. No town in Judah has been found to have been continuously occupied throughout the exilic period." — *Illustrations from Biblical Archaeology*, pp. 70-73.

prophecies were fulfilled to the letter when Zedekiah saw Babylon's king, but entered the city of Babylon both bound and
blinded.

In the meantime, the starved survivors in Jerusalem, reduced
in some cases to cannibalism by the prolonged siege (Lam. 4:
8-10; cf. Jer. 37:21; 38:9; 52:6), were brutally mistreated by
Babylonian soldiers (II Chron. 36:17; Jer. 38:22-23; Lam. 5:11-
13), and then herded together and chained like wild animals
for deportation to Babylon (Jer. 39:9; 40:1).[17] The only ones
that were not deported were poor country people who were left
to care for vineyards and orchards (Jer. 39:10); Gedaliah to
serve as the governor of this pitiful remnant; certain guerilla
fighters who had been hiding in the hills (Jer. 40:7-8); and a
few other Jews who had fled to surrounding countries and were
now returning (Jer. 40:11-12).

As for Jeremiah, Nebuchadnezzar gave strict instructions that
he was to be well cared for (Jer. 39:11-14) because of his
great help to the Babylonians in weakening Jewish resistance
(cf. Jer. 38:4).[18] Doubtless many deserters had spoken to the
Babylonians of Jeremiah's impassioned sermons, and it also
seems possible that Daniel warned Nebuchadnezzar against mis-
treating this great prophet of Jehovah. In the general confusion
that followed the fall of the city, however, Jeremiah was accidentally put into chains and led five miles north to Ramah before the error was discovered and he was released (Jer. 40:1-
6). Not only was he given the choice to stay or to leave, but
he also received a food allowance and "a present" (Jer. 40:5).
If his own nation rejected him, God had other means of honoring
His faithful servant in a material way.[19]

This public honoring of Jeremiah by the Babylonians must

---

[17]According to Jer. 52:29, over eight hundred Jews were taken captive
the year before Jerusalem fell. In addition to these, apparently, were many
Jews who had deserted to the Babylonians (in response to Jeremiah's appeals?). Zedekiah was particularly afraid of falling into the hands of
these deserters (cf. Jer. 38:19; 39:9).

[18]In a similar way, Daniel was honored by Cyrus after the fall of Babylon in 539 B.C. (Dan. 6:2-3).

[19]Cf. Matt. 13:57 — "A prophet is not without honor, save in his own
country, and in his own house."

have been the final proof to many Jews that Jeremiah was indeed a traitor (cf. Jer. 37:11-15). But the tears he shed over the fallen city (Lam. 1:16; 2:11, 18), his refusal to leave the land when given the opportunity to enjoy great honors in Babylon (Jer. 40:4), and his lengthy and vigorous denunciations of pagan Babylon (Jer. 50-51), must have made it perfectly clear to all unprejudiced minds that Jeremiah, so far from being a traitor, was the embodiment of God's deep love for His people.

From August 15 to 18, about a month after the city was taken and the captives deported, a Babylonian general named Nebuzaradan began the systematic destruction of Jerusalem (II Kings 25:8; Jer. 52:12). The walls were broken down; the temple, palace, and chief houses burned to the ground; and all the sacred vessels that had not been taken in 605 B.C. and 597 B.C. were now processed for shipment to Babylon. Even as Ezekiel described the reluctant and gradual departure of the Shekinah Glory from the temple seven years earlier (Ezek. 8–11), so now the inspired writer takes a final sad look at his beloved temple, lingering over the details of its destruction (Jer. 52:17-23).

But the measure of tragedy was not yet full. Two months after the city was burned, Gedaliah, the worthy governor of Judah,[20] and many people with him, were brutally slain by an ambitious Jewish prince named Ishmael (Jer. 41:1-10). Johanan, a guerilla captain, had warned Gedaliah about Ishmael, but to no avail (Jer. 40:13-16). Now Johanan's forces succeeded in rescuing Jeremiah and others from the hands of Ishmael, and fearing reprisals from the Babylonians, led the entire group of survivors down to Egypt against the strong protests and warnings of Jeremiah (Jer. 41:11—43:7). "It is difficult to conceive any situation more painful than that of a great man, condemned to watch the lingering agony of an exhausted country, to tend it during the alternate fits of stupefaction and raving which precede its dissolution, and to see the symptoms of vitality disap-

---

[20]Presumably Gedaliah was a friend of Jeremiah, because his father Ahikam once rescued Jeremiah from certain death (Jer. 26:24; cf. 39:14; 40:5-6). It was for this reason that Gedaliah did not oppose Babylonian rule and thus was placed in a position of authority. It was because he trusted unworthy men that he lost his life.

pear one by one, till nothing is left but coldness, darkness, and corruption."[21]

The first phase of Israel's experience as a divinely-established theocratic kingdom on earth had come to an end. The period of Babylonian captivity and of Gentile dominion now began, and Jehovah's purposes for His people Israel took a new course. "For the children of Israel shall abide many days without king, and without prince, and without sacrifice . . . afterward shall the children of Israel return, and seek their God, and David their king, and shall come with fear unto Jehovah and to his goodness in the latter days" (Hos. 3:4-5).[22]

Why did God permit Judah to suffer the horrors of Babylonian captivity? The Chronicler lists three reasons. *First,* Zedekiah refused God's Word through Jeremiah and broke his oath to Nebuchadnezzar (II Chron. 36:12-13). *Second,* the priests and the people adopted heathen customs, polluted the temple, and scoffed at God's prophets (II Chron. 36:14-16). And *third,* God's provision for the sabbatical year (cf. Lev. 25:4; 26:34) had been neglected for centuries; therefore, "as long as it lay desolate it kept sabbath, to fulfill threescore and ten years" (II Chron. 36:21).

The history of Israel from Solomon to the Babylonian Exile is a four-hundred-year demonstration of God's faithfulness to His Word in both promise and warning. He is a God who never changes (Mal. 3:6). He can be depended upon from generation to generation. And what He proved Himself to be for Israel, He proves Himself to be for us, as we heed His warnings and put our complete trust in His gracious promises. "Now these things happened unto them by way of example; and they were written for our admonition, upon whom the ends of the ages are come. Wherefore let him that thinketh he standeth take heed lest he fall . . . but God is faithful . . ." (I Cor. 10:11-13).

---

[21]Quoted from Streane's commentary on Jeremiah by G. Campbell Morgan, *Studies in the Prophecy of Jeremiah* (London: Oliphants Ltd., n.d.), p. 9.

[22]For a thorough study of the future phase of Israel's experience as a theocratic kingdom, see Alva J. McClain, *The Greatness of the Kingdom* (Chicago: Moody Press, 1968), pp. 135-515.

BIBLIOGRAPHY

Adams, J. McKee. *Biblical Backgrounds*. Nashvillè: Broadman Press, 1934.

Aharoni, Yohanan. "Arad: Its Inscriptions and Temple." *Biblical Archaeologist* 31, no. 1 (Feb. 1968).

————. "Hebrew Ostraca from Tel Arad." *Israel Exploration Journal* 16, no. 1 (1966).

————. *The Land of the Bible*. Translated by A. F. Rainey. Philadelphia: Westminster Press, 1962.

————, and Avi-Yonah, Michael. *The Macmillan Bible Atlas*. New York: Macmillan, 1968.

Albright, W. F. *Archaeology and the Religion of Isarel*. Baltimore: Johns Hopkins Press, 1953.

————. *The Archaeology of Palestine*. Baltimore: Penguin Books, 1961.

————. *The Biblical Period from Abraham to Ezra*. New York: Harper & Row, 1949.

————. *From the Stone Age to Christianity*. Baltimore: Johns Hopkins Press, 1957.

————. "New Light on the Early History of Phoenician Colonization." *Bulletin of the American Schools of Oriental Research* 83 (Oct. 1941).

Alleman, H. C., and Flack, E. E. *Old Testament Commentary*. Philadelphia: Fortress Press, 1954.

Anderson, Bernhard W. "The Place of Shechem in the Bible." *Biblical Archaeologist* 20, no. 1 (Feb. 1957).

————. *Understanding the Old Testament*. Englewood Cliffs, NJ: Prentice-Hall, 1957.

Archer, Gleason L. *A Survey of Old Testament Introduction*. Chicago: Moody Press, 1964.

Baly, Denis. *The Geography of the Bible*. New York: Harper & Bros., 1957.

Baxter, J. Sidlow. *Judges to Esther*. Explore the Book, vol. 2. Grand Rapids: Zondervan, 1960.

Bensen, Joseph. *Bensen's Commentary*. New York: Carlton and Porter, n.d.

Bettan, Israel. *The Five Scrolls*. Cincinnati: Union of American Hebrew Congregations, 1950.

Bright, John. *A History of Israel*. Philadelphia: Westminster Press, 1959.

Brown, Francis; Driver, S. R.; and Briggs, Charles A. *A Hebrew and English Lexicon of the Old Testament*. Oxford: Clarendon Press, 1952.

Bruce, Frederick Fyvie. *Israel and the Nations*. Grand Rapids: Wm. B. Eerdmans, 1963.

Buck, Harry M. *People of the Lord*. New York: Macmillan, 1966.

Burney, C. F. *The Book of Judges*. 2nd ed. London: Rivingtons, 1930.

Burrows, Millar. *What Mean These Stones?* New York: Meridian Books, 1957.

Clarke, Adam. *Clarke's Commentary*. New York: Carlton and Phillips, 1854.

Cook, F. C., ed. *The Holy Bible with Explanatory and Critical Commentary*. New York: Scribner, Armstrong & Co., n.d.

Crosby, Howard. *Expository Notes on the Book of Joshua*. New York: Robert Carter & Bros., 1875.

Davidson, A. B. *The Theology of the Old Testament*. New York: Charles Scribner's Sons, 1907.

Davidson, Francis; Stibbs, A. M.; and Kevan, E. F., eds. *New Bible Commentary*. Grand Rapids: Wm. B. Eerdmans, 1953.

Davis, John D. *A Dictionary of the Bible*. Grand Rapids: Baker Book House, 1954.

Davis, John J. *Biblical Numerology*. Grand Rapids: Baker Book House, 1968.

————. "The Patriarchs' Knowledge of Jehovah." *Grace Journal* 4, no. 1 (1963).

————. "Tombs Tell Tales." *Brethren Missionary Herald* 31, no. 10 (May 1969).

DeHaan, M. R. *The Romance of Redemption*. Grand Rapids: Zondervan, 1958.

Dever, William G. "The Water Systems at Hazor and Gezer." *Biblical Archaeologist* 32, no. 3 (1969).

Douglas, George C. M. *The Book of Judges*. Edinburgh: T. & T. Clark, 1881.

Douglas, J. D., ed. *The New Bible Dictionary*. Grand Rapids: Wm. B. Eerdmans, 1962.

Driver, G. R. *Canaanite Myths and Legends*. Edinburgh: T. & T. Clark, 1956.

Driver, S. R. *Notes on the Hebrew Text of the Books of Samuel*. Oxford: Clarendon Press, 1913.

Edersheim, Alfred. *The Bible History: Old Testament*. 2 vols. Grand Rapids: Wm. B. Eerdmans, 1949.

Eissfeldt, Otto. *The Hebrew Kingdom.* Cambridge: Cambridge University Press, 1965.

Ellicott, Charles, ed. *Ellicott's Commentary on the Whole Bible.* Grand Rapids: Zondervan, n.d.

Exell, Joseph S., and Spence, H. D. M., eds. *The Pulpit Commentary.* Vol. 4. Grand Rapids: Wm. B. Eerdmans, 1950.

Fay, F. R. *Commentary on the Holy Scriptures: Joshua.* Translated by Philip Schaff. Grand Rapids: Zondervan, 1915.

Finegan, Jack. *Handbook of Biblical Chronology.* Princeton: Princeton University Press, 1964.

————. *Light from the Ancient Past.* Princeton: Princeton University Press, 1959.

Free, Joseph P. *Archaeology and Bible History.* Wheaton, IL: VanKampen Press, 1950.

Freedman, David N. "The Second Season at Ancient Ashdod." *Biblical Archaeologist* 26, no. 4 (Dec. 1963).

Freeman, Hobart E. *An Introduction to the Old Testament Prophets.* Chicago: Moody Press, 1968.

Freiderberg, S. *Joshua: An Annotated Hebrew Text.* London: William Heinemann, 1913.

Garstang, John. *Joshua-Judges: The Foundation of Bible History.* New York: Richard R. Smith, 1931.

————, and Garstang, J. B. E. *The Story of Jericho.* Rev. ed. London: Marshall, Morgan & Scott, 1948.

Gill, John. *An Exposition of the Old Testament.* Vol. 2. London: Wm. H. Collingridge, 1853.

Glueck, Nelson. "Ezion-geber." *Biblical Archaeologist* 28, no. 3 (Sept. 1965).

Goldman, S. *Samuel.* Soncino Books of the Bible. London: Soncino Press, 1951.

Gordon, Cyrus. *Ugaritic Literature.* Rome: Pontifical Bible Institute, 1949.

————. *The World of the Old Testament.* London: Phoenix House, 1960.

Guthrie, Donald; Motyer, J. Alec; Stibbs, Alan M.; and Wiseman, Donald J. *The New Bible Commentary.* Rev. ed. Grand Rapids: Wm. B. Eerdmans, 1970.

Harrison, R. K. *Introduction to the Old Testament.* Grand Rapids: Wm. B. Eerdmans, 1969.

Heicksen, Martin H. "Tekoa: Excavations in 1968." *Grace Journal* 10, no. 2 (Spring 1969).

Heinisch, Paul. *Theology of the Old Testament.* Collegeville, MN: Liturgical Press, 1955.

Ironside, H. A. *Addresses on the Book of Joshua.* New York: Loizeaux Bros., 1950.

Jamieson, Robert; Fausset, A. R.; and Brown, David, eds. *Commentary on the Whole Bible.* Grand Rapids: Wm. B. Eerdmans, 1948.

Josephus, Flavius. *Complete Works.* Translated by William Whiston. Grand Rapids: Baker, 1974.

Kaufman, Yehezkel. *The Biblical Account of the Conquest of Palestine.* Jerusalem: Hebrew University Magnes Press, 1935.

Keil, C. F., and Delitzsch, Franz. *Biblical Commentary on the Old Testament.* Vol. 4: *Joshua, Judges, Ruth;* vol. 5: *Samuel;* vol. 6: *Kings;* vol. 7: *Chronicles.* Grand Rapids: Wm. B. Eerdmans, 1950.

Kenyon, Kathleen. *Archaeology in the Holy Land.* New York: Frederick A. Praeger, 1960.

———. *Digging Up Jericho.* London: Ernest Benn, 1957.

Kitchen, K. A. *Ancient Orient and the Old Testament.* Chicago: Inter-Varsity Press, 1966.

Krummacher, F. W. *Elijah the Tishbite.* Grand Rapids: Zondervan, n.d.

Lacheman, Ernest. "Notes on Ruth 4:7–8." *Journal of Biblical Literature* 61 (1937).

Laetsch, Theodore. *Bible Commentary: Jeremiah.* St. Louis: Concordia Publishing House, 1952.

LaSor, William Sanford. *Great Personalities of the Old Testament.* Westwood, NJ: Fleming H. Revell, 1959.

Lloyd, John. *The Book of Joshua.* London: Hodder and Stoughton, 1886.

McClain, Alva J. *The Greatness of the Kingdom.* Chicago: Moody Press, 1959.

McGee, J. Vernon. *Ruth: The Romance of Redemption.* Findlay, OH: Dunham Publishing Co., 1962.

McKenzie, John L. *The World of the Judges.* Englewood Cliffs, NJ: Prentice-Hall, 1966.

Maclaren, Alexander. *Maclaren's Expositions of Holy Scripture.* Vol. 2. Grand Rapids: Wm. B. Eerdmans, 1952.

Malamat, A. "Aspects of the Foreign Policies of David and Solomon." *Journal of Near Eastern Studies* 22, no. 1 (Jan. 1963).

———. "The Kingdom of David and Solomon in Its Contact with Egypt and Aram Naharaim." *Biblical Archaeologist* 21, no. 4 (Dec. 1958).

Marcus, Ralph. "The Word Sibboleth Again." *Bulletin of the American Schools of Oriental Research* 87 (Oct. 1942).

Mauro, Philip. *Ruth: The Satisfied Stranger*. Swengel, PA: Bible Truth Depot, 1963.

Mendelson, I. "Samuel's Denunciation of Kingship in the Light of the Akkadian Documents from Ugarit." *Bulletin of the American Schools of Oriental Research* 143 (Oct. 1956).

Mendenhall, George E. *Law and Covenant in Israel and the Ancient Near East*. Pittsburgh: Biblical Colloquium, 1955.

Merrill, Eugene H. *An Historical Survey of the Old Testament*. Nutley, NJ: Craig Press, 1966.

Morrison, James. *The Pulpit Commentary*. Vol. 4. Grand Rapids: Wm. B. Eerdmans, 1950.

Nichol, Francis D., ed. *The Seventh-day Adventist Bible Commentary*. Vol. 2. Washington, DC: Review and Herald, 1954.

Noth, Martin. *The History of Israel*. New York: Harper & Row, 1960.

Oehler, Gustave F. *Theology of the Old Testament*. Grand Rapids: Zondervan, n.d.

Orr, James, ed. *The International Bible Encyclopedia*. Grand Rapids: Wm. B. Eerdmans, 1960.

Payne, J. Barton. *The Theology of the Older Testament*. Grand Rapids: Zondervan, 1962.

Pfeiffer, Charles F. *The Divided Kingdom*. Grand Rapids: Baker Book House, 1967.

————, and Harrison, Everett F., eds. *The Wycliffe Bible Commentary*. Chicago: Moody Press, 1962.

Pink, Arthur W. *Gleanings in Joshua*. Chicago: Moody Press, 1964.

Pritchard, James B. *Gibeon, Where the Sun Stood Still*. Princeton: Princeton University Press, 1962.

————. "Industry and Trade at Biblical Gibeon." *Biblical Archaeologist* 23, no. 1 (Feb. 1960).

————, ed. *Ancient Near Eastern Texts Relating to the Old Testament*. Princeton: Princeton University Press, 1955.

Rea, John. "New Light on the Wilderness Journey and the Conquest." *Grace Journal* 2, no. 2 (1962).

————. "The Time of the Oppression and the Exodus." *Grace Journal* 2, no. 1 (1961).

Ridout, Samuel. *Lectures on the Books of Judges and Ruth*. New York: Loizeaux Bros., 1958.

Rowley, H. H. *The Rediscovery of the Old Testament*. Philadelphia: Westminster Press, 1946.

———. *The Servant of the Lord*. 2nd ed. rev. Oxford: Basil Blackwell, 1965.

Simons, J. *The Geographical and Topographical Texts of the Old Testament*. Leiden: E. J. Brill, 1959.

Simpson, C. A. *Composition of the Book of Judges*. Oxford: Blackwell, 1957.

Sinclair, Lawrence A. "An Archaeological Study of Gibeah (Tell el-Ful)." *Biblical Archaeologist* 27, no. 2 (May 1964).

Slotki, J. R. *The Five Megilloth*. Edited by Abraham Cohen. London: Soncino Press, 1952.

Smith, James. "The Life and Thoughts of the Pre-Literary Prophets." *Seminary Review* 13, no. 4 (Summer 1967).

Smith, Louise P. "The Book of Ruth." *The Interpreter's Bible*, vol. 2. New York: Abingdon Press, 1953.

Speiser, E. A. "Of Shoes and Shekels." *Bulletin of the American Schools of Oriental Research* 77 (Feb. 1940).

———. "The Shibboleth Incident (Judges 12:6)." *Bulletin of the American Schools of Oriental Research* 85 (Feb. 1942).

Terry, Milton S. *Biblical Hermeneutics*. Grand Rapids: Zondervan, n.d.

Thiele, Edwin J. *The Mysterious Numbers of the Hebrew Kings*. Rev. ed. Grand Rapids: Wm. B. Eerdmans, 1965.

Thomas, D. Winton, ed. *Documents from Old Testament Times*. New York: Harper & Bros., 1961.

Totten, Charles A. *Joshua's Long Day and the Dial of Ahaz*. Haverhill, MA: Destiny Publishers, 1941.

Unger, Merrill F. *Archaeology and the Old Testament*. Grand Rapids: Zondervan, 1954.

———. *Biblical Demonology*. Wheaton, IL: VanKampen Press, 1952.

———. *Israel and the Aramaeans of Damascus*. London: James Clarke & Co., 1957.

———, ed. *Unger's Bible Dictionary*. Chicago: Moody Press, 1957.

Ussishkin, D. "King Solomon's Palace and Building 1723 in Megiddo." *Israel Exploration Journal* 16, no. 3 (1966).

Velikovsky, Immanuel. *Worlds in Collision*. New York: Macmillan, 1950.

Watson, Robert A. *The Expositor's Bible: Judges and Ruth*. New York: A. C. Armstrong and Sons, 1899.

Whitcomb, John C., Jr. *Chart of the Old Testament Kings and Prophets.* 4th rev. ed. Chicago: Moody Press, 1968.

Whyte, Alexander. *Ahithophel to Nehemiah.* Bible Characters, vol. 3. London: Oliphants, n.d.

Williams, George. *The Student's Commentary on the Holy Scriptures.* London: Oliphants, 1949.

Wilson, Robert Dick. "What Does 'The Sun Stood Still' Mean?" *Princeton Theological Review* 16 (1918).

Wiseman, Donald J. *Chronicles of Chaldaean Kings.* London: The Trustees of the British Museum, 1956.

————. *Illustrations from Biblical Archaeology.* Grand Rapids: Wm. B. Eerdmans, 1958.

Wood, Leon James. *Elijah, Prophet of God.* Des Plaines, IL: Regular Baptist Press, 1968.

Wright, G. Ernest. *Biblical Archaeology.* Philadelphia: Westminster Press, 1957.

————. "Fresh Evidence for the Philistine Story." *Biblical Archaeologist* 29, no. 3 (Sept. 1966).

————. "Philistine Coffins and Mercenaries." *Biblical Archaeologist* 22, no. 3 (Sept. 1959).

————. "The Stevens' Reconstruction of the Solomonic Temple." *Biblical Archaeologist* 18, no. 2 (May 1955).

Yadin, Yigael. "The Fifth Season of Excavations at Hazor." *Biblical Archaeologist* 32, no. 3 (1969).

————. "Let the Young Men, I Pray Thee, Arise and Play Before Us." *Journal of the Palestine Oriental Society* 21 (1948).

Young, Edward J. *My Servants the Prophets.* Grand Rapids: Wm. B. Eerdmans, 1955.

————. *Studies in Isaiah.* Grand Rapids: Wm. B. Eerdmans, 1954.

NAME/SUBJECT INDEX

Aaron(ic), 26, 191–193, 292, 330, 359, 392, 443
Abdon, 105, 130, 176
Abel, 381, 399, 419
Abiathar, 239–241, 251, 263, 273, 330, 332, 335
Abigail, 243, 263, 275, 315
Abihu, 191
Abijah, 362
Abijam, 329, 363 n, 365–367
Abimelech, 117–119, 224, 236
Abinadab, 233, 291
Abishag, 329, 331
Abishai, 244
Abner, 185, 245, 276, 278–282, 315
Abraham (Abram), 35, 40, 88, 96, 113, 127, 159, 195, 235, 294, 353, 355, 392, 394, 397, 407 n, 427, 439
Absalom, 280, 306–307, 310–319, 329–331, 357, 367
Achan, 52, 55, 85, 206, 301, 378, 389
Achish, 236, 246, 248–249, 259–262
Acre, Plain of, 110
Adam, 301, 396, 397, 399
Adam (city), 36, 38
Adoni-Bezek, 98
Adonijah, 192, 240, 329–332, 438
Adoniram, 335
Adoni-zedec, 63–65
Adullam, 237
Aegean (Sea), 179, 195
Africa, 346, 354
Agag, 220–221, 239, 393
Ahab, 51, 264, 266, 329, 354, 373, 376–386, 388–389, 393, 398–399, 403, 411, 416, 419, 420, 421, 423, 425, 426, 435, 436, 453, 478
Ahaz, 127, 356, 430, 444–447, 450, 463, 464, 475, 481
Ahaziah, 327, 329, 373, 384, 385 n, 399–400, 412, 420, 425, 436–437
Ahijah, 328 n, 351, 356, 362, 364, 366
Ahikam, 493 n
Ahimelech, 233, 235, 238–239, 244, 297
Ahinoam, 263, 275, 307
Ahithophel, 271 n.68, 313, 315–316
Ahitub, 233
Ai, 22, 24, 49, 52–62, 63, 150, 219, 378
Aijalon, 130
Ain-Jalud, 260
Ajalon (Valley), 218
Akhenaton, 19, 95, 333
Akkad(ian), 450, 481, 483
Alalakh, 202
Allah, 354
Altar, 60, 84–87, 114
Amalekite(s), 24, 107, 113, 115, 130, 181, 212, 219–221, 239, 263–264, 266, 270–272, 282, 378
Amarna (letters), 19, 21, 48, 55, 59, 63, 64, 75
Amasa, 161, 316, 318, 331
Amaziah, 426, 440–442
Amen, 95
Amenhotep II, 19
Amenhotep III, 19, 48
America, 393, 467
Amminadab, 170
Ammon(ites), 105, 107, 120–124, 128, 160, 181, 199, 203, 206–207, 212, 298–300, 302, 306,

503

SCRIPTURE INDEX

12:19-21—262
12:23-40—285
Chaps. 13-16—290-
292
13:1-4—291
13:6—291
14:12—289 n.79
14:16—289 n.80
15:18-24—292
15:29—293
18:1—295
18:12—296
18:15—335
18:17—297
19:6—298
20:1—300
20:3—306
20:5—319-320
21:1—321
21:1-6—321
22:2—336
22:3—216
22:8—294
24:1-2—192
24:3—330
25:1—407
26:4 ff.—292
27:1—32 n
28:3—294
29:22—285
29:27—285
29:29—183, 238, 293

II Chronicles

II Chron.—269
2:3—288
2:11 ff.—336
3:10-13—342
5:9-16—287-288
7:1—392
8:17-18—343

9:25—336
9:29—293, 328 n, 351
Chaps. 10-12—364-
365
11:4—366
11:13-15—360, 365
11:16—360, 433
11:17—360, 364, 365,
366
11:18-23—365
12:1-4—365
12:6—366
12:12—365, 366
12:13—353
12:14—364
12:15—328 n
Chap. 13—363 n,
365-366
13:4-11—359 n
13:4-12—366
13:7—353 n, 366
13:8—366
13:9—365, 366
13:11—194 n
13:12—366
13:20—366
13:22—328 n
Chaps. 14-15—367-
369
14:1—367
14:5-7—367
14:6—367, 369
14:9—213, 371
14:11—367
14:14—367
14:15—367
15:3-6—368
15:7—368
15:9—368, 369, 441 n
15:10—369
15:17—371
15:18—371
15:19—369

Chap. 16—369-372
16:1—369, 391
16:10—399
16:14—436
Chaps. 17-20—372-
374
17:1—372
17:3—372
17:9—372, 472
17:11—373
18:1—373, 381
18:2—381
18:28-34—266
18:31—383
19:2—373, 384
19:3—384
19:4—373
19:4-11—373
20:14-17—373
20:23—405
20:29—373
20:35-37—373, 405
20:37—400
Chaps. 21-22—435-
437
21:2—435
21:3—435
21:4—374, 435
21:6—381, 435
21:8-10—435
21:12-15—374, 436
21:13—435
21:16—437
21:17—384, 437
21:19—385, 436
21:20—436
22:2—381
22:3—381, 435, 436
22:3-5—436
22:8—385
22:9—437
22:10—385, 437
22:10-12—385

Zephaniah

1:4—474
2:5—297, 438 n

Haggai

2:23—485

Zechariah

1:1—440 n
4:10—410
6:13—443
10:2—144, 253
12:8—378
12:11—478
13:2—382
13:3—393
13:4—400

Malachi

2:6-7—472
3:6—494
4:6—46

II Maccabees

7:27—189 n
8:28-30—265

Matthew

1:3-6—157
1:5—50
1:12—485
1:20—250
3:4—400
4:19—398
6:26-27—50-51
6:33—352, 387
7:14—397
8:10—387
10:30—408
11:8—400

12:24—400
12:33-35—476
12:42—351
12:43—476
13:57—492 n.19
15:19—476
17:3—257
17:8—402
17:27—410
18:3—413
18:25—409
19:5—352
19:8—353
19:27-30—161
22:29—459
23:15—393
23:32-36—381
23:35—440 n
26:59-67—381
27:5—271 n.68
28:19-20—31

Luke

1:7—132
1:15—188
1:32—294
1:33—294
1:46-55—190
2:36—433, 473
3:31—437
3:32-33—157
4:25—386, 387
5:27-29—398
8:35—441
9:27-36—402
9:30, 31—257
9:55—397
9:61-62—398
12:27—351
14:31-32—448
16:25—257
16:26—258

16:28-31—258
17:15—413
23:42-43—141
23:42, 43—188

John

1:35-42—398
3:3-8—397
3:14-15—447
4:9—434
7:32—416
7:46—416
9:3—387
9:6—465
10:27—380
12:40—74
13:27—417
15:2—462
15:7—351
19:15—203
21:21-23—418

Acts

8:18-20—413
13:21—176
17:5—404
17:16, 29—391
18:18—413
19:19-20—447
21:9—473
21:26—413
26:7—433

Romans

1:16—413
1:24-32—382
3:7-8—425
3:9-30—397
5:12—399
5:20—355